MCSD: Access 95 Study Guide Companion CD-ROM

For ___ 98, and NT4 users, this *autoplay* CD-ROM automatically displays the Sybex MCSD interface ___ the different products on the CD. Just pop it in the CD-ROM drive and let the autoplay CD ___ ___terface. You'll find the following software products on the CD:

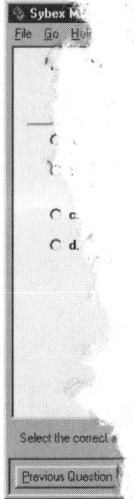

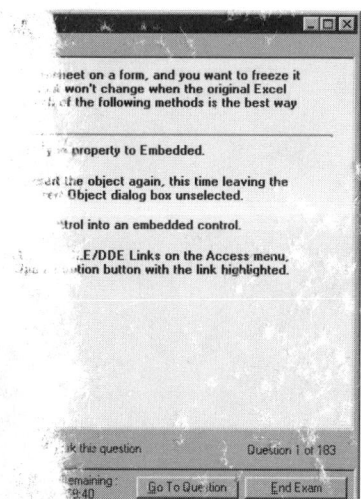

The Exclusive Sybex MCSD ExamReady Test Engine. All the questions and answers in this book are included on the Sybex MCSD ExamReady Test Engine, an easy-to-use program for test preparation.

MCSD Offline Update. The latest Microsoft information on the MCSD certification program. Internet Explorer 4 is required to run this HTML-based document.

Internet Explorer 4.01. Just in case you don't have it or feel like downloading it, we've included this powerful browser, which you can use to view the Microsoft offline information.

MCSD on the Web. Popular MCSD Web sites listed in order of importance to MCSD students.

Using ___ ___ MCSD ExamReady Test Engine

The Sybex ___ ___ an autorun test engine created exclusively for the Sybex MCSD Study Guides. To prepare for ___ ___:

1. Install ___ ___dy test engine from the Sybex interface, or double-click SETUP.EXE In the CD's \EXAM ___ ___tory. Reboot!

2. Start ___ Tes ___ ___ne by looking in the Start menu under Programs ➢ Sybex Study Guide ➢ ExamR ___ vll2 ___.

3. When the ___ ___ine starts, click Name and enter your name, then press Enter.

4. Click Exam, ___ n Timed Exam to begin the timed, mock MCSD exam.

5. You're ready to ___! Start the timer, then answer the questions one by one. Click Next Question at the bottom of the screen to proceed. (Remember to press the F9 Key for Exhibit button if the question includes a code listing or a table.)

To access other elements on the CD, use Windows Explorer (File Manager).

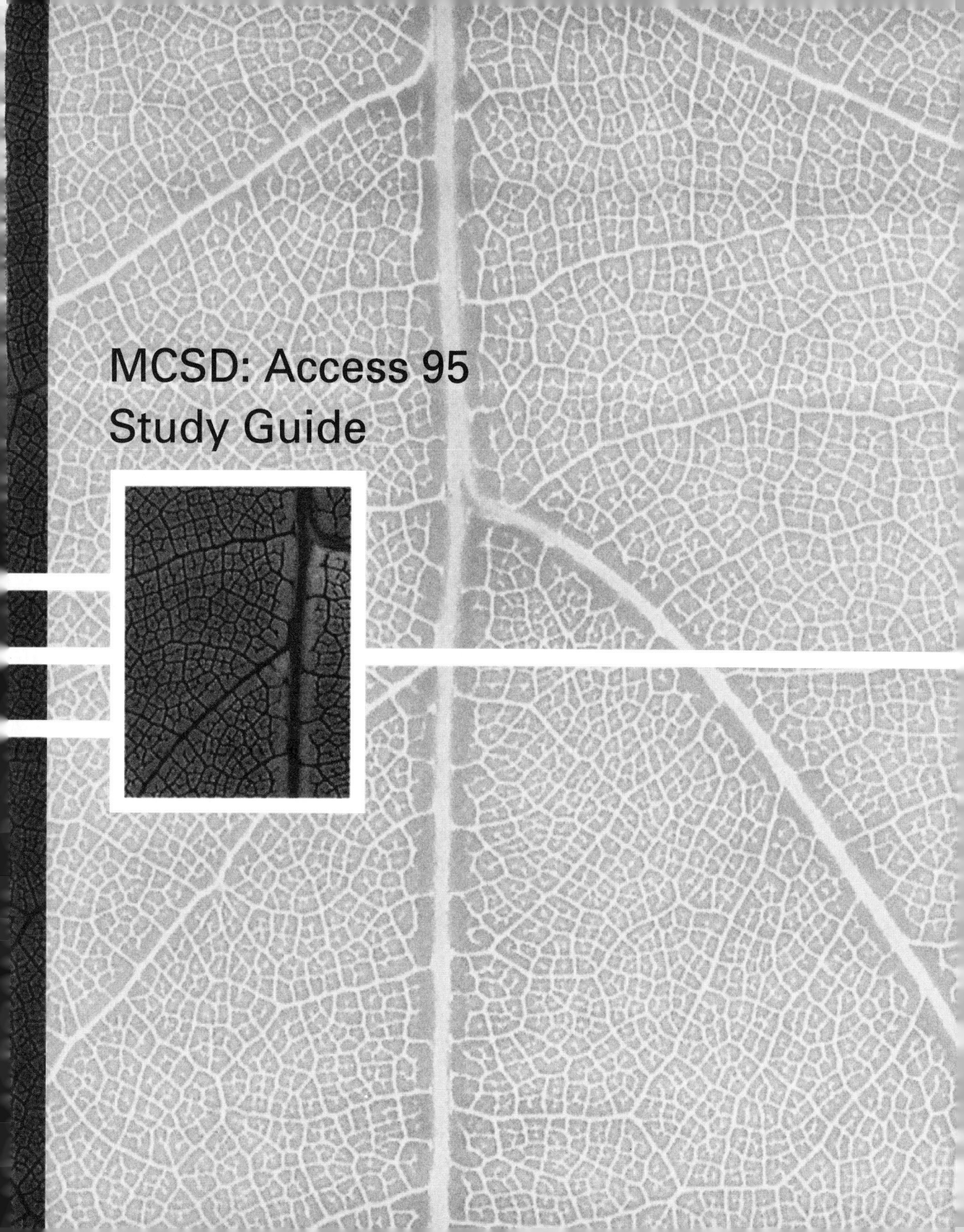

MCSD: Access 95
Study Guide

MCSD: Access® 95
Study Guide

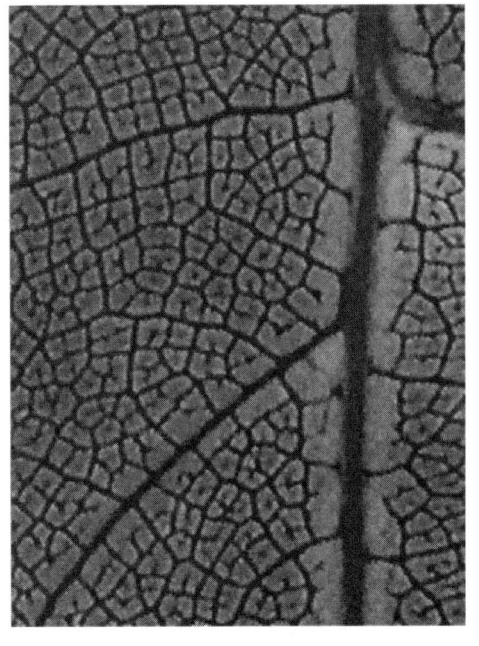

Peter Vogel
Helen Feddema

San Francisco • Paris • Düsseldorf • Soest

Associate Publisher: Gary Masters
Contracts and Licensing Manager: Kristine Plachy
Acquisitions & Developmental Editor: Melanie Spiller
Editor: Vivian Perry
Project Editor: Shelby Zimmerman
Technical Editors: Helen Feddema and Rima Regas
Book Designer: Patrick Dintino
Graphic Illustrators: Michael Gushard and Tony Jonick
Electronic Publishing Specialists: Maureen Forys, Happenstance Type-O-Rama and Cyndy Johnsen, Sybex Inc.
Production Coordinators: Eryn Osterhaus and Jefferson McClure
Indexer: Ted Laux
Companion CD: Molly Sharp and Ginger Warner
Cover Designer: Design Site
Cover Photographer: Design Site

Screen reproductions produced with Collage Complete. Collage Complete is a trademark of Inner Media Inc.

SYBEX, Network Press, and the Network Press logo are registered trademarks of SYBEX Inc.

TRADEMARKS: SYBEX has attempted throughout this book to distinguish proprietary trademarks from descriptive terms by following the capitalization style used by the manufacturer.

The CD Interface music is from GIRA Sound AURIA Music Library ©GIRA Sound 1996.

The author and publisher have made their best efforts to prepare this book, and the content is based upon final release software whenever possible. Portions of the manuscript may be based upon pre-release versions supplied by software manufacturer(s). The author and the publisher make no representation or warranties of any kind with regard to the completeness or accuracy of the contents herein and accept no liability of any kind including but not limited to performance, merchantability, fitness for any particular purpose, or any losses or damages of any kind caused or alleged to be caused directly or indirectly from this book.

SYBEX is an independent entity from Microsoft Corporation, and not affiliated with Microsoft Corporation in any manner. This publication may be used in assisting students to prepare for a Microsoft Certified Professional Exam. Neither Microsoft Corporation, its designated review company, nor SYBEX warrants that use of this publication will ensure passing the relevant exam. Microsoft is either a registered trademark or trademark of Microsoft Corporation in the United States and/or other countries.

Library of Congress Card Number: 98-84540
ISBN: 0-7821-2282-5

Manufactured in the United States of America

10 9 8 7 6 5 4 3 2 1

CERTIFIED PROFESSIONAL

Approved Study Guide

November 1, 1997

Dear SYBEX Customer:

Microsoft is pleased to inform you that SYBEX is a participant in the Microsoft®
Independent Courseware Vendor (ICV) program. Microsoft ICVs design, develop,
and market self-paced courseware, books, and other products that support Microsoft
software and the Microsoft Certified Professional (MCP) program.

To be accepted into the Microsoft ICV program, an ICV must meet set criteria. In
addition, Microsoft reviews and approves each ICV training product before
permission is granted to use the Microsoft Certified Professional Approved Study
Guide logo on that product. This logo assures the consumer that the product has
passed the following Microsoft standards:

- The course contains accurate product information.
- The course includes labs and activities during which the student can apply
  knowledge and skills learned from the course.
- The course teaches skills that help prepare the student to take corresponding
  MCP exams.

Microsoft ICVs continually develop and release new MCP Approved Study Guides.
To prepare for a particular Microsoft certification exam, a student may choose one or
more single, self-paced training courses or a series of training courses.

You will be pleased with the quality and effectiveness of the MCP Approved Study
Guides available from SYBEX.

Sincerely,

Holly Heath
ICV Account Manager
Microsoft Training & Certification

MICROSOFT INDEPENDENT COURSEWARE VENDOR PROGRAM

This is my first book so it's dedicated to the people who had to put up with me first: my father, my mother, and my brother. Thank you.
—Peter

To my high school English teacher, Mrs. Norris, who taught me to be specific—a good piece of advice for writing a computer book.
—Helen

Acknowledgments

It's always tempting to look at the authors' names on the front of the book and assume that they alone are responsible for it. This book is the result of an enormous amount of work by a lot of people. In addition to the authors, three editors deserve credit for getting this book into your hands: Shelby Zimmerman, Melanie Spiller, and Vivian Perry. Technical editing was handled by Helen Feddema and Rima Regas. Thanks also to production coordinators Jefferson McClure and Eryn Osterhaus for orchestrating the production of the book deftly, and Maureen Forys, desktop publisher, for laying out the book beautifully and in record time. This book has been greatly enhanced thanks to all their Herculean efforts.

When it came time to write this book, Peter and Helen received some help. Mary Chipman did the chapters on security and replication. Tech editor Rima Regas contributed the chapter on client/server issues. Ours thanks to these contributors.

Peter: On a personal note, I also need to recognize the support and understanding that I have received from my wife, Jan, and my two boys, Jamie and Christopher. No one could have a better family than the one that I have been blessed with.

Helen: I would like to thank the many Access users and developers on the old MSACCESS CompuServe forums and the new Internet newsgroups, for their help and encouragement (and the challenging questions and problems they provided to work on). All of these things helped me develop my skills as an Access programmer.

Contents at a Glance

Table of Contents

Table of Exercises

Introduction

If you've purchased this book, you are probably chasing one of the Microsoft professional certifications: MCP, MCSD, or MCT. All of these are great goals, and they are also great career builders. Glance through any newspaper and you'll find employment opportunities for people with these certifications—these ads are there because finding qualified employees is a challenge in today's market. The certification means you know something about the product, but more importantly, it means you have the ability, determination, and focus to learn—the greatest skill any employee can have!

You've probably also heard all the rumors about how hard the Microsoft tests are—believe us, the rumors are true! Microsoft has designed a series of exams that truly test your knowledge of their products. Each test not only covers the materials presented in a particular class, it also covers the prerequisite knowledge for that course. This means two things for you—that first test can be a real hurdle and each test *should* get easier since you've studied the basics over and over.

This book has been developed in alliance with the Microsoft Corporation to give you the knowledge and skills you need to prepare for one of the key exams of the MCSD certification program: Microsoft® Access for Windows® 95 and the Microsoft® Access Developer's Toolkit. Reviewed and approved by Microsoft, this book provides a solid introduction to Microsoft development technologies and will help you on your way to MCSD certification.

What Does This Book Cover?

This book will provide you with the information that you need to create database applications with Microsoft Access. We begin with what you need to know to start designing your application and continue right through to show you all the ways to distribute your finished product. On this journey, you'll learn how to use Access forms and reports, how to create tables to store your data, and how to write VBA code to tie it all together. We've pooled our experience to provide some cool tips and warnings along the way.

Your Key to Passing Exam 70-069

This book provides you with the key to passing Exam 70-069, Microsoft® Access for Windows® 95 and the Microsoft® Access Developer's Toolkit. Inside, you'll find information relevant to this exam and practice questions, all designed to make sure that when you take the exam, you are ready.

To help you prepare for certification exams, Microsoft provides a list of exam objectives for each test. This book is structured according to the objectives for Exam 70-069, designed to measure your understanding of Microsoft Access 95 and development.

Is This Book for You?

If you want to pass the MCSD exam, this book is for you. We cover all the exam topics. We've included exercises so you can try out the material covered in this book. Each chapter ends with questions that will allow you to test your understanding of the material in the chapter. The information in this book, combined with your experience using Microsoft Access, will prepare you for the exam.

Most importantly, this book will prepare you to use Microsoft Access. Like any good test, the Access certification exam isn't a random collection of questions. The exam is designed to probe your knowledge of Access and force you to demonstrate that you know how to use this powerful product. To pass the exam you must know how to use Access. Our goal is to ensure that you know exactly that.

Understanding Microsoft Certification

Microsoft offers several levels of certification for anyone who has or is pursuing a career as a network professional working with Microsoft products:

- Microsoft Certified Professional (MCP)

- Microsoft Certified Solution Developer (MCSD)

- Microsoft Certified Systems Engineer (MCSE)

- Microsoft Certified Professional + Internet

- Microsoft Certified Systems Engineer + Internet
- Microsoft Certified Trainer (MCT)

The one you choose depends on your area of expertise and your career goals.

Microsoft Certified Professional (MCP)

This certification is for individuals with expertise in one specific area. MCP certification is often a stepping stone to MCSE certification and allows you some benefits of Microsoft certification after just one exam.

By passing one core exam (meaning an operating system exam), you become an MCP.

Microsoft Certified Solution Developer (MCSD)

The MCSD certification identifies developers with experience working with Microsoft operating systems, development tools, and technologies. To achieve the MCSD certification, you must pass four exams:

1. Windows Architecture I
2. Windows Architecture II
3. Elective
4. Elective

Some of the electives include:

- Microsoft Visual Basic 5.0
- Microsoft Access for Windows 95
- Implementing a Database Design on Microsoft SQL Server 6.5
- Developing application with C++ and MFC
- Microsoft FoxPro 3.0

Microsoft Certified Systems Engineer (MCSE)

For network professionals, the MCSE certification requires commitment. You need to complete all of the steps required for certification. Passing the exams shows that you meet the high standards that Microsoft has set for MCSEs.

 The following list applies to the NT 4.0 track. Microsoft still supports a track for 3.51, but 4.0 certification is more desirable because it is the current operating system.

To become an MCSE, you must pass a series of six exams:

1. Networking Essentials (waived for Novell CNEs)

2. Implementing and Supporting Microsoft Windows NT Workstation 4.0 (or Windows 95)

3. Implementing and Supporting Microsoft Windows NT Server 4.0

4. Implementing and Supporting Microsoft Windows NT Server 4.0 in the Enterprise

5. Elective

6. Elective

Some of the electives include:

- Internetworking with Microsoft TCP/IP on Microsoft Windows NT 4.0

- Implementing and Supporting Microsoft Internet Information Server 4.0

- Implementing and Supporting Microsoft Exchange Server 5.5

- Implementing and Supporting Microsoft SNA Server 4.0

- Implementing and Supporting Microsoft Systems Management Server 1.2

- Implementing a Database Design on Microsoft SQL Server 6.5

- System Administration for Microsoft SQL Server 6.5

Microsoft Certified Trainer (MCT)

As an MCT, you can deliver Microsoft certified courseware through official Microsoft channels. The number of exams you are required to pass depends on the number of courses you want to deliver. Certification is granted on a course-by-course basis.

In addition to passing exams for the courses that you want to deliver, you must also attend a trainer skills course that is approved by Microsoft. You must also demonstrate that you have prepared adequately for each new class. This can be done by either attending the class or completing a self-study checklist and sending it to Microsoft.

For the most up-to-date certification information, visit Microsoft's Web site at www.microsoft.com/train_cert.

Preparing for the MCSD Exams

To prepare for the MCSD certification exams, you should try to work with the products as much as possible. In addition, a variety of resources from which you can learn about the products and exams are available:

- You can take instructor-led courses.

- Online training is an alternative to instructor-led courses. This is a useful option for people who cannot find any courses in their area or who do not have the time to attend classes.

- If you prefer to use a book to help you prepare for the MCSD tests, you can choose from a wide variety of publications. These include study guides, such as the Network Press *MCSD Study Guide* series, which cover the core MCSD exams and key electives.

For more MCSD information, point your browser to the Sybex Web site, where you'll find information about the MCP program, job links, and descriptions of other quality titles in the Network Press line of MCSD-related books. Go to www.sybex.com and click on the MCSD logo.

Scheduling and Taking an Exam

Once you think you are ready to take an exam, call Prometric Testing Centers at (800) 755-EXAM (755-3926). They'll tell you where to find the closest testing center. Before you call, get out your credit card because each exam costs $100. (If you've used this book to prepare yourself thoroughly, chances are you'll only have to shell out that $100 once!)

You can schedule the exam for a time that is convenient for you. The exams are downloaded from Prometric to the testing center, and you show up at your scheduled time and take the exam on a computer.

Once you complete the exam, you will know right away whether you have passed or not. At the end of the exam, you will receive a score report. It will list the six areas that you were tested on and how you performed. If you pass the exam, you don't need to do anything else—Prometric uploads the test results to Microsoft. If you don't pass, it's another $100 to schedule the exam again. But at least you will know from the score report where you did poorly, so you can study that particular information more carefully.

Test-Taking Hints

If you know what to expect, your chances of passing the exam will be much greater. The following are some tips that can help you achieve success.

Get there early and be prepared   This is your last chance to review. Bring your book and review any areas about which you feel unsure. If you need a quick drink of water or a visit to the restroom, take the time before the exam. Once your exam starts, it will not be paused for these needs.

When you arrive for your exam, you will be asked to present two forms of ID. You will also be asked to sign a piece of paper verifying that you understand the testing rules and that you will not disclose the content of the exam to others.

Before you start the exam, you will have an opportunity to take a practice exam. It is not related to Windows NT and is simply offered so that you will have a feel for the exam-taking process.

What you can and can't take in with you   These are closed-book exams. The only thing you can take in is scratch paper provided by the testing center. Use this paper as much as possible to diagram the questions. Many times, diagramming questions will help make the answer clear. You will have to give this paper back to the test administrator at the end of the exam.

Many testing centers are very strict about what you can take into the testing room. Some centers will not even allow you to bring in items like a zipped purse. If you feel tempted to take in any outside material, beware that many testing centers use monitoring devices such as video and audio equipment (so don't swear, even if you are alone in the room!)

Prometric Testing Centers take the test taking process and the test validation very seriously.

Test approach   As you take the test, if you know the answer to a question, fill it in and move on. If you're not sure of the answer, mark your best guess, then "mark" the question.

At the end of the exam, you can review the questions. Depending on the amount of time remaining, you can then view all of the questions again, or you can view only the questions about which you were unsure. Double-check your answers, just in case you misread any of the questions on the first pass. (Sometimes half of the battle is in trying to figure out exactly what the question is asking you.) You may find that a related question provides a clue for a troublesome question.

Be sure to answer all questions. Unanswered questions are scored as incorrect and will count against you. There is no penalty for guessing. Also, make sure you keep an eye on the remaining time so that you can pace yourself accordingly.

If you do not pass the exam, note everything that you can remember while the exam is still fresh on your mind. This will help you prepare for your next try. Although the next exam will not be exactly the same, the questions will be similar, and you don't want to make the same mistakes.

After You Become Certified

Once you become an MCSD, Microsoft kicks in some goodies, including:

- A one-year subscription to the Microsoft Beta Evaluation program, which is a great way to get your hands on new software. Be the first kid on the block to play with new and upcoming software.

- Access to a secured area of the Microsoft Web site that provides technical support and product information. This certification benefit is also available for MCP certification.

- Permission to use the Microsoft Certified Professional logos (each certification has its own logo), which look great on letterhead and business cards.

- An MCP certificate (you will get a certificate for each level of certification you reach), suitable for framing, or sending copies to Mom.

- A one-year subscription to *Microsoft Certified Professional Magazine*, which provides information on professional and career development.

What's on the CD?

The Sybex MCSD ExamReady CD contains the following tools to help you prepare for exam 70-069:

- Sybex Exam Ready Test Engine. The fastest way to prepare for the real exam. Contains the practice test questions and answers from each chapter.

- MCSD on the Web. Links to the best MCSD sites on the Web.

- Microsoft Offline Update. Microsoft's latest-breaking information on the MCP Certification Program.

- Internet Explorer 4. Latest Microsoft browser which you will need to read the Microsoft Offline Update included on the CD.

For details on how to install and run these programs, see the front inside cover of this book.

About the Authors

Peter Vogel was one of the first MCSDs in Canada. He took the time to prepare for the exams for one reason: he thought it would be good for his career. In the two years since he earned his certification, he has found that he was right. Within a year of getting his certification, he started a successful consulting practice that has allowed him to do more of the things that he wanted to do than he had thought possible (and make more money at it, too).

There's one programming tool that Peter uses more than any other: Microsoft Access. He considers Access to be the most productive tool on the market for creating database applications. Not surprisingly, then, the Access certification exam was the first exam that he took. He had been using Access since version 1.0, so he didn't do much preparation for the Access 2.0 exam—he just showed up at the testing center and took the test. Well, he passed, but it wasn't by a lot. Peter discovered that in a product as powerful as Access, there was a great deal that he didn't know. Access 95 is a considerably more complicated tool than Access 2.0 and, at least from his experience, the certification exams have gotten a lot tougher, too.

Peter learned from his experience with the Access exam. For the subsequent exams, he didn't rely just on his hands-on work with the Microsoft tools in question. Instead, he thoroughly researched each of the products before taking the test. Since there were no study guides at that time, that meant searching out and reading a variety of books, white papers, and technical articles.

In 1996, Peter took over as editor of the *Smart Access* newsletter. *Smart Access* is the leading newsletter for in-depth technical information on Microsoft Access (you can check it out at `www.pinpub.com`). The founding editor of the newsletter, Paul Litwin, co-wrote the standard reference for Access developers, *The Access Developer's Handbook*. Regular contributors include recognized experts in the field. As editor of *Smart Access,* Peter has been exposed to some of the best information on how Access works and how to get the most from it.

Helen Feddema grew up in New York City. She was ready for computers when she was 12, but computers were not ready for her yet, so she got a B.S. in Philosophy from Columbia and an M.T.S. in Theological Studies from Harvard Divinity School. It was at HDS that she got her first computer, an Osborne, and soon computers were her primary interest. She started with word processing and spreadsheets, went on to learn dBASE, and did dBASE development for six years, part of this time as a corporate developer. Eventually, she started doing independent consulting and development, using dBASE, ObjectVision, WordPerfect and Paradox.

Always looking for something new and better, Helen beta tested Access 1.0, and soon recognized that this was the database she had been looking for ever since Windows 3.0 was introduced, and she saw the gap waiting to be filled by a great Windows database. Since then she has worked as a developer of Microsoft Office applications, concentrating on Access, Word, and Outlook.

Helen has been a regular contributor to Pinnacle's *Smart Access* and *Office Developer* journals, *Woody's Underground Office* newsletter, PC Magazine's *Undocumented Office*, and the *MS Office and VBA Journal*. Her most recent article is a three-part series on writing Access add-ins for *Smart Access*.

Helen is a big-time beta tester, sometimes running seven or eight betas at once, mostly from Microsoft, but with some from other vendors as well.

She lives in the mid-Hudson area of New York state with three cats and three computers.

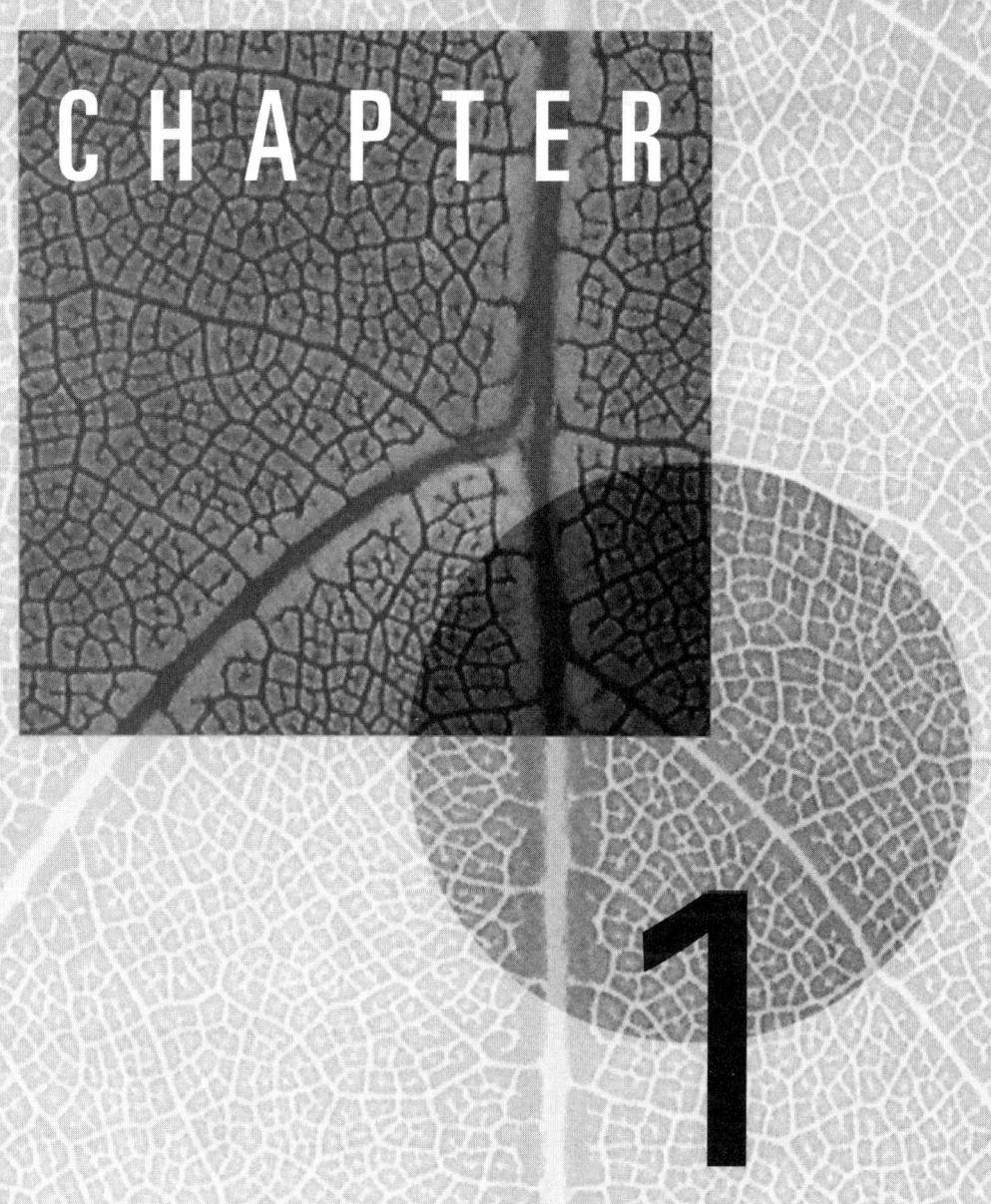

CHAPTER

1

Introducing the Access Database

Microsoft Exam Objectives Covered in This Chapter:

- Apply the basic concepts of normalization.

- Use the cascade update and cascade delete options.

Access is a complete environment for developing database applications. With Access you can define your database, build forms and reports for accessing or displaying the data stored in your database, and create programs in Visual Basic to manipulate the data. While Access comes with a database system of its own, Access isn't limited to using just that database. You can create Access applications with any database—from dBase to Oracle.

The first step in designing any Access application is deciding what data you will be storing in your database and how best to organize this information. In this chapter you'll be introduced to a method for designing databases and the fundamental rules that you should follow in order to build efficient Access applications.

In this chapter, you will learn:

- How to determine what data you need to store.

- What a relational database is and how to create one.

- How to organize the data you need for your application into relational tables.

- How to make the best use of Access to help you manage your data, including how to set up appropriate relationships between the database's component elements and data structures.

Access 95 and Data

Working with Microsoft Access means working with data. There are lots of programming tools available, but there is no better product for building database applications than Microsoft Access. In this chapter you'll get an introduction to the fundamentals of database design and see how to use Access to start creating the databases and tables for a sales order management application.

What Is a Database Application?

A *database application* is an application that is primarily concerned with storing, manipulating, and retrieving information. Access provides a complete environment for managing data and creating applications that use that data. Access has built-in tools for creating tables that store your data and also for building queries to display and update that data. Access also has tools for designing forms and reports, and an integrated programming environment that allows you to build applications that will do anything that you might need.

Businesses create database applications for a variety of reasons. In the early days of computerization, companies saw computers as a way to save money. By having the computer store and retrieve information, rather than recording data on paper forms, the business could reduce the number of clerks it employed. More recently, companies have come to realize that access to business information can have strategic importance for them; data is a valuable resource for business planning.

With this shift in emphasis, it has become more important that the data captured by an application be stored in a way that makes it available to people throughout the company, possibly in different locations.

Example: A Sales Order System

One typical example of a database application is a sales order system. A sales order system records information about customer orders for the purchase of company products. Figure 1.1 shows an Access form that can be associated with a paper-based order system. The problem with a paper-based system is that the data isn't generally available for review analysis—only the person with access to the file cabinet with the completed forms can provide any information about company sales.

Nor should a sales order system just record orders—to be really useful, the system must also record information about the company's customers and products. Once you start storing a variety of information in your system, you

FIGURE 1.1

Sample sales order forms and inventory records

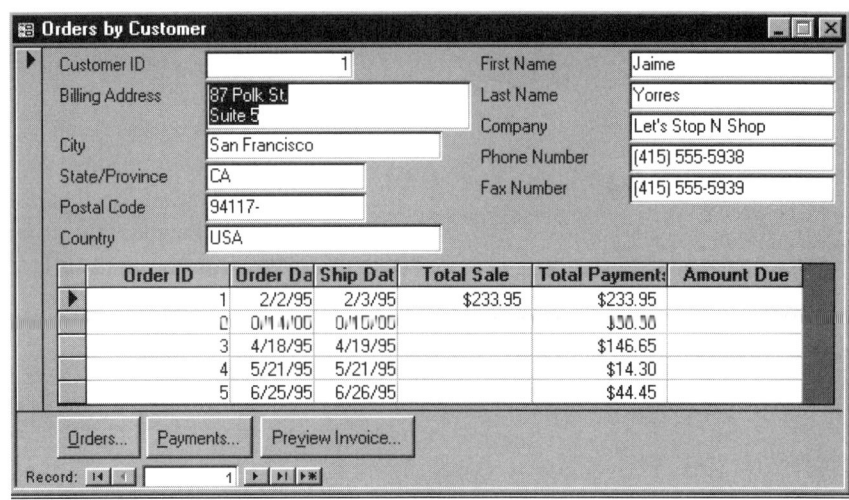

must separate the sales information from the customer information, and the customer information from the product information. If you don't separate the customers and product data, then every time you enter an order, you will have to re-enter the customer and product data in order to complete the order. Not only would this be time-consuming, it's also likely to lead to errors.

By separating the different kinds of data you also make it easier to retrieve data. It's a lot easier to find all the customers in Connecticut when the customer data is stored separately from the product data. However, when you divide your data up you must also set up links between customers and products, and the sales orders that they depend on.

A well-designed database system lets you easily retrieve the system's data in a variety of formats. The data can be used to determine who is buying which products, and how often they order. This information can then be used to ensure that the right products are in stock, that the right advertising is being used and the right investments are being made in research and development projects.

As the data designer for a sales order database application, it is your responsibility to decide which information the application will store and to create the data structures to store the information, the queries to filter it, the forms to display it, and the reports to print it. The way you design the database components has a profound effect on the company's ability to make effective use of the information stored in the database.

Database Design

Figure 1.2 shows the three stages in the process of designing your database: investigation of the company's needs, design of the database, and creation of your database. In the investigation stage you try to determine which information will be stored in your database. In the second stage, you design the data structures to hold the information about those items. And, of course, after you design your database, you must eventually create it with its component objects—tables, queries, forms, reports, and supporting VBA code.

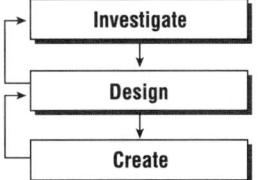

FIGURE 1.2

The three stages in designing and creating your database

The stages for creating a database are not strictly sequential. Even at the beginning of your investigation you will find yourself making preliminary designs based on what you learn. Later, you will find that setting up the data structures in your database will raise questions that require you to go back to your design, ask more questions, and make modifications to the database design. You will find that this process is never really complete—as the company changes and grows (or shrinks) the demands on the database will also change. Those changes will often result in changes to your data design.

Which Entities?

As your investigation proceeds, your first design decision will be to determine which items (or *entities*) you will store information about, as shown in Figure 1.3. In database terminology, an entity is an object or event important to a process, such as a customer, a product, a sales call, or an invoice. In some cases, you will have a specifications document detailing the information to be stored in the database, and perhaps the types of reports to generate from the data. In other cases, you will need to figure out what data should be stored in your database by talking to users of the present system and examining paper records.

FIGURE 1.3

The first step in the design process is determining data entities.

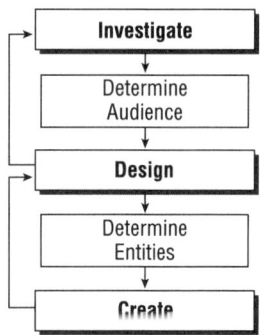

Some of the entities that must be involved in a sales order application are obvious, because they are part of the description of the system. You would expect any sales order application to track information about customers, their orders, and the products the customers buy. Other entities are not so obvious. Will the bills sent to the customers for their purchases be part of the system? If they are, then you will need to add them to the list of entities you will store information about.

That's only the beginning, though. Designing a database is not an exercise in abstract thought. Every database is designed to meet the needs of some set of users (it's hard to get funding for an application if no one is going to use it). In deciding what information will be stored in the database, the audience and users of the system must be considered. To do this, you must identify the database's audience. This is the first step of the investigation, as shown in Figure 1.3.

The System Audience

In our hypothetical sales order system, sales orders are phoned in from sales representatives while they are out visiting customers. If the only people using the system are the clerks who receive the orders and record them, then you will only need to store the minimum information necessary to process an order. This might consist of just the customer name and address, the list of products purchased, and the total price.

It would be an unusual system that had so few users, though. A more likely design for a sales order system would include order fulfillment and shipping. As a result, the shipping department would also need some of the information in the system. The shipping department would want the system to match orders to inventory to make sure that (at the very least) the company doesn't accept orders for non-existent products.

It also wouldn't be surprising if the vice-president of sales were to take an interest in the system. If so, she would want to be able to retrieve information about the orders that would help her analyze the customers who buy the company's products. For instance, she'll want to know how many orders are being placed by each customer segment (seniors, professionals, suburbanites, and so on) and what the trends for each segment are. If that's the case, your database will also need to store information about the customer segments that are relevant to your company's line of products.

System Scope

Determining the *scope* of the application is an important part of building a database and hinges on determining the project's audience (see Figure 1.4). Application scope is a major factor in controlling which entities will have their information stored in the database. In our example, the sales order system used only by the sales clerks has a very narrow scope. On the other hand, the sales order system that involves the shipping department, inventory, and the vice-president of sales would have a very broad scope (and that's without handling invoicing).

FIGURE 1.4

As your investigation proceeds, you can determine which information is to be stored.

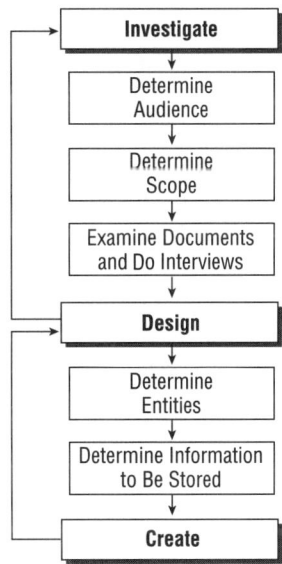

The scope of the application should be determined by the needs of its users. As a result, limiting the number (or more precisely, the categories) of different users will help control the scope of the application and the number of entities to be tracked. You should remember that the narrower you keep the scope, the more likely it is that you will be able to complete the application. On the other hand, too narrow a scope will result in delivering a database application too limited to be of any real use.

No matter how carefully you (and the potential users) determine who will be using the system and for what purposes, after the system is deployed new groups of users will probably find they have a use for it. They will make new demands on the system. Planning ahead for standard requirements, such as reports, invoicing, and customer lists, can save time later on—even if users don't initially request these features.

Including Relevant Information

After determining which entities will be included in your application, you need to decide what information about those entities will be stored in your database. In most cases you will be building a system to supplement or replace an existing system that doesn't share data well (either a paper-based system or one running on a mainframe computer using a legacy database application). The business will already have some process in place for taking orders from its customers. So, as Figure 1.4 shows, you can begin determining what data must be stored by gathering the documents and records already being used.

For the sales order system in our example, this will mean getting a copy of the sales order forms, the inventory records, the catalogue of products, and so on. Every place on those forms and records where information can be written or displayed corresponds to a potential data item that you may need to record in your database.

You'll also need to talk to all of the people who are involved in processing sales orders. It frequently turns out that much of the information that people use is never written down, but is passed orally. For example, the current sales order forms may not have an "Urgent" box on them that employees could use to indicate a rush order. In your investigation, though, you may find that sales representatives frequently call in with "high priority" orders.

You may also find people using information from the system in unexpected ways. For instance, the accounting department may keep track of the total purchases for each customer for the last six months in order to determine the customer's credit worthiness. Sales reps may make note of customers' birthdays so they can send them birthday cards. If so, you'll also be expected to keep this information in your database.

Defining Entities

By this point in the process you've decided what entities make up your database and what information you need to store. As your investigation proceeds, you will start assigning information to entities, as Figure 1.5 shows. During this part of the process, you will formally define the entities that make up the system by deciding which data belongs with which entity. Some of these decisions are easy: the sales order form has an order date on it—you will need to store the order date as part of the sales order.

FIGURE 1.5

After the investigation is complete, you can assign information items to entities.

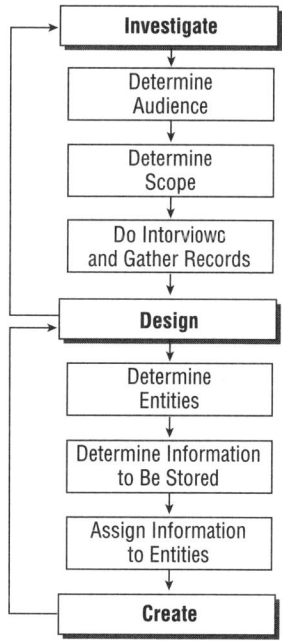

Frequently, you will find data that could be stored as part of two different items in your database. The sales order form will have a shipping address that differs from the billing address, for instance. As part of designing the database you'll have to answer the question, "Is the shipping address part of the sales order information or part of the customer information?"

Unfortunately, at this stage there are no hard and fast rules about deciding which information belongs with which items. One way of making these decisions is to consider whether the information is likely to be different every time the user enters data. In the Sales Order system, to determine which entity the shipping information belongs to, you would ask "Should the user re-enter the shipping address every time a sales order is created?"

The answer depends on the way the business is run. If sales orders are likely to be shipped to a different customer every time, then entering the shipping address with every sales order makes sense. In this situation, the shipping address is part of the sales order information and is created with each new sales order.

On the other hand, if your business tends to sell its products to the same customers over and over again, you probably won't want to re-enter the customer's address for each order. Instead, when you enter the customer's name or identifying code, you will want the customer's address to be automatically retrieved. Where you have the same customers making purchases on a regular basis, the shipping address belongs with the rest of the customer information.

The Physical Database

Up until this point you have been working with the logical design of your database. A logical data design is done on paper or, in the case of very small projects, in your head. A logical design is independent of the constraints that may be imposed by the database system used to store the data.

After the planning and analysis phase is completed, as Figure 1.6 shows, you begin to create your database using Microsoft Access. At that point you move from working with a logical data design to using Access to create a database on your computer. Like the shift from investigating to designing, moving from logical to physical database design isn't a one-way process. During the creation of the database you will shift back and forth between physical and logical design. As you cycle between the logical and physical design of your database you will make many modifications to your database as you refine your design.

F I G U R E 1.6

Near the end of the design phase you can create a preliminary version of your database.

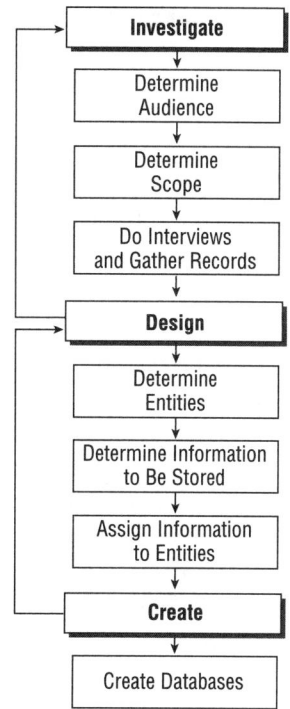

Revising your physical database as you refine your logical design requires a powerful, flexible database system. Some database management systems recommend that you don't move to the physical design until you have finalized your logical design, because it is so difficult to make changes to the database. In the real world, this is unrealistic.

Access makes it easy to modify your design so that you can use Access to help you refine your logical database even while you are starting to construct your database. You can even use Access to prototype an application: creating interface elements (primarily forms) on which users can run tests and comment. Early feedback from your users will aid you in deciding what data you need to have in your database and which entities they belong with.

With older database products, this would be difficult or impossible. More inflexible systems often require the database designer to use a separate prototyping product to design the application's interface. Access forms are so easy to design that you don't need a separate prototyping product to show users how their application will work. Nor do your users need to learn how to work with your prototyping tool and then how to work with your database tool. With Access you can use one tool both as your development tool and as your production system.

Creating Databases

Once you have determined your data needs, you are ready to create your database—or databases. One of the greatest temptations in creating a database application is to put all of the information that you require for your application into one giant database. This is almost always a mistake. You can bet that the customer information used by the sales order system will be required by some other application in the future. By placing your customer data in a separate Access database you make it easier to reuse your data.

So, when you create a database, the first thing you must do is decide what data will (and won't) go into it. Most applications require several databases. For instance, in order to support the sales order application, you should create a database to hold customer information, another to hold product information, and a third to hold information about sales orders. A fourth database to hold invoicing data might also be required.

There is one very important reason to separate your application into at least two databases: one Access database containing all of the application's tables and another holding its forms, reports, and other interface elements. This separation greatly simplifies updating forms and reports as users request changes in the application's interface. With the user interface elements stored in a separate database you can simply replace that database whenever you need to update a form, report, or the system's programming. However, if your company's data is stored in the same database as your forms and reports, you can't replace the database without also wiping out the data stored in it.

To prevent this problem, you should divide the database into two components: one database for the data tables, and another for all the other database components, such as forms, reports, queries, and code modules. The database that contains the forms and reports can use Access' ability to share tables from other databases to link to the tables in the database containing the system's data.

Using the Relational Model

Once you've created your database, the next step is to create the structures within the database to hold your data. As Figure 1.7 shows, this happens simultaneously in the design phase and the create phase. While it might be possible to completely design your database on paper before creating it, Access is such a powerful and flexible tool for refining your database that you should use it as part of your designer's toolkit.

FIGURE 1.7

Access allows you to normalize your tables by actually creating them in your database.

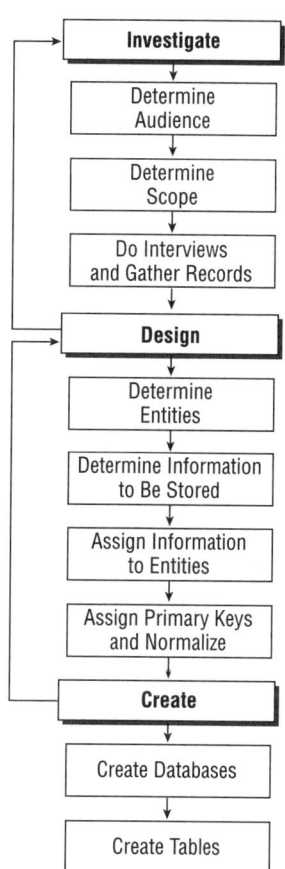

Tables

Many different models have been suggested for storing data. Access uses the relational model. In the relational model, data is organized into tables. If you've ever looked at a multiplication table or a train schedule, you've seen this kind of data structure before. A table organizes data into a set of rows and columns. In the relational model, each row represents a set of related information, while columns represent the kind of data stored in each row.

The train schedule in Figure 1.8, for instance, is an excellent example of a relational database table. Each row in the schedule represents a different train. Each column holds the time the train arrives at each station (train 531 arrives in Guelph at 7:00, for instance).

FIGURE 1.8

A train schedule is an example of a relational table.

Train Number	Toronto	Guelph	Kitchener	London	Sarnia
420	4:20	5:00	6:05	8:30	9:21
426	5:20	6:00	7:05	9:30	10:21
531	6:20	7:00	8:05	10:30	11:21
001	7:20	8:00	9:05	11:30	12:21
907	10:00	10:40	10:45	12:40	N/A

Columns

Rows ⟶

It's common for the rows in a relational table to be referred to as *records* and the columns as *fields*. Since that's what the Access documentation does, that's the convention used in this book.

The relational model is attractive because, thanks to its basis in mathematics, the rules for working with it are very well defined (and you don't have to learn the math). Because there is industry-wide acceptance of the relational model, once you understand the Access relational database you are ready to work with a relational database from any vendor.

To convert your data design to the relational model, your entities (sales orders, customers, products) become tables in the database, and the information about those items (dates, addresses) becomes fields in the table.

Relational Tables

The difference between a relational table and a multiplication table is that the relational table has a *primary key*. A primary key is a field (or group of fields) that uniquely identifies each record in the table. In the train schedule, for instance, the train number would be a good choice as a primary key, as no two trains will have the same number.

Table 1.1 shows an initial design for the customer table of a sales order system. You might have created this table design by reviewing all the forms and reports for the existing system and noting every field that seemed to hold customer-related data.

At this point the table is in design mode; no data has been entered into it. It is often valuable to enter some test data into these tables to support the sample forms you are using to get advice from your users. However, making changes to these tables can cause data to be lost, so you shouldn't start filling the table with your company's actual data until you are certain that the design of the tables is final.

Once you have decided which fields will make up the table, you need to select which field (or fields) should make up the table's primary key. Most tables will have a number of *candidate keys*. In this customer table, for instance, you might use the customer first name plus customer last name as the primary key for the record. There are problems with this choice because you might have two customers with the same name. Since this would violate the rule that a primary key must uniquely identify each record in the table, you wouldn't be able to use the customer's name as the table's primary key.

Sometimes there is no combination of fields in a table that can function as a primary key. As a result, many database designers resort to assigning a unique and arbitrary number to each record and using that as a primary key. If that is the case, Access offers a built-in data type—the AutoNumber data type—that makes it easy to create unique record IDs even when there is no field that has guaranteed unique data. An AutoNumber field generates a new number in the field each time a record is added to the table.

In the tblCustomer table in Table 1.1, a CustomerID field of the Auto-Number data type guarantees that customer records will be unique and offers a convenient single key field for linking to other tables.

T A B L E   1.1:   The Customer Table (tblCustomer)

Field Name	Data Type	Length	Field Description	Primary Key
CustomerID	AutoNumber		Unique identifying ID	Yes
CustomerLastName	Text	15	Customer's last name	No

TABLE 1.1: The Customer Table (tblCustomer) *(Continued)*

Field Name	Data Type	Length	Field Description	Primary Key
CustomerFirstName	Text	15	Customer's first name	No
CustomerAge	Number–Single		Customer's age in years	No
CustomerBirthDate	Date/Time		Date customer was born	No
BillingStreet	Text	25	Street address for invoicing	No
BillingCity	Text	15	City to send invoice to	No
BillingState	Text	15	State to send invoice to	No
BillingPostalCode	Text	11	Postal code to send invoice to	No
ShippingStreet	Text	25	Street Address to send goods to	No
ShippingCity	Text	15	City to send goods to	No
ShippingState	Text	15	State to send goods to	No
ShippingPostalCode	Text	11	Postal Code to send goods to	No
SalesRep	Text	25	Name of sales rep who made the sale	No
SalesArea	Text	25	Sales area serviced by the sales rep	No
SegmentName	Text	10	Segment of population the customer is in	No
Phone1	Text	25	Phone number	No
Phone2	Text	25	Fax number	No

In Exercise 1.1 you'll create a customer table and define the primary key for it.

EXERCISE 1.1

Creating a Customer Table and Defining a Primary Key

1. Start Access and create a database called Customer. In the Customer database create a tblCustomer table to match the one in Table 1.1.

2. Click on the gray record selector to the left of the CustomerID field. The field line will display in inverse video to indicate that it is selected.

3. Click on the Primary Key button. A small key appears in the gray record selector to the left of the CustomerID field to indicate that it is now the record's Primary key.

4. Close the table, saving your changes.

Congratulations! You've created an Access table that, because it has a primary key, is a part of the relational model.

The standard prefix tbl is used for tables, as part of a naming convention which makes the database self-documenting.

Normalizing the Database

In the initial stages of your database design, there were few rules to help you decide which items you needed to store information about. Once you begin to move your design to the point where you are creating relational tables, that all changes. The relational model defines a set of rules to help you create a well-designed database.

Microsoft Exam Objective

Apply basic concepts of normalization.

Within the relational model there is a hierarchy of five table designs, called the *normal forms*, which define the characteristics of a good relational table. Typically, after you design a table you will examine your design to see if it meets the criteria of the first of the normal forms. If it doesn't, you will modify your design to move the table into first normal form. Once that's done, you will repeat the process for each of the remaining four normal forms. This process of refining your table design to move it up through the five normal forms is called "normalizing" your data.

Normalizing Your Data

The relational model and the five normal forms were defined in order to make programmers more productive. By refining your table design using the normal forms, you reduce problems that may occur in updating your databases. As you'll see in this chapter, each normal form is designed either to make your data more usable or to reduce problems when records are added to or deleted from your tables. (The latter applies in the case of creation of duplicate customer entries with different address data.)

Despite the general usefulness of the normal forms, not all the normal forms are used in every business situation. A data warehouse, for instance, might be left in first normal form. It's unusual to see a database left in second normal form, and fourth and fifth normal forms are not typically used in business situations. The result of applying the normal forms (as shown in Figure 1.9) is that you end up with more (and smaller) tables than you have before you normalize your design.

First normal form makes it possible for data to be retrieved from the database easily. First normal form can create problems, though, when records are changed or deleted. In a data warehouse environment, these problems aren't considered important, because while records may be added to the warehouse they are seldom removed or changed. Since the primary purpose of a data warehouse is reporting, and first normal form facilitates data retrieval, first normal form is appropriate for a data warehouse.

While the first normal form may be acceptable by itself, it is very unusual to leave a database in second normal form. Second normal form eliminates some, but not all, of the problems that can occur when data is changed or deleted. To fully eliminate these problems, a database must be moved to third normal form. As a result, if a database is going to be subject to changes and deletions, it should be moved through second normal form into third normal form. In this chapter, second and third normal form will be considered together since they can be combined to make one, simpler rule.

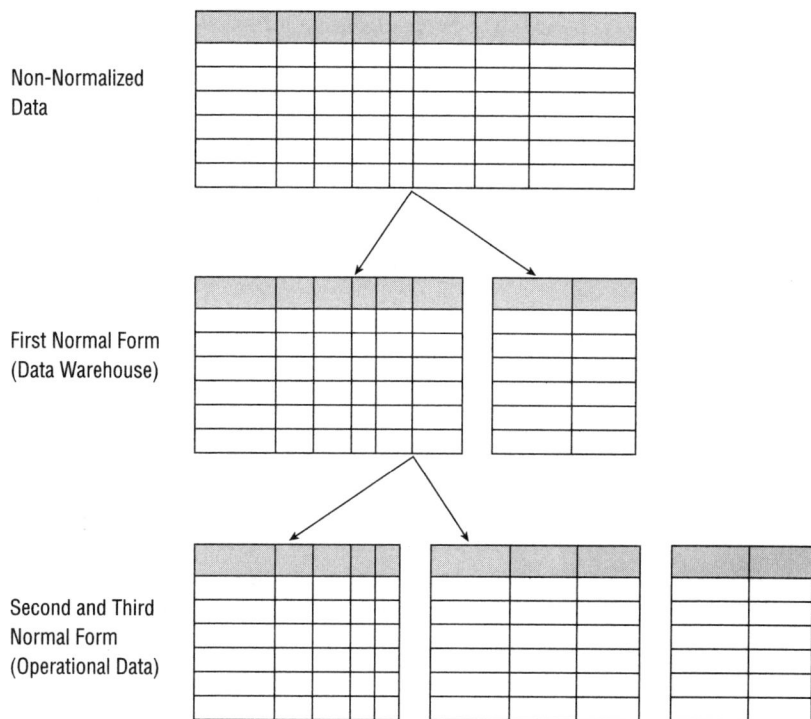

FIGURE 1.9

The standard business system normal forms

Non-Normalized Data

First Normal Form (Data Warehouse)

Second and Third Normal Form (Operational Data)

While the relational model defines a fourth and fifth normal form, in a typical business situation tables are usually left in third normal form. Normalizing your tables typically results in the creation of more tables. Since fourth and fifth normal forms handle relatively obscure situations, the extra tables generated by moving to those forms are regarded as an unnecessary complication for most business applications.

So, what are the normal forms? The easiest way to understand the normal forms is to take a relational table and move it through the first, second, and third normal forms. As the table is design is refined you'll be able to see not only how to normalize a table, but also what problems are eliminated by normalization.

First Normal Form

First normal form specifies that the table must not contain any repeating fields. Repeating fields occur when there are two or more fields that hold the same kind of information. Table 1.1 showed a proposed layout for tblCustomer, a table in the Sales Order system that would hold customer data. There are at least two sets of fields in the tblCustomer table that can be considered repeating fields: the two sets of address fields and the two phone fields.

Leaving repeating fields in a table is probably the most common design error made in creating a database. It's also an error that is will create problems as the demands on the database change over time.

Handling Changes

Imagine, for instance, that you need to store a third address for a customer (an address to send advertising information to, for instance). With the repeating address fields of the tblCustomer table, the only way to handle the new address is to add another set of address fields to the table. While you are making this change, no one else will be able to use the table. If you are storing data in an Access MDB file, this process will take only a few minutes, so the data will be unavailable only for a short period of time.

If you are using Access to work with data in a SQL Server database, the change becomes more burdensome. Adding those new fields will require you to unload all the data in the table, re-create the table with the new fields, and reload the data. If the table contains thousands of customer records, this process of dumping and unloading data will take several hours. And, as with the MDB file, while you are dumping and reloading the data, the table can't be used by anyone else.

Suppose also that the government increases the size of the postal code portion of the address—you must alter the postal code field for both the billing and mailing addresses. A typical error that occurs in changing repeating fields is that only some of the fields get changed. If this happens in adjusting the size of the postal code files there will be problems when address data is updated. The fields that were enlarged would store the new code in full but the fields that were missed would truncate the data.

Retrieving Data

The most important problem with repeating fields is that they make it difficult to get to the data you want, because information is stored in too many places. For instance, trying to find the customers with an address of any kind in Michigan will be difficult because of the repeating address fields in this table. In a design with multiple address fields, you must check the Sent-ToState and the BillingState for every customer to see if either address is in Michigan. And every new address type that is added requires you to check yet another State address field to find the customers in Michigan.

The same kinds of problems occur with the Phone fields: if you decide to keep track of mobile phone numbers, you would have to redesign the table; a query to find phone numbers in a particular area code will require searching both Phone fields.

Recognizing Repeating Fields

It's not always easy to spot repeating fields in your table design. For instance, do the fields "First Name" and "Last Name" make up a set of repeating fields?

One way to test if a field is repeating information is to ask if the number of the fields could be increased indefinitely. Although the company is storing only two phone numbers now, is there any reason why the company wouldn't want to store three or four phone numbers (perhaps adding mobile and radio phones) 12 or 18 months in the future? Probably not. In the case of name fields (FirstName, Middle-Name, LastName), although there are two (or three) name fields, they represent different types of information, and each person can have only one first name, (possibly) one middle name, and one last name, so these are not repeating fields. Address, phone, and online ID fields are repeating data, because one person can have multiple addresses, multiple phone numbers, and multiple online IDs.

Another test for identifying repeating fields is to imagine trying to find a record in the table based on a value in any of the suspect fields. If the audience the database serves will ask those kinds of questions, then the fields should be considered to be repeating fields. The questions "Find the record where any address is in Michigan" and "Find the record where any purchase field is greater than $1000" are typical examples of this kind of check. You would probably be surprised to find that your business frequently asks to "Find the record where any part of the customer's name is 'Sharon,'" though, which suggests that the name fields are not repeating fields.

Even if it is not initially requested during the design phase, it is an excellent idea to break down any name data in a table into Salutation, FirstName, MiddleName, LastName, and Suffix fields. This permits maximum flexibility in displaying, sorting, and printing data in different formats later on.

Similar to determining the scope of your database project, deciding if two fields are repeating information depends on the needs of your business.

Moving a Table into First Normal Form

Moving a table into first normal form, as shown in Figure 1.10, consists of creating another table where the fields do not repeat. Thus, instead of having two Phone fields in one table, you will have a separate table for phone numbers, with one phone number per record. This process turns the repeating fields of the original table into repeating records in the new table.

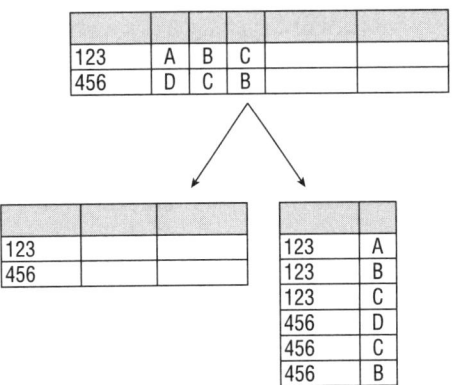

For instance, to move the tblCustomer table into first normal form, the customer address fields must be removed from the tblCustomer table and placed in a table of their own. In this new table, the address fields do not repeat. Instead, one record in the table will hold the billing address for the customer and a second record will hold the shipping address.

In order to link the addresses in this new table back to the customer they belong to, the CustomerID field is also added to the new CustomerAddress table. This allows you to retrieve the CustomerAddress records for any tblCustomer record by matching the IDs in the two records.

To match a field of the AutoNumber data type, use a Long Integer field in the related table.

Finally, a field is added to the new table to distinguish between the various kinds of addresses. This field will contain a "B" when the address is a billing address and an "S" for shipping addresses. Since users will need to know what these codes mean, another field (the AddressDescription field) is also added to the tblCustomerAddress table.

The process is repeated for the Phone1 and Phone2 fields: a new tblCustomerPhone table with a single phone number field is created, the CustomerID field is added to tie the data to a specific customer, and a Description field is added.

Tables 1.2, 1.3, and 1.4 show the results of moving the tblCustomer table to first normal form.

TABLE 1.2 The tblCustomer Table in First Normal Form	**Field Name**	**Field Description**	**Primary Key**
	CustomerID	Unique identifying ID	Yes
	CustomerLastName	Customer's last name	No
	CustomerFirstName	Customer's first name	No
	CustomerAge	Customer's age in years	No
	CustomerBirthDate	Date customer was born	No
	SegmentName	Segment of population the customer is in	No
	SalesRep	Name of SalesRep who made the sale	No
	SalesArea	Sales area serviced by the SalesRep	No

TABLE 1.3 The tblCustomer Address Table	**Field Name**	**Field Description**	**Primary Key**
	CustomerID	Unique identifying ID	Yes
	AddressType	Type of address (Billing, Shipping, etc.)	Yes

T A B L E 1.3 *(cont.)* The tblCustomer Address Table	**Field Name**	**Field Description**	**Primary Key**
	AddressDescription	Description of the Address Type	No
	Street	Street Address	No
	City	City	No
	State	State	No
	PostalCode	Postal Code	No

T A B L E 1.4 The tblCustomer-Phone table	**Field Name**	**Field Description**	**Primary Key**
	CustomerID	Unique identifying ID	Yes
	PhoneNumber	Phone number	Yes
	Description	Type of phone number (voice, fax, and so on)	No

By breaking the tblCustomer table up in this way, you avoid a number of problems. To begin with, adding a new address type requires no change to table design. To add a new address, you only need to define a new AddressType ("A" for advertising, for instance) and add the new records.

In addition, there is now only one PostalCode field, so there's only one field to change if the government increases the size of the postal code. Finally, finding all of the customers with an address in Michigan just means looking at the State field of the tblCustomerAddress table.

There are similar benefits in moving the phone number fields to a table of their own. Now you can store as many phone numbers as necessary for each customer, just by typing in the appropriate description for each number.

In Exercise 1.2 you'll modify the tblCustomer table to bring it into first normal form while creating the tblCustomerAddress and tblCustomerPhone tables.

EXERCISE 1.2

Moving a Table into First Normal Form

1. Start Access, open the Customer database, and click on the Tables tab.

2. Click on the tblCustomer table to select it, and select Edit ➤ Copy to copy the table (or press Ctrl+C). Select Edit ➤ Paste to paste the table back into the database (or press Ctrl+V).

3. The Paste Table As dialog box will appear. Enter **tblCustomerAddress** in the Table Name field. Click on the OK button. The tblCustomerAddress table is added to the list of tables in your database.

4. When pasting a table, you have three choices. Choosing Structure Only will create a new table just like the one you copied, but empty of data. Selecting Structure and Data will create a copy of the table plus all the data that was in the table that you copied. Choosing Append Data to an Existing Table will copy the data from the original table to the end of the table whose name you enter in the dialog box (the two tables must have very similar structures).

5. Now you need to remove the extra fields from the tblCustomerAddress table. Click on the tblCustomerAddress table to select it.

6. Click on the Design button to open the table in Design view. Select the fields CustomerAge and CustomerBirthDate, and then press the Delete key. (To delete a group of fields you must first select them.) Repeat the process to select and delete the fields from ShippingStreet to Phone2. The table should now just have the CustomerID and the billing address fields.

7. Since the address fields are no longer dedicated to holding just billing address information, the names for these fields are no longer accurate. You need to alter these field names to describe their more general nature. Click in the BillingStreet field and change the name of the field to Street. Repeat for the other Billing address fields by removing the word *Billing* from their names.

Once your tables are normalized you need to define a primary key for the new tables that you created as part of the normalization process. Since the customer ID field uniquely identifies customer records, this field will also be

---

Setting the Arrow Key Option

You may have noticed that you can't use the arrow keys on your keyboard inside a field—those keys move you from field to field instead of from character to character. If you find this annoying, here's how to make your arrow keys move the cursor from character to character:

1. Select Tools ➢ Options.

2. Select the Keyboard tab.

3. In the Arrow Key Behavior box, select Next Character and click on the OK button.

---

part of the key that identifies customer address records. But since a customer can have many addresses, the customer ID is not enough to uniquely identify an address record. In Exercise 1.3 you'll add a new field to the address record to identify which kind of address each record is. You'll then create a primary key that includes the CustomerID field and the new AddressType field to uniquely identify each record in the table.

EXERCISE 1.3

Creating Primary Keys to Link Tables

1. Click on the gray record selector to the left of the Street field name to select it. Press the Insert key on your keyboard to add a new, blank field line to your table design.

2. In the new line, add a new field called *AddressType*. It should be a Text field with a Field Size of 1, its description should be "Type of address (Billing, Shipping, etc)." Repeat the process for the AddressDescription field, which should be a Text field with a field size of 15 and a description that says "Description of address type."

3. Select the CustomerID and AddressType fields. Click on the Primary Key button to make these fields the primary key for the table.

4. Close the tblCustomerAddress table, saving your changes.

5. In a similar manner, create the tblCustomerPhone table from the tblCustomerAddress table, with three fields: CustomerID, PhoneNumber, and Description.

6. Close the tblCustomerPhone table, saving your changes.

You have now moved the tblCustomer table to first normal form. One of the additional effects of this exercise is that you have added two more tables to your database.

Redundant Data

If you look at the tblCustomer table design you'll see that the table isn't in third normal form. The first potential update anomaly can be found with the CustomerAge and CustomerBirthDate fields. The age field is dependent on the birthdate field because changing the data in the CustomerBirthDate field requires that the CustomerAge field also change. Technically, you would say that the record is storing *redundant data*.

The update anomaly occurs when you change one field but not the other. For instance, if you alter the CustomerBirthDate data without also changing the CustomerAge, it won't be clear how old your customer actually is. This problem can be handled by eliminating the CustomerAge field, which also eliminates the redundancy (you can calculate the customer's age from their birthdate when you need it).

Embedded Records

The tblCustomer record still isn't in third normal form. The tblCustomer record has the name of the sales rep who made the sale to the customer and the area that the particular sales rep services. As in the previous problem, changing the SalesRep field would require you to change the area serviced by the sales rep, or vice versa, which means the table is not in third normal form.

In this situation you cannot simply remove one of the fields, because there is no way to determine the SalesArea from the sales rep's name. The SalesRep fields in the tblCustomer record are really information about one of the entities in the sales order system (SalesReps) that are embedded in another item's (the tblCustomer's) data. Really, the SalesRep information belongs in a table of its own.

This violation of the normal forms goes beyond the simple data redundancy problem found with the CustomerBirthDate and CustomerAge fields. By having the information about a SalesRep stored in a tblCustomer record there is a real possibility that the information about the SalesRep could be lost accidentally. For instance, if all of the customers for a particular SalesRep were deleted you would lose the information that tells you which SalesArea that SalesRep services.

The problem doesn't stop there. Since the SalesRep/SalesArea information is repeated on every record, when SalesReps change their area, every record they appear on must be changed. When that is done, it's certainly possible that one or more records will be missed. The result would be a SalesRep with an area of "Michigan" on one record and "Alaska" on another. How could you tell which one was correct?

To solve this problem, a new table must be created that will hold the SalesRep information (in this case, that's just the SalesRep name and SalesArea fields). Figure 1.11 shows the result of this separation. In order to link the SalesRep to the appropriate tblCustomer Records, the SalesRep field is left in the tblCustomer table. Tables 1.5 and 1.6 show the layout of the two tables.

FIGURE 1.11

In this table, the sales rep area field doesn't depend on the CustomerId.

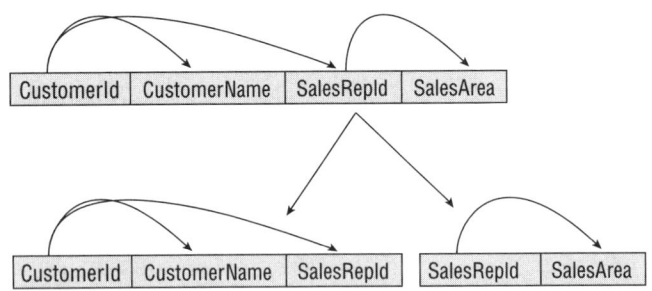

Field Name	**Field Description**	**Primary Key**
CustomerID	Unique identifying ID	Yes
CustomerLastName	Customer's last name	No
CustomerFirstName	Customer's first name	No
CustomerAge	Customer's age in years	No
SalesRep	Name of SalesRep who made the sale	No

TABLE 1.5

The tblCustomer Table in Second Normal Form

TABLE 1.6	Field Name	Field Description	Primary Key
The tblSalesRep Table	SalesRep	Name of sales rep who made the sale	Yes
	SalesArea	Sales area serviced by the sales rep	No
	SegmentName	Segment of population served by the sales rep	No

The Primary Key

At this point you may feel that all of the data in the tables for the Customer database depend on their primary keys. For a table to be in third normal form, though, the fields must be dependent on the *whole* primary key and that's not yet true. In the CustomerAddress table, while every field is dependent on the primary key, the AddressDescription field is dependent only on part of the primary key: the AddressType field.

The problems with tables dependent on part of the primary key are similar to the problems with tables that have fields dependent on each other. Should the description for an address type change, one record with AddressType B may have a different AddressDescription than another record of AddressType B. And removing all of the records of type B would eliminate the ability to retrieve the description for type B records.

As with the SalesRep/SalesArea fields, the solution is to create a new table consisting of AddressType and AddressDescription fields. The AddressType field remains in the CustomerAddress record to link the tables, as shown in Tables 1.7 and 1.8.

TABLE 1.7	Field Name	Field Description	Primary Key
The tblCustomer-Address Table in Third Normal Form	CustomerID	Unique identifying ID	Yes
	AddressType	Type of address (Billing, ShippingSendTo, etc.)	Yes
	Street	Street Address	No
	City	City	No
	State	State	No
	PostalCode	Postal Code	No

	Field Name	Field Description	Primary Key
TABLE 1.8 The Address-Description Table	AddressType	Type of address (Billing, Shipping, etc.)	Yes
	AddressDescription	Description of the Address	No

Creating a Table in Third Normal Form

You can boil down the process of creating a table into five steps:

1. Create the table.

2. Add the required fields.

3. Select a primary key.

4. Remove repeating fields (first normal form).

5. Remove fields dependent on other fields (second and third normal forms).

Fourth and Fifth Normal Forms

Fourth and fifth normal forms are more esoteric than the first three normal forms. Fourth normal form requires that fields in the same record have a necessary relationship with each other.

In our database example, you might add a field to the tblSalesRep record to hold the product line that the SalesRep specializes in. Now the record contains both a SalesArea and a SalesProductLine field, though there is no real connection between the SalesRep's current SalesArea and the product line they support. To put the record in fourth normal form, a tblSalesRepProductLine table should be created containing SalesRep and ProductLine fields. By doing this, your system can now handle SalesReps that support several product lines.

Fifth normal form is used when there are external conditions that would force you to have to create many records to store a single piece of information. For instance, the company might insist that a SalesRep who specializes in snowblowers must also know how to use any other snow removal equipment. As a result, adding one snowblower record to the tblSalesRep table would require the creation of a number of other records for the other snow removal tools the SalesRep must know. In this case, to keep the table in fifth normal form, it might be worthwhile to create a table of product line groupings and have the SalesRep support a product line group rather than a long list of individual products.

Table References

Once you have defined these tables, you'll see that there are relationships between them. For any customer record, for instance, you will want to be able to retrieve the corresponding address records. You made this possible by embedding the primary key for the tblCustomer table in the CustomerAddress table.

Many people (experienced developers are often among them) suffer under the misconception that the term relational refers to the ability of tables to reference each other. After all, these tables are "related" to each other. Don't believe these people! The term *relation* refers to the mathematical basis of the database model that Access is based on. Tables are said to refer to each other rather than relate to each other. The ability of tables to reference each other gives us the term *referential integrity*.

When the primary key for one table is embedded in another table it's called a *foreign key*. In this case, CustomerID (the primary key in the tblCustomer table) is a foreign key in the tblCustomerAddress table.

The Relationships Window

The next step in designing your database is to record relationships. In Access, this can be done using the Relationships window (Figure 1.12 shows the Access Relationships window). Later in this chapter, you will use special relationship options to get Access to help you maintain your data.

In Exercise 1.4 you'll document the relationships in your database using the Relationships window.

FIGURE 1.12

The Access Relation-
ships window allows
you to specify refer-
ences between tables.

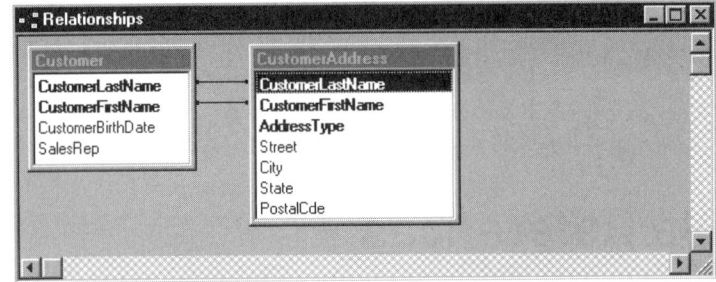

EXERCISE 1.4

Using the Relationships Window

1. Start Access and open the Customer database. Select Tools ≻ Relationships to display the Relationships window and the Add Table
   dialog box.

2. Click on the tblCustomer table in the Add Table dialog box to select it.

3. Click on the OK button to add the tblCustomer table to the Relationships window. Add the tblCustomerAddress table to the Relationships
   window. Click on the Close button to close the Add Table dialog box.

4. Click on the CustomerID field in the tblCustomer table window and
   drag it to the CustomerID field in the tblCustomerAddress table window. The Relationship dialog box appears. Click on the Create button
   to create the new link.

5. The Relationships window shows that Access now recognizes the link
   between the two CustomerID fields.

6. Add the tblCustomerPhone table; create the relationships between it
   and the tblCustomer table, using the CustomerID field again; and
   close the Relationships window.

You have now documented the foreign key relationships among the three
tables in your database. Now you can use those relationships to aid in
linking data on forms and reports.

WARNING

Once you establish relationships between tables, Access will make it more difficult for you to change your table designs if the change would violate relational rules. Access won't let you delete a table involved in a relationship, for instance, or change the size of a text field that is used in a relationship. You should only use the Relationship window when you are sure that you have completed your logical database design and have fully normalized your tables.

Reference Types

As you've seen, one table can be linked to several other tables. A database consisting of many tables will have many different relationships linking the tables together. The tblCustomer table, for instance, is linked to both the tblCustomerAddress and the tblCustomerPhone tables. In the relational model, though, only the links between two tables are considered at any one time. So, the relationship between tblCustomer and tblCustomerAddress is considered to be independent of the relationship between tblCustomer and tblCustomerPurchase table.

When two tables are linked, the link is always implemented through primary and foreign keys: one table's primary key will appear as a foreign key in the other table. There are only three ways that these tables can be joined together (see Figure 1.13):

- **One to one:** In this kind of relationship there is one record in the foreign key table for each record in the table with the primary key.

- **One-to-many:** Here there are many records in the foreign key table for each record in the primary key table.

- **Many-to-many:** There is no explicit many-to-many relationship in Access, but you can create a many-to-many relationship between two tables by creating a junction table, as discussed later in this chapter.

NOTE

See the Northwind sample database for an example of a many-to-many relationship between the Orders and Products tables (one order can have many products, and each product appears on many orders).

F I G U R E 1.13

The relational model
supports three types
of relationships.

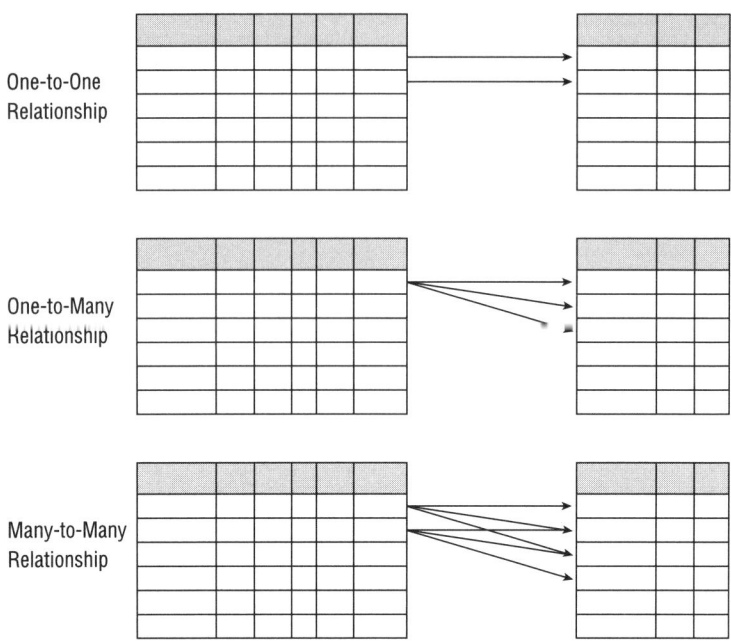

One-to-One
Relationship

One-to-Many
Relationship

Many-to-Many
Relationship

Primary and Foreign Keys

The terms *one-to-one*, *one-to-many*, and *many-to-many* don't refer to how many records are actually tied together in the database. Instead, they refer to how many records could be involved in the links, which is controlled by the involvement of primary and foreign keys in making the references between the tables.

In the Customer database, a quick inspection may show that each customer has exactly one address record. But, because of the way the tables are set up, each customer could have many tblCustomerAddress records at some time in the future. The CustomerID field that is used to join the two tables is the primary key in one table (the tblCustomer table) and a foreign key in the other (the tblCustomerAddress table).

As a primary key, the CustomerID field must be unique, meaning that there will only be one record for any customer in the tblCustomer table. On the tblCustomerAddress side, the CustomerID field is not the complete primary key, and so may repeat over many records. The result is that each tblCustomer record could have many tblCustomerAddress records, making this a one-to-many relationship.

One-to-One Relationships

A one-to-one relationship occurs when the tables are linked through their primary keys and there is only one record in the second table linked to each record in the first table.

Consider a situation in the Customer database where you add a table that lists information about how to contact each customer. Table 1.9 shows this tblCustomerContact table. Since each customer will have only one contact record, the primary key for this table is the tblCustomer CustomerID field—the same key as in the tblCustomer table itself, though its data type is Long Integer rather than AutoNumber.

In some situations multiple contacts might be permitted, and a one-to-many relationship would be called for; but if company policy requires a unique contact for each customer record, a one-to-one relationship is required between tblCustomer and tblCustomerContact.

	Field Name	Field Description	Primary Key
T A B L E 1.9 The tblCustomer Contact Table	CustomerID	Unique identifying ID	Yes
	ContactLastName	Contact's last name	No
	ContactFirstName	Contact's first name	No
	PhoneNumber	Contact's phone number	No
	ContactHours	Hours customer can be contacted	No

The CustomerID field links the tblCustomer and tblCustomerContact tables. Since these fields are the primary keys of their records (and primary keys may not be duplicated), there can be only one record in each table for any CustomerID. This is the definition of a one-to-one relationship.

Unless your one-to-one relationship would create an unreasonably large table, you should probably combine any tables in a one-to-one relationship into a single table. Normally, one-to-one relationships are recommended only when the fields in one record are split into two different tables for some reason other than normalizing the data. This might happen if, for instance, the size of the tblCustomer record exceeded the maximum allowed size for the database system (Access 95 limits records to a maximum of 2KB of actual data, for example). Should this occur, the only choice the table designer has is to add a new table to the database in a one-to-one relationship with the original table. Effectively, the single table in the logical design of the database is broken into two physical tables as part of implementing the physical database design.

One-to-Many Relationships

This is the most typical relationship between two tables. In this relationship the primary key for one table appears as a foreign, non-primary key in another table. Since a non-primary key may occur many times in a table, there can be many records in the foreign key table for each record in the primary key table.

One-to-many relationships are created as part of the process of normalizing your data. You'll notice that when you normalized the tblCustomer table, you created several one-to-many relationships. Since the first step in normalizing a table is to remove repeating fields, it's not surprising that normalizing produces a new table with many records for each record in the original table.

In moving to third normal form, you pulled the SalesRep information out of the tblCustomer record. One of the problems with leaving the SalesRep data in the tblCustomer record was that the data for one sales representative was duplicated on many tblCustomer records. That duplication was eliminated by putting the information in a separate tblSalesRep table. Instead, a relationship of one tblSalesRep record to many tblCustomer records was created.

Many-to-Many Relationships

Access doesn't have an explicit many-to-many relationship type, which is why you won't see this choice when you create a join in the Relationships window. But sometimes you need a many-to-many relationship when there are two entities, each of which can be related to multiple records of the other. For example, students and teachers in a school are related many-to-many since each student can have several teachers, and each teacher has many students.

While Access does not have a many-to-many relationship type, you can create one out of two one-to-many relationships. Exercise 1.5 shows how the student-teacher many-to-many relationship can be implemented through two complementary one-to-many relationships, with a junction table to link the key fields in the two tables (see Figure 1.14). Frequently, you will find that there is some data that can only be stored in the junction table. In Exercise 1.5, for instance, the information on the course that the student takes with the teacher is stored in the junction table.

FIGURE 1.14

Resolving a many-to-many relationship with a junction table

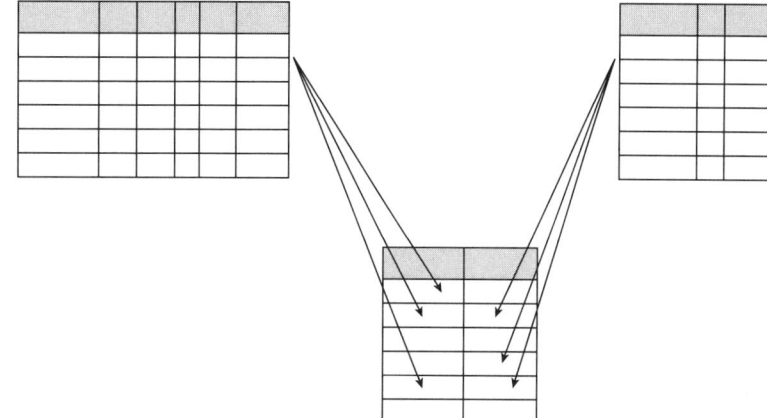

EXERCISE 1.5

Creating a Many-to-Many Relationship

1. Create a tblStudent table with StudentID (AutoNumber data type) as the primary key.

2. Create a tblTeacher table with TeacherID (AutoNumber data type) as the primary key.

3. Create a tblStudentTeacher junction table with two fields of Long Integer type: StudentID and TeacherID. Also add a text field called CourseName that is 15 characters in length.

4. Link tblStudent to tblStudentTeacher in a one-to-many relationship on the StudentID field.

5. Link tblTeacher to tblStudentTeacher in a one-to-many relationship in the TeacherID field.

Referential Integrity

Once you have linked your tables in one-to-many or one-to-one relationships, you may still have problems with your data that cannot be addressed by normalization alone. If, for instance, you delete a tblCustomer record, you would orphan all of the records in the other tables that refer to it—obviously not a good situation. But you needn't delete the tblCustomer record to create a problem. If you had used the CustomerLastName field as part of the key that links the tables together, just changing a customer's last name would disconnect it from its related records in the other tables. In our sales order system we won't have this problem because we used an AutoNumber field for our CustomerID and AutoNumber fields can't be changed.

These problems with maintaining the relationships between records fall under the heading of maintaining *referential integrity*. For one-to-one and one-to-many relationships, Access can prevent referential integrity problems from occurring, if you select the appropriate option when creating a link between tables. In Exercise 1.6 you'll set the referential integrity options for the tblCustomer to tblCustomerAddress relationship and see how Access can help manage your data.

EXERCISE 1.6

Enforcing Referential Integrity

1. Open the Customer database, open the Relationships window, and add tblCustomer and tblCustomerAddress to it (if they are not there already). Drag the CustomerID field from tblCustomer to the CustomerID field in the other table; the Relationships dialog box will open.

2. Click on the Enforce Referential Integrity checkbox and then click on the OK button to create a one-to-many link between the tables. Close the Relationships window.

3. Open the tblCustomerAddress table that you created in Exercise 3.1 in datasheet mode and try to add a record to it. When you leave the record, or try to close the table while on the new record, you will get an error message telling you that you "can't add or change record. Referential integrity rules require a related record in table 'tblCustomer'."

4. Open the tblCustomer table, and add a record to it; and then add a record for the same customer to the tblCustomerAddress table. Now there won't be an error when you save the record and close tblCustomerAddress, since there is a matching record in tblCustomer.

How do you know if there are referential integrity problems in a database which already contains data—perhaps one you have taken over after it was created by an end user unfamiliar with database design? If you try to set up a one-to-many link with referential integrity between two tables in the Relationships window and you get an error message saying "Microsoft Access can't create this relationship and enforce referential integrity," this means that there are records incompatible with the link you are trying to set up, typically records in the "many" table that don't have matching records in the "one" table.

To set up a relationship with referential integrity, you have to clean up the records that are causing the problem before you can create the link. Access provides two queries which are useful for dealing with such situations: the Find Duplicates Query and the Find Unmatched Query. After finding the unmatched records, and deleting (or changing) them, you can now link the two tables in a relationship with the Enforce Referential Integrity option checked.

Cascade Updates and Cascade Deletes

Microsoft
✓ *Exam*
Objective

Use the cascade update and cascade delete options.

In addition to the Enforce Referential Integrity option, there are two other important options you can set when creating a link between tables in the Relationships window: Cascade Updates and Cascade Deletes.

Returning to the Relationships Window

When you joined two tables in the Relationships window, you used the Relationships dialog box to specify the fields involved in the join. *Join* is the term for the link between tables, represented by the line linking two tables in the Relationships window. In the lower part of the Relationships dialog box, the type of join is displayed ("one-to-one," "one-to-many," or "indeterminate" for many-to-many).

In the Relationships dialog box, you can check the Enforce Referential Integrity checkbox to have Access prevent problems caused by updating or deleting records that reference each other. Checking the Enforce Referential

Integrity checkbox enables the checkboxes below it: Cascade Update Related Fields and Cascade Delete Update Related Fields (usually referred to as Cascade Update and Cascade Delete).

Preventing Problems

As noted earlier, selecting Enforce Referential Integrity causes Access to turn on some powerful control features. With Enforce Referential Integrity checked, Access will not allow you to add a record to the table on the "many" side of a relationship until you have added a corresponding record on the "one" side. For example, in the Customer database with referential integrity enforced, Access would not allow you to add a tblCustomerAddress record unless there is a corresponding record in the tblCustomer table. With Enforce Referential Integrity checked, the record on the "one" side of the relationship must always be added before any records are added on the "many" side.

The Enforce Referential Integrity option will also prevent you from orphaning records by deleting records on the "one" side of a relationship or changing the primary key data. Attempting to delete a tblCustomer record that has related tblCustomerAddress records, for example, will cause Access to display an error message and prevent the deletion. With Enforce Referential Integrity checked, the records on the "many" side of the relationship must always be deleted before any records on the "one" side.

During the design phase, while using Access to prototype your database, you will probably want to leave this box unchecked. Once you start enforcing referential integrity, making changes to your database becomes more complicated. Once you move out of the design phase though, you'll want to have this feature enabled.

WARNING Sometimes it may seem that enforcing referential integrity isn't desirable. For example, company policy may require order records be archived even after a customer record has been deleted. However, this purpose is better served by writing code to archive the orders records into a special archival set of tables, rather than disabling referential integrity. Turning off referential integrity to allow customers to be deleted will either lead to customer records being deleted inappropriately (damaging the integrity of your data) or will require you to write additional code to ensure that customer records are only deleted during archive operations.

Coping with Problems

Access's referential integrity options can be used to resolve problems that occur when you make changes to related records. When you select Cascade Update or Cascade Delete (or both), Access will take care of the records on the "many" side of a relationship when a record on the "one" side is deleted or has its primary key changed. Here's what the two options do:

- **Cascade Update:** When Cascade Update is selected, any change to the primary key of the record on the "one" side of the relationship will automatically be performed on the corresponding field of the records on the "many" side. In other words, changing the CustomerLastName field in a tblCustomer record will cause Access to automatically change the CustomerLastName field in the corresponding records in the tblCustomerAddress table.

- **Cascade Delete:** Selecting this option will cause any records on the "many" side of the relationship to be deleted when the record on the "one" side is deleted. With this option selected, deleting a tblCustomer record will automatically delete all of the tblCustomerAddress records for that customer. Access will warn you when Cascade Delete will trigger the deletion of related records.

More Integrity?

Other database systems offer more options for enforcing referential integrity, some of which may appear in future versions of Access.

One referential integrity option offered by many other systems is Cascade Null. Using Cascade Null, when a record on the "one" side of a table is deleted, the database sets the keys of the corresponding "many" records to Null. This allows records orphaned by the deletion of the "one" record to be processed at a later date.

Some systems also offer the ability to automatically generate the "one" record in a relationship when a record is added to the table on the "many" side. This could be helpful in a real-world situation where a clerk has to enter an order for a new customer.

 Changing the value of a primary key when Access is enforcing referential integrity is not an easy task. To change the data in a table's primary key field you must first copy the record to a new record (changing the primary key field), then copy the related records in any referenced tables (also changing the primary key fields), and finally delete the original records. Turning on Cascade Updates makes this process much simpler: you just change the value in the key field.

Summary

Access is a tool for developers to create database applications; it provides the tools to create and store data according to the relational database model. The relational database model organizes data into tables made up of rows and columns—or records and fields in Access terminology. Each record should have a primary key of one or more fields that uniquely identifies a record.

The relational model also identifies five normal forms for a table. The first through third forms are the most commonly used. To place a table in first normal form, all repeating fields must be removed from the record. Moving a table to second and third normal form means removing any fields that aren't affected when the primary key of the record changes.

Typically, in moving a record to second and third normal form, new tables are created. To link these tables back to the data in the original table, the primary key for the original table is included in the new table. When this happens, those fields are called foreign keys because they point to a record in another table.

Fourth and fifth normal forms provide additional refinements to the relational model, but are not commonly used.

When multiple tables are created with primary and foreign keys, you have defined a relationship between them that is typically one-to-many: one record's primary key can appear as the foreign key in many records of another table. One-to-many relationships can be used in Access to help you display, edit, and print records based on their links to records in other tables, such as printing a customer's phone numbers and addresses on a Customer List report.

One-to-one relationships are needed when database requirements force logical records to be split up into multiple tables. Many-to-many relationships are simulated by two one-to-many relationships to a linking junction table.

Access can efficiently maintain the relationships between records in one-to-many and one-to-one relationships. With Enforce Referential Integrity selected, Access will prevent records from being orphaned through the deletion or update of records on the "one" side of a relationship. With Cascade Update and Cascade Delete also selected, Access will delete or update related records when the record on the "one" side of a relationship is updated or deleted.

Review Questions

1. Below is the table design for a library; it contains information about books and borrowers. Which fields should be in a separate Book table?

   A. Title, DateLastBorrowed, Address

   B. Title, DateLastBorrowed, BookID

   C. Title, BookID, PhoneNumber

   D. Title, BookID, Address

T A B L E 1.1 Library Table Design Elements	Field Name	Field Description
	BookID	Book's unique identifier in the library
	Name	Library member's name
	Title	Book title
	Address	Library member's address
	PhoneNumber	Library member's phone number
	DateLastBorrowed	Last time the book was borrowed by a library member

2. Which field(s) should be removed from the following table design to put the table in first normal form?

   A. LastName, FirstName, MiddleName

   B. BirthDate, HireDate, StartDate, TerminationDate

   C. Hours1WeekPrior, Hours2WeeksPrior, Hours3WeeksPrior

   D. DepartmentCode

T A B L E 1.2	Field Name	Field Description
First Normal Form Elements	EmployeeId	Employee number
	LastName	Employee Last Name
	FirstName	Employee first name
	MiddleName	Employee middle name
	Birthdate	Employee Birthdate
	HireDate	Date employee hired
	StartDate	First date employee worked
	TerminationDate	Date employee left employ
	Hours1WeekPrior	Hours worked last week
	Hours2WeekPrior	Hours worked 2 weeks ago
	Hours3WeekPrior	Hours worked 3 weeks ago
	DepartmentCode	Department employee assigned to

3. When building a new database you should

   A. Cycle between investigation and design before creating your database

   B. Cycle between investigation and design and creation

   C. Complete the investigation before beginning the design stage

   D. Defer creating the database until the design is complete

4. An entity is

   A. A record in a table in your database

   B. Something that you store information about

   C. A database

   D. A complete information item

5. A database system with narrow scope

   A. Has a small audience

   B. Has very few tables

   C. Takes up very little room on your hard disk

   D. Has a small user interface

6. To determine which entity a piece of information belongs to

   A. Apply the rules of normalization

   B. Create a sample database to test performance

   C. Investigate the way the business works

   D. None of the above

7. With Microsoft Access, you shouldn't create your database until after you have completed the design stage because

   A. It is very difficult to make changes in the database after it is created

   B. If the database is created too early, it causes the design stage to be poorly done

   C. The database design isn't fully ready to be implemented until after the design stage

   D. With Access you can create the database before the end of the design stage

8. A table is a relational table only if it

   A. Consists of rows and columns

   B. Is fully normalized

   C. Has a primary key

   D. Is stored in a relational database

9. A candidate key is a key that

   A. Consists of only one field

   B. Could be used as a primary key

   C. May or may not use fields in the table

   D. Is small enough to be used effectively

10. Tables are frequently left in

   A. First normal form

   B. Third normal form

   C. Both of the above

   D. Neither of the above

11. First normal form

   A. Eliminates repeating fields

   B. Ensures that all fields depend on the primary key

   C. Eliminates redundant data

   D. Ensures that update anomalies do not occur

12. When a table is moved to first normal form and a new table is created

   A. The old table's primary key is expanded to include the key of the new table

   B. The new table's primary key becomes a foreign key in the old table

   C. The new table's primary key includes the old table's primary key

   D. None of the above

13. A foreign key is

   A. A primary key with multiple fields

   B. A key that is not used to enforce referential integrity

   C. A key that allows duplicates

   D. A key that is a primary key in another table

14. You change the value of a field in a record. As a result, the foreign keys of several other tables are also changed. This is an example of

   A. Cascading Updates

   B. Cascading referential integrity

   C. Referential integrity using foreign keys

   D. Cascading Deletes

15. You are unable to enforce referential integrity when creating a relationship in the Access Relationships window. The most probable cause is

   A. The data in the tables is inconsistent

   B. The database is corrupt

   C. Cascading Deletes has not been selected

   D. Cascading Deletes has been selected

CHAPTER

2

Programming

Microsoft Exam Objectives Covered in This Chapter:

- Declare variables in modules and procedures.

- Declare arrays, and initialize elements of arrays.

- Given a scenario, use arithmetic, comparison, logical, concatenation, and pattern-matching operators.

- Use Visual Basic for Applications loop statements.

- Use form methods.

- Open multiple instances of a form and refer to them.

- Use the Property Set and Property Let statements to assign values to form properties.

- Assign event-handling procedures to controls in a form.

Visual Basic for Applications (VBA) is the dialect of Visual Basic used in Access 95. In this chapter, you'll learn how to write separate code modules composed of VBA procedures to add functionality to your Access applications, and also how to write procedures for Code Behind Forms (CBF) modules for forms and reports. When you've finished reading this chapter, you'll know about the declaration of variables and the use of the built-in Access functions and logical constructs to allow your code to perform different actions in different circumstances.

In this chapter, you will learn:

- To understand the relationship between Visual Basic for Applications (VBA), used by Access as its programming language, and Visual Basic.

- Which parts of a VBA statement are optional and which are required.

- That VBA is object-oriented and what that means. You'll learn how objects are integrated with VBA and how you work with objects in VBA.

- Which data types are available in VBA. You'll learn what you should watch out for when moving data from the database into VBA variables and how you can create your own data types.

- How arrays are handled in VBA and how you initialize array values. You'll learn about changing array sizes on the fly.

- Where and when to use VBA operators in VBA and learn what they do.

- How sequential processing, branching, and looping are supported in Visual Basic. You'll learn how VBA implementation differs from implementations in other languages.

- How forms can be treated as objects in Access and how you can create your own properties and methods for your form objects.

What Is VBA?

With Access 95, Access acquired a new programming language—sort of. The programming language used in Access had always been Basic, but it was a special version called, appropriately enough, Access Basic. Since Microsoft wanted to have one language—Visual Basic—used across all of its applications, the fact that Access used its own version of Basic became a problem.

The differences between Access Basic and Microsoft's flagship product, Visual Basic, weren't many, but some of them were significant. The syntax of the two languages was identical, for instance, but Access Basic included a number of keywords that Visual Basic did not. To meet its goal of using one language across all Microsoft Applications, Microsoft developed Visual Basic for Applications (VBA), which was first implemented in Excel 5.0.

Visual Basic for Applications is a version of Basic that allows forms to be created by dragging and dropping controls on a blank form. VBA also supports "event-driven programming" where Basic code is run in response to some event in the environment. With Access 95, however, VBA uses the Access form system and responds to the events that Access triggers.

VBA incorporates a form of object-oriented programming. VBA's objects let programmers work with a variety of tools by setting properties and invoking methods. VBA's objects allow the language to be extended seamlessly. When used in Access, for instance, VBA is extended to pick up the Access keywords that Visual Basic lacked.

From a developer's point of view, the transition to using VBA in Access 95 was almost invisible—all of the old Access Basic code continued to run in VBA. In fact, from the developer's point of view, the major changes in going to VBA were to the menus in the Access editor. These menu changes have almost become a standard in Access upgrades—every version of Access from 1.0 to 97 has required a different set of keystrokes to bring up the Debug window, for instance.

Visual Basic Everywhere

With the release of Access 95, Microsoft was well on its way to making VBA the standard application development language in all of its products. Of the applications included in Microsoft Office 95, only Word doesn't use VBA (a problem that was corrected in Word 97, though the latest addition to Office, Outlook, uses a simplified version of VBA called VBScript).

As you'll see in Chapter 5, it's possible for every OLE server application to expose its component objects for manipulation by an OLE controller (or client) application. VBA provides several functions that let you work with OLE objects to control the application. When VBA is used inside Access, the objects that make up Access are automatically available to VBA. The same is true of Excel; the objects that make up Excel are automatically available when you start VBA from within Excel. You can even use Excel objects from VBA in Access, provided that you have set a reference to the Excel type library and that you add the two or three lines of code necessary to make Excel's objects available to VBA in Access.

From a developer's point of view, when you buy an Office product, you're really just buying VBA. If you buy Excel, you get a copy of VBA. With Excel, you also get a set of objects for working with spreadsheets and graphs. Similarly, when you buy Access you now get VBA, along with a set of objects for working with forms and reports. Even Microsoft's flagship product, Visual Basic, uses VBA. When you buy Visual Basic you get VBA plus a standalone development environment and a compiler (there are also some additional objects and controls in the box).

Due to Microsoft's effort to standardize on VBA as the single application programming language, you can write programs in any Microsoft application that supports VBA and copy that code to any other Microsoft application that supports VBA.

Access: VBA and Data

So, what does Access bring to VBA? Access provides a user-friendly development environment for creating VBA modules. Access also provides a set of forms and controls that can be tied to tables and queries.

Access provides two object models for VBA to work with:

- The objects that make up the Access user interface (forms, reports, and macros)

- A set of objects for working with data (Data Access Objects, or DAOs)

There isn't much discussion of Access in this chapter—the focus is on VBA. At the end of this chapter, when we look at how VBA code interacts with forms and reports, we'll turn our attention back to Access.

A Quick Review of VBA Syntax

As a developer, you've probably written quite a lot of VBA code by the time you begin to think about getting certified. This section is a review of the fundamentals of VBA syntax to ensure that the vocabulary you're using matches the one we're using.

Statement Syntax

A VBA program is made up of statements. A statement can contain:

- Variables

- Literals

- VBA keywords

- Operators

- Objects and their methods or properties

The following statement contains the VBA keywords If and Then, the variable UserName, the literal "Peter," the equal sign operator (=), and a reference to the Application object with one of its methods, CloseCurrentDatabase:

```
If UserName = "Peter" Then Application.CloseCurrentDatabase
```

Statement Format

A statement can be broken up over many lines by using the VBA continuation characters (a blank followed by an underscore). This statement is identical to the previous one, except that it extends over many lines:

```
If _
strUserName = "Peter" _
Then Application.CloseCurrentDatabase
```

With two exceptions, VBA statements begin with a VBA keyword. The first exception is a VBA statement that assigns a value to a variable:

```
strUserName = "Peter"
```

This only seems to be an exception, though. When a statement does not begin with a VBA keyword, VBA assumes the keyword Let. You could write the previous line of code as:

```
Let strUserName = "Peter"
```

The second exception occurs when a statement is invoking a method for an object, as in this statement:

```
Application.CloseCurrentDatabase
```

Omitting Objects

As in the case of the Let keyword, when using a method or property you can omit the object. VBA will search through its list of known objects to find an object with the method or property that you used in your code. This code, for instance, omits the Application object when calling the CloseCurrentDatabase method:

```
If strUserName = "Peter" Then CloseCurrentDatabase
```

Of course, leaving out the object name means that you run the risk of invoking a method for an object other than the one you intended, and it makes your code harder to understand.

Omitting the object when using a method or property is particularly confusing when the object is a form. You can use the Me keyword to reference the current form or report in procedures in a form. When you leave out the Me keyword others reading your code may not be able to tell whether you are referring to a control on a form, a field from the form's record source, or a function.

Understanding Data Declarations

Most VBA code involves working with variables, so the best place to start with VBA is declaring variables. In this section you'll learn about the different types of data supported by VBA, how to create your own data types, and how VBA lets you declare and work with arrays.

Microsoft
✓ ***Exam***
Objective

Declare variables in modules and procedures.

Data Types

Most variables used in Access programs hold a specific type of information, generally either numeric or character information. If you don't specify a data type when declaring a variable, VBA defaults to the Variant type, which can hold any kind of data. By declaring a variable as holding a specific type of data, you improve the performance of your program because VBA will handle the data more efficiently. In addition, VBA will abend if you make an error, such as assigning character data to a numeric field. While abends are unpleasant, they also make it easier to find and fix those errors. Figure 2.1 shows the hierarchy of VBA data types.

FIGURE 2.1

The VBA data type hierarchy

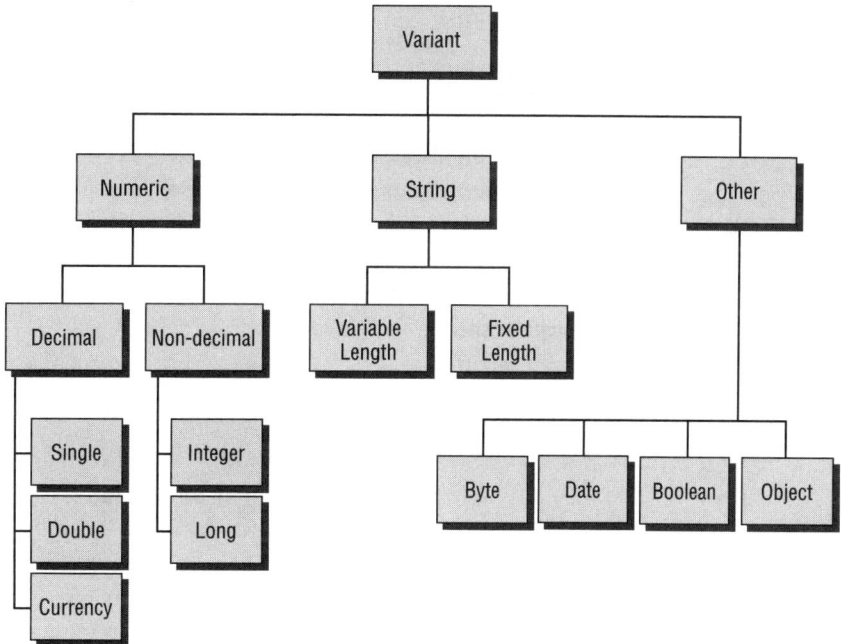

In this chapter you'll find out about the String data type and the variety of numeric data types that VBA supports. You'll also get a look at the data types VBA provides for working with dates, logical values, and other special purposes.

Before using a variable you should declare it. Declaring a variable allocates memory for storing the data, specifies the data type to be stored, and assigns a name to use when accessing the data. The syntax for declaring a variable is the same for all data types:

```
Dim variablename As datatype
```

Multiple variables can be declared on the same line, provided that the declarations are separated by commas.

```
Dim variablename As datatype, variablename As datatype
```

Each variable name must have a data type assigned to it. The following statement only declares the `strLast` variable as a String. The rest of the variables have no data type specified and will be declared with VBA's default data type (which is Variant):

```
Dim strFirst, strSecond, strLast As String
```

To declare all three variables as strings you would write:

```
Dim strFirst As String, strSecond As String, strLast As String
```

Variable naming rules in VBA are so flexible it's easy to forget that there are any. The four restrictions on a variable name are: the name must be less than 200 characters in length; the name must begin with a letter of the alphabet; the name can't contain special characters other than the underscore (_); and the name can't be a VBA keyword.

Most programmers follow a naming convention that controls which names they assign to variables. A naming convention identifies the kind of data stored in a variable and the use the variable is put to. When a naming convention is used, variable names become self documenting. The variables in this book all follow a simplified version of the naming convention defined by Greg Reddick. The Reddick naming convention specifies a set of prefixes and suffixes for Access variable names and is itself a modification of the Hungarian notation popular among C and Visual Basic programmers. In this book, only the prefixes that indicate the type of data are used (str for String and int for Integer, for instance).

Numeric Data Types

There are five numeric data types: Integer, Long, Single, Double, and Currency. As shown in Table 2.1, they differ in how large (or small) a value they can store and whether they can handle decimal data.

	Data Type	Range
TABLE 2.1 The Five Numeric Data Types and Their Characteristics	Integer	–32,768 to 32,767
	Long (long integer)	–2,147,483,648 to 2,147,483,647
	Single (single-precision floating-point)	–3.402823E38 to –1.401298E-45 for negative values; 1.401298E-45 to 3.402823E38 for positive values
	Double (double-precision floating-point)	–1.79769313486232E308 to –4.94065645841247E-324 for negative values; 4.94065645841247E-324 to 1.79769313486232E308 for positive values
	Currency (scaled integer)	–922,337,203,685,477.5808 to 922,337,203,685,477.5807

The five numeric data types are:

- **Integer:** Integer variables hold numbers that range between –32K and 32K (see Table 2.1 for the exact limits). Integer variables have no decimal places. If you try to store a number with decimal information in an integer variable, the decimal portion will be lost. After this code executes, for instance, the variable intTest will contain the number 3:

```
Dim intTest As Integer
intTest = 3.97
```

- **Long:** The name for this variable is short for Long Integer. A long variable can hold numbers ranging from –2 million to 2 million. Like Integers, Longs cannot hold decimal places. If you are multiplying two integers together, you might well require a Long variable to hold the result:

```
Dim intTest as Integer
Dim lngTest as Long
intTest = 32567
lngTest = intTest * intTest
```

Most CPUs will process Integers and Longs faster than Singles or Doubles.

- **Single:** Singles are one of the three variable types that can hold decimals. Singles can also hold numbers both larger and smaller than Integers or Longs. A Single can hold a number as large as a 3 with 38 zeros after it (both positive and negative). For decimals, Singles can hold numbers with 48 zeros after the decimal point. Singles lose precision as they get very large or very small. In other words, if you are storing the distance to the nearest star, use a Single but recognize that the result may be rounded to the nearest hundred thousand miles. In the following code, for instance, the number stored in sngRight will be stored exactly as shown, but the number in sngClose will be rounded and lose the 1 in the last position.

```
Dim sngRight as Single
Dim sngClose as Single
sngRight = 3000001
sngClose = 30000001
```

- **Double:** Like the Single, the Double can hold decimals. Doubles can also handle numbers both larger and smaller than Singles. Like the Single, the Double becomes less precise as you approach the outer limits of its range. In the following example, dblClose will lose the 1 in the final position but dblRight will not:

```
Dim dblRight as Double
Dim dblTest as Double
dblRight = 300000000000001
dblClose = 3000000000000001
```

Single and Double variables have such wide ranges that their limits are normally expressed in scientific notation. The upper limit for a Single is normally written as 3.402823E38, which translates as 3.402823 multiplied by 10 raised to the 38th power. As the values stored in Singles and Doubles get larger, Access will display the values in scientific notation.

- **Currency:** This data type is not just for holding dollar amounts. The Currency data type can handle very large numbers, though not as large as the Single (Currency is limited to 15 positions to the left of the decimal). Currency can also handle decimals with up to 4 positions to the right of the decimal point. Unlike Singles and Doubles, the Currency data type does not lose precision as numbers get very large or very small. In the following code, while `sngClose` will lose the 1 in the final position, `curRight` will not:

```
Dim curRight as Currency
Dim sngClose as Single
sngClose = 3000000000000001
curRight = 3000000000000001
```

 Use the Integer data type when you are working with numbers that don't have decimals (unless the value stored will exceed 32K, in which case you should use a Long). If you require decimals, use the Currency data type. Use Single and Double only if you are working with numbers that require more than 15 positions to the left of the decimal or 4 positions to the right.

The String Data Type

String is the most commonly used Access data type. String variables are used to hold either character data or numeric data that will not be used for calculations, such as ID numbers or phone numbers.

Strings can be declared using the same format as other data types:

```
Dim strTest As String
```

Declared like this, a String variable can hold up to 2 billion characters. This declaration creates a variable-length string whose memory requirements vary with the number of characters in the string.

Strings can also be declared in a fixed-length format that specifies the maximum number of characters that can be put in the string. The amount of memory used by a fixed-length string does not vary with the number of characters in the string.

The first line in the following code declares a string variable with a maximum of five characters. The second line attempts to store the word "Surprise" in the variable, but only the first five letters ("Surpr") will actually be stored:

```
Dim strTest As String*15
strTest = "Surprise"
```

Fixed-length strings are limited to 65KB in size.

WARNING Don't confuse the String data type in VBA with the Text data type you use when designing tables. When you don't enter any data in a field in a table, the special value Null is stored in the field. While the Text data type can hold a Null value, the String variable cannot. In VBA, only the Variant data type can hold a Null value.

Other Data Types

There are five other data types that you can use within Access. While not used as frequently as the various numeric data types or the String data type, they can be very useful. Table 2.2 shows the characteristics of these types (and the String data type), and the list that follows in this section provides additional details about them.

T A B L E   2.2

Other Data Types and
Their Characteristics

Data Type	Range
Byte	0 to 255
Boolean	True or False
Date	January 1, 100 to December 31, 9999
Object	Any Object reference
String (variable-length)	0 to approximately 2 billion
String (fixed-length)	1 to approximately 65,400
Variant (with numbers)	Any numeric value up to the range of a Double
Variant (with characters)	Same range as for variable-length String

These other data types are:

- **Boolean:** The Boolean data type is used to store the results of a test and so contains either the value True or False. You can treat a Boolean variable as if it were an Integer and store numerical data in it. If you do, –1 will be treated as True and 0 will be treated as False.

```
Dim bolTest As Boolean
bolTest = (userName = "Peter")
If bolTest Then Application.CloseCurrentDatabase
```

- **Byte:** Bytes store numerical data without decimals or signs and can hold a value ranging from 0 to 255. Bytes are typically used to store binary data returned from some other program.

```
Dim bytTest As Byte
bytTest = 240
```

- **Date:** Date variables, not surprisingly, contain dates and times. While a date variable can hold any time from 12:00 midnight to 11:59:59 p.m., there are limits to the range of dates that can be held. VBA cannot work with dates before January 1, 100 or dates after December 31, 9999.

Like Strings, literal dates must be enclosed in delimiters. The date delimiter is the hash sign (#). VBA will convert a remarkable number of date formats to valid dates provided they are enclosed in hash signs. All of the following statements cause the date of January 1, 1997 to be stored in the dteTest field:

```
Dim dteTest As Date
dteTest = #January 1, 1997#
dteTest = #1 Jan 1997#
dteTest = #1/31/97#
dteTest = #31/1/97#
```

Where the date is ambiguous (such as 1/2/97), VBA determines which number is the month by using the information in the Date tab under Regional Settings in the Windows Control Panel.

Bearing in mind all the problems with converting computers to recognize dates as of the year 2000, you might want to remember that the VBA Date field will fail on December 31, 9999. On the other hand, that date may be beyond your planning horizon.

- **Object:** The Object data type is used to hold references to the objects that you are using in your program. This data type will be discussed in more detail in Chapter 5.

- **Variant:** The Variant data type provides all the functionality of all of the other data types. If a variable is declared without a data type, VBA will assume that it is a Variant. The Variant data type actually stores two pieces of information: the data itself and a number indicating what format the data is stored in (Double, Long, String, etc.). Only a variable declared as variant could be used in the following code because of the variety of data types stored in the variable:

```
Dim varTest as Variant
varTest = 2
varTest = "My name"
varTest = #1/1/97#
```

You should always place Option Explicit in the Declarations section at the top of your form or code modules. Without this line, Access will allow you to use variables without having to declare them with a Dim statement . While this may sound like a way to save some time, the result is that when you mistype the name of a variable, Access will not flag it as an error. When your code does not behave as expected you will be forced to try to find where in your code you've made the typing error. Rather than try to remember to add Option Explicit, the best thing to do is to select Tools ➢ Options and check Require Variable Declaration on the Module tab. This will cause Access to put Option Explicit at the top of each new module you create.

Arrays

An array is like a list: it contains several ordered items referred to by a single name (see Figure 2.2). Arrays allow you to store several data items of the same type in a single variable. Each item is assigned a position to distinguish it from the other data items in the array.

F I G U R E   2.2

Like grocery lists, arrays let you refer to a group of items with one name.

Grocery List

1.) Bread
2.) Milk
3.) Cheese
4.) Fruit
5.) Vegetables
Get ALL 5 Items

Dim Grocery(4) As String

0:	Bread
1:	Milk
2:	Cheese
3:	Fruit
4:	Vegetables

Declaring an Array

The syntax for declaring an array is almost identical to the syntax for declaring an ordinary variable. The only difference is that you must specify the position of the last element in the array between parentheses after the variable name:

```
Dim sngTestArray(10) As Single
```

Microsoft ✓ **Exam Objective**

Declare arrays, and initialize elements of arrays.

Since the first position in the array is normally position 0, an array declared with a final position of 1 can hold two pieces of data (position 0 and position 1). This code declares an array that has position 5 as the last position in the array, so the array can hold six items:

```
Dim strTestArray(5) As String
strTestArray(0) = "First Item"
strTestArray(1) = "Second Item"
strTestArray(2) = "Third Item"
strTestArray(3) = "Fourth Item"
strTestArray(4) = "Fifth Item"
strTestArray(5) = "Sixth Item"
```

Using an Array

You can use an array variable exactly as you would an ordinary variable of the same type, except that you must specify the element in the array that you want to work with. This code, for instance, adds the item in position 6 of the array to the item in position 7, and stores the result in position 8:

```
Dim ingTestArray(10) As Integer
ingTestArray(6) = 5
ingTestArray(7) = 4
ingTestArray(8) = inTestArray(6) + ingTestArray(7)
```

The simple routine in Exercise 2.1 allows you to create an array, initialize it, and display the array's contents.

EXERCISE 2.1

Creating and Initializing an Array

In this exercise you will create an array, load it with some values, and print them in the Debug window. Over the course of this chapter, you'll gradually enhance this routine to create a copy of any array.

Open Access, select the Modules tab, and click on the New button. Enter this code into the module:

```
Sub DisplayArray()
Dim DispArray(5) As Integer

DispArray(0) = 1
DispArray(1) = 2
DispArray(2) = 3
DispArray(3) = 4
DispArray(4) = 5
DispArray(5) = 6

Debug.Print DispArray(0)
Debug.Print DispArray(1)
Debug.Print DispArray(2)
Debug.Print DispArray(3)
Debug.Print DispArray(4)
Debug.Print DispArray(5)

End Sub
```

Open the Debug window, type **DisplayArray**, and press ↵. The contents of the array are displayed in the Debug window.

You can use Ctrl+G as a hot key to open the Debug window.

Changing an Array's Size

When you declare an array, you can omit the last position of the array and set that later in your program using the ReDim keyword, as shown in Exercise 2.2. This code, for instance, sets an array to have 10 positions after the array has been declared:

```
Dim lngArray() As Long
ReDim lngArray(9)
```

Using the ReDim command by itself not only redimensions the array but also causes all the data in the array to be discarded. By using the optional Preserve keyword you can change the size of an array without losing the data stored in it. In this code, for instance, the element lngArray(5) will still contain 250 after the ReDim Preserve statement:

```
Dim lngArray() As Long
lngArray(5) = 250
ReDim Preserve lngArray(9)
```

EXERCISE 2.2

Modifying an Array's Dimensions

In this exercise, you'll modify the array's dimensions.

Modify the DisplayArray routine to this:

```
Sub DisplayArray()
Dim DispArray() As Integer

ReDim DispArray(2)
DispArray(0) = 1
DispArray(1) = 2

ReDim DispArray(6)
Debug.Print "Values after ReDim"
Debug.Print DispArray(0)
Debug.Print DispArray(1)

DispArray(0) = 1
DispArray(1) = 2
```

```
DispArray(2) = 3
DispArray(3) = 4
DispArray(4) = 5
DispArray(5) = 6

ReDim Preserve DispArray(5)
Debug.Print "Values after ReDim Preserve"
Debug.Print DispArray(0)
Debug.Print DispArray(1)
Debug.Print DispArray(2)
Debug.Print DispArray(3)
Debug.Print DispArray(4)
Debug.Print DispArray(5)

End Sub
```

Open the Debug window, type **DisplayArray**, and press ↵. The contents of the array after a ReDim are displayed, followed by the contents of the array after a ReDim Preserve.

In this version of the routine, you started to use the ReDim commands to alter the size of your array.

Multiple Dimensions

The arrays we've looked at so far have all been of one dimension. An array with one dimension is like a list: a set of items recorded one after another. You can also create arrays of multiple dimensions. While an array of one dimension looks like a list, an array of two dimensions resembles a table with a set of rows and columns as shown in Figure 2.3.

To declare an array of two dimensions you simply specify the final position for each dimension. This code declares an array of two dimensions:

```
Dim strArray(5,9) As String
```

The first dimension of strArray can hold six items and the second dimension can hold 10. One way to think about this array is to consider it as a table with five rows and nine columns. You can place data in any position of the

FIGURE 2.3

A two-dimensional
array

Schedule

Train	Toronto	Guelph	Kilchenar	London	Sarnie
420	4:20	5:00	6:05	8:30	9:21
426	5:20	6:00	7:05	9:30	10:21
531	6:20	7:00	8:05	10:30	11:21
891	7:20	8:00	9:05	11:30	N/A

Dim Schedule (5,4) As String

0,0	420
0,1	4:20
0,2	5:00
0,3	6:05
0,4	8:30
0,5	9:21
1,0	426
1,1	5:20
1,2	6:00
1,3	7:05
1,4	9:30
1,5	10:21
2,0	531
2,1	6:20

array by specifying the row and column. For instance, this code puts data in the sixth column of the third row:

```
strArray(2,5) = "Peter"
```

ReDim can be used with an array with multiple dimensions to change the size of any of the dimensions. If you use ReDim Preserve, though, you can only change the upper bound of the last dimension of the array. To put it another way, if the array is declared as follows:

```
Dim strArray(2,4 to 8)
```

you can use ReDim Preserve only to change the second dimension (the one declared 4 to 8 and only the upper bound (the 8) can be altered. If you change the first dimension (the 2) or the lower bound of the second dimension (the 4) then the data in the array will be discarded.

This code declares a two-dimensional array, ReDims it to five rows and eight columns, stores some data in the array and then ReDims the array's last column without losing any of the data:

```
Dim intArray(,) As Integer
ReDim intArray(4,7)
intArray(3,4) = 100
ReDim Preserve intArray(3,10)
```

Arrays can be declared with up to 60 dimensions or to the limit of memory available on your computer, whichever is lower.

Array Bounds

You're not required to have your arrays start at 0. You can have your array elements run from any convenient number that you want. You need only specify the start and end positions for each dimension of your array when you declare the array. This code declares an array of 64 elements beginning with element 32 and ending with element 95:

```
Dim intArray(32 to 95) As Integer
```

You can even declare arrays with negative bounds:

```
Dim strArray(-5 to 10) as String
```

Regardless of what bounds you set on your array, attempting to use an element outside of the bounds of the array will generate an error ("Subscript out of range"). As you will see in Chapter 7, VBA has two functions that will let you check the upper and lower bounds of your arrays so that you can ensure that the array element that you want to use really does exist.

You can force your arrays to begin at 1 by adding Option Base 1 to the Declarations section of your module. But because the VBA standard is to begin arrays at 0, using this option will probably just confuse anyone who has to maintain your program.

User-Defined Data Types

Sometimes the data types provided by VBA aren't enough for what you need to do. VBA allows you to define new data types made up of the VBA-defined ones.

For example, in the customer database there may be several pieces of customer information that you will generally use together. An obvious example is the CustomerFirstName and CustomerLastName fields. Rather than requiring that you set up two separate String variables to hold these values, VBA allows you to create a new data type that can hold them both.

The first step in using a new data type is to define it using the Type keyword. To define a CustomerName data type, you would add this code to the Declarations section of a module:

```
Type udtCustomerName
strFirstName As String
strLastName As String
End Type
```

Now that you've defined the data type you can declare variables of that type in the same way that you would declare variables to be String or Integer. This code declares the variable NewName as being of the type CustomerName:

```
Dim udtNewName as udtCustomerName
```

Finally, you can access the individual data fields within your variable by referring to them by name:

```
udtNewName.strFirstName = "Peter"
udtNewName.strLastName = "Vogel"
```

You can use your CustomerName variable anywhere that you can use variables declared with Access' native data types:

```
MsgBox "Hello " & udtNewName.strFirstName &
udtNewName.strLastName
```

In Exercise 2.3, you'll create a user-defined type to hold information about your array.

EXERCISE 2.3

Creating and Using a User-Defined Data Type

1. In the Declarations section of your module add this Type definition:

```
Type udtArrayInfo
intLowerBound As Integer
intUpperBound As Integer
End Type
```

2. Modify the DisplayArray routine to use the ArrayInfo type:

```
Sub DisplayArray()
Dim DispArray() As Integer
Dim ArrayInfo As udtArrayInfo

ReDim DispArray(2)
DispArray(0) = 1
DispArray(1) = 2

ReDim DispArray(6)
Debug.Print "Values after ReDim"
Debug.Print DispArray(0)
Debug.Print DispArray(1)

DispArray(0) = 1
```

EXERCISE 2.3 (CONTINUED)

```
DispArray(1) = 2
DispArray(2) = 3
DispArray(3) = 4
DispArray(4) = 5
DispArray(5) = 6
udtArrayInfo.intLowerBound = LBound(DispArray)
udtArrayInfo.intUpperBound = UBound(DispArray)
ReDim Preserve DispArray(5)
Debug.Print "Values after ReDim Preserve"
Debug.Print DispArray(0)
Debug.Print DispArray(1)
Debug.Print DispArray(2)
Debug.Print DispArray(3)
Debug.Print DispArray(4)
Debug.Print DispArray(5)

Debug.Print "Original Array size:", _
  udtArrayInfo.intLowerBound, _
  udtArrayInfo.intUpperBound
End Sub
```

3. Open the Debug window, type **DisplayArray**, and press ↵. The contents of the array after a ReDim are displayed, followed by the contents of the array after a ReDim Preserve.

Using Operators

Operators are used to perform simple operations on variables. VBA's operators can be divided into three categories: Arithmetic, Comparison, and Logical. Figure 2.4 shows the VBA operators organized by type.

Microsoft ✓ *Exam Objective* **Given a scenario, use arithmetic, comparison, logical, concatenation, and pattern-matching operators.**

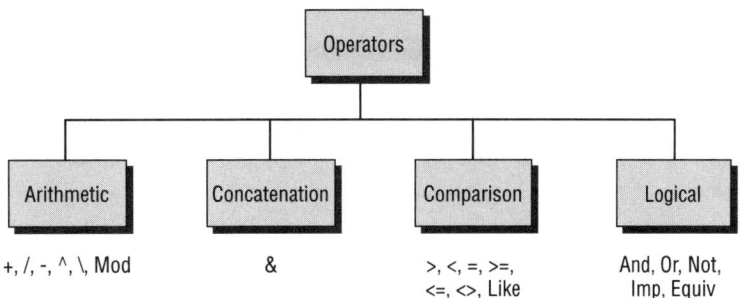

FIGURE 2.4

Classifying the VBA operators

Arithmetic/Concatenation

Five of VBA's arithmetic operators correspond very closely to the ones you learned in school. Table 2.3 shows the basic arithmetic operators.

TABLE 2.3

Basic Arithmetic Operators

Operator	Name	Sample	Result
+	Addition	IntNewValue = 3 + 4	7
-	Subtraction	IntNewValue = 100-2	98
*	Multiplication	IntNewValue = 4 * 2	8
/	Division	IntNewValue = 100/25	4
^	Exponentiation	IntNewValue = 5^3	125

Two of VBA's arithmetic operators require some special explanation:

- The \ operator performs integer division, which means that the \ operator discards the remainder (if any) of the division operation. For example, 5\3 will give 1 as a result.

- The Mod operator also performs division but returns only the remainder; 5 Mod 3 will yield 2 as a result.

The concatenation operator (&) is used to join two or more Strings together to make a larger String. This code puts "cat and dog" in the variable strAnimals:

```
strFirstWord = "Cat"
strSecondWord = "Dog"
strAnimals = strFirstWord & " and " & strSecondWord
```

WARNING

It is possible to use the plus sign (+) to concatenate two strings. This is an old practice, though, and not recommended because it can make for ambiguous code. For instance, which of the following code snippets returns "22" and which returns 4: "2" + "2"; 2 + 2; "2" + 2; 2 + "2"?

Order of Operations

The operators in an arithmetic operation are not processed in left-to-right order. Instead, some operations (exponentiation, multiplication, division) are done before others (addition, subtraction). For instance, this calculation equals 35, not 98:

3 + 4^2 * 2

The arithmetic order of operations raises the 4 to the power of 2 first, then multiplies the result by 2 before adding the 3.

Rather than try to remember the order that operations are done in, it's better to place parentheses around the activities that you want done first. Not only does this ensure that you get the result you want, it indicates to whoever might be making changes to your program what you expect to have done. If you wanted the addition done first and the exponentiation done second, you could have written the previous formula as:

((3 + 4)^2) * 2

to yield 98.

In Exercise 2.4 you will modify the DispArray routine to perform some basic arithmetic operations on the contents of the array.

EXERCISE 2.4

Using Arithmetic Operators

1. Modify the DisplayArray routine to average the contents of the array:

```
Sub DisplayArray()
Dim DispArray() As Integer
Dim intTotal As Integer
Dim intAverage As Integer
Dim udtArrayBounds As udtArrayInfo
```

```
ReDim Preserve DispArray(5)
DispArray(0) = 1
DispArray(1) = 2
DispArray(2) = 3
DispArray(3) = 4
DispArray(4) = 5
DispArray(5) = 6

intTotal = DispArray(0) + DispArray(1) + DispArray(2) + _
        DispArray(3) + DispArray(4) + DispArray(5)

udtArrayBounds.intLowerBound = LBound(DispArray)
udtArrayBounds.intUpperBound = UBound(DispArray)

intAverage = intTotal/(udtArrayBounds.intUpperBound + 1)
Debug.Print "Average of array contents: ", intAverage
End Sub
```

2. Open the Debug window, type **DisplayArray**, and press ↵. The average of the contents of the array is displayed.

This version of the routine processes the contents of the array using some simple arithmetic operators.

Comparison

The comparison operators are used to compare two expressions to determine if they are equal, greater, lesser, or not equal to each other. Again, these operators will be familiar to you from grade-school arithmetic. All of the tests in Table 2.4 are True, for instance.

	Operator	Name	Sample
T A B L E 2.4 Basic Comparison Operators	=	Equal To	$3 = 4 - 1$
	>	Greater Than	"Fox" > "Dog"
	<	Less Than	$14 < 21$

The three basic operators can be combined in pairs. The combination >= provides a "greater than or equal to" comparison and <= provides "less than or equal to." All of these tests are true, for instance:

```
bolTest = ("A" <= "B")
bolTest = (5 <= 3 + 2)
bolTest = ("Dog" >= "Cat")
bolTest = (100 >= 10^2)
```

The <> combination is read as "not equal to" and is used to test for inequality (VBA has no single inequality operator). This test is True because the two items are not equal:

```
bolTest = ("A" <> 4)
```

The Like Operator

The most powerful comparison operator, Like, requires a more extensive explanation than the other operators. The Like operator is used to match an expression to a pattern. A pattern is a String that includes special characters that can match one or more characters in the expression being tested.

The asterisk (*)when used in a pattern, matches any number of any characters. The following test will be true regardless of what is stored in the variable strTest because the asterisk will match anything:

```
bolTest = (strTest Like "*")
```

The asterisk can be used at the beginning, middle, or end of a pattern. These tests are all also True:

```
bolTest = ("Taste" Like "T*e")
bolTest = ("Taste" Like "*ste")
bolTest = ("Taste" Like "Tas*")
```

The question mark is a more limited version of the asterisk: it matches only to a single letter (not any character). The following tests are all true because the question mark permits any letter in the second position of the word:

```
bolTest = ("Cot" Like "C?t")
bolTest = ("Cat" Like "C?t")
bolTest = ("Cut" Like "C?t*")
```

Since the question mark only permits one matching letter, this test fails:

```
bolTest = ("Chat" Like "C?t")
```

The hash sign (#) functions like the question mark, but matches only the digits 0 to 9.

The most flexible tool in pattern matching is formed with the left and right brackets ([]). Any character enclosed in the brackets is considered an acceptable match to the pattern. To match "Cat" and "Cot" but not "Cut," you would use the pattern "C[ao]t." In the following code, the first two tests are True and the last one is False:

```
bolTest = ("Cat" Like "C[ao]t")
bolTest = ("Cot" Like "C[ao]t")
bolTest = ("Cut" Like "C[ao]t")
```

To match a range of letters you specify the first and the last letter, separated by a hyphen. The pattern [F-I] matches the letters F, G, H, and I.

The Option Compare Statement

When you are comparing strings you have to decide if you want your comparisons to be based on the value of the letter of the alphabet or the internal representation of the letter in your computer's memory.

When a comparison is made on the value of the letter of the alphabet, upper- and lowercase letters are considered to be equal (that is, *B* is equal to *b*). When a comparison is made on the value of the letter's internal representation, *B* will be less than *b* rather than equal to it.

In VBA, comparisons are controlled using the Option Compare statement. To ensure a comparison based on the value of the letters in your Strings, add this line to the Declarations section of your module:

```
Option Compare Text
```

If you would prefer comparisons based on the letter's internal representation, add this line to the Declarations section:

```
Option Compare Binary
```

Access has a special version of the Option Compare statement: Option Compare Database. This option compares letters based on the sort order of the locale id stored in the database. The locale id is part of the Windows internationalization system, and it specifies a variety of information about the way alphabets, numbers, dates, time, and money are handled. By using Option Compare Database (which is Access' default) you help ensure that your database will function correctly when used with languages other than English.

Logical Operators

The logical operators are used to combine tests to get a single result. A logical operator appears between two tests and returns a value based on combining the results of the two tests.

Three of the logical operators (Not, And, and Or) will be familiar to you already and are summarized in Table 2.5 (the sample statements in Table 2.5 are all True).

	Operator	Name	Sample	Notes
T A B L E 2.5 Basic Logical Operators	Not	Switches False to True and True to False	Not (2 = 3)	Since 2 = 3 is False, the Not swaps the value to True.
	And	True if both tests are True	(2 = 3 – 1) And "Fox" > "Dog"	Since both tests are True, the whole statement is True.
	Or	True if either test is True	(2 = 3) Or "Fox" > "Dog"	While the first test (2 = 3) is False, the second test is True, making the whole statement True.

There are three other logical operators that are slightly out of the ordinary:

- **Xor:** This operator's name is short for "exclusive or." An exclusive or is True when one (and only one) of the tests is True. If both of the tests joined by the Xor are True then Xor returns False.

- **Imp:** This operator's name is short for "implied." Imp is true for almost every combination of tests except when the first test is True and the second test is False. In this situation only, Imp returns False.

- **Eqv:** This operator's name is short for Equivalence. Eqv returns True when both tests are True or both tests are False.

Working with Programming Constructs

Now that you are comfortable with the different kinds of variables you can create and the operators you can use, it's time to write some code.

All programs can be broken down into three different kinds of processing, shown in Figure 2.5. They are:

- **Sequential Processing:** One statement after another, each performing an action.

- **Branching:** One or more statements that may not be processed depending on specific conditions.

- **Looping:** One or more statements executed repeatedly.

In this section you'll see how VBA implements each of these types of processing.

Sequential Execution

Sequential execution is the simplest kind of processing that can take place in VBA code. The most common type of sequential processing is a series of assignment statements. An assignment statement consists of a variable, the equals sign, and an expression. When the statement executes, the expression is evaluated and its value is stored in the variable. Typical assignment statements look like this:

```
intMaxHours = 40
strCarModel = "Firebird"
Text1.Text = "California"
bolAgeOK = (intUserAge > 21)
curPay = (EmpHours - 40 * 1.5 * curPayRate) + 40 *
curPayRate
strUserSuppliedPassword = GetUserPassword()
```

FIGURE 2.5

The three programming constructs (illustrations of sequential, branching and looping)

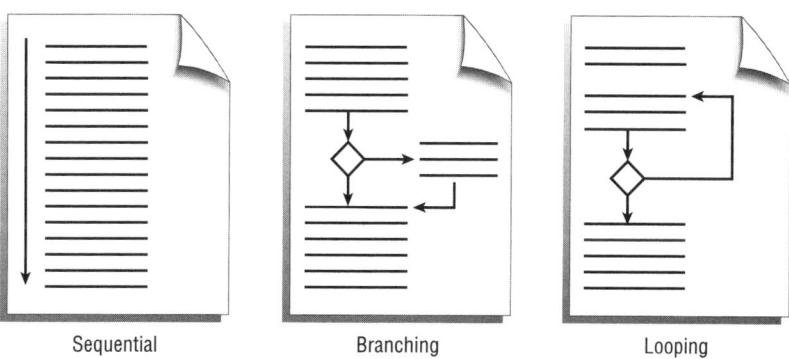

Sequential   Branching   Looping

Any set of statements executed one after another constitutes sequential processing. In VBA, those statements that aren't assignment statements (or branching or looping control statements) will be:

- Calls to subroutines
- Statements to call the method of some object
- Statements beginning with VBA keywords

Some typical nonassignment statements are:

```
Application.CloseCurrentDatabase
CheckUserPrivileges strUserName
Debug.Print "Check Value: " & strTestValue
```

Branching

Branching is used in code when there is some part of the code that shouldn't be executed under some conditions. VBA provides a number of different ways to break your sequential code up into blocks and control which code blocks are executed. Figure 2.6 shows flowcharts for the different ways that VBA handles branching.

The If...Then Statement

A VBA procedure often has one or more lines of code that don't need to be executed every time the program is run. VBA provides the If...Then statement to control when the code will be executed.

The If...Then construct performs a test and, if the result is True, executes the code following the Then portion of the statement. This code, for instance, sets the strUserType variable to "Administrator" if the strUserName variable contains the value "Peter".

```
If strUserName = "Peter" Then strUserType = "Administrator"
```

If there is more than one line of code to be executed, a block If should be used. In a block If, when the If test is True, all the lines between the If statement and the next matching End If are performed. In this code, the variables strUserType and strUserGroup are both set when the If test is True:

```
If strUserName = "Peter" Then
    strUserType = "Administrator"
    strUserGroup = "Admins"
End If
```

In a block If, nothing can appear in the statement after the Then keyword.

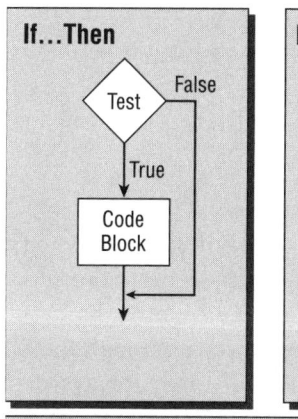

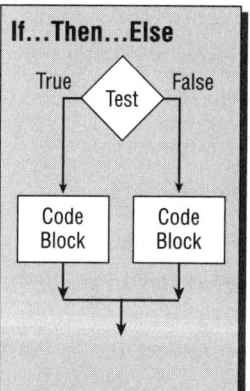

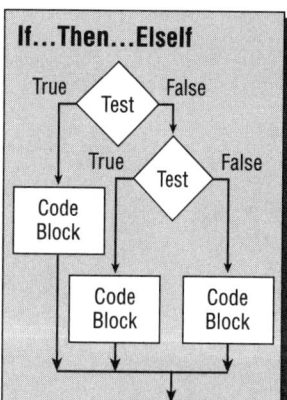

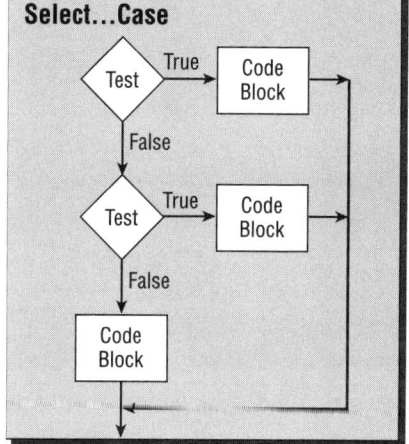

In a block If the lines of code are generally indented three or four characters. The effect of this additional white space is to make the block If stand
out from the sequential code around it. As a result, common programming
practice is to use a block If even when only one line of code is to be executed, to make the If easier to spot when reading code.

If blocks can be nested within each other. In this code, if the strUserName
variable contains "Peter" then a second test is done against the strUser-
LoginName variable:

```
If strUserName = "Peter" Then
    strUserType = "Administrator"
```

```
      strUserGroup = "Admins"
      If strUserLoginName = "VogelP" Then
        MsgBox "Good Morning, Mr. Vogel"
      End If
    End If
```

The Else Keyword

Another common branching operation occurs when there are two blocks of code that may be executed. In this scenario one block of code is executed under a certain set of conditions and another block is executed when the conditions aren't met. VBA supports this through the Else keyword. This code calculates the employee's pay two different ways, depending on whether the employee has worked more than 40 hours or not:

```
If intHoursWorked > 40 Then
  curHoursOver = intHoursWorked - 40
  curEmpNormalPay = 40 * curPayRate
  curEmpOverPay = curHoursOver * curOverRate
  curEmpPay = curEmpNormalPay + curEmpOverPay
Else
  curEmpPay = intHoursWorked * curPayRate
End If
```

In Exercise 2.5 you'll enhance the DispArray routine to provide either the total or the average of the contents of the array. The new version of DispArray will accept a parameter that indicates which calculation should be performed.

EXERCISE 2.5

Choosing a Processing Type

1. Modify the DisplayArray routine to display either the average or the total of the contents of the array:

```
Sub DisplayArray(strCalcType As String)
Dim DispArray() As Integer
Dim intTotal As Integer
Dim intAverage As Integer
Dim udtArrayBounds As udtArrayInfo
```

```
ReDim Preserve DispArray(5)
DispArray(0) = 1
DispArray(1) = 2
DispArray(2) = 3
DispArray(3) = 4
DispArray(4) = 5
DispArray(5) = 6

intTotal = DispArray(0) + DispArray(1) + DispArray(2) + _
        DispArray(3) + DispArray(4) + DispArray(5)

udtArrayBounds.intLowerBound = LBound(DispArray)
udtArrayBounds.intUpperBound = UBound(DispArray)

If strCalcType Like "*Add*" Then
Debug.Print "Total of array contents: ", intTotal
Else
intAverage = intTotal/(udtArrayBounds.intUpperBound + 1)
Debug.Print "Average of array contents: ", intAverage
End If
End Sub
```

2. In the Debug window, type **DisplayArray("Add")** and proce ↵. The total of the array is displayed.

3. By using the Like operator, you have allowed the routine to accept a variety of parameters. In the Debug window, type **DisplayArray("Do an add")** and press ↵.

4. To get the average of the contents, type **DisplayArray("")** and press ↵.

The Select Case Statement

The Select Case statement is used when a single expression controls which block of code is to be executed. An employee's pay rate may vary depending on how many years they have worked for the company: the more years, the higher the rate. The Select Case statement in the following code selects among the different calculations:

```
Select Case intYearsEmployed
  Case 0
    CurEmpPay = intHoursWorked * curStartPay
  Case < 5
    curEmpPay = intHoursWorked * curEmpPay
  Case 5 to 10
    curEmpPay = intHoursWorked * curEmpAdvancedPay
  Case 11, 12
    curEmpPay = intHoursWorked * curEmpAdvancedPlusPay
  Case Else
    curEmpPay = intHoursWorked * curEmpSeniorPay
    curEmpPay = curEmpPay + curSeniorityBonus
End Select
```

The Select Case statement begins by specifying an expression that will be used to control which code block will be executed. In the example above, the `intYearsEmployed` variable is specified in the Select statement as the expression to be tested:

```
Select Case intYearsEmployed
```

Each Case statement between the Select Case and the End Case statements tests one or more expressions against the expression in the Select Case statement. If the test is True, then the code in that Case block is executed and the rest of the Case blocks are ignored. If an employee had worked 11 years, for instance, their pay would be calculated using this Case block:

```
Case 11, 12
curEmpPay = intHoursWorked * curEmpAdvancedPlusPay
```

If no Case statement passes the test, the code in the Case Else block is executed. The Case Else block is optional.

The Case statement provides a variety of ways of testing against the expression in the Select Case clause. These include:

- Comparing against a single value for equality, as shown in the first Case block. This statement will cause the Case block to be executed if `intYearsEmployed` is equal to 0:

```
Case 0
```

- Comparing against a single value for inequality, as shown in the second Case block. When `intYearsEmployed` is less than 5, this Case block will be executed:

```
Case < 5
```

- Comparing against a range of values, as shown in the third Case block. Here, if the expression `intYearsEmployed` has any of the values 5, 6, 7, 8, 9, or 10, the Case block will be executed:

```
Case 5 to 10
```

- The various comparisons can be combined in a single Case statement. The fourth Case block combines two tests for equality. The first of the two following Case blocks will be executed if the expression `intYearsEmployed` is equal to 11 or 12. The second Case statement has combined four tests:

```
Case 11, 12
Case 11, 12, 15 to 25, > 50
```

Finally, if several Case blocks would test True only the first one in the list is actually executed. In the sample code an employee who just started would have 0 years employed. While both the first and second Case blocks would test True for this employee, once the first Case block tested True all the subsequent Case blocks would be ignored.

The ElseIf Statement

On occasion, branching can get quite complicated, with several different code blocks to be executed depending on a variety of different variables. For example, an employee's pay may vary depending not just on the hours worked but on whether the employee is on salary. An IfElse...EndIf statement won't handle this situation because there are more than two code blocks to choose among (salary, non-salary and over 40 hours, as well as non-salary and 40 hours or less). And, while there are a number of code blocks to choose from, a Select Case statement can't be used because there is more than one variable to test.

Under these circumstances the ElseIf statement can be used to choose between a variety of options, supplying a different test for each code block. Here's the code to handle the employee pay:

```
If strEmpPayType = "Salary" Then
   curEmpPay = curSalaryAmount
```

```
ElseIf strEmpHours > 40 Then
  curHoursOver = intHoursWorked - 40
  curEmpNormalPay = 40 * curPayRate
  curEmpOverPay = curHoursOver * curOverRate
  curEmpPay = curEmpNormalPay + curEmpOverPay
Else
  curEmpPay = intHoursWorked * curPayRate
End If
```

The ElseIf statement allows you to add a test to the Else portion of an If to check for a second set of conditions.

Looping

Other than sequential processing and branching, the only other programming construct is *looping* (or, more technically, *iteration*). Looping is the ability to perform a block of code until some condition is achieved.

Microsoft ✓ ***Exam Objective*** **Use Visual Basic for Applications loop statements.**

Every loop consists of three items:

- An end condition that will terminate the loop

- A block of code to repeat

- Some activity that will satisfy the end condition at some point

When creating a loop it's important to make sure that the end condition for the loop will be reached, otherwise the loop will not terminate (the resulting condition is known as the *infinite loop*). Normally, the code block inside the loop will eventually generate the condition that will terminate the loop. It's not unusual, though, for a code block to execute until some condition outside the program is reached—the user pressing a key, for instance.

The Do...Loop Tool

The most flexible looping tool in VBA is the Do...Loop. In the Do...Loop construct, the code block is enclosed between the Do statement and the Loop statement. The end condition is specified as a test (like the If statement) either in the Do or the Loop statement. Figure 2.7 shows flowcharts for the two different formats of the Do...Loop.

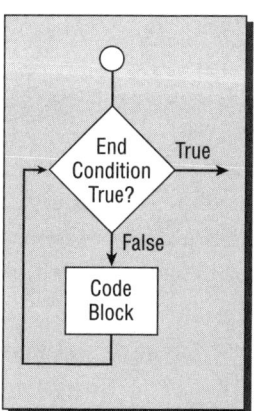 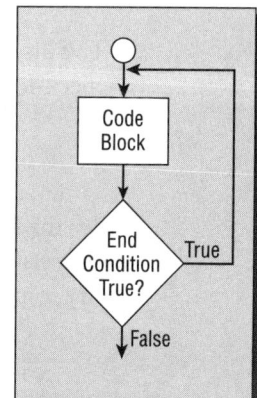

When the test is in the Do statement, the test is checked before the first statement in the code block is performed. If the end condition is satisfied at that point, the loop is never executed. In this code, for instance, if the variable `strUserSuppliedPassword` already contains the password, the InputBox statement isn't executed:

```
Do While strUserSuppliedPassword <> strCorrectPassword
    strUserSuppliedPassword = InputBox("Please enter a
    ➥ password")
Loop
```

On the other hand, if `strUserSuppliedPassword` doesn't contain the correct password, the code block is executed. The code block uses the InputBox function to request a password from the user and assign it to the variable `strUserSuppliedPassword`. The loop won't be exited until the user supplies the correct password (or the computer is turned off).

When the test is in the Loop statement, the test is performed after the first pass through the loop, guaranteeing that the code block will be performed at least once. Using the password example, if you wanted to force the user to enter a password, you would use this code to ensure that the password would be requested at least once:

```
Do
    strUserSuppliedPassword = InputBox("Please enter a
    ➥ password")
Loop While strUserSuppliedPassword <> strCorrectPassword
```

VBA even lets you specify the end condition two different ways:

- Continue looping as long as the test is True (using the While keyword)

- Continue looping as long as the test is False (using the Until keyword)

The While keyword in the password example requires the loop to continue until the test (`strUserSuppliedPassword <> strCorrectPassword`) becomes False. If the Until keyword is used, the loop continues as long as the condition is False. The password loop looks like this with the Until keyword:

```
Do
    strUserSuppliedPassword = InputBox("Please enter a
    ➥ password")
Loop Until strUserSuppliedPassword = strCorrectPassword
```

Whether you use While or Until depends on the situation. Generally, programmers are more familiar with Do While, so using Do While makes it easier for other programmers to read your program. Frequently, though, as in the password examples, using While requires a negative test ("not equal to"). By using Until in the password loop, the test could be rephrased as a positive test ("equal to"). Positive tests are generally easier to understand than negative tests.

The For...Next Loop

Many times, a code block simply needs to be executed a specific number of times. In these cases, the simplest construct is the For...Next loop. The For...Next loop combines the end condition test and the code to reach the end condition in one For statement. This For...Next loop initializes the variable `intCount` to 1, increments the variable on each pass through the loop, and sets the end condition to be when `intCount` is greater than 10 (the Next statement marks the end of the code block). Figure 2.8 shows the flowchart for the For...Next loop. No other code is required to create a loop that will be processed 10 times:

```
For intCount = 1 To 10 Step 1
Next
```

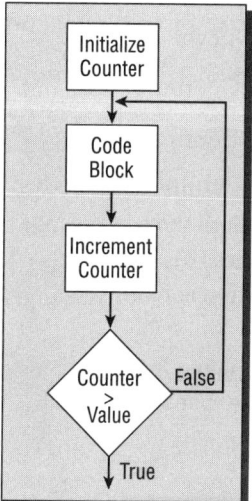

Of course, a loop with no code block in it isn't much good. For...Next loops are frequently used to process all the elements of an array. This loop prints out the first 11 elements of the strEmployee array to the Debug window:

```
For intCount = 0 To 10 Step 1
    Debug.Print strEmployee(intCount)
Next
```

The Step portion of the For statement is optional (if you omit it, the variable will have 1 added to it on each pass through the loop). Normally, the Step portion is provided only when the counter is to have some number other than 1 added to it. This code, for instance, prints out the even numbers between 0 and 100:

```
For intCount = 0 to 100 Step 2
    Debug.Print intCount
Next
```

In Exercise 2.6 you'll use the For...Next loop to reduce the number of lines of code used to initialize your array. Later in the routine you'll use Do...Loop to make your routine flexible enough to handle a routine of any size.

EXERCISE 2.6

Using a For...Next Loop

1. Modify the DisplayArray routine to use For...Next and Do...Loop:

```
Sub DisplayArray(strCalcType As String)
Dim DispArray() As Integer
Dim intTotal As Integer
Dim intAverage As Integer
Dim intPosition as Integer
Dim curMultTotal As Currency
Dim udtArrayBounds As udtArrayInfo

ReDim Preserve DispArray(5)
For intPosition = 0 to 5
  DispArray(intPosition) = intPosition + 1
Next

udtArrayBounds.intLowerBound = LBound(DispArray)
udtArrayBounds.intUpperBound = UBound(DispArray)

Select Case strCalcType
    Case "Add","Sum"
    intPosition = udtArrayBounds.intLowerBound
Do While _
   intPosition <= udtArrayBounds.intUpperBound
  intTotal = intTotal + DispArray(intPosition)
  intPosition = intPosition + 1
Loop
Debug.Print "Total of array contents: ", intTotal
Case "Average","Avg"
intPosition = udtArrayBounds.intLowerBound
```

```
Do While _
   intPosition <= udtArrayBounds.intUpperBound
   intTotal = intTotal + DispArray(intPosition)
   intPosition = intPosition + 1
Loop
intAverage = _
intTotal/(udtArrayBounds.intUpperBound + 1)
Debug.Print "Average of array contents: ", intAverage
Case "Multiply"
curMultTotal = 1
intPosition = udtArrayBounds.intLowerBound
Do While _
   intPosition <= udtArrayBounds.intUpperBound
   curMultTotal = curMultTotal * DispArray(intPosition)
   intPosition = intPosition + 1
Loop
Debug.Print "Multiplied result of array contents: ",
curMultTotal
Case Else
Debug.Print "Invalid calculation type:", strCalcType
End Select
End Sub
```

2. In the Debug window, type **DisplayArray("Multiply")** and press ↵. The result of multiplying the contents of the array is displayed.

3. To get the average of the contents, type **DisplayArray("Avg")** and press ↵.

Exit Statements

It's often necessary to exit a loop without processing all of the statements in the code block. The Exit Do and Exit For statements allow you to do this. In the code samples below, a loop is used to add up the first 100 elements of an array, stopping if the total reaches 1000:

```
Do While intEmpCounter <= 100
   intTotalHours = intTotalHours + intEmpHours(intEmpCounter)
```

```
If intTotalHours > 1000 Then
  Exit Do
End If
intEmpCounter = intEmpCount + 1
Loop
For intEmpCounter = 0 to 100
intTotalHours = intTotalHours + intEmpHours(intEmpCounter)
If intTotalHours > 1000 Then
Exit For
End If
Next
```

When the Exit statement is used, processing resumes after the line that marks the end of the loop (that is, after the Loop or Next statement).

Using Objects

In a typical VBA program a great deal of the code that you write will reference one or more objects. Interacting with an object consists of just three activities:

- Setting and reading properties
- Calling methods
- Responding to events

An object's properties provide you with information about the object or a means to control the object. An object's method, when invoked, causes the object to carry out some activity. Events provide a way for an object to communicate information to the program that is using it.

Setting and Reading Properties

Any place that you can use a variable, you can use an object property. This code sets a command button's Caption property to "Click Here":

```
cmdButton.Caption = "Click Here"
```

This code displays the button's caption concatenated with a string literal:

```
MsgBox "The button's caption is " & cmdButton.Caption
```

Calling Methods

Methods of objects are invoked by naming them. This is the code to close the current database but leave Access running:

```
Application.CloseCurrentDatabase
```

Some methods must be passed parameters in order to carry out their task. The CompactDatabase method of the DBEngine object requires the name of a database to compact and the name of the new database to create:

```
DBEngine.CompactDatabase "C:\Old.MDB", "C:\New.MDB"
```

Some methods return a value, much like a function does. The OpenDatabase method of the DBEngine object returns a database object:

```
Dim dbs as Database
Set dbs = DBEngine.OpenDatabase ("C:\New.MDB")
```

Responding to Events

An object triggers events as a way of communicating with the program that is using it. Events allow an object to inform the controlling program that something has happened that the program may want to deal with. Not all objects trigger events (Data Access Objects don't trigger events, for instance, nor do custom OLE controls).

To respond to an event you must write an event handler. An event handler is a subroutine that is called by the object at the time the event occurs. In VBA, event handlers have predefined names made up of the name of the object, an underscore, and the name of the event that the subroutine is to handle. A subroutine to close the form when the cmdExit command button fires its Click event looks like this:

```
Sub cmdExit_Click()
   DoCmd.Close
End Sub
```

Event handlers can have parameters passed to them by the object. These parameters provide a way for the object to share information about the event with the handler. In some event handlers, those parameters can be changed in order to pass information back to the object from the event handling routine.

Forms as Objects

In Access 95, forms can be treated as objects. Each form has a code module associated with it that holds the event handlers for events fired by the form. (You can also put subroutines and functions to be called from the event handlers in the form's code module). The form's code module also holds code to respond to the events triggered by the controls on the form.

You can set the form's properties and call its methods from the form's code module or other modules in the Access application. By using Property Let and Set procedures you can create new, read-only properties for the form. Finally, the New keyword, used for creating new objects, allows you to load a form multiple times.

Using Form Events

A form can trigger about 30 different events. This section looks at the ones that are used most frequently and their order of execution.

Open and Close Event Order

When a form is opened or closed, a series of events is fired. Each event has a specific purpose that controls when in the series it will occur. In addition to the Load and Unload events, these events include Open, Activate, Deactivate, and Close.

The order of events in the life of a form is shown in Figure 2.9. On the left side are the events that occur when a form opens. After whatever processing takes place, the form is closed, triggering the events shown on the right side of the figure.

When a form opens, the Open event fires before the first record has even been loaded to the form or the form has been displayed. The Load event fires next, after the data for the first record is loaded to the form. The Activate event fires last, as the form gets the focus.

The order of events when a form is closed is not a mirror image of the form open events. When a form closes the Unload event fires first because, like the Load event, it fires while the data is still available on the form. The Deactivate event fires as the form is removed from the screen. The Close event fires last, after the form's data has been removed and the form is no longer displayed.

F I G U R E   2.9

Form Open and
Close events

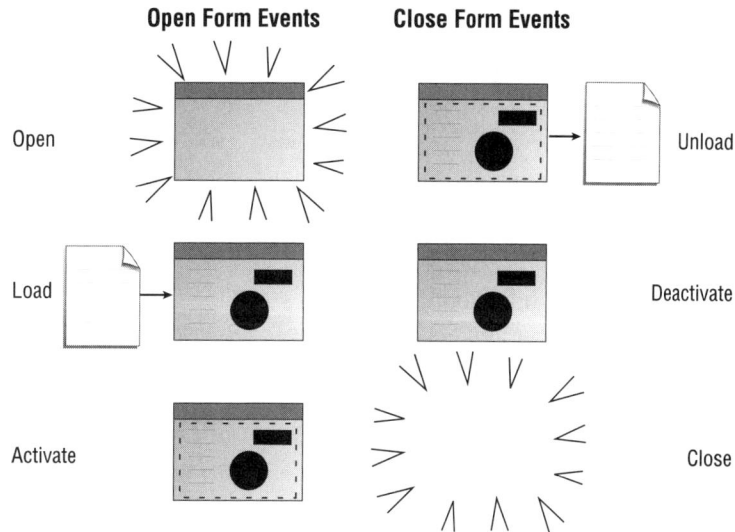

Form Switching Events

The Activate event doesn't just fire when the form is loaded. The Activate event also fires every time a user switches to the form from another open form (or report) in the same database. Similarly, the Deactivate event for a form fires when the user switches away to another open form (or report) in the same database. The full sequence of events as you shift from one form to another is:

- LostFocus for the control on the current form
- Deactivate for the current form
- Activate for the form being switched to
- GotFocus for the control on the form getting the focus.

The Activate and Deactivate events are normally used in applications that have many forms open at the same time. In that situation, the Activate and Deactivate events are used to control the forms as control is switched between them.

The Activate event does not fire when you switch from another application's window to the Access window.

The Form Load Event

The form's Load event is fired after the form is brought into memory and the first record's data is loaded to the controls on the form. The Unload event is the first event fired as a form is closed.

Typically, a Load event handler is used to initialize variables, or to load controls on the form that don't contain data from the record being displayed. This code shows a form Load event that opens a log file to record the activity that occurs on the form:

```
Sub Form_Load()
   Open "C:\Accesslog.txt" For Append As #1
End Sub
```

The Unload event for the same form closes the log file:

```
Sub Form_UnLoad(Cancel As Integer)
   Close #1
End Sub
```

Exercise 2.7 allows you to see the order in which a form's events fire.

EXERCISE 2.7

Investigating Events

1. Open the Customer database, click on the Forms tab, and then click on the New button. Select Design view and click on the OK button to open a new form.

2. Select View ➢ Code to display the code module for this form. In the Object drop-down list box at the top of the Module window select Form. Access creates a Form_Load event by default. Add a MsgBox "Form Load" statement to make the routine look like this:

```
Private Sub Form_Load()
MsgBox "Form Load"
End Sub
```

3. From Proc drop-down list, select Activate. Add a MsgBox "Form Activate" line to the routine so that it looks like this:

```
Private Sub Form_Activate()
MsgBox "Form Activate"
End Sub
```

4. Repeat step 3, selecting the Close, Deactivate, GotFocus, Load, Lost-Focus, Open, and UnLoad events, adding a MsgBox to each one that displays the event name. Close the Module window.

5. Select View ➤ Form and note the order in which the events fire. Switch to the Database window and note the events that fire as the form loses focus. Return to the form to see the events that fire as the form gains focus. Close the form to see the last set of events.

6. Save the form as **frmTestEvent**.

Data-Related Events

Access forms trigger a number of events as data is moved from the form back to the database. If you change data in the form, for instance, the BeforeUpdate event is fired just before the data is written back to the database. The After-Update event is fired immediately after the record is written to the database. There are corresponding events for inserting and deleting new records.

The events that fire before data is written to the database have the ability to prevent the updates by changing a parameter passed to the event. An Integer parameter is passed to the BeforeUpdate event, for instance. If the event handler sets this parameter to True, the update to the database will not be made.

Typically, the BeforeUpdate event is used to do any final editing of the record before it is written to the database. This routine, for instance, checks that the customer has been given either a SalesRep or a mailing address for advertising material. If the customer doesn't have either, a message box is displayed and the update is canceled:

```
Private Sub Form_BeforeUpdate(Cancel As Integer)
If Me![txtSalesRep] = "" And _
   Me![txtAdvertisingAddress] = "" Then

   MsgBox "Please supply a SalesRep name or mailing address."
   ➥ Cancel = True
End If
End Sub
```

Other data-related form events fire:

- Before and after a record is inserted (BeforeInsert, AfterInsert)
- Before any record is deleted (Delete)
- Before and after a user is asked to confirm the deletion of one or more records (BeforeDelConfirm, AfterDelConfirm)

Only one event fires as data is moved from the database to the form. The Current event fires after record data is moved to the controls on the form. Typically, the Current event is used to set properties on the form based on data in the record. This code enables or disables the command button to display SalesRep information, depending on whether there is a SalesRep name displayed:

```
Private Sub Form_BeforeUpdate(Cancel As Integer)
If Me![txtSalesRep] <> "" Then
    cmdSalesRepInfo.Enabled = True
End If
End Sub
```

When a form is opened, the Current event fires just after the Activate event. Exercise 2.8 allows you to see the order in which a form's data-related events fire.

EXERCISE 2.8

Investigating Data-Related Events

1. Open the Customer database, click on the Forms tab, and then the frmTestEvent form. Click on the Design button to open the form in Design view.

2. If the Properties List dialog box isn't visible, select View ≻ Properties to display it. Enter **Customer** in the RecordSource property. Select View ≻ Field List to display the list of fields in the table. Drag the CustomerLastName and CustomerFirstName fields from the field list to the form to create text boxes. Close the Field List.

3. Select View ≻ Code to display the code module for this form. In the Object drop-down list box at the top of the Module window select

Form. In the Proc drop-down list select Current. Add a MsgBox "Form Current" statement to make the routine look like this:

```
Private Sub Form_Current()
  MsgBox "Form Current"
End Sub
```

4. Repeat step 3, selecting the AfterDelConfirm, AfterUpdate, BeforeDel-Confirm, BeforeUpdate, and Delete events, and then adding a MsgBox to each one that displays the event name.

5. Select View ➢ Form and note the order in which the events fire. Change the name in the CustomerLastName field, and then click on the CustomerFirstName field to see which events fire as you change fields. Close the form to see the last set of events.

6. Click on the record selector for the form and press the Delete key to delete the record. Note the order in which the events are fired.

Form Methods

Microsoft ✓ **Exam Objective**

Use form methods.

The most important Access form methods are data related:

- **Refresh:** The form's Refresh method re-fetches the currently displayed record from the database. This method allows a user to see any changes that might have been made to the record by other users on the system. If new records have been added to the database the Refresh method won't cause them to be displayed. The Refresh method just re-fetches the data for the records associated with the form.

- **Requery:** The Requery method reruns the query that retrieved the records for the form. Unlike a Refresh, a Requery can find new records that should be displayed on the form. A Refresh will also discard any records that have been deleted since the record was first displayed.

Access forms have relatively few methods compared to the forms used with Visual Basic. (On the other hand, Access forms have a lot more events than Visual Basic forms have).

- **Undo:** The Undo method discards any changes made to the record currently being displayed and restores the original data to the form. Once the record has been saved, because the user moved to a new record or selected Records ➤ Save Record, the Undo method has no effect.

You can overcome this limitation of Undo by writing code on the Current event to store the original value of each control in a set of variables. This allows you to restore it from code on a command button later on, even if the user has saved the record in the interval.

You can allow your user to use the Refresh, Requery, or Undo changes on the form, by providing them with a set of three command buttons that call these methods:

```
Sub cmdRefresh_Click()
  Refresh
End Sub
Sub cmdRequery_Click()
  Requery
End Sub
Sub cmdUndo_Click()
  Undo
End Sub
```

Two form methods are useful in handling the display of the form:

- **SetFocus:** The SetFocus method allows you to move the focus to any form in the application. If the form isn't open, it will be opened. To move the focus to the CustomerUpdate form from some other form you would use this code:

```
Form_CustomerUpdate.SetFocus
```

When referring to a form from some other form or code module, prefix the form's name with Form_.

- **Repaint:** Access will often defer the redisplay of a form while it's running your code. If you want to force a form to be redisplayed before your code is run, you can use the Repaint method at the start of the code block:

```
Repaint
```

Creating New Forms

VBA includes the New keyword for creating objects. Since Access treats forms as objects, you can use the New keyword to load multiple copies of a form. The New keyword returns an object variable that you can use to work with the form's methods and properties from outside of the form's code module.

Microsoft Exam Objective

Open multiple instances of a form and refer to them.

This capability allows you to create Multiple Document Interface (MDI) applications in Access. You're probably most familiar with MDI applications from working with Word or Excel. Both of these applications allow you to have several documents open at the same time and switch between them. In our Sales Order application, for instance, you might want to be able to view the information for several customers or orders at the same time. By using the New keyword, you have the ability to open as many copies of a form as your application needs.

This code, for instance, loads two copies of the CustomerUpdate form and sets their caption properties so that each form will have a different name in its title bar. Since forms created with the New keyword open invisibly, the code also sets the Visible property of each form to True so that you can see the form:

```
Dim frm1 As Object
Dim frm2 As Form

Set frm1 = New Form_frmTest
Set frm2 = New Form_frmTest

frm1.Caption = "Test Form 1"
frm2.Caption = "Test Form 2"

frm1.Visible = True
frm2.Visible = True
```

When forms are created with the New keyword, they close when the procedure ends, unlike forms opened with DoCmd.OpenForm. In the above code, frm3 is opened with OpenForm, while frm1 and frm2 are created with the New keyword. When the function ends, only frm3 remains open.

In Exercise 2.9 you'll add a button to your form that will allow you to create a new copy of it.

EXERCISE 2.9

Working with New Forms

1. Open the frmTestMethods form in Design view.

2. If the toolbox isn't visible, select View ➤ Toolbox to display it. If the upper-right button showing the magic wand is depressed, click on it. This will turn off the Control Wizard. Drag a command button to the form.

3. Right-click on the first button and select Build Event. From the Choose Builder dialog box, select Code Builder and click on the OK button. In the Click event procedure, enter this code:

```
Sub Command4_Click()
   Dim frm As Form
   Set frm = New Form_frmTestMethods
End Sub
```

4. Return to the form and set the command button's caption property to **New**. Select View ➤ Form to display your form.

5. Click on the New button to create a new copy of your form. Use the PageDn key to page through the records in the Customer table.

6. Return to the first form and change the CustomerFirstName field. Page to the next record to cause Access to save your change.

7. Return to the second version of the form and page to the record that you changed to see your change. If your change isn't visible, click on the Refresh button.

Form Properties

Unlike most Access objects, forms support the creation of new properties. In fact, each of the controls on your form acts as a property for the form. From a code module you can display the CustomerLastName text box on the CustomerUpdate form with this code:

```
MsgBox Form_CustomerUpdate.CustomerLastName
```

You can also add properties by declaring a variable in the Declarations section of your form's code module. This line of code, added to the Declarations section of the CustomerUpdate form, gives the form a Counter property:

```
Global Counter as Integer
```

Now, from any other form or code module you can use that property by referencing the form by name:

```
Form_CustomerUpdate.Counter = Form_CustomerUpdate.Counter + 1
```

Property Let, Property Set

There are times when you will want to have some code execute when a property that you've added to your form is changed by a program manipulating the form. To do that, you can create properties by using Property Let or Set procedures in your form's code module. Property Let and Set procedures look very much like subroutines that accept one or more parameters.

*Microsoft
Exam
Objective*

**Use the Property Set and Property Let statements to assign
values to form properties.**

This routine creates a property called LogEntry and writes a record to a
log file whenever the property is set:

```
Public Property Let LogEntry (strValue As String)
    Open "C:\FormFile.Log" For Append As #1
    Print #1, strValue
    Close #1
End Property
```

The Property Let procedure has the same name as the property that it
defines. The LogEntry property that this Property Let procedure defines
could be used from a code module to add a line to the log file by using this
statement:

```
Form_CustomerUpdate.LogEntry = "About to do update"
```

A Property Let statement always accepts at least one parameter, which is
the value that the property is being set to in the statement that sets the property. In the earlier example, the parameter strValue will be set to "About to
do update."

The data type of the property is set by the data type of the parameter that
the property procedure accepts. In the previous example, the LogEntry property would be a String property because that's the data type of the strValue
parameter. The Counter property that follows would appear as an integer
property:

```
Property Let Counter (intValue as Integer)
```

If the property is declared with the Object data type, though, you must use
a Property Set routine:

```
Property Set ReferenceDatabase (dbs as Database)
```

Property Get

You cannot mix properties defined through variables and properties defined
through Property Let and Set statements. If you define a property by using a

Property Let or Set routine then you must define a Property Get routine if your users are to be able to read the property. A Property Get procedure has the same name as the property it defines. At some point in the Property Get routine the name of the procedure must be set to some value. It is this value that will be returned to the program that is reading the property.

Here is a Counter property that adds whatever value is passed to it to an internal variable (intCounter). The Property Let procedure is run when the Counter property is set, the Property Get procedure is run when the Counter property is read:

```
Dim intCounter as Integer
Public Property Let Counter(intValue As Integer)
   intCounter = intCounter + intValue
End Property
Public Property Get Counter() As Integer
   Counter = intCounter
End Property
```

To set the property (and run the Property Let procedure) you would use:

```
Form_CustomerUpdate.Counter = 4
```

To read the property (and run the property Get) you would use:

```
intValue = Form_CustomerUpdate.Counter
```

Multiple Parameter Properties

You can create Property procedures that accept more than one parameter, in which case the first parameters appear as subscripts to the property. A Property procedure declared like this:

```
Property Let ListItem(intPosition as Integer, _
 strValue as String)
```
could be used like this:

```
Form_CustomerUpdate.ListItem(1) = "Car"
```
The parameter intPosition would contain the value 1 and the parameter strValue would contain the value "Car". The extra parameters don't have to be numeric.

Control Events

Like forms, intrinsic controls in Access also fire events. Here are some of the more commonly used events for controls:

- **Click:** The Click event is associated with a number of controls but is most commonly used with command buttons. The Click event fires when the user presses down on the left mouse button over a control and then releases the mouse button. This code would close the form whose code module it appears in:

```
Sub cmdExit_Click()
  DoCmd.Close
    End Sub
```

Microsoft
Exam
Objective

Assign event-handling procedures to controls in a form.

- **GetFocus, LostFocus:** These events fire whenever a control gets and loses focus. Typically, the GetFocus and LostFocus events are used to edit the data in the control.

```
Sub txtSalesRep_LostFocus()
If Me![txtSalesRep] = "" Then
  MsgBox "Please enter a Sales Representative's name"
  Me! txtSalesRep.SetFocus
End If
End Sub
```

The Enter and Exit events are similar to the GetFocus and LostFocus events but do not fire in as many situations. The Exit and Enter events fire as the user enters or exits a control. The Exit and Enter events will not fire when the user switches from one form to another if the user does not change the current control (as happens if the user clicks on the form's title bar to switch to the form).

- **BeforeUpdate, AfterUpdate:** These events fire as the control loses focus if the data in the control has been changed and the control is displaying data from the database. The BeforeUpdate event is passed a parameter which can be used to cancel the update. These events do not fire when a record is deleted.

The BeforeUpdate and AfterUpdate events are the best events to use if you want to take some action when data in a control is changed (though not when the data in the control is changed from code). The Change event is not as useful as its name suggests. The Change event does not fire if the data in the control is changed from code. The Change event also fires with every keystroke in the field.

Exercise 2.10 allows you to see the order in which a form's control data-related events fire.

EXERCISE 2.10

Investigating Control Data-Related Events

1. Open the Customer database, click on the Forms tab, and then the frmTestEvent form. Click on the Design button to open the form in Design view.

2. Select View ➢ Code to display the code module for this form. In the Object drop-down list box, select the CustomerLastName field. Add Msgbox statements to its BeforeUpdate and AfterUpdate events:

```
Private Sub CustomerLastName_BeforeUpdate(Cancel As Integer)
  MsgBox "Field BeforeUpdate"
End Sub
```

3. Select View ➤ Form, and note the order in which the events fire. Change the name in the CustomerLastName field and then click on the CustomerFirstName field to see which events fire as you change fields. Close the form to see the last set of events.

Summary

Visual Basic for Applications (VBA) is Microsoft's application development language. VBA is used in Access as a hosted language. A program is made up of a series of statements that consist of object references, VBA keywords, operators, and variables.

VBA variables are declared using the Dim keyword. The Integer and Long data types are used for non-decimal data, the Single and Double data types are used for decimal data (with some loss of precision with very large and very small numbers). The Currency data type provides support for decimal data in the range of numbers used in business applications. The String data type is used to store character information. The other data types in VBA are Boolean, Byte, Date, Object, and Variant. VBA also allows you to create your own data types from the native VBA types.

You can declare arrays of one or more dimensions of any data type in VBA. When you declare an array you specify the position of the last element in the array. Since the first array element is normally 0, the number of elements in the array is always one more than the number the array is declared with.

The operators supported by VBA include arithmetic, concatenation, logical, and comparison.

The arithmetic operators support the common math functions (addition, subtraction, multiplication, and division), and four less common operators. The comparison operators allow for the common comparisons (equal to, greater than, and less than), and the use of three less common operators. The comparison operators also include the Like operator, which is used with wild cards in pattern matching comparisons. The logical operators are used to join tests and include Not, And, and Or, and three less common operators.

VBA has keywords that implement branching and looping. Branching is supported through the If...Then...Else/ElseIf and Select...Case constructs. Looping is supported by the For...Next and Do While/Until...Loop keywords.

VBA code is run in response to events triggered by objects—primarily forms and controls. The code run in response to an event interacts with objects by setting and reading properties, or calling object methods. VBA code can be used to give new properties and methods to forms.

Review Questions

1. To declare a string and two integer variables you would use:

   A. Dim strName as String
       Dim intOne, intTwo As Integer

   B. Dim strName As String
       Dim intOne As Integer, intTwo As Integer

   C. Dim strName As String
       Dim intOne As Integer; intTwo As Integer

   D. Dim strName As String
       Dim intOne As Integer, Dim intTwo As Integer

2. What will be displayed when the following code executes?

```
Dim strValue As String*3
strValue = "Peter Vogel"
Debug.Print strValue
```

   A. "Pet"

   B. "Peter"

   C. "Peter Vogel"

   D. An error will occur

3. Adding Option Explicit to your Module will:

   A. Require you to declare all your variables

   B. Start all arrays with position 1

   C. Compare strings based on their actual values

   D. Compare strings based on their characters

4. An array is declared as `Dim DispArray(5) As String`. The array can hold how many items?

   A. 4

   B. 5

   C. 6

   D. None, this is an improper declaration

5. To test that the value in intTest is greater than 200 you would use:

   A. If intTest > 200 Then

   B. If intTest >= 199 Then

   C. If intTest < 200 Then

   D. If intTest <= 199 Then

6. In your comparisons you do not want "S" to be equal to "s". You should add which statement to your module?

   A. Option Compare Text

   B. Option Compare Exact

   C. Option Compare Binary

   D. Option Explicit

7. If you want to ensure that a loop is executed at least once, you should:

    A. Not put the code in a loop

    B. Use the Skip keyword

    C. Put the test in the While statement

    D. Put the test in the Loop statement

8. How many times will this loop be executed?

```
For intCounter = 3 To 8 Step 2
Next intCounter
```

    A. 2

    B. 3

    C. 4

    D. 5

9. To create a read-only property on a form you would:

    A. Add Property Get and Property Let procedures to your form

    B. Add only a Property Get procedure to your form

    C. Add only a Property Let procedure to your form

    D. You can't create a read-only property

10. To open a second copy of the CustomerUpdate form you would use:

    A. DoCmd.OpenForm CustomerUpdate

    B. DoCmd.OpenForm "CustomerUpdate"

    C. Set frm = New Form_CustomerUpdate

    D. CustomerUpdate.New

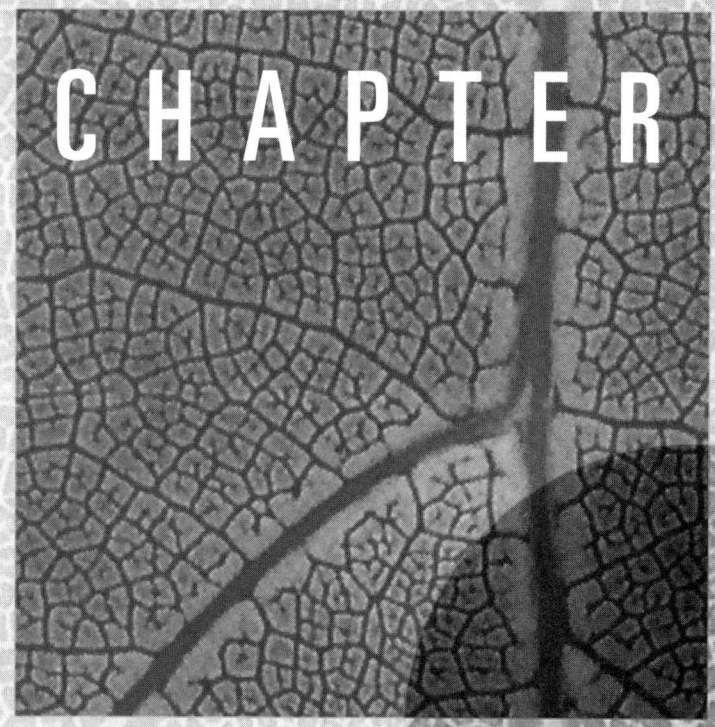

CHAPTER

3

Forms, Controls, and Reports

Microsoft Exam Objectives Covered in This Chapter:

- Choose which form-specific and report-specific properties to set.
- Choose which control properties to set.
- Set properties for custom controls.

The topic of this chapter, the form, is probably the most important component to the entire Access puzzle. Were there no forms there would be no access to data. The form is the interface for Access; and if you plan on developing Access solutions, you'll rely on the form more than any other single component in Access. Of course, you might also say that without the control, the form would not exist. It is the control that gives the form all of the power it has to make queries, sort data, and organize other forms. It's sort of a chicken and egg proposition. In this chapter, we've chosen to consider these two important elements together. In this chapter, you will learn:

- The forms and controls that make up your application have an enormous number of properties that affect their behavior. You'll learn which ones are important, which ones you should change, and the effects of changing those properties.

- How you can handle several people updating the same record and the effect that will have on the application's performance.

- Which of the controls that come with Access to use on your forms, and how to add new controls to Access.

- The differences between Access forms and reports.

- The basics of tying forms to a table or query, and the relationship between form controls and fields in the form's record source.

- The difference between a bound and an unbound control.

- How you can make a form control that does a calculation based on the contents of other controls. (Not all of the data on a form necessarily comes from the underlying table.)

Access Forms

Ever since Visual Basic 1.0 came along, applications have been based on forms. Windows applications developed with Visual Basic or Access typically consist of a series of forms displayed on the screen to the user. The user then works with those forms by clicking on buttons, entering data, selecting choices, or interacting in a variety of other ways. Access allows you to generate application forms that use data faster than any other development system.

To understand forms, you need to understand their properties. Using Access forms effectively means knowing which properties are available, what the effect of setting those properties will be, and how those properties interact.

Form Structure

Forms are divided into three sections: header, detail, and footer. Headers and footers come in two varieties: form and page. You can display form headers and footers by selecting which ones you want from the View menu in Design view.

The form header appears at the top of the form on the screen (or on the page if the form is printed). The form header is always visible; it does not scroll on a form that displays multiple records. As a result, the header section is generally used to display the form's title (or other static information) and for command buttons, which let users perform actions, or combo boxes, for selecting a specific record. A button to close the form is often placed in this area. The form footer appears at the bottom of the form and also does not scroll, so it is a good location for information that should remain in view and for command buttons.

A form can also have a page header and footer. Page headers and footers do not display on the screen and only appear when the form is printed.

The form detail section is generally used to display data from tables in your database. With the capability Access has to create a continuous form, you can repeat a form's detail section so that several records are displayed at once.

All of these sections fit in a single form page. A form has only one page, which can be up to 22 inches high (although, realistically, that size is not recommended). You can use page break controls to divide forms into logical pages, though this method is not used very much since the development of the Tab control, which provides a superior paged interface.

Form Properties

To control the appearance and behavior of the form, you set the form's properties. For instance, if you don't want your form to have either vertical or horizontal scrollbars, you set the form's ScrollBars property to Neither.

Form properties have a critical impact in Access on the way your application will work. Form properties control which records are displayed in a form and how those records are shared between users in a multiuser environment.

Working with Properties

The simplest way to view a form's properties in Design view is to right-click in the upper-left corner of the form and select Properties from the pop-up menu. There are properties sheets not just for the form but also for the individual sections that make up a form (header, footer, and detail) and for controls as well. To view the properties sheet for any form section, right-click on the form inside the appropriate section, as shown in Figure 3.1.

Microsoft
✓ *Exam*
Objective   **Choose which form-specific and report-specific properties to set.**

The form properties sheet is divided into five tabs: a list of all the form properties (the All tab) and four categorized lists (Format, Data, Event, and Other). Within each tab, related properties are grouped together.

Since Access is a tool for creating database applications, the most important properties to understand are those that control how Access works with data. Most (but not all) of those properties appear on the Data tab.

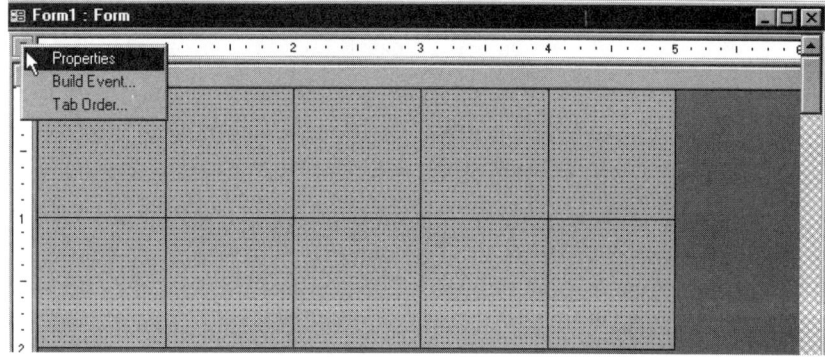

FIGURE 3.1

A new form in Design
view displaying the
Form context menu

Data Properties

The data properties allow you to associate records from your database
with a form. Among other things, these properties control what happens
when you have several users all accessing the same records at the same time.

Data Selection Properties

The most important property in this section is the Record Source property,
which binds the form to a collection of records drawn from one or more
tables in the database. Other properties allow you to control which records
in the Record Source are displayed and what kind of updates are allowed.
The following is a list of those properties:

- **Record Source:** This property allows you to associate a form with a
  collection of records. The Record Source property accepts a variety of
  settings that specify a set of records. You can enter the name of a table,
  the name of a query, or even a valid SQL statement as the Record
  Source for a form.

  - Once you've set the Record Source property of a form, any bound
    controls that you add to the form can be used to display individual
    fields in the records that make up the Record Source. In addition,
    any changes made to the data displayed in those controls will
    result in the data in the table being changed also.

- **Recordset Type:** This property sets the kind of Record Source that is used to manage the data in the record. This property takes three values: Dynaset, Dynaset (Inconsistent Updates), and Snapshot:

  - **Dynaset:** If the Record Source contains information from only one table, the user is allowed to change the data displayed in the controls. If the Record Source displays data from more than one table, the user will not be able to make changes to the data if the result would violate the database's referential integrity rules.

  - **Dynaset (Inconsistent Updates):** The user is allowed to make changes to the data even if it would violate the referential integrity rules for the database.

  - **Snapshot:** The user can only view the data displayed in the form.

- **Allow Filters:** Controls whether the user is allowed to create and apply filters to the form's Record Source at run time. This property accepts either Yes or No as its values.

  - **Yes:** The user can apply filters at run time.

  - **No:** The user cannot apply filters at run time.

Figure 3.2 shows a user creating a filter to limit the number of customers about whom information is displayed.

- **Filter:** This property accepts a test that limits the records that are displayed. A filter consists of a test of one or more fields in the Record Source. For instance, `[CustomerLastName] > 'S'` would limit the records displayed in the form to customers with last names beginning with the letters *T* through *Z*. The form's FilterOn property (which can only be set from code) must be set to True for the filter to take effect. To apply the filter, click the Apply Filter button on the toolbar.

- **OrderBy:** Controls the order in which records are displayed in the form. If you enter the name of one or more of the fields from the Record Source in this property, the records in the form will be sorted by those fields (multiple fields must be separated by semicolons). To sort the records by the customer's last name and first name, you would enter `CustomerLastName;CustomerFirstName` in the OrderBy property. The form's OrderByOn property (which can only be set from code) must be set to True for the records to be sorted by OrderBy property.

FIGURE 3.2

A form displaying all the records in a record-set is shown above.

Then the filter is applied (middle).

The result is the filtered form shown at the bottom.

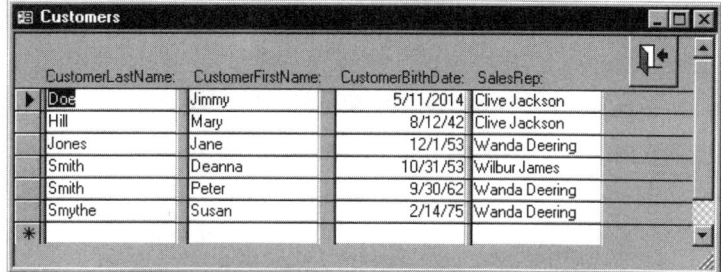

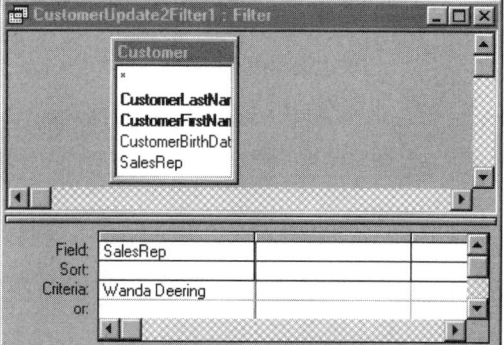

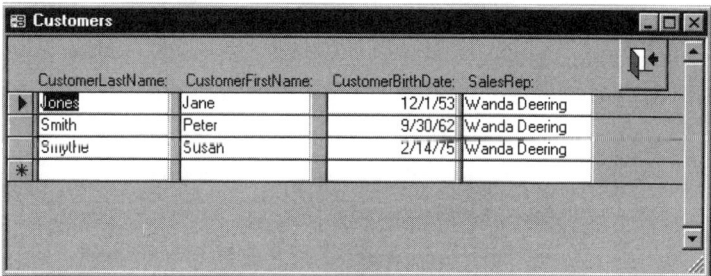

The Missing OrderByOn and FilterOn Properties

The OrderByOn and FilterOn properties aren't listed in the properties sheet for forms (although they are for reports). As a result, they can only be set using a macro or VBA code. Since both of these properties default to False you must add these lines to the Form_Load event of your form for your entries in Filter and OrderBy properties to take effect:

```
Me.FilterOn = True
Me.OrderByOn = True
```

In Exercise 3.1 you'll create a form, associate it with a table, and add controls to the form to display the data.

EXERCISE 3.1

Creating a Form Bound to a Table

1. Start Access and open the database that you created in Chapter 1 (the Customer database). Open a new Form in Design view. When the new, blank form displays, right-click in the upper-left corner of the form to display the form's pop-up menu, and select Properties from the menu. In the Record Source property, enter **Customer** (or select the Customer table from the drop-down list).

2. Click on the Format tab to display just the Format properties. Click in the Caption field and enter **Customers** (the text you enter in the Caption property will be displayed in the title bar of your form).

3. Select the Default View property and click on the drop-down arrow to display all of the Default View options. Select Continuous Forms.

4. The next step in defining the form is to add some fields to it. Access provides a list of fields from the Record Source to let you drag and drop fields onto your form. Leave the Properties list and select View ➤ Field List, or click on the Field List button on the toolbar. A window displaying the list of fields in the Customer table appears.

5. Click on CustomerLastName, drag it over to the form and drop it on the form. Drag the rest of the fields in the table to the form and arrange them so that they are all visible. To move the fields around on the form, click on the field and drag it to its new location.

6. Now that you've created a form to view and update Customer table data, use it to enter the records in Table 3.1 into the table.

7. Close the form. You will be asked if you want to save your changes to the form. Click on Yes to save your changes. The Save As dialog box appears asking you to give the form a name. Enter **frmCustomerUpdate** as the form name and click on the OK button to save your form.

8. The form would be more useful if it displayed multiple customers. To make that change, return to Design view by selecting View ➤ Form Design. Set the DefaultView property to Continuous forms. Select View ➤ Form to see the effect of your change.

9. Now you'll set the form to display the records in a useful order. In Design view, enter **[SalesRep]** in the OrderBy property. Note that the records are now sorted by Sales Rep.

You've now created a form based on a table, modified its properties, and used it to view your table's records.

T A B L E 3.1: Sample Customer Records

CustomerLastName	CustomerFirstName	CustomerBirthDate	SalesRep
Jones	Jane	12/01/53	Wanda Deering
Smith	Peter	9/30/62	Wanda Deering
Doe	Jim	5/11/14	Clive Jackson
Smythe	Susan	2/14/75	Wanda Deering
Hill	Mary	8/21/42	Clive Jackson

As a shortcut for switching between Form and Design view, use the View drop-down list on the left of the Access toolbar.

You can move several fields at once by holding down the Shift key or the Ctrl key while you click on them. Click on one field then hold the Shift key. When you click on another field all the fields in between will become selected. Holding the Option key lets you select fields in any order you wish. To drag the group of fields to the form, click on any one of the highlighted fields and drag it to the form.

Data Entry Properties

Data entry properties control the way your users can enter data. You can, for instance, prevent your users from using a form to add records or you can dedicate the form to just adding records. The properties are as follows:

- **Allow Edits/Deletions/Additions:** These three properties control what actions the user may perform on the data in the Record Source. These properties accept two values: Yes and No. The choices are:

  - Allow Edits permits modification to data in the record.

  - Allow Deletions lets the user delete records.

  - Allow Additions lets the user add new records.

  If you set all of these properties to No, you convert your form into a read-only view of the Record Source.

WARNING   Note that when the Allow Edits/Deletions/Additions properties are set to True, no error messages are generated when your users try to update the data in the form—their keystrokes just don't have any effect.

- **Data Entry:** This property causes the form to open, displaying a new blank record instead of the first record in the Record Source. The user will be able to add new records (and review the records they enter) but will be unable to see records already present in the Record Source. The property accepts two values: Yes and No. The choices are:

  - Yes: The user can only use the form to add records

  - No: The user can use the form to work with existing records.

  The Allow Additions property must be set to Yes if you set the Data Entry property to Yes (otherwise the form displays with only its header and footer sections and no detail section, which is very disconcerting). The Allow Edits property must also be set to Yes or the user won't be able to change the records after they enter them.

In Exercise 3.2 you'll work with form properties to control the way data is handled in your form. In the process, you'll create two variations on your form to be used when you want to control which kinds of updates the user is allowed to do.

EXERCISE 3.2

Changing the Data Properties of a Bound Form

1. Begin by converting your customer update form to a data-entry-only form. Open the frmCustomerUpdate form that you created in the last exercise in Design view and open the form's property sheet.

2. Set the DataEntry and Allow Additions properties to Yes.

3. Switch to Form view and note that you can't navigate through previously added records.

4. Add a new record. Select File ➢ Save As/Export to display the Save As dialog box. Enter **frmCustomerAdd** as the form name and click on the OK button.

5. Switch back to Design view and set the AllowEdits, AllowDeletions, and AllowAdditions properties to No.

6. Switch back to Form view and note that you can't edit data or delete or add records; the form is now read-only. Save this form as **frmCustomerView**.

 You may want to give the user a visual cue that the form is read-only, perhaps by changing the text box special effect or background color.

In this exercise you generated two more forms that display the same data as your update form but that prevent the user from making changes to existing records.

Record Locking

There's only one property discussed in this section, but in a multiuser environment it's the most important property a form has.

In an environment where many people are using the same database, there is a real possibility that two people will attempt to update a record at the same time. If you don't take control of this process, your users will end up repeating this three-step scenario:

1. A user displays a record and starts making changes to it.

2. A second user displays the same record, makes their changes more quickly than the first user, and saves the record.

3. The first user saves their changes without seeing the changes made by the other user and wipes out the other user's changes by overwriting them with theirs.

There are two ways to handle this problem:

- Don't allow the second user to make changes while the first user is looking at the record.

- Allow the second user to make changes, but advise the first user that the record was altered while they were working with it.

Both choices are available in Access (plus an even more restrictive choice); they are implemented through the form's Record Locks property.

The Record Locks property controls whether users are permitted to make changes to a record that is being viewed by another user. This property accepts three values: No Locks, All Records, and Edited Records:

- **No Locks:** Users are allowed to make changes to the displayed data even if another user is viewing the record. If two users are viewing a record and both make changes to it, the person who saves their changes last will get a message indicating that the record has been changed by someone else. The user can choose to save their results anyway (wiping out the first person's changes), view the new record, or copy their version of the record to the Clipboard.

- **All Records:** As long as the form is displaying a record, anyone attempting to change any of the records in the Record Source will find that they can't. When a user tries to change a locked record, the status bar will display a message that the recordset is not updateable.

- **Edited Records:** If the form is being displayed and a change has been made to the displayed record, anyone attempting to change the record will find that their keystrokes have no effect on the displayed data. No message is displayed, but a circle with a line through it will be displayed on the record selector of the form of the person trying to make the change.

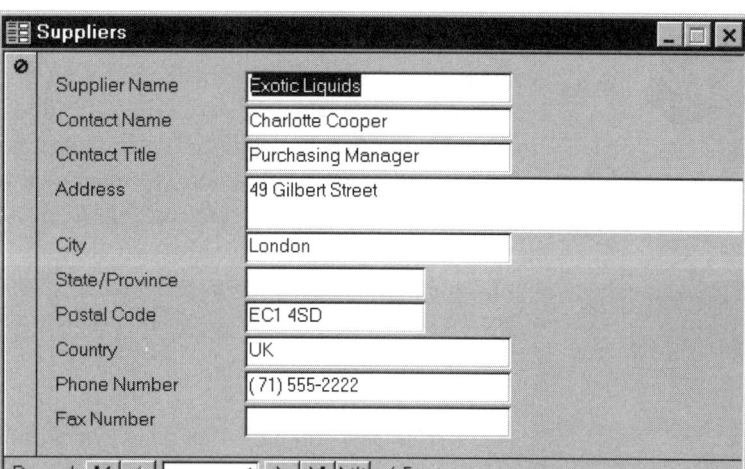

Optimistic and Pessimistic Locking

Setting the Record Locks property to No Locks implements *optimistic locking*. If you take the optimistic view that two people will never be working on the same record or, if they are, that most people won't be changing the records they are looking at, this setting makes sense. But, with optimistic locking, a user can make changes to a record, try to save their changes, and get an ugly message that their changes will not be saved because some other person has changed the record. This can be very frustrating.

Setting the Record Locks property to Edited Records implements *pessimistic locking*. If you take the pessimistic view that people will frequently be trying to change the same record, you'll want to use this setting because it prevents users from making changes and then discovering that they can't save them—as will happen under optimistic locking. In pessimistic locking a user won't be allowed to make changes to a record if it is being displayed in the form by some other user. This can be frustrating if the other user isn't actually going to make changes to the record, or has displayed the record and then left for lunch.

Access's locking process is made slightly more complicated than it might appear because Access doesn't just lock the record being displayed. Access locks the record being displayed and all the records in a 2KB page around it. As a result, a user who is viewing one record can actually lock other users out of several records, depending on how many of the table's records fit in a 2KB page.

What are the best settings for the RecordLocks property? It depends on the situation. To begin with, if you're not in a multiuser situation, you can ignore the RecordLocks property. In a multiuser setting you should use No Locks for read-only and data-entry forms. The Edited Records setting should be used for most other forms unless you are absolutely certain that no record will ever be accessed by two people at the same time. Finally don't use All Records on forms. All Records should be used on reports, where it's essential that no records in the table be changed while a report is running.

In Exercise 3.3, you'll change the way that your form works with its Record Source and see how two forms that share the same data interact.

EXERCISE 3.3

Locking Data Shared between Two Forms

1. Create a new form based on the Customers table, as you did in Exercise 3.1. Save it as **frmCustomerUpdate2**.

2. Open both frmCustomerUpdate and frmCustomerUpdate2 in Design view. Set both forms' RecordLocks property to No Locks to implement optimistic locking.

3. Open frmCustomerUpdate in Form view and change the data in one of the text boxes for the displayed record. Press Shift+↵ to save the changed record.

4. Switch to frmCustomerUpdate2, and make a change to the same record, then press Shift+↵.

5. The Write Conflict dialog box pops up, offering the user a choice of Save Record, Copy to Clipboard, or Drop Changes. Save Record will overwrite the changes you made in frmCustomerUpdate, Drop Changes will abandon the change you just made in frmCustomerUpdate2, and Copy to Clipboard will copy frmCustomerUpdate2's data to the Clipboard, presumably so that you can paste it back into the form and try the update again at some later time.

6. Click on Drop Changes and close both forms to unlock the Customer table.

7. In order to prevent your users from seeing a cryptic dialog box, you can change the RecordLocks property of the form. Open the frmCustomerUpdate form in Design view and change its RecordLocks property to All Records. Switch to Form view and change the data in one of the text boxes.

8. Open the frmCustomerUpdate2 form, and try to change the data in a control on the other form; you should hear a beep and not be able to edit the data.

In this exercise you have explored the effect of working with optimistic and pessimistic locking. Although you are only one user working with two forms, Access behaves the same way if one user accesses a table via two forms, or two different users access the same table via the same form in two different databases in a multiuser environment.

Format Tab Properties

The properties on the Format tab of the properties sheet control the appearance of the form—an important part of your application's user interface. These properties control whether the form displays just one record from the Record Source at a time or if the user is given a set of records to work with. These are some of the more important form format properties:

- **Default View:** Controls how the form appears to the user when it is first displayed. There are three settings for this property: Continuous Forms, Single Form, and Datasheet, as shown in Figure 3.3.

  - **Continuous Forms:** One copy of the detail section of the form is displayed for every record associated with the form. This is limited only by available space in the form's detail section.

  - **Single Form:** One copy of the detail section of the form is displayed.

  - **Datasheet:** Uses a table format to display the records associated with the form.

FIGURE 3.3

The Format tab from the Form properties sheet showing the Default View choices

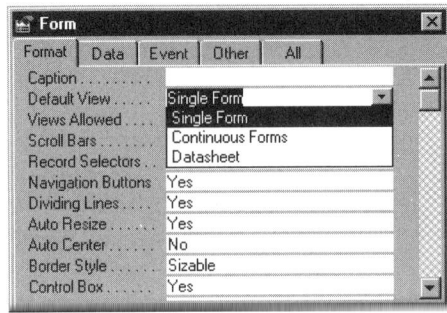

- **Views Allowed:** Normally a user can select different views of a form from the View menu. Setting the Views Allowed property controls which views the user is allowed to select. The three choices for this property are Datasheet, Form, and Both:

  - **Datasheet:** The user can only display the form in Datasheet view.

  - **Form:** The user can only display the form in Form view (either continuous or single, depending on the setting of Default View).

  - **Both:** The user can switch between Datasheet and Form view.

Only if Views Allowed is set to Both does Default View matter. If Views Allowed is set to Form or Datasheet, it doesn't matter what Default View is set to—the form will be displayed according to the Views Allowed setting.

Other Tab Format

Two properties on the Other tab also control the appearance of the form:

- **Popup:** Setting this property to Yes causes the form to display on top of any other form in Access.

- **Modal:** Setting this property to Yes prevents the user from doing anything else in Access until this form closes. That includes closing the form, unless you have a command button to close it.

If a form is set to display as a Datasheet, and Popup is set to Yes, it will display as a single form. Continuous Forms will display the same way with Popup set to Yes. Whatever the Default View property is set to, if the form's Popup property is set to Yes, the user can't change the view type in the interface.

Using Popup to Create User Manuals

Setting a form's Popup property to Yes actually frees it from Access. Normally all of your forms in Access are treated as children of the Access window. Popup forms, on the other hand, are independent of the Access window. If you take a screen snapshot by pressing Alt+PrintScrn (you should find the PrintScrn button to the right of the F12 key on your keyboard) while using your form, you will get a snapshot of the Access window with your form displayed in it. If you set the form's Popup property to Yes and press Alt+PrintScrn, you will get a snapshot of just your form. If you are preparing documentation for your Access application, this can be very useful, as you can paste the screenshot directly into Word with Ctrl+V.

Setting both Popup and Modal to Yes gives you a form that behaves just like a Windows dialog box.

In Exercise 3.4 you will see how some of the form properties interact.

EXERCISE 3.4

Setting Views in a Form

1. Open the frmCustomerUpdate form created in Exercise 3.1. Set the form's DefaultView property to Datasheet, and Views Allowed to Form.

2. Select View ➢ Form to view the form. It opens as a form despite the Default View setting of Datasheet.

3. Select View from the Access menu bar and note that you have a choice of Design, Form, and Datasheet, with a bullet next to Form, indicating that it is the current view. Datasheet is grayed out, indicating that it cannot be selected.

4. Return to Design view and set Modal to Yes. Return to Form view. Now Datasheet view is not selectable.

5. Return to Design view and set Popup to Yes. The View list has disappeared from the toolbar, so you can't select another view.

After working with various combinations of views and properties, you now know how to achieve the following effects with the following combinations of property selections:

- Read-only: Set the form's Allow Edits, Allow Deletions, and Allow Additions properties to No.

- Allow user to choose any view: Set the form's Views Allowed property to Both, Popup to No, and Modal to No.

- Limit the user to one view only: Set the form's Views Allowed to the setting that you want.

- Make a form float over all other windows: Set the form's Popup property to Yes.

- Require the user to close the form before moving the focus to any other part of the your application: Set the form's Modal property to Yes.

Using Controls

Creating an Access application consists of creating a set of forms and other objects and then populating those forms (and possibly reports) with controls for the user to interact with. A form is only useful if it has some controls on it.

A *control* is an object which can be placed in a container (in Access, the relevant containers are forms and reports). Controls are used to display data from a record source; to display informational text; to allow the user to make choices; or just for decoration.

You can add a control to a form by selecting it in the toolbox and then clicking (or drawing a rectangle) on the form where it is to appear; or, alternatively, you can drag a field from the Field List to create a new control bound to that field. The act of placing the control on the form creates the control object that your application will use.

Controls, Objects, and Classes

Anything in Access that has properties or methods, or that triggers events, is an object. Controls are just one of the types of objects that you can use in building Access applications.

On a form, you can have many different controls and many instances of the same control (it's an unusual form that has just one text box, for instance). All of the text boxes on your form work the same way because they all use the same underlying code. That underlying code forms the definition of a text box: which properties and methods it has, what happens when you set a property or call a method, and so on.

The definition of a kind of object is called a *class.* Technically speaking, what you see in the toolbox is not a text box but the TextBox class from which any particular text box is created. A text box doesn't become a real object until it is drawn on the form and is actually created.

Designing Forms

As the first exercise of this chapter showed, you can't do much with a plain form. In the first exercise, just to display data from the Record Source, you added several text boxes and labels to your form.

Good form design means picking the right controls to carry out the form's intended tasks. Getting the control to do what you want means understanding its properties and setting them appropriately. The only people capable of deciding if your form is well-designed are the people who will use it. In an ideal world you could give a select group of your users a copy of Access and ask them to build the forms they needed to do their job.

Unfortunately, your users will probably lack the knowledge to work with the Access form designer effectively. In our less than ideal world, it's your responsibility to work closely with your users to help them get the user interface that they need to work with your application. As an Access developer, you will provide the technical knowledge required to work with Access, and your users will provide the knowledge of the way their business works and feedback on the usability of the application's forms and reports.

Types of Controls

Controls can be categorized in many ways, but a fundamental difference between different controls is whether they are intrinsic or custom.

Intrinsic Controls

An *intrinsic control* is one that is included as part of the Windows 95 operating system. Many of the controls initially displayed in the Access toolbox (see Figure 3.4) are Windows 95 intrinsic controls that you can use in designing Access forms. An intrinsic control does not require any additional files other than those included in Windows 95. This also means that the text box control that you use is the same one used by every other Windows application. Fortunately, you don't have to know which controls are intrinsic and which are not in order to use them—Access treats them all alike.

F I G U R E 3.4

The Access Toolbox with its initial set of controls

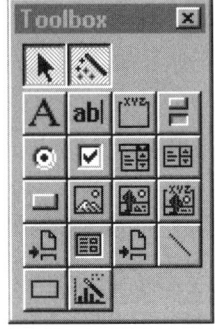

Custom Controls

Microsoft
Exam
Objective

Set properties for custom controls.

When you add a custom control to a form, it is placed inside an OLE control. As a result, the properties sheet that appears does not display the properties for the custom control. Instead, the properties sheet displays the properties for the OLE control.

In order to access the properties for the custom control, you must bring up the control's custom properties sheet. To do this, right-click on the control after adding it to the form. This will bring up the OLE control's context menu. One of the choices will be *Controlname* for ActiveX Control, where *Controlname* is the name of the custom control. Selecting this choice will display a menu with the choice Properties and display the properties sheet for the custom control.

You won't see the term "custom controls" turn up much outside of Access 95. That doesn't mean they've gone away—it's just that Microsoft keeps changing their name. For a while they were called "OLE controls," and they are currently called "ActiveX controls." Since many controls are delivered in files that have an .OCX extension you may also hear them referred to as "OCX controls" or just "OCXs."

Where do custom controls come from? Lots of places. Microsoft provides some with Access 95 and the Access Developer's Toolkit. Among these controls are the TreeView and Calendar controls.

See Chapter 12 for a more detailed discussion of using custom controls.

The specification for custom controls is a very general one and is not specific to Access. As a result, controls delivered with other products (like Visual Basic) can also be used with Access, though there are some compatibility problems. There is also a flourishing industry in providing custom controls. The companies in this industry range from small startups offering one or two controls to large software companies selling packs of 10 or 20 controls. A few of the major providers of Access custom controls are listed in Table 3.2.

T A B L E 3.2 Third-Party Access Custom Control Providers	Provider Name	Web Address
	FMS	`www.fmsinc.com`
	Cary Prague Books & Software	`www.caryp.com`
	The Component Café	`www.componentcafe.com`

WARNING   Not all custom controls work in all environments. If you are thinking about buying a control to work with Access, check with the vendor and make sure that it will work with Access 95.

Adding a custom control to your computer in order to use the control with Access 95 can be very simple: just run the setup program that installs the control on your disk. This program will copy the necessary files to your hard disk and update the Windows Registry.

Custom Controls and the Windows Registry

Access has to know what custom controls are installed on your computer before you can use them. Access gets that information by searching the Windows Registry. The Registry is part of Windows 95 and acts as a database about the hardware and software on your computer. A custom control must add the necessary entries in order to put itself on the list of installed custom controls and provide Windows with enough information to start the control when you need it. The process of updating the Registry for a new control is called "registering" the control.

In addition to the information Windows needs, the control may store other information that it needs in the Registry. If the Setup program asks for your name or company name, that information will typically be stored in the Registry, for instance. Many controls will store control information and user customization options in the Registry also.

After running the control's setup program, you should check that the necessary Registry entries have been made. If they haven't been made, you'll need to make the entries yourself by registering the control through Access. To check that a control is registered correctly, follow these steps:

1. Select Tools ➤ Custom Controls. The custom controls dialog box appears (see Figure 3.5).

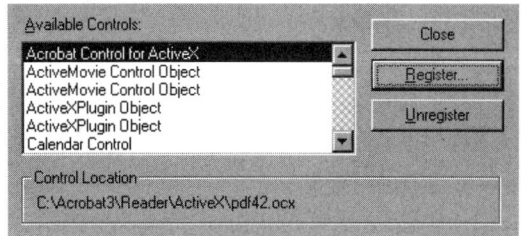

2. Scan the list for your control. If it doesn't appear, go on to step 3, otherwise you're done.

3. Click on the Register button to display the Add Custom Control dialog box.

4. Navigate to the directory where the OCX or DLL file that implements your control is located (check your documentation to find out which file this is and where it was installed on your hard disk).

5. Select the file and click on the OK button to register the control.

Your Toolbox

Since the number of controls available to Access is unlimited, you can't be expected to be familiar with all of them. It's important that you develop a toolbox of controls that you understand well and use frequently. Over time you can add to your toolbox, but there will always be a small set of controls that you use most.

In the next section you'll be introduced to the controls that most developers use frequently. As you will see, controls tend to share a number of properties, making it easier to adopt a new control when you need it.

Control Properties

As with forms, using a control effectively means knowing what properties it has and what will happen when you change those properties. Also (like forms) the simplest way to get to a control's properties is to right-click on the control and pick Properties from the pop-up menu.

Microsoft
✓ *Exam*
Objective

Choose which control properties to set.

The most commonly used controls in building Access applications are:

- **Text box:** Used to display information from a Record source and allow users to update that information or to show a calculation's results.

- **Command button:** Provides a way for users to start some activity, by running VBA code or a macro.

- **Label:** Used to display information, such as a description of a text box control.

- **List box:** Allows users to select from a set of predefined choices.

- **Combo box:** Allows users to select from a set of predefined choices, or enter new text manually.

- **Option group:** A frame enclosing a group of Option Buttons, giving the user a choice among various alternatives. Only one option in an option group can be selected at a time.

- **Option button:** A circular control that is clicked to indicate that an option is chosen (also known as radio button). Option buttons are added to option groups to define the choices within the group.

- **Checkbox:** A box that is checked to indicate a choice.

In this section you'll get a look at the most important properties of each of these controls. (A property that is shared by many controls will be discussed in the section that covers the control it is most often used with.)

Text Boxes

Like most Access controls, a text box can be "bound." This means that you can associate the text box with a field in the Record source of the form that the control is placed on. When you bind a control to a field, Access moves the data for the field out of the table and into the control when the user moves to a new record. When changes are made to the text box, the updated data is moved from the text box back into the field in the table before the next record is displayed. Figure 3.6 shows the properties sheet for a text box.

In addition to its data properties, the text box has a number of properties that affect its behavior and appearance.

F I G U R E   3.6

This properties sheet
is showing the settings
for the Data properties
of a text box.

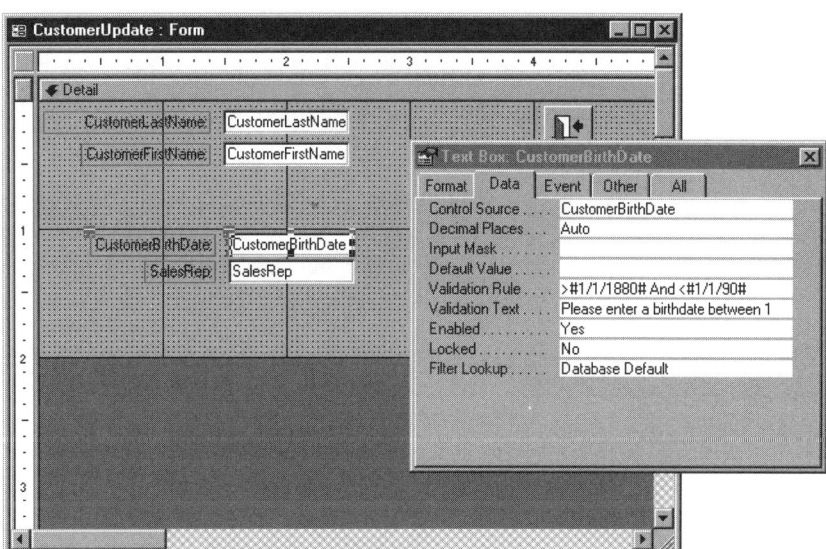

Data Properties

The Data tab of the text box's properties sheet allows you to control what data is displayed in the text box and what data is passed back to the database. Some of the options are:

- **Control Source:** The Control Source specifies which field in the form's Record Source will be bound to the text box. When you click on this property in the properties sheet, a drop-down list of available fields appears. You can select the field from this list or enter an expression, beginning with an equals sign (=). You can enter a valid VBA expression, including one that manipulates the fields that appear in the drop-down list. You might want to have the text box display just the customer's first initial, for instance. In that case you would enter the following expression as the text box's Control Source:

```
=Left(FirstName,1)
```

When you use an expression in the Control Source property, your users won't be able to change the contents of the text box.

It is a good idea to give calculated controls a different background color or special effect to indicate to the user that they can't be edited.

- **Default Value:** Setting this property to an appropriate value causes Access to pre-fill the text box with that value when you are adding new records to the database. For numeric fields, you might choose to set this property to 0 so that any textbox that the user does not change will be set to 0.

The Default Value property only applies to new records being added to the database. Default Value will not, for instance, pre-fill the text box for empty fields in an existing record.

- **Validation Rule/Text:** These two properties work together to control which data will go to your database from the text box. The Validation Rule property is set to a test that will be applied against the data entered in the text box. The Validation Text is the message that is displayed should the data fail the test. If you wanted to do a reasonableness check on the sales person's salary you might give the text box a Validation Rule of `> 25000 and < 90000`. This would require that the salary be greater than $25,000 and less than $90,000. An appropriate setting for the Validation Text property for this test would be

```
Please enter a salary between $25,000 and $90,000.
```

The Validation Rule is checked only if the data in the text box changes. As a result, adding a Validation Rule after the data has been entered will not clean up your data files. Nor will the data be checked against the Validation Rule if the data is entered through another form or entered directly into the table itself. To ensure that all data is edited correctly, use the Validation Rule property of the field in the table itself.

In general, using the Validation Rule property in a form is not a good idea. In the salary example, for instance, if the salary range for a salesperson is expanded, every form that uses this rule must be found and changed. It's a better idea to use the Validation Rule properties of the table, as you'll see in Chapter 5.

- **Enabled/Locked:** These two properties are frequently confused as they both prevent the user from making an entry in the text box. They work very differently, though. Both accept only one of two possible values: Yes and No.

  - **Yes:** Setting the Locked property to Yes prevents the user from typing in the text box. Users will still be able to tab to the text box, and clicking on the text box will trigger events. The appearance of the text box is unchanged. The only effect of setting the Locked property to Yes is to prevent users from changing the contents of the text box. The Enabled property is normally set to Yes.

  - **No:** Setting the Enabled property to No makes a number of changes to the behavior of the text box. The Enabled property determines whether or not the text box can receive any events. When the Enabled property is set to No, your users will not be able to tab to the text box and nothing will happen when they click on it. In addition, the box will appear grayed out on the screen. The Locked property is normally set to No.

Exercise 3.5 will give you a chance to see how Validation Rules work.

EXERCISE 3.5

Controlling Data Entry

1. Open the frmCustomerUpdate form in Design view, select the CustomerBirthDate text box and enter **> #1/1/1960#** in the Validation-Rule property. Enter **Customer birth dates must be greater than January 1st, 1960**.

2. Switch back to Form view and navigate among the records. Note that any existing data that violates the new rules remains unchanged.

3. Select a customer and change their birth date to some date prior to 1960 to see your validation message displayed.

4. Go to back to Design view. Set the CustomerLastName text box's Enabled property to No. Set the CustomerFirstName text box's Locked property to Yes. Display the form.

5. Notice the difference between the CustomerFirstName text box (locked) and the CustomerLastName text box (not enabled). The locked text box looks like any other text box, but the disabled CustomerLastName text box is grayed out.

6. Attempt to tab to the CustomerLastName text box or click on it to shift focus to it. Because the field is disabled, it cannot get the focus.

7. Tab to the CustomerFirstName field and attempt to change the data in it. Notice that while a locked field can get the focus, the data in it cannot be changed.

As you have seen, the Validation Rule property only edits your data when you change it.

Other Tab Properties

Every control is automatically given a name as it is added to the form. You can change that name through the Name property of the control properties sheet's Other tab. To bring up the properties sheet for a control, right-click on the control and select Properties from the pop-up menu. The Format tab is displayed as part of the control's properties sheet.

In addition to the Name property, several properties on the text box's Other tab affect the way the text box works. These properties include the Tab Stop, Tab Index, and Status Bar Text properties. The Other tab also has the Tag property, which has no effect on the text box in the user interface, but can be very useful in VBA code. Here are some of the important properties listed on the Other tab.

- **Tab Stop:** This property is used to prevent a user from being able to tab to a control. Tab Stop can be set to Yes or No. The user can still move to the control by clicking on it, but they can't tab to it.

- **Tab Index:** This property is used to control the order in which the user will visit the controls when pressing the Tab key. This property accepts a numerical value and the controls will be visited in numerical order.

The order in which controls are visited as the user tabs through the form (the tab order) defaults to the order in which the controls were added to the form. Rather than attempt to get the tab order you want by setting the individual controls' Tab Index properties, select View ➤ Tab Order and use the Tab Order dialog box to set the order. Clicking on the dialog box's Auto Order button will set the tab order to visit the controls from the upper-left control to the lower-right control by zig-zagging left to right, top to bottom through the form.

- **Status Bar Text:** This property can be set to any string. The message you type in here will be displayed in Access' status bar at the bottom of the screen when the user enters the text box. Unfortunately, the status bar text is rarely noticed by the users. The new Access 95 Control Tip property is much more useful for alerting users about important information about a control.

- **Tag:** The Tag property has no effect on the control's appearance. It is typically used in VBA code by programmers to hold information about the control. The Tag property lets you associate any information that you want with a control. For example, the function below cycles through all controls on all open forms, saving each control's name to its Tag property, which is handy for reference in case you

change the control's name and then find you need to know what it was
called before the change:

```
Public Function NameToTag()

    Dim frm As Form
    Dim ctl As Control

    For Each frm In Forms

        For Each ctl In frm.Controls
        ctl.Tag = ctl.Name
        Next ctl
        MsgBox "Form name: " & frm.Name & " processed"
    Next frm

End Function
```

- **Enter Key Behavior:** This property has two settings: New Line in Field and
  Default. When set to New Line in Field, pressing ↵ will always cause a new
  line to be added to the text box—just like the ↵ key does in a word pro-
  cessor. Setting the property to Default causes the ↵ key's behavior to match
  Access's default behavior for ↵ (see the sidebar "The ↵ Key in Access").

The ↵ Key in Access

Access offers a variety of choices when it comes to deciding what the cursor
will do when you press ↵. You can pick the behavior you want by selecting
Tools ➢ Options ➢ Keyboard (see Figure 3.7). The option box Move After
Enter in the resulting dialog box lets you specify what pressing ↵ will do to the
position of your cursor. You have three choices: Don't Move (pressing ↵ has
no effect on the position of the cursor), Next Field (pressing ↵ moves the cursor to the next field or control in the table or form), Next Record (pressing ↵
makes the next record in the recordset the current record).

When you set a text box's Enter Key Behavior property to Default, then
pressing ↵ in that text box will cause the cursor to move according to the
setting you make in this option box.

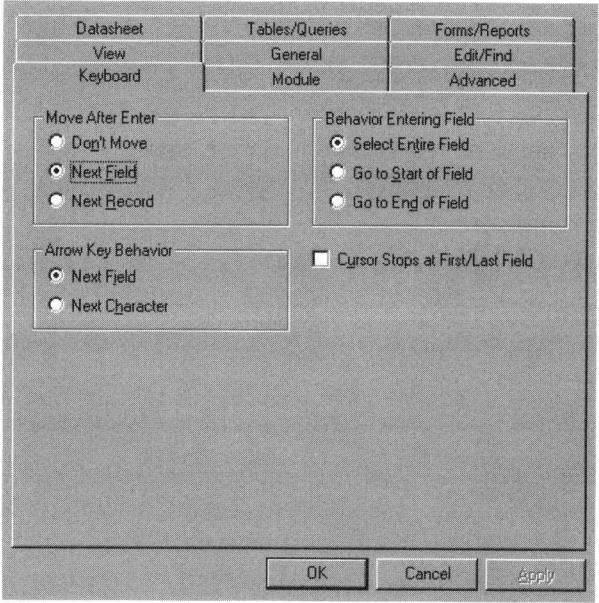

- **Name:** The name of the control, which can be used to refer to the control in VBA or Access macros. If you place a text box on the form by dragging it from the Field List, the name of the control will be set to the name of the field it is bound to. If you add a text box by dragging it from the toolbox, the name will be set to Text*x* where *x* is an arbitrary number.

Your code will be considerably easier to read and maintain if your give all your controls meaningful names. VBA code that refers to the control Last-Name is a lot easier to understand than code that refers to control Text12. (Naming the control txtLastName is even better, as it tells you the control is a text box.) Since the typical program costs six times as much to maintain than it does to create, anything you can do to make maintenance easier has a big payback.

- **Control Tip:** Displays text in a floating yellow box, similar to the one that appears over tools on the toolbar.

- **Cycle:** Gives you a choice (Current Page, All Records, Current Record) of what happens when the user tabs out of the last control on a form. Setting this property to Current Record is generally the most useful; it prevents the user from inadvertently going to the next record, or creating a new record, when they tab out of the last field on your form.

In Exercise 3.6 you will work with a text box to see how its properties can be used to change the ↵ key's behavior.

EXERCISE 3.6

Working with Text Box Properties

1. Open the Customer table and add a field called **Memo**. Select the Memo data type for the field.

2. Open the frmCustomerUpdate form and add a text box. Give it the name **txtMemoBox** and a control source of Memo. Set the Enter Key Behavior to New Line in Field.

3. Open the form in Form view and type some paragraphs of data in the memo field. Use the ↵ key to create new paragraphs as you enter your text.

4. Reopen the form in Design view and set the Enter Key Behavior property to Default.

5. Switch to Form view, type more text in the txtMemo control, then press the ↵ key. Notice that pressing the ↵ key does not create a blank line in the text box. The action that is taken depends on the setting in Tools ➢ Options ➢ Keyboard, which we'll look at next.

6. Go to Tools ➢ Options ➢ Keyboard and set Move After Enter option to Next Record (if this option already is set to Next Record, change it to Next Field). Return to the form and try using the ↵ key in the text box again. Now that you've changed the ↵ key's default behavior, you will get a different response to pressing the ↵ key.

7. Return to Tools ➢ Options ➢ Keyboard and restore the original setting in the Move After Error option box (normally Next Field).

Users generally expect to be able to use the ⏎ key to start a new paragraph in text, so if your form has lots of text boxes where users need to enter paragraphs of data, the New Line in Field selection is a good setting. Otherwise, you should leave the Enter Key Behavior property set to Default so that your form behaves the way that the rest of Access does.

Format Tab Properties

The Format tab of the text box's properties list provides the most properties for controlling the appearance of the data in the text box. The Format tab includes a full range of Font properties, for instance. There are a number of other properties that control whether the control appears on the form, and a set of special effects to alter the appearance of the control. The Format tab includes the following properties:

- **Format:** This property accepts a wide variety of settings that allow you to control how data is displayed. Here are some examples.

  - Table 3.3 shows how the date 1/1/80 could be displayed with different settings for the Format property.

  - Table 3.4 shows how the number 375 appears in various Formats.

T A B L E 3.3 One Date in Different Formats	Format	Display
	General Date	1/1/80
	Long Date	Tuesday, January 1, 1980
	Medium Date	01-Jan-80

T A B L E 3.4 A Number in Various Formats	Format	Display
	General Number	375
	Currency	$375.00
	Percent	37500.00%

- **Visible:** This property has two settings, Yes and No. Visible determines whether the control appears on the form. The main reason to use this property is to hide or show a control when a condition is met—for example, you want to make a control containing overtime hours visible only if the employee is in the Hourly category.

- **Can Grow/Can Shrink:** These properties allow the text box to increase or decrease vertically from the size you set in Design view, depending on the amount of data in the field. These properties only apply to text boxes (and some other controls) used on reports.

- **Special Effect:** This property has six settings: Flat, Raised, Sunken, Etched, Shadowed, and Chiseled. Figure 3.8 shows the results of applying those settings to a form.

F I G U R E   3.8

The text box's Special Effects settings

Command Buttons

Command buttons are placed on a form to allow the user to start an action (including closing the form). Typical command button activities include saving changes to a record, confirming a deletion, or opening a form. The most common user activity in Access, after entering data in a text box, is probably clicking on a command button.

Command buttons have many of the properties of text boxes. However, they can't be bound to a data field, and they lack most of the appearance-related properties, apart from Caption font properties. An Access command button appears in the same color as a generic Windows command button (usually light gray). The command button shares most of the Other tab properties, including Name, Tab Index, Tab Stop, and Tag. The command button has several unique properties of its own, though.

Format Tab Properties

The command button has the following properties to give you some flexibility in the button's appearance:

- **Picture:** Clicking on this property lets you select a bitmap to appear on the button. You can use any of the bitmaps used in Access, or select a bitmap file from your hard disk.

- **Picture Type:** This property controls how the bitmap selected in the Picture property is stored if you select a file from your hard disk. The property has two settings:

  - **Embedded:** This option causes the bitmap to be incorporated into your Access MDB.

  - **Linked:** The bitmap is left on the hard disk and is loaded into memory only when the button is displayed.

Since setting the Picture Type property to Embedded causes the bitmap to be stored inside your MDB file, the bitmap can't be shared with any other application. In addition, your MDB file will get larger by at least the size of the bitmap file (and possibly by twice the size of the bitmap file). On the other hand, using Linked may slow down form display as the bitmap is read from the file on the disk. Moving or renaming a Linked bitmap file will also break the link and you will have to re-enter the property to pick the file up again.

- **Transparent:** This property accepts two values, Yes and No:

  - **Yes:** The command button is invisible. Unlike when the Visible property is set to False, though, the button can still be used.

  - **No:** The command button appears as usual.

You can use the Transparent property of a command button to give controls that don't have a Click event (like labels) all the events of a command button. To do this, just position the transparent command button over the object you want the user to click on. Now, anyone clicking on the object will, in fact, trigger a Click event in the button. To keep users from tabbing to the button, you should set the button's Tab Stop property to False.

- **Display When:** You should use this property if you are planning on printing your form as a report (which is not a good idea, in general). It takes three values: Always, Print Only, and Screen Only:

  - **Always:** The button is visible on the screen and the printed version of the form.

- **Print Only:** The button appears only when the form is printed and does not appear on the screen. The button also cannot be used on the form.

- **Screen Only:** The button appears on the form but does not appear when the form is printed.

In Exercise 3.7 you'll experiment with the format settings of the command button.

Changing the Format Settings of the Command Button

1. Open frmCustomerUpdate form in Design view. From the toolbox, select Command Button and add it to the form. When the Wizard appears, select Application from the first column and select Run Notepad from the second column. Click on the Finish button to close the dialog box and add the button to your form.

2. Right-click on the button and select Properties. Click on the Format tab. Notice that the Picture property is set to Bitmap to display the Notepad icon on the button. Set the caption property to **&Click Here**.

3. Switch to Form view. Notice that the Notepad bitmap is displayed on the button and not the &Click Here caption that you entered. When a bitmap and a caption are both specified for a command button, only the bitmap is displayed. However, your shortcut key will still work. Press Alt+C and you will see the button depress and Notepad start running. Close Notepad.

4. Return to Design view and set the Transparent property of your new button to Yes. Return to Form view and notice that the button no longer appears. However, it can still be activated through its shortcut key. Press Alt+C and Notepad will start running. Shut down Notepad. If you remember where you placed the button on the form you can also activate the button by clicking on the area of the form where you know the command button is located.

5. Return to Design view and set the Visible property of your new button to No. Return to Form view and notice that the button still can't be seen. Press Alt+C and notice that Notepad does not start running. Setting a button's Visible property to No also disables the button.

You've now seen some of the differences between the Transparent and Visible properties. As noted above, you can use Transparent to add button-type functionality to parts of your form that don't have it (like labels). Since you can use the Visible property to not only make a control invisible but also to disable it, you should use the Visible property to effectively add and remove controls from your form at run time, using VBA to set the Visible property.

Changing the Visible property of a text box can be very useful when you want a certain text box to be visible on a record only if it meets certain criteria. In the code sample below the txtOvertime text box is visible if the employee's JobCategory is Hourly, but invisible if the category is other than Hourly (this code is put in the Form's Current event which is fired each time the form moves to a different record):

```
Private Sub Form_Current()

    If Me![JobCategory] = "Hourly" Then
        Me![txtOvertime].Visible = True
    Else
        Me![txtOvertime].Visible = False
    End If

End Sub
```

Other Tab Properties

In addition to the properties available to most controls on this tab, the Other tab contains two properties specific to command buttons: Cancel and Default.

- **Control Tip Text:** This property appears on the Other tab of most controls. The text you enter here will appear as a floating label when the user moves their mouse over the control, like a ToolTip for a button on the toolbar.

- **Cancel:** You can use this property to tie a command button to the Esc key on the keyboard. The property accepts two values, Yes and No:

  - **Yes:** When the user presses the Esc key this button will get a Click event. To put it another way, when this property is set to Yes, pressing the Esc key is exactly the same as clicking on the command button.

  - **No:** The button is not tied to the Esc key.

- **Default:** You use this property to tie the command button to the ↵ key. The property accepts two values, Yes and No.

  - **Yes:** When the user presses the ↵ key this button will get a Click event. To put it another way, when this property is set to Yes, pressing the ↵ key is exactly the same as clicking on the command button, even if another control has the focus.

  - **No:** The button is not tied to the ↵ key.

Only one button on the form can have its Default property set to Yes. If you set a button's Default property to Yes, any other button that had its Default property set to Yes will have it set to No. The same is true of the Cancel property.

List and Combo Boxes

List boxes allow the user to select one or more pre-defined items, which are displayed in a fixed-height list format. List boxes have a special set of properties associated with displaying and managing lists.

Combo boxes are a combination of the list box and the text box, with a drop-down list that folds up to a single line once the user has made a selection from it. As a result, the combo box includes properties used both by the list box and the text box. Combo boxes use less form real estate than list boxes, so they are much more widely used.

List Box

The items displayed in a list box can be loaded into the list box in two different ways. You can set the list box's items in the form's Design view by using the Row Source and Row Source Type properties. But a list box's entries can also be loaded from a table or query. When you load a list box from a table, the list box's entries are set when the form is run, based on the data in the table it is bound to.

Specifying a list box's values in Design view is usually a bad idea. If you ⭠ enter a set of values in Design view, the form will have to be reopened in Design view should those values ever need to be changed. You will probably not want your users to do this, as it will force your users to call you (or the database administrator) whenever the list box's entries need to be updated. If there are list boxes on a number of different forms with this data, a change in the system's requirements will require all of these forms to be found and changed.

If you load list box data from a table or query, though, these problems go away. With a list box loaded from a table, new entries can be added (and old ones deleted or changed) by changing the contents of the table. You can even provide your users with a dialog form that allows them to make changes to the list box's table on-the-fly. The only real problem that occurs when a list box is bound to a table is that the data in the table could be changed or deleted unintentionally; however, you could protect against this by providing an interface for adding to the table with a confirmation dialog box, as described in the following section.

In Exercise 3.8, you'll create a combo box that draws its entries from a table. In addition, you'll add the code that will allow a user to add a new entry to the table from the combo box.

EXERCISE 3.8

Creating a Combo Box

1. Import the Categories and Employees tables from the North-wind.MDB database and rename it **tblCategories**. (You'll create an employee form that allows you to assign each employee to one of the entries in the tblCategory table.)

2. Add a field called **CategoryID** to the tblEmployees table with a type of Long Integer. This field will hold the key of the entry in the tblCategory table that your user selects.

3. In the Forms tab of the database, click on the AutoForm button on the New Object drop-down list on the toolbar to make an autoform based on tblEmployees; name the form **frmEmployees**. Change the form's Cycle property to Current Record.

4. Switch frmEmployees to Design view, and use the Command Button Wizard to create a combo box with tblCategories as its row source; bind the combo box to the new CategoryID field. The combo box displays the Category name, but stores the Category ID to tblEmployees. Name the combo box **cboSelect**. By default, the combo box's Limit to List property is set to Yes; change it to No.

5. Switch to the form's code module and insert the following event procedure:

```
Private Sub cboSelect_NotInList(strNewData As String,
➥ intResponse As Integer)

    Dim intResp As Integer
    Dim strTitle As String
    Dim intMsgDialog As Integer
    Dim strMsg1 As String
    Dim strMsg2 As String
    Dim strMsg As String
    Dim ctl As Control
    Dim dbs As Database
    Dim rst As Recordset
    Dim strTable As String
    Dim strEntry As String

    strTable = "tblCategories"
    strEntry = "Category"
    Set ctl = Me![cboSelect]

    'Display a message box asking if the user wants to add
    'a new Category entry
    strTitle = strEntry & " Not in List"
    intMsgDialog = vbYesNo + vbExclamation + vbDefaultButton1
    strMsg1 = "Do you want to add "
    strMsg2 = " as a new " & strEntry & " entry?"
    strMsg = strMsg1 + strNewData + strMsg2
    intResp = MsgBox(strMsg, intMsgDialog, strTitle)

    If intResp = vbNo Then
        intResponse = acDataErrContinue
        ctl.Undo
        Exit Sub
```

```
    ElseIf intResp = vbYes Then
        'Add new record to lookup table
        Set dbs = CurrentDb
        Set rst = dbs.OpenRecordset(strTable)
        rst.AddNew
        rst![CategoryName] = strNewData
        rst.Update
rst.Close

        'Continue without displaying default error message.
        intResponse = acDataErrAdded

    End If

End Sub
```

6. In the cboSelect properties sheet's Event tab, you should see [Event Procedure] in the On Not in List event; if not, click on the drop-down list and select that option to activate the code you just added.

7. Switch to Form view and select an existing category from the combo box, to see how the combo box normally works.

8. Now type in a new category called **Sawdust**, and press ↵; a dialog box appears asking you if you want to enter Sawdust as a new Category entry; click on Yes. The NotInList event runs, adding Sawdust to tblCategories. Sawdust is also entered as the Category for the current record.

9. Close frmEmployees and open tblCategories, where you will see the new record for Sawdust.

Data Properties

As with any bound control, the properties on the control's Data tab are important to understand when using the control. The list box can be bound in two ways: one method determines which entries are displayed in the list box, the other method determines which field is updated when the user selects an entry from the list box. You might think of these methods as telling where the data comes from, and where it goes. Typically, these locations are two different tables in the database. For example, you might select a region from tblSalesRegion to enter into a field in the tblAccountRep table.

The properties on the Data tab that you will need to work with to bind a control to a data source are:

- **Row Source Type:** This property accepts three values: Value List, Table/Query, and Field List.

  - **Value List:** This choice effectively makes the entries in the list box unbound. The list box will display the list of items entered into the Row Source property in Design view.

  - **Table/Query:** This choice binds the display of entries in the list box. The list box will display the data in the table, query, or SQL statement specified in the Row Source property.

  - **Field List:** This option causes the list box to display the names of the fields in the table or query, instead of the data in those fields.

- **Row Source:** The choices for this property vary depending on the setting for the Row Source Type property.

  - If Row Source Type is set to Value List, the Row Source property must contain a list of values separated by semicolons (text information must be enclosed in double quotes and date information enclosed in hash marks). Here are some examples using first a set of strings, then a set of dates, and finally a set of numbers:

    ```
    "Finance";"Sales";"Manufacturing"
    #01/01/97#;#01/04/97#;#01/07/97#;#01/10/97#
    1;12;144
    ```

  - If the Row Source Type is set to Field List or Table/Query, then the Row Source property must contain the name of a table, a query, or a valid SQL statement. Here are some examples:

    ```
    tblCustomer
    Select * from Customer where SalesRep = "Wanda Deering"
    CustomerAddressQuery
    Select CustomerLastName, CustomerFirstName from
    ➥ tblCustomer
    ```

- **Control Source:** The Control Source property specifies which field is to be updated when the user makes a selection in the list box. This property is set to the name of a field in the form's Record source property.

Handling Multiple Columns

A list box or combo box can display multiple columns of information (as shown in Figure 3.9). You can decide which column(s) are displayed and which column (only one) is used to update the table to which the form is bound. This requires the coordinated use of a number of the properties of the list or combo box.

Unlike most numeric sequences in Access, column numbering in the Bound Column property starts with 1, not 0. However, when you reference columns in VBA code, using the Me![cboSalesRep].Column(n) syntax, the numbering starts with 0.

FIGURE 3.9

Examples of single column and multi-column list boxes

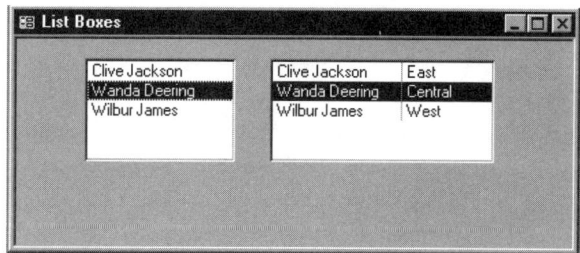

The following properties are relevant when working with multiple column lists:

- **Column Count:** If the table or query specified in the Row Source has more than one field in it, you can set this property to determine how many of the columns you want to have displayed. You must display adjacent columns starting with the first column in the table or query.

The Column Count property can be set to a number larger than 1 when Row Source Type is Value List or Field List. When the Column Count is set to 2, for instance, the first two items in the Value List or Field List are displayed on the same line in the list box.

- **Column Widths:** This property controls how much space in the list box is given to each column (normally in inches, although you can use another unit of measure by using its abbreviation, such as cm). The column widths are separated by semicolons. You can set a column width to 0 to hide a column in the list box, as in Exercise 3.9, typically to hide a cryptic code needed for linking the data.

- **Bound Column:** If you set Column Count to a number larger than 1, you need to decide which column in the list box will be used to update your record. The Bound Column property on the Data tab is used to set the column that will update the field in the Control Source property.

You can set any of the columns in the list box to be the Bound Column, even if its width has been set to 0″ to hide it. This is particularly useful when you have a table of codes and code descriptions to be displayed in a list box. Your list box's row source could include both the code and the description, but with the code column's width set to 0″ to hide it. The user would see a list of descriptions rather than codes, but when they made a selection from the list, the hidden key field column would be used to update the form's table.

A typical situation might be a field that is to be updated with a Product ID (a code). Rather than have the user select from a list of codes, though, you want to present a list of Product Descriptions and Product Managers and have the user select the correct entry from that list. The table that you want to display this information from (tblProducts) contains the fields Product Id, Product Description, Product Image, and Product Manager. To get the list box to work the way you want, you would set up the combo box's properties as shown in Table 3.5.

T A B L E 3.5 The Properties of a Combo Box with Multiple Columns	**Property**	**Value**
	ControlSource	ProductID
	Row Source/Type	Table/Query
	Row Source	tblProducts
	Column Count	4
	Column Widths	0″;1″;0″;1″
	Bound Column	1

In Exercise 3.9 you will have a chance to add a bound combo box to your form to make it easier to select a valid salesperson for a customer.

Using a Combo Box

1. Open the Customer database and add the sales people in Table 3.6 to the SalesRep table.

2. Open the frmCustomerUpdate form in Design view and delete the SalesRep text box so that we can replace it with a combo box.

3. In the upper-right corner of the form toolbox there is a button with a magic wand on it. This activates the Control wizard. In order for you to work directly with the control properties, you need to turn off the wizard. Click on the button to put it in the "up" state.

4. Click on the combo box control and draw it on the form where the SalesRep text box used to be. Right-click on the combo box and select Properties.

5. Set the Row Source Type property to Table/Query. Enter **tblSalesRep** for the Row Source property. The values to be displayed in the combo box will now be pulled from the tblSalesRep table.

6. Set the Control Source property to SalesRep to bind this field to the Sales-Rep field in the tblCustomer table. Name the combo box **cboSalesRep**. Switch to Form view and try out your new combo box.

7. Now that you know that your combo box is working properly, you should change it to prevent the wrong salesperson from being selected. Salespeople are assigned to a customer if the customer is in the sales person's sales area. You'll now alter the combo box so that it displays the sales areas, to allow the person entering the customer information to select the right area. However, the box will still store the salesperson's name in the tblCustomer table's SalesRep field. Return to Design view and select the combo box.

8. Set the Column Count property to 2. This will cause the first two columns of the tblSalesRep table (SalesRep and SalesArea) to display. Set the Column Widths property to 0;1.25″. This will cause the first column to have a width of 0 inches, preventing it from displaying. However, the second column will now have a width of 1.25 inches, allowing the Sales-Area to display. Set the List Width property to 1.25″ to allow the columns to display.

9. Check that the bound column is still set to 1 so that the first column (SalesRep) is still the column to be stored in the field specified in the ControlSource field. Switch to Form view and select a new area in your combo box to change the salesperson for this customer. Switch to the database window and open the Customer table to confirm that the SalesRep field has been changed.

TABLE 3.6	**SalesRep**	**SalesArea**
Sample Customer Records	Wanda Deering	North
	Clive Jackson	South
	Connie Jones	East
	Mark Rodgers	West

In this exercise you have used the combo box's properties to display a list of values from a table in the database.

Other Tab Properties

The list box has a property on its Other tab that is shared only with the List-View control. The Multi-Select property can be used to create a list box where the user can select more than one entry. The Multi-Select property accepts the values None, Simple, and Extended:

- **None:** When the Multi-Select property is set to None, the user can select only one value in the list. Selecting a second value automatically deselects any previously selected item.

- **Simple:** Simple selection allows the user to select multiple items on the list. Each item the user clicks on is selected (unless the item is already selected, in which case the item is deselected).

- **Extended:** Extended selection allows the user to select multiple items from the list box by holding down the Shift or Ctrl key.

WARNING You don't want to use Simple or Extended selection on a list box whose Control Source binds it to a field. Regardless of whether your user selects one or more items from the list box, the data in the bound field is wiped out.

Using the Select Property

If you set the Multi-Select property to Simple or Extended, you need some way to determine which items in the list box the user has chosen. This can only be done from VBA code by making use of the list box's Selected property. This property has a value of True for each selected item in the list. A simple code segment to display a message box for each selected item in a list box called lstSalesRep would look like this:

```
Dim intItem As Integer
For intItem = 0 To Me!lstSalesRep.Count - 1
    If Me!lstSalesRep.Selected(intItem) = True Then
        MsgBox Me!lstSalesRep.Column(0,intItem)
    End If
Next intItem
```

Using Reports

While forms let users enter and edit data, *reports* are used to print out the data, often grouped and sorted in a variety of ways. You can also preview a report on screen, which in some cases can be a useful way of displaying a limited amount of data.

While it may be tempting to plan to just print out the forms you are creating for data entry and update, that is rarely a satisfactory approach. When you print out a form you also print out the form's background and controls. In addition, a continuous form may only display four or five items from a large list. When you print a form only those four or five records are printed. A report, on the other hand, will print all of the records in the recordset.

Reports have several useful properties lacking in forms. With a report you can provide subtotals and running totals, for instance. The Access report writer is very easy to use and comes with a number of wizards to make it even easier to generate reports. As a result, with a little training, your end users could use Access to generate their own reports.

Reports share many properties with forms. Reports, like forms, have a Record source property that binds the report to a set of records and a caption that displays in the title bar of the report's window in Print Preview.

But reports make less use of the variety of controls available than forms. Generally, report controls tend to be limited to labels, text boxes, and the occasional picture control. On the other hand, reports have more flexibility than forms in the way they use headers and footers.

There are a number of controls that don't make any sense when they appear on a report. Text boxes for entering data, for instance, or command buttons used for executing VBA code. Access won't prevent you from placing these non-functional controls on reports.

Report Structure

Unlike a form (which has only three sections), a report has a detail section, a page header and footer, a report header and footer, and one or more group sections as you desire (each with its own header and footer). Group sections are used to supply totals and headers for subsets of data in the reports (for instance, to break up a report of customers into the customers served by each sales person).

With reports, as with forms, you turn on Report and Page headers and footers from the View menu, and they are selected in pairs. You must have a header with a footer, and you can't suppress one or the other (though you can reduce its size to zero, so it isn't visible in Form view). However, report group headers and footers can be enabled or disabled separately for each group level.

Figure 3.10 shows a report with all of its standard sections visible and with one group section.

FIGURE 3.10

A report with a
group section

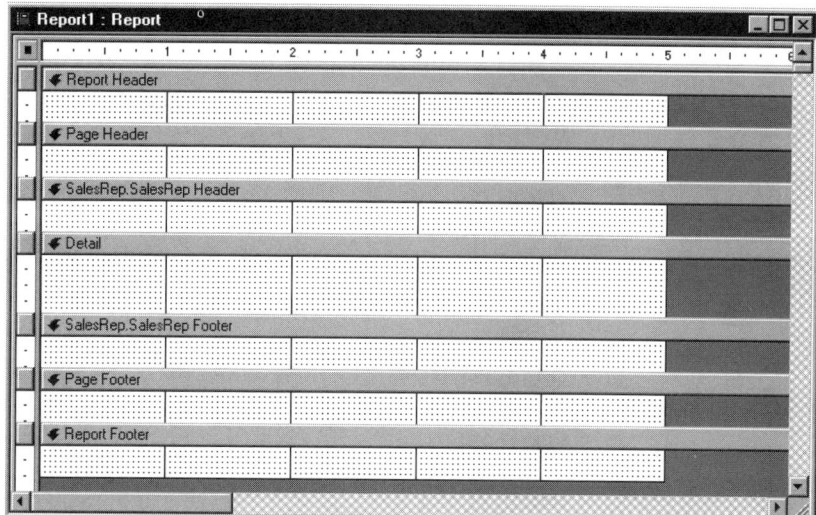

Report Sections

Report sections are used to control when, in the process of printing a report, data should be printed. Information (such as the report's title) that should appear only at the beginning of the report goes in the report header. Information (such as a grand total of numeric data) that is needed at the very end of a report goes in a report footer. Report sections are also used to control data formatting and layout.

The report page header and footer (similar to Word headers and footers) print data at the top and/or bottom of each page—typically column headers, the report's name (perhaps in an abbreviated form or smaller font than in the report header), the date printed, and current page number.

Access allows report data to be organized into groups based on the nature of the data. In a report that lists individual sales for customers, you could group the report by SalesRep and print total sales for all of the customers for a SalesRep. Within that group, you could also group information by customer, allowing you to display the total sales for each customer. Group headers and footers are used to print information related to each group level, such as the field data (the state name for a report grouped by states, for example), or a group subtotal for numeric data. You can have a maximum of 10 group sections in a single report.

You can determine which pages the page headers and footers appear on by selecting the desired value for the report's page header or page footer property. Table 3.7 lists all of the report sections and when each is printed.

	Report Section	When Printed
T A B L E 3.7 Report Sections	Report Header	Once, at the start of the report
	Page Header	Printed at the top of each page
	Group Header	Printed at the start of each group
	Group Footer	Printed at the end of each group
	Page Footer	Printed at the bottom of each page
	Report Footer	Printed once at the end of the report

Sorting and Grouping

Typically, you will want to group and sort the data in all but the simplest reports. A marketing report, for example, might be sorted by Country, Region, State, and Sales Rep. Typically, each report group is sorted alphanumerically (the sort order is ascending by default, but you can sort in descending order, too). A simple report that doesn't need grouping can just be sorted without any grouping.

To sort by a field in some arbitrary order that is neither alphabetic nor numeric, add a numeric field to the table called SortOrder, enter numbers in it that would sort the records in the desired order, and sort the report by that new field.

In addition to grouping by a field, you can group by an expression by entering it directly into the Sorting/Grouping dialog box (shown in Figure 3.11). If your report is based on a query, you can create a new column containing the expression in the query and select that calculated field as the grouping field. For example, you could sort by the first letter of the company's name using this expression:

```
Left[CompanyName, 1]
```

FIGURE 3.11

The Sorting and Grouping dialog box

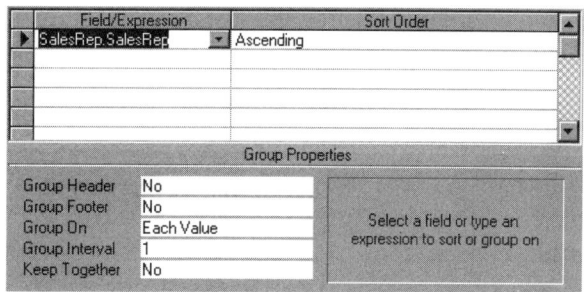

WARNING If you've bound your report to a query or SQL statement that has a sort order, you might expect the report to be sorted in the order specified by the query or the SQL statement. Access does not guarantee this—the only way to be sure what order a report's data will be in is to set the sort order in the Sorting and Grouping dialog box.

Report Pages

While a form has only one page, reports have as many pages as necessary to display or print all the data in the report's underlying Record source. Each report page is created dynamically based on the amount of data that will fit into the page height, less the size of the page header and footer (if any), and taking into account the spacing, height, and font size of the controls on the report. If a report includes sorting and grouping, the number of groups printed and the number of header and footer lines generated by each group is also taken into account by Access when fitting data to the page.

Report Properties

When a report is open in Design view, you can view its properties the same way you would a form: right-click in the upper-left of the report window and select Properties from the pop-up menu. The following properties are available:

- **Page Header/Footer:** These two properties each accept four entries: All Pages, Not With Report Header, Not With Report Footer, and Not With Report Header/Footer:

  - **All Pages:** A page header or footer is printed on every page.

  - **Not with Report Header:** The page header/footer is not printed on the same page with the report header (typically, the first page of the report).

  - **Not with Report Footer:** The page header/footer is not printed on the same page with the report header (typically, the last page of the report).

  - **Not with Report Header/Footer:** The page header/footer is not printed on the same page with either report header or footer (typically, the first and last pages of the report).

The Not With... options are typically used when the first and last pages of the report are significantly different from all the other pages of the report. If you use the report header to create a title page that doesn't include the data printed in the detail section of the rest of the report, you will want to select the Not with Report Header option. The same is true if you are using the report footer to print summary data on a separate page at the end of the report.

Data-Driven Section Properties

You can divide the Report sections into two groups:

- **The Report Header/Footer, Detail, and Group Header/Footer:** The appearance of these sections is controlled by the way your data is organized. A new detail section is generated for each record, for instance, along with a new group.

- **Page Header/Footer:** These sections appear based on the number of pages in the report; they are not as dependent on the structure of the data being reported (other than the number of records: more records means more pages).

The data-driven sections (Report Header/Footer, Detail, and Group Header) share a number of interesting properties for controlling the display of your data. They are:

- **Force New Page:** This property allows you to tell Access to start a new page of a report even though the current page isn't full. This lets you organize the data in your report onto separate pages. This property has four settings:

  - **Before Section:** Access will start a new page before printing any of the data in the section. If you set the Report Header section to this setting, for instance, the report will begin with a blank page.

  - **After Section:** Access will start a new page immediately after printing all of the data in the section.

  - **Before & After:** Access will print all of the information in this section on a separate page.

  - **None:** No special page breaking is done.

- **New Row or Col:** This property only applies when you have used the Access print options to create a report with multiple columns. The settings are the same as for Force New Page.

- **Keep Together:** When this property is set to Yes, Access will not print the section on the page if there isn't enough room on the page to print the whole section. If the section is longer than a page, Access will start the section on a new page.

- **Can Grow, Can Shrink:** If a multiple-line text box is included in a section, the amount of space that the data needs in order to be displayed can change as the number of lines in the text box increases or decreases. By setting these two properties to True, the section can expand and contract from the height set at Design time to accommodate the size of the text box controls in the section.

Frequently, in designing a report, you will want to start new groups of data on a new page (or screen, if you only intend to view the report and not to print it), to set apart the groups of data. The easiest way to do this is to create a group footer in the Sorting and Grouping dialog box, and then set the report's Force New Page property to After Section. Be aware that this will also cause the report footer to print on a separate page at the end of the report. You can also set Force New Page to Before Section on a group header, which will cause a blank page to be printed before the first page of the report.

Reports with Multiple Columns

If you select File ➢ Page Setup ➢ Layout, you can tell Access that you want your report to be printed in columns by setting the Items Across box to some number larger than 1. Once that is done, Access will repeat the detail section of your report across the width of the report to provide the number of columns you specified in Items Across.

In a multicolumn report you must also tell Access what direction to use when filling those columns. The default is to have Access fill rows before columns by printing successive copies of the detail section across the page, before going down and printing a new row (Across, then Down). You can also tell Access to fill columns first by printing successive copies of the detail section down the length of the page, before returning to the top of the page and starting the next column (Across, then Down).

The setting you pick for New Row or Column interacts with the direction you pick in printing the reports columns. If you select Across, then Down, and Before & After Section, the section will be printed on a row by itself. If you pick Down, then Across, and Before & After Section, then the section will be printed in a column by itself.

In Exercise 3.10 you'll work with some of the special report properties. In order for this exercise to be effective, you'll need a lot of data. Rather than enter it, we'll link to tables in the Northwind database that was installed when we installed Access.

EXERCISE 3.10

Creating a Report

1. Open the Customer database and use the Get External Data command on the File menu to create a link to the Products table in the Northwind.MDB database.

2. Click on the Reports tab and start a new report. Display the properties list for the report and set the Record Source property to Products. Select View ➤ Field List. From the Field List drag the SupplierId, CategoryId, and ProductName fields into the Detail section of the report. Close the Field List.

3. Adjust the size of the Detail Section of your report by clicking the Page Footer bar near the bottom of the report and dragging it up to the fields you just added. Select View ➤ Print Preview to view your report. Click on the Close button to return to Design view.

4. Select View ➤ Sorting and Grouping to display the dialog box for setting grouping options. In the first line of the dialog box enter **CategoryId** (or select it from the drop-down list). In the options at the bottom of the dialog box set Group Header to Yes.

5. In the second line of the Sorting and Grouping dialog box enter **SupplierId** (or select it from the drop-down list). Close the Sorting and Grouping dialog box to return to your report. Notice that a new section has been added called CategoryId Header.

6. Drag the CategoryId field from the Detail section to the CategoryId Header section. Right-click on the CategoryId Header bar and select Properties from the pop-up menu. Set the Force New Page property to Before Section. Close the Properties dialog box.

7. Select View ➤ Print Preview to display the report. Notice that the products are now organized by category (each on a separate page) with the category name displayed before each group. Within each category, the products are sorted by supplier.

Summary

Forms and reports are key to building applications in Access. Forms allow you to display and update your data, while reports allow you to display or print large amounts of data in an organized fashion. Using forms and reports effectively means understanding their properties and the results you get when using them.

The most important properties for forms and reports are the data properties. The Record Source property allows you to bind a form or report to a table or query, causing Access to automatically handle moving the data from the form or report to the table, and back again.

Since forms allow you to change the data in the Record source, it's important to pay attention to the Record Locks property. The Record Locks property allows you to switch between pessimistic locking (records cannot be changed if they are being viewed by another user) and optimistic locking (record changes are only forbidden while the record is being changed by another user). If you select optimistic locking, Access will advise a user if the record has been changed by another user since it was first displayed.

Once you have created a form, you must populate it with a set of controls to display your data and allow your users to interact with the form. Like Access forms and reports, controls can be bound to data through their Control Source property. This property can also be used to evaluate expressions and display their results. Normally, however, a Control Source specifies a field from the form or report's Record Source that is to be displayed and updated through the control.

Unlike forms, reports also have the ability to group data through the Sorting and Grouping dialog box. This dialog box allows you to generate a group section whenever data is in a specific field. You can use these sections to organize the data on your report.

Review Questions

1. Which of the following is not a section in an Access form?

   A. Form Header

   B. Page Footer

   C. Group Header

   D. All are valid sections

2. When does a form's Form Header appear?

   A. When the form is displayed on the screen

   B. When the form is printed

   C. Both A and B

   D. Neither A nor B

3. To tie a form to a table or query you would use the form's _____ _____ property.

   A. Record Source

   B. Row Source

   C. Control Source

   D. None of the above

4. You have set the form's Filter property but the form still displays all of the records. You must:

   A. Set the FilterOn property on the properties list.

   B. Set the FilterOn property using VBA.

   C. Select Filter ➢ View.

   D. Do nothing. The filter must be incorrect.

5. You have set a form's Record Lock property to No Locks. As a result:

   A. No record locks will be used on the recordset.

   B. Optimistic locking will be used on the recordset.

   C. Pessimistic locking will be used on the recordset.

   D. The recordset will be a snapshot.

6. When a user is unable to change a record because it is being viewed by another user, this is called:

   A. Optimistic locking

   B. Pessimistic locking

   C. Table level locking

   D. No Locks

7. The smallest level of locking for the Jet database engines is:

   A. Field level

   B. Record level

   C. Page level

   D. Table level

8. When a form's default view is set to Form and its Views Allowed is set to Datasheet, how will the form initially display?

   A. As a Datasheet

   B. As a Form

   C. Neither, an error is raised

   D. Either, depending on how the user opens the form

9. You want a user not to do anything else in your application until they have completed all the entries in a form and closed it. You should:

   A. Set the form's Dialog property to No.

   B. Set the form's Popup property to Yes.

   C. Set the form's Modal property to Yes.

   D. This can't be done in Access (without a Windows API call).

10. To remove a command button from a form at runtime using VBA code, you would:

A. Set the Transparent property to True

B. Set the Locked property to True

C. Set the Visible property to False

D. Use VBA to delete the control

11. You have set the Cancel property of a command button to True. You now set another button's Cancel property to True. The result is:

A. Both buttons will be activated when the user presses the Esc key.

B. Neither button will be activated when the user presses the Esc key.

C. The first button set will be activated when the user presses the Esc key.

D. The second button set will be activated when the user presses the Esc key.

12. To have a list box display only the second field of a query but update the field it is bound to with the first field in the query, you must set the following properties:

A. Bound Column = 2, Column Count = 2, Column Widths = 1;1

B. Bound Column = 1, Column Count = 2, Column Widths = 0;1

C. Bound Column = 2, Column Count = 1, Column Widths = 0;1

D. Bound Column = 1, Column Count = 2, Column Widths = 1;0

13. To create a list box that would allow the user to select multiple entries using the Ctrl and Shift keys, you would:

A. Set the Select property to Extended

B. Set the Multi-Select property to Extended

C. Set the Select property to True

D. Set the Multi-Select property to True

14. A report will display data in the order of

   A. The primary key of the table.

   B. The sort order of the underlying Record Source.

   C. The order in the Sorting and Grouping dialog box.

   D. It depends on how the report is opened.

15. To prevent the page header from displaying on the first page of the report, you would:

   A. Set the Page Header/Footer property to Not with Report Header

   B. Set the Page Header/Footer property to Skip First Page

   C. Set the First Page Property to False

   D. Use VBA code

16. You have grouped your data by department and want to have each department print on a separate page, with the first page of the report displaying the first department. To do this, you would:

   A. Create a department header and set its Force New Page property to After Section.

   B. Create a department header and set its Force New Page property to Before Section.

   C. Create a department footer and set its Force New Page property to After Section.

   D. Create a department footer and set its Force New Page property to Not With Report Header.

17. To prevent a group from printing only some of its entries at the bottom of a page, you would set:

   A. The Widows/Orphans property to Yes

   B. The Widows/Orphans property to Keep Together

   C. The Keep Together property to Yes

   D. The Keep Together property to Widow/Orphan Control

CHAPTER

4

SQL

Microsoft Exam Objectives Covered in This Chapter:

- Differentiate between single-field and multiple-field indexes.
- Use Access SQL to write common queries.
- Refer to objects by using Access SQL.
- Restructure queries to allow faster execution.
- Optimize queries by using Rushmore technology.
- Use union queries.

Access lets you work with a version of the industry standard data access language, SQL, to manipulate your data. With SQL you can create tables and update or retrieve the data stored in those tables. You can also use SQL to create the indexes on those tables that will speed access to your data. In this chapter you'll learn what SQL is and how to use it with Microsoft Access.

If you've come from a programming background that didn't include SQL, you may be tempted by the Access programming environment into writing a great deal of VBA code to retrieve and update your data. Using SQL effectively can reduce the amount of code you write while speeding up your applications. If you are used to using SQL you may use the Access graphical query designer to create all of your SQL statements. However, there are a number of SQL statements that you can't create with the query designer (any statement that creates or modifies a table, for instance). In this chapter you'll learn how to create SQL statements without the query designer and so put yourself in a position to harness the full power of this part of Access.

In this chapter, you will learn:

- What SQL is and how to use it in Access.
- What tasks SQL can handle.
- How to use SQL to read and update the data in your database.
- How to optimize your SQL queries.
- How to use SQL to create tables in your database.
- The relationship between SQL and Access queries.

The Universal Language: SQL

There are a variety of programming languages available for developing applications, but there is one language that has become the universal standard for working with data: Structured Query Language (SQL, sometimes pronounced "Sequel"). SQL was originally designed to provide a way of working with data in relational databases. Since that time, as illustrated in Figure 4.1, many database systems using other storage models have adopted SQL as their standard data manipulation language. Microsoft's latest data initiative, OLE DB, will use SQL to retrieve and update in non-relational data stores including e-mail, imaging, and document management systems.

FIGURE 4.1

The same SQL statement can be used on many databases.

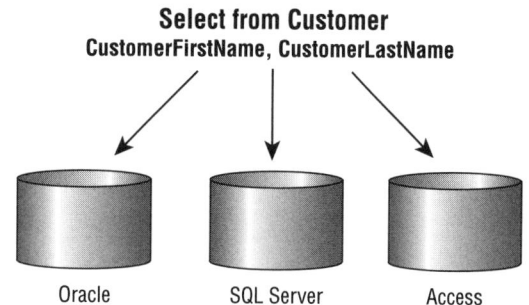

Access comes with a version of SQL called, appropriately enough, Access SQL. You can use Access SQL to efficiently read and update data in Access. And, since Access can work with data stored in almost any database system, you can use Access SQL to access data almost anywhere.

What's SQL?

SQL lets you perform all essential database update and retrieval activities. In addition, the SQL language includes the commands needed to create the table structures that your data will be stored in. SQL has become the dominant data language because it has several interesting characteristics, which are discussed in the next section. SQL is both non-procedural and non-navigational, two characteristics which may require you to think about accessing your data in a different way than you may have done in the past. If you have been working with dBase, for instance, you are used to specifying which tables to open, which record to move to, and so on. With SQL those activities are taken care of for you.

Readable

Simple SQL statements can be easily read and understood by people with very little training in SQL (originally, the language was called SEQUL for Structured *English* Query Language). The following SQL statement, for instance, extracts the data in two fields from a table:

```
Select LastName, FirstName
From Employees
```

As the example shows, when fields and tables in a database are given meaningful names, SQL commands can be very easy to read. As SQL commands get more complicated, it becomes increasingly difficult for the uninitiated to read them:

```
Select A.LastName, A.FirstName, Department.Department
From Employees As A Left Join Department
On A.Department = Department.Department
Where Department > Some
(Select Avg(B.Salary)
From EmployeeArchive As B
Where B.Department = A.Department)
And Department.Department Is Null
```

Structured

The SQL language has a simple structure (see Figure 4.2) that controls the format of all SQL statements. In the SQL language each statement begins with one of just seven SQL verbs (Drop, Create, Select, Update, Delete, Insert, or Alter) followed by the keywords parameters. The rest of a SQL statement consists of a series of clauses, each of which begins with a SQL keyword. These clauses (Where, From, Order By, Group By, and Having) have a fixed order when used with one of the seven SQL verbs.

The following SQL statement begins with the Delete verb followed by the asterisk parameter indicating that all the fields in a table are to be deleted. The statement also uses the From and Where clauses to select which records from a table of employees are to be deleted:

```
Delete *
From Employees
Where Department = 'Finance'
```

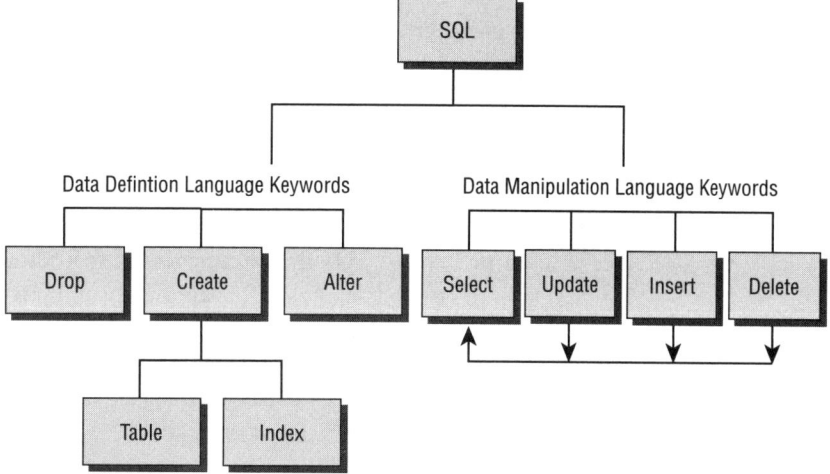

The structure of this Select statement is very similar to the SQL statement to retrieve the same records:

```
Select *
From Employees
Where Department = 'Finance'
```

The SQL language also allows SQL statements to be nested within other SQL statements. This SQL command contains a nested Select statement that determines the average sales made by all employees. That number is then used to determine which Employees are to get a 10 percent raise:

```
Update Employees
Set Salary = Salary + (Salary * 1.10)
Where Sales >
 (Select Avg(Sale)
 From Employees)
```

Non-Procedural

New users of SQL may find it surprising that SQL contains no commands for determining how the data is to be retrieved or updated. Using the SQL language you can describe only which records you want to be retrieved or updated. You can't tell SQL which records to retrieve first or last, or even which table to begin processing with. It is the responsibility of the database system that processes your SQL request to determine the most effective means of retrieving the records that meet your request.

Non-Navigational

A SQL statement implies no order of processing on the records that it retrieves or updates. Instead, SQL operates on sets of records and, as much as possible, SQL appears to update all the records in a set simultaneously. There are no SQL commands to process records one at a time. The SQL command contains no commands to process the "next" or the "previous" record. If you are used to reading and writing records from a file, this set-oriented way of dealing with the rows in a table will seem odd to you.

Relational

The result of a SQL statement, operating on one or more relational tables, is another relational table (though not necessarily one stored on a hard disk). Every SQL command, if it returns data, returns the data in a row and column format that corresponds to the format of a table in a database (see Figures 4.3 and 4.4). You may have noticed when working with Access, for instance, that a query in Datasheet view looks very much like a table in Datasheet view.

The result of this similarity is that a SQL command returns values that can be processed by other SQL commands.

FIGURE 4.3

An Access table from which a SQL statement can extract data

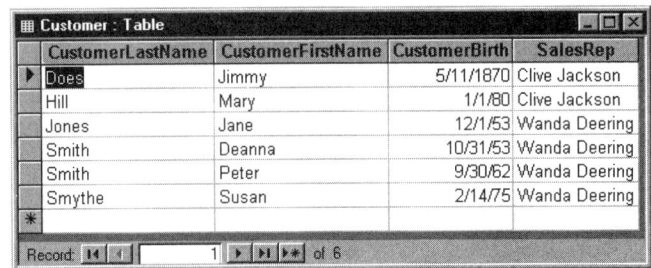

In this book the output of a SQL query will be referred to as records since SQL treats a query's output just like the records in a table.

FIGURE 4.4

The results of extracting the data from the table shown in Figure 4.3, presented by SQL as another table

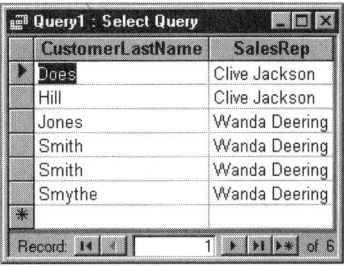

Complete

All of the activities involved in retrieving or updating data can be done with SQL. In theory, any set of procedural code for updating or retrieving data, no matter how complicated, could be replaced with one or more SQL statements.

Using SQL in Access

If you've ever created a query in Access, you've worked with SQL. While you may create Access queries by dragging and dropping tables and links in Query Design view, the end result of your work is a SQL statement. Before you run or save your query, Access scans your design and creates the appropriate SQL statement for it. In the Query Design window, you can view the SQL statement you have generated by selecting View ➤ SQL.

If you want to create your queries in SQL you can switch directly to the SQL view and enter your SQL statements there. When you switch back to Design view, Access will to convert your SQL statement into the graphical representation that you see in the Query Design window.

In Exercise 4.1 you'll create a simple SQL query in Access.

EXERCISE 4.1

Creating a SQL Query

1. Start Access and click on the Query tab. Click on the New button to start a new query, select Design View, and click on the OK button.

2. The Show Table dialog box is displayed, but you're not going to add any tables. Click on the Close button to close the Show Table dialog box.

3. From the View menu, select SQL to display the SQL entry window.

4. Enter **Select * From Customer** in the query window, replacing the text already present. From the View menu, select Datasheet to see the results of your query.

5. From the View menu, select Query Design to see your query in the Access graphical design view. Drag SalesRep down to the Field row of the query grid and enter **Wilma Deering** in the Criteria row.

6. From the View menu, select Datasheet to see the results of your query. From the View menu, select SQL to see the SQL statement that Access generated from your graphical design.

In this exercise you got a chance to create a query in Access and see how Access converts from SQL to graphical mode and back again.

DDL Commands

Any complete data manipulation language must contain commands both for defining data structures and for working with the data stored in those structures. The part of the language used for creating and modifying data structures is called the Data Definition Language (DDL). The part of the language for retrieving and updating the data in those structures is referred to as the Data Manipulation Language (DML). SQL contains all the necessary commands to make up a complete set of DML and DDL.

In the relational model, there is only one data structure: the table. SQL contains all the DDL commands that you will need to create and destroy tables in the database. In addition, SQL contains commands for working with indexes, which are used by the database engine to speed up your access to data.

There are three DDL verbs in SQL: Create, Drop, and Alter. The Create command is used to define new tables and indexes. Once a table is created, the Alter command is used to modify it. The Drop command is used to remove tables and indexes from the database.

Create Table

Before storing data in a database you must create the tables to hold the data. In SQL you use the Create Table statement to add a new table to the database. The syntax for the Create Table statement is:

```
CREATE TABLE table name (field definition [, field
➡ definition [, ...]] [, multifieldindex [, ...]])
```

The easiest way to understand the Create Table statement is to look at it piece by piece. The best place to begin is the field definition, which defines one field in the table's record. The field definition gives a field a name and specifies its data type. Table 4.1 lists the data types that you can use in creating fields with SQL. While some of the SQL data types are similar to the ones used in VBA (both VBA and SQL have an Integer type, for instance), SQL does have its own special formats (such as Counter).

T A B L E 4.1: SQL Data Types

Data Type	Type of Data	Size (in Bytes Unless Otherwise Stated)
Binary	Any type of data	1 byte per character.
Byte	Integer	1 byte (an integer value between 0 and 255).
Char, Text, VarChar	Text, or combinations of text and numbers; as well as numbers that don't require calculations, such as phone numbers.	Up to 255 characters or the length set by the FieldSize property, whichever is less. Char is fixed length while Text and VarChar are variable length.
Longtext	Lengthy text or combinations of text and numbers.	Up to 64,000 characters.
Integer, Long, Double, Single, Currency	Numeric data used in mathematical calculations.	2 (Integer, Single), 4 (Long) 8 (Double, Currency) (16 bytes for ReplicationID only).

T A B L E 4.1: SQL Data Types *(Continued)*

Data Type	Type of Data	Size (in Bytes Unless Otherwise Stated)
DateTime	Date and time values for the years 100 through 9999.	8.
Counter	A unique sequential (incremented by 1) number or random number assigned by Microsoft Access whenever a new record is added to a table. AutoNumber fields can't be updated.	4 (16 for ReplicationID only).
Bit	Yes and No values and fields that contain only one of two values (True/False, On/Off).	1 bit.
GUID	A unique identification number used with remote procedure calls.	128 bits.
Longtext	Text.	Zero to 1.2 gigabytes.
Long Binary	An object (such as a Microsoft Excel spreadsheet) linked to or embedded in a Microsoft Access table.	Up to 1 gigabyte (limited by available disk space).

If you wanted to use terms from the relational model, you wouldn't use the term *field*. Instead, you would say that each definition defines a new column in the table. Access documentation, however, tends to use the terms *field* and *record*.

The simplest possible table contains a single field. To create a table called Dummy with a single Integer field called FirstField, you would use this statement:

```
Create Table Dummy (FirstField Integer)
```

Tables created with the Create Table command won't appear in the Tables window until you click on another tab and then return to the Tables tab.

The other numeric types (Double, Long, and so on) are declared the same way. However, if you want to create a field that holds character information, you can specify not only the data type of the field but the field's size as well. This statement defines a text field that is five characters in length:

```
Create Table Dummy (FirstCharField Text(5))
```

If you run a DDL Create Table query and there is already a table of that name, you will get an error message.

There are three different kinds of text fields that you can create in Access SQL: Char, Text, and VarChar. Char fields are fixed length, which means that a field defined as Char(5) will always take up five characters in the database, no matter how few letters you actually store in it. Text and VarChar (Variable Character) are variable length fields. If you define a field as Var-Char(5) or Text(5), the field will take up less than five spaces in the database if you put less than five characters in it. The character fields can be declared without a size, in which case they will default to 255 characters.

It's a good idea to use Text and VarChar wherever possible to reduce the size of your database.

Most tables have more than one field defined. You can specify as many fields as you want for your table with each field, separating definitions with commas, up to the limit of the database system:

```
Create Table Customer (LastName Text(15), FirstName Text(15),
➥ NumberOfVisits Integer)
```

Access tables are limited to 255 fields. If you have a database design that requires more than 255 fields in a table in Access, you'll have to break your logical table up into two physical tables and create a one-to-one relationship between them.

SQL statements have no particular format. Spaces in a SQL statement, other than one space between each word, are ignored, as are line breaks. The result is that you can format your SQL statements anyway you want and spread them over several lines, as desired. The standard is to begin each clause on a new line.

Exercise 4.2 demonstrates how to create a table using the SQL Create Table command.

EXERCISE 4.2

Creating a Table Using SQL

1. Open the Access Query Designer in SQL view, as you did in Exercise 4.1.

2. Enter **Create Table SimpleCustomer (CustomerName Text, Age Integer, SalesRep Text)**.

3. From the Query menu, select Run, or click on the Run button on the toolbar.

4. Switch to the Database window and click on the Tables tab to see your table. Click on the SimpleCustomer table to select it. Click on the Design button to review the fields created by the SQL statement. Switch to Datasheet view and enter some data into the table.

With a single SQL statement, you've created an Access table with three fields.

Single-Field Constraints

In addition to the field name and data type, a field can include one or more constraints. A *constraint* specifies a limitation on the values that can be stored in the field.

To specify a constraint on a field in the Create Table statement, you follow the field data type with the keyword Constraint, the name of the constraint, and one of the three constraint type keywords (Unique, Primary Key, or References):

```
fieldname datatype [(size)] [Constraint constraintname {Unique
➡| Primary Key | References foreigntable [(foreignfield)]}
```

Here's what each constraint will do:

- **Unique:** This constraint prevents two records in the same table from having the same value in this field. To put it another way, the Unique constraint prevents records from duplicating in this field. In the following SQL statement, the CustomerId field has the Unique constraint, which prevents any two records from having the same CustomerId:

```
Create Table Customer
(CustomerID Integer Constraint CID Unique,
 LastName Text(15),
 FirstName Text(15))
```

- **Primary Key:** This constraint performs the same function as the Unique constraint, but also specifies that the field must always have a value (that means when a new record is created, this field *must* be filled in). While a table can have many fields with the Unique constraint, there can be only one Primary Key constraint on a table:

```
Create Table Customer
(CustomerID Integer Constraint PK Primary Key,
 LastName Text(15),
 FirstName Text(15))
```

WARNING   In order to make effective use of Access you will need to define a Primary Key for every table you create.

- **References:** This constraint (see Figures 4.5 and 4.6) links a record in a table to one or more records in another table. The References constraint effectively implements the relational model's concept of the foreign key (but it doesn't implement referential integrity). A References constraint includes the name of the table and field being referenced by the field in the field definition. In this SQL statement, the CustomerNum field is being created so that it references the CustomerId field of the Customer table:

```
Create Table CustomerAddress
(CustomerNum Integer
       Constraint FK References Customer(CustomerID),
 AddressType Text(1),
 Street Text(20),
 City Text(15))
```

When two fields reference each other they must be of the same data type
and size. If the field being referenced is the Primary Key field of the other
table, you can omit the field name in the Constraint:

```
Create Table CustomerAddress
(CustomerNum Integer
        Constraint FK References Customer,
   AddressType Text(1),
   Street Text(20),
   City Text(15))
```

The References constraint enforces referential integrity without cascading
updates or deletes. Once the References constraint is applied, records can't be
added to the CustomerAddress table for a customer until that customer is added
to the Customer table. Similarly, customers can't be deleted from the Customer
table until their addresses have been removed from the CustomerAddress table.

In Exercise 4.3 you'll create a table with constraints using the SQL Create
Table command.

EXERCISE 4.3

Using Constraints

1. Open the Access Query Designer in SQL.

2. Enter **Create Table SimpleSalesRep (SalesRep Text Constraint PK Primary Key, SalesRegion Text)**.

3. From the Query menu, select Run or click on the Run button on the toolbar.

4. Switch to the Database window and click on the Tables tab to see your table.

5. Click on the SimpleSalesRep table to select it. Click on the Design button to review the fields created by the SQL statement.

6. Switch to Datasheet view and enter some data into the table. Try making two entries for the same SalesRep. Make sure that the Customer names that you enter are customers from the SampleCustomer table you created in Exercise 4.2.

In this exercise you've created a table with a Primary key constraint.

Access, like most database management systems, implements constraints by creating indexes on the fields that are constrained.

There are several special operators for detecting the Null value. In VBA you can use the IsNull function to check to see if a field contains Null:

```
If IsNull(rst("AField")) Then….
```

In SQL, you can use the Is Null test to find fields containing Null:

```
Select *
From Employees
Where Status Is Null
```

You can also use the Nz function in VBA to convert Nulls to zeroes, zero-length strings, or other appropriate values.

Multiple-Field Constraints

Up to this point in our discussion, all the constraints applied to the table have applied to only one field. Constraints can also be specified to include several fields (see Figure 4.7). These constraints are written at the end of the Create Table statement, following all the field definitions.

The syntax for table-level constraints is almost identical to the syntax for single-field constraints. The major difference is that you must specify a list of the fields involved for each constraint.

This Create Table command establishes two fields (LastName and First-Name) as the primary key for the table:

```
Create Table Customer
(LastName Text(15),
 FirstName Text(15),
 TotalPurchases Double,
Constraint PK Primary Key (LastName, FirstName))
```

When a primary key contains two fields, neither field can contain a Null value and the combination of the two fields must not be duplicated (that means you can't have two customers named Mary Smith, but you can have two customers named Mary provided that they have different last names).

The syntax for a Unique constraint that includes multiple fields is very similar to the syntax for a single-field Unique constraint:

```
Create Table Customer
(LastName Text(15),
 FirstName Text(15),
 TotalPurchases Double,
Constraint UK Unique (LastName, FirstName))
```

The syntax for a References constraint is slightly different for multiple field constraints than the single-field constraint. You must add the keywords Foreign Key and a field list after the constraint name and before the References keyword. The field list that follows the Foreign Key keyword specifies the fields in the table that participate in the constraint. As with the single-field References constraint, the field list that follows the References keyword specifies the fields in the other table.

```
Create Table CustomerAddress
(LastName Text(15),
 FirstName Text(15),
 AddressType Text(1),
 Street Text(20),
 City Text(15),
Constraint FK Foreign Key (LastName, FirstName)
References Customer (LastName, FirstName))
```

WARNING The field in the References clause must have either the Unique or Primary Key constraint, or an index with the same properties.

Drop Table

In addition to being able to add tables to a database, you'll also need to be able to remove them from a database. The Drop Table statement removes a table from a database. The syntax for the command is:

```
Drop Table tablename
```

To remove the Customer table from your database you would use:

```
Drop Table Customer
```

Create Index

It's unusual to retrieve or update all the records in a table. Most queries or updates to your database will be to retrieve or update only specific records in a table. As a result, the database will spend a great deal of time finding the records in your tables that you want to see or update. If you have more than a few hundred records in the database, this process of finding records can be very time consuming.

In order to speed up the process of finding records, you can create an index on a table. A table's index functions just like an index in a book. If someone handed you a 1,000-page history book and asked you find all the pages that mentioned Napoleon, you could start at the first page and flip through the book to find all the relevant pages. It would be a lot faster to go to the book's index, look up Napoleon in the index's alphabetically sorted list, get the page numbers, and then flip directly to the relevant pages.

The database system that manages your data will use indexes to find records in your tables in exactly the same way. In the absence of an index, the database system is obliged to read through every record in a table to find the records you want. If there is an index on the table that can be used, the database system will avoid reading every record and, instead, use the index to go directly to the records you want. In Figure 4.8, the index on City links directly to the three customers who live in New Your City. This allows SQL to find those three records by reading the New York City record from the index and then go directly to the relevant customers. Without the index, SQL would have to read every record in the Customer table to find the customers in a specific city.

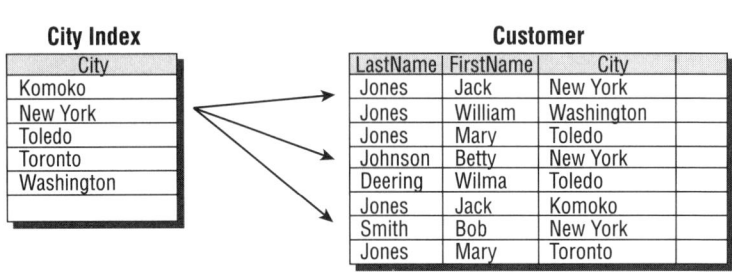

FIGURE 4.8

Using the City index to find the customers in New York City

The syntax to create an index on a table is:

```
CREATE [ UNIQUE ] INDEX indexname
ON tablename (fieldname [ASC|DESC][, fieldname [ASC|DESC],...])
[WITH { PRIMARY | DISALLOW NULL | IGNORE NULL }]
```

To create an index on the City field of the CustomerAddress table, you would use this SQL statement:

```
Create Index CityIndex
On CustomerAddress (City)
```

The previous example created a single field index. You can also create an index on multiple fields to make a multiple field index:

```
Create Index CityState
On CustomerAddress (City, State)
```

If you want to make sure that the index contains no duplicate records, you can use the Unique keyword to tell Access that:

```
Create Unique Index CustName on Customer (LastName, FirstName)
```

When you create a unique index on a field (or set of fields), Access will prevent you from adding records that would create duplicate entries in the index.

There are some additional options on the Create Index statement that you should be aware of:

- **Asc, Desc:** You can specify that a field in an index is to be indexed in ascending or descending order (ascending is the default). Creating a index sorted in descending order can speed queries that retrieve data sorted in that order:

```
Create Index PurchDate
On Purchases (PurchaseDate Desc)
```

- **With Disallow Null:** If you specify the Disallow Null option, Access will not allow you to add records to the table where the indexed field is Null.

- **With Ignore Null:** The Ignore Null causes records with Null in the indexed field to be left out of the index. As a result, searches for records with Nulls in those fields won't be able to use the index and will run more slowly. However, if many records have Nulls in the indexed fields, using this option can decrease the size of the index and speed up finding those records that do have values in the indexed fields.

- **With Primary:** This option is identical to specifying the Primary Key constraint in the Create Table command or creating a Unique index with Disallow Null. In order for Access's object-oriented methods to be able to update your records, you must have at least one index on the table that does not permit duplicates or Null values. Using the With Primary option when creating an index is one way to do this. You can't use With Primary if the table was created with a Primary Key constraint.

You may be tempted to create a lot of indexes on a table in the assumption that, sooner or later, each index will be useful to some query. You should remember that every index is, in effect, another table in your database that must be updated and maintained. Whenever you add or delete a record, or change the value of an indexed field, the indexes on the table must also be updated. If you have five indexes on a table, an update to that table can result in five additional updates to each of the indexes.

In Exercise 4.4 you'll add a primary key index to the SampleCustomer table.

EXERCISE 4.4

Creating a Primary Key

1. In SQL view, enter **Create Index PK On SimpleCustomer (Customer-Name) With Primary**.

2. From the Query menu, select Run or click on the Run button on the toolbar.

3. Open the SimpleCustomer table and attempt to add a duplicate customer record. Because the index you created does not allow duplicate entries, you will not be able to add this second record.

This SQL statement has allowed you to add a primary key to an existing table.

Drop Index

There may come a time when you feel that you have an index on your table that isn't providing much support to your application. You can remove an index from a table with the Drop Index statement.

To remove the City index from the CustomerAddress table, you use:

```
Drop Index CityState
On CustomerAddress
```

Alter Table

There may also come a time when you find that your table's structure requires some changes. You can use the Alter Table statement to add or delete columns or constraints.

The format of the Alter Table statement is:

```
Alter Table tablename
[Add fielddefinition | constraintdefinition]
[Drop Column fieldname | Constraint constraintname]
```

The field and constraint definitions are identical to the ones used in the Create Table command.

To add a City field that doesn't allow duplicates to the SalesRep table, for instance, you could use an Alter statement like this:

```
Alter Table SalesRep
Add City Text(20) Constraint CityU Unique
```

To remove the CityU constraint you would use:

```
Alter Table SalesRep
Drop Constraint CityU
```

You cannot use the Alter Table statement to change the size or data type of a column. To do that you must create a new table that duplicates the original table but has the new column definition. You can then copy the data from the old table to the new table (using the SQL Insert statement), delete the original table, and rename the new table to the old name. If the old table has relationships with other tables, those relationships must be deleted before you can delete the old table.

In Exercise 4.5 you'll add a foreign key reference to the SalesRep table from the SalesRep field in the Customer table.

EXERCISE 4.5

Creating a Foreign Key

1. In SQL view, enter **Alter Table SimpleCustomer Add Constraint FK Foreign Key (SalesRep) References SalesRep**.

2. From the Query menu, select run or click on the Run button on the toolbar.

3. In the SimpleSalesRep table, try to add a record for a customer that doesn't exist. In the SimpleCustomerTable, try to remove a customer that has a SalesRep record.

In this exercise you've used the Alter statement to create a constraint to enforce referential integrity between your two tables.

The MSys* Tables

One of the central tenets of the relational model is that the data about the tables and indexes in the database is also stored in the database. The relational model also requires that this "data about data," or *metadata,* be stored in the same table structures that the rest of the data is stored in.

You don't update these metadata tables yourself. Instead, as you issue the various DLL commands, the database system updates the tables to reflect the changes to your database.

In Access, the tables that contain the information about the data all have names beginning with MSys*. Normally, these tables are hidden from view, but you can view them by selecting Tools ➢ Options and then checking System Objects on the View tab. Figure 4.9 shows a database with the system tables displayed. The most important of the Microsoft system tables is MSysObjects. The MSysObjects table lists every object in the database, from individual fields through tables to the modules that hold your VBA code.

WARNING You shouldn't make changes to the Jet system tables—changing the data in these tables can cause Jet to corrupt your database.

FIGURE 4.9

The Access database window showing the system tables

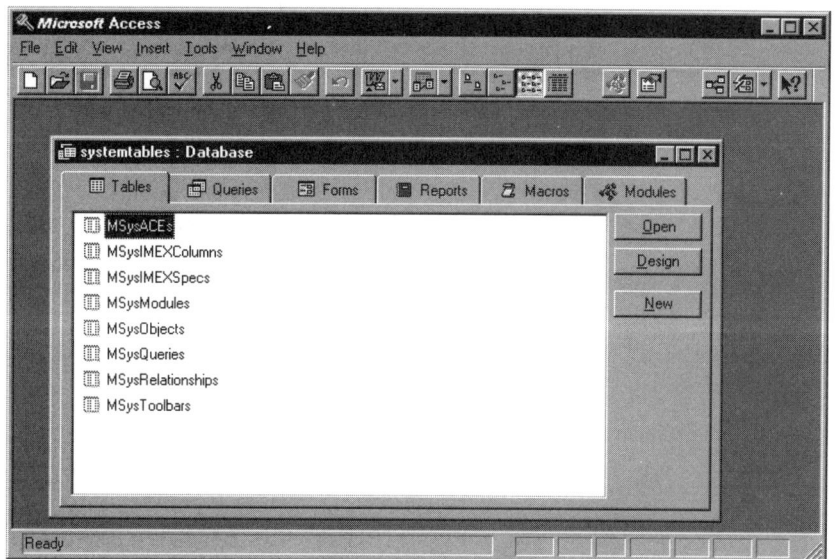

 You can create hidden tables of your own by prefixing their names with USys.

DML Commands

Microsoft ✓ *Exam Objective*   **Use Access SQL to write common queries.**

While the DDL commands are essential to creating your database, they're not the ones you use the most. The vast majority of the SQL commands that you'll use will be the Data Manipulation Language commands that allow you to read and update your data.

SQL's DML commands consist of the Select statement for retrieving records from your tables and the three update commands (Insert, Delete, and Update) for changing the data in your tables.

Select

The Select statement is probably the most frequently used SQL command. You'll use the Select statement to retrieve records or, along with other SQL statements, to select which records are to be updated. Figure 4.10 shows the options for the Select keyword. Its syntax is:

```
SELECT predicate selectionlist
FROM tableexpression
[WHERE... ]
[GROUP BY... ]
[HAVING... ]
[ORDER BY... ]
[WITH OWNERACCESS OPTION]
```

FIGURE 4.10

The Select statement options

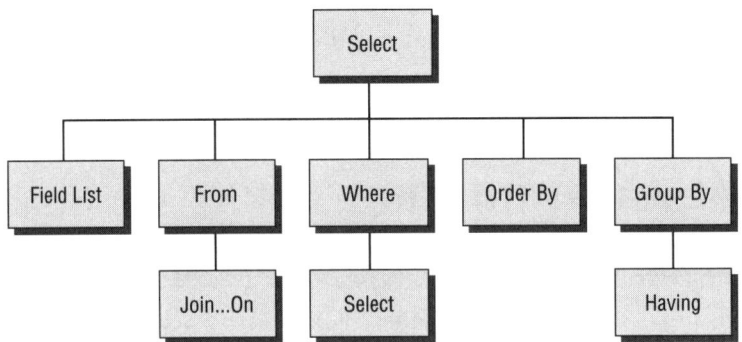

The selection list is usually a list of fields from the tables from which the Select statement is drawing data. The From clause specifies from which table (or tables) the data is to be drawn.

This Select statement will display the FirstName and LastName fields from the Customer table:

```
Select FirstName, LastName
From Customer
```

If you want all of the fields from the database, you can use an asterisk (*) in the select list:

```
Select *
From Customers
```

Of course, the more fields you select from a table, the longer it will take your query to run.

You're not limited to just field names in the selection list, though. You can use any valid expression in the selection list, including:

- String and numeric literals ("Your name", 4)

- Valid VBA expressions (3 + 2, "Your" & "Name")

- User-defined functions ("CalcCustomerBalance()")

- Access objects

This Select statement includes:

- An expression that uses fields from the database

- A string literal

- A user-defined function (GetRating()) whose argument is the CustId field from the table:

```
Select  FirstName & " " & LastName, "has a credit rating
➥ of", GetRating(CustId)
From Customers
```

The result of this query might look like this:

| John Smith | has a credit rating of | Very Good |
| Leslie Jones | has a credit rating of | Excellent |

Use the With OwnerAccess option when you create a query to be run by a user whose security won't let them access the table. If you add the With OwnerAccess option, the user gets your security access for the tables the query runs against.

In Exercise 4.6 you'll experiment with a simple Select statement.

EXERCISE 4.6

Using the Select Statement

1. In SQL view, enter **Select "Customer Name", CustomerName, Age From SimpleCustomer**.

2. From the Query menu, select Run, or click on the Run button on the toolbar.

3. In the resulting query, change the ages of some of your customers.

4. Return to SQL view, and alter your Select statement by replacing Age with **DateAdd("y",Now,Age*-1)**.

5. Run your query and attempt to change the customer's birthdate. The message in the status bar will tell you why you can't change this field. Notice the name of the column with the customer's birthdate in it.

6. Return to SQL view, and alter your Select statement by adding **As BirthDate** after the birthdate calculation. Rerun the query and look at the name of the birthdate column now.

7. Switch to Query Design view to see your query in a graphical view.

Selecting Records

With most queries you won't want to retrieve all the records in the table. SQL's Where clause allows you to specify which records in the table you want to retrieve. The Where clause looks very much like the If statement in VBA: it consists of one or more tests joined together with logical operators.

The simplest Where clause compares a field in the table to some value in order to restrict the records to those where the field matches the specified value. This Where clause extracts all the records for customers in New York City:

```
Select *
From Customers
Where City = 'New York City'
```

In Exercise 4.7 you'll add a Where clause to your Select statement.

EXERCISE 4.7

Adding Criteria to a Select Statement

1. Reopen the query from Exercise 4.6 and return to SQL view. Alter your Select statement to **Select "Customer Name", CustomerName, DateAdd("y",Now,Age*-1) As BirthDate From SimpleCustomer Where BirthDate < #1/1/1970#.**

2. Open your SimpleCustomer table and alter your customer's ages until you have some customers born before 1970 and some after. Rerun your query and you'll see that you now only retrieve those customers born before January 1, 1970.

Microsoft
✓ *Exam*
Objective

Refer to objects by using Access SQL.

You can also use objects in the Access environment in your SQL Where clause. This SQL query uses the value of the City textbox from the Customer form to select Customer records:

```
Select *
From CustomerAddress
Where City = Forms!Customer!City
```

To refer to a control on a form you must specify the form that the control is on (in this case, the Customer form) and the collection that the form is part of (all open forms are members of the Forms collection).

If you refer to an Access object in a SQL query, the object must be available at the time the query is run. If you run a query that refers to Form!Customer!City from the database window and the Customer form isn't open, Access will pop up a message box asking the user to enter the parameter Forms!Customer!City. If you run the query from within a program and the form isn't open, you will get the message "Too few parameters. Expected 1."

More complicated Where clauses combine several tests by using logical operators. For example, this query extracts all the customers in New York City, but only if their birthdate is prior to 1980:

```
Select *
From CustomerAddress
Where City = "New York"
And BirthDate < #01/01/1980#
```

Restructuring Queries

Microsoft ✓ *Exam Objective*	**Restructure queries to allow faster execution.**

Since the queries are so important in Access it is critical to be aware of the ways you can optimize queries for the fastest possible operation. The faster users can access the data they seek, the more productive the entire system can be. First on the list of techniques for query optimization is *compacting*. Compacting your database allows Access to organize the applications tables in the most efficient manner. It does this by attempting to locate pages in order based on the table's primary key, placing the relevant pages next to each other. This allows for more efficiency as the query works its way through the data. Of course, compacting the database is a good move in general.

Here are a few tips that work well for most query optimizations:

- Use the most efficient data types for each field in your database. This cuts down on data returns that are unnecessarily large. Applying a unique ID number to each record in a table makes large searches very fast.

- Keep the expression count as low as possible. Instead, include those expressions in the form related to the query. Of course, this means more work for you, but keeping the bulk of the expressions local cuts down significantly on parsing time.

- Do not add criteria to non-indexed or calculated fields unless it is absolutely necessary. A field that is not indexed will require more parsing time. This is also true of calculated fields, which require that the additional time be dedicated to resolving the calculation and returning the value.

- In a similar vein, avoid querying calculated fields when your queries are nested. If you must build calculations into your queries, keep the line count down as much as possible.

- Use Make Table queries. This technique builds a custom table from the query criteria, putting all the most often needed data in one, custom-built table. This is faster than querying each table for the same data each time you need it. This works best with data that rarely changes, so the custom table does not need to be rebuilt all the time.

WARNING   Not all of the techniques outlined in this section work with all queries. Test all optimizations before you deploy your application.

Indexes are great boons to environments that need fast access to data. There are, however, only a few things you can do with indexes that truly improve query response time. Indexing adds processing time to the back-end, as it must update, insert, and delete entries more often.

You should use as many indexes as you need to improve system operation, speed, and usability. (Remember, though, that there are some limitations to the use of indexes.) You can index both sides of a Join, giving you faster access to all of the data in case you need to modify the query. You should only add fields that will be helpful to the user. The more data that must be transferred, the more network traffic there will be.

Here are a couple of operationally-oriented modifications you can make to your queries and applications that will often improve your query performance:

- Indexes can't be used when a query string begins with a wildcard character (*). Modify the query to include a wildcard at the end of the string and reap the benefits of using indexes.

- Count(value) is faster than specifying a field name when evaluating for like content. The Count operation simply tallies the number of items that evaluate to the value. If you specify a field name, the query will attempt to evaluate all fields to that criteria, a much slower process.

There are only a few things you can do to optimize the query that is sent to the back-end. Once you have had some practice you will find it is easier to incorporate these strategies into your original design schema, saving you a lot of time in the installation phase. In the next section we take a look at Rushmore, a great optimizer around which to develop your system.

Using Rushmore

Microsoft
✓ *Exam*
Objective

Optimize queries by using Rushmore technology.

Jet stores the information in its indexes using a technology called Rushmore. If you construct your Where clauses correctly, Jet can find your records faster by using Rushmore to reduce the number of records that are read from the database file.

It's very easy to take advantage of Rushmore. A Where clause typically consists of a field that is compared to some value or to some other field.

Here are some typical examples of Where clauses:

```
Where LastName = 'Smith'
Where Age < HireDate
```

To use Rushmore, your Where clause must follow two rules:

- The field being tested must be indexed (preferably in ascending order—if the table is in descending order, Rushmore will only work if the test uses '=').

- The test must use <, >, =, <=, >=, <>, Between, or In. (You can also use Like, provided the expression following it doesn't begin with a wildcard.)

Rushmore works with both single and multiple field indexes. However, when the field is part of a multiple field index, you must, in your Where clause, use the fields in the same order as they appear in the multiple field index, starting with the first field in the index.

Rushmore technology can still be used even when the Where clause is made up of several tests—provided that the tests are combined through And and Or. Rushmore is most effective when all of the tests follow the two rules listed above. Rushmore can speed up your queries even if only one of the tests is "Rushmore-compatible," provided that the tests are joined together with an And. Rushmore also helps out when you use the Count(*) function to determine the number of records that meet a condition.

While Rushmore will work with Microsoft Access, FoxPro, and dBase tables, you can't use Rushmore with ODBC data sources.

Joining Tables

One of the results of normalizing your tables is that most queries will draw on several tables in order to get the desired result. As a result, most of the queries you create will need to combine two or more tables. In Access SQL, tables are combined through the use of the Join keyword.

The syntax for the Join statement is:

```
table1 Inner Join table2
On joincriteria
```

The first part of the Join statement (*table1* Inner Join *table2*) specifies which tables are to be joined. The relational model specifies that the first step in creating a join is to generate the Cartesian product of the two tables. The Cartesian product for two tables is another table that contains records made up of every possible combination of records from the two joined tables (see Figure 4.11).

FIGURE 4.11

The Cartesian product of two tables

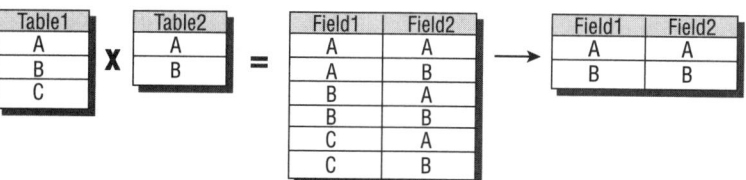

SQL then extracts from the Cartesian product every record that meets the join criteria. A typical join will require that a field in one table match a field in the other table. This query's join, for instance, specifies that the only records to be used from the Cartesian product are the records where the SalesRep field from the Customer table matches the SalesRep field from the SalesRep table:

```
Select LastName, FirstName, SalesArea
From Customer Inner Join SalesRep
On Customer.SalesRep = SalesRep.SalesRep
```

Where fields in the two tables being joined have the same name, you must prefix the field name with the name of the table that you want to draw the field from. In the previous example, Customer.LastName indicates that the LastName field is to be the field in the Customer table—not the Customer-Address table.

The Join criteria can, like the Where clause, include multiple tests by using the logical operators to combine those tests. This query joins the Customer table and the CustomerAddress table on both the LastName and FirstName fields:

```
Select LastName, FirstName, Street
From Customer Inner Join CustomerAddress
On Customer.LastName = Customer.LastName
And Customer.FirstName = Customer.FirstName
```

As with a single table query, a Where clause can be used to select records from the result of the join. This SQL query shows only those addresses where the AddressType field is equal to "Billing":

```
Select Customer.LastName, Customer.FirstName, Street
From Customer Inner Join CustomerAddress
On Customer.LastName = CustomerAddress.LastName
And Customer.FirstName = CustomerAddress.FirstName
Where AddressType = "Billing"
```

Repeated Records

Because a join begins with the generation of a Cartesian product, if a table has a one-to-many relationship with another table, data will be repeated when the tables are joined.

For instance, in the Sales Order system, each customer can have many address records in the CustomerAddress table. The Cartesian product of these two tables will match every Customer record with every Customer-Address record. As a result, each CustomerAddress record will get its own copy of the information for its customer.

After records that don't meet the Join criteria are removed, each Customer-Address record for a customer will still have a copy of its corresponding Customer record. When the results of the join are displayed, the Customer data will be duplicated for each address.

The records returned by this query will duplicate the information from the Customer table (LastName, FirstName) for each address that a Customer has:

```
Select LastName, FirstName, City
From Customer Inner Join CustomerAddress
```

```
On Customer.LastName = CustomerAddress.LastName
And Customer.FirstName = CustomerAddress.FirstName
```

A typical result for this query might be:

Jones Mary	New York City
Jones Mary	Birmingham
Smith Jack	New York City
Brown Jane	Los Angeles
Brown Jane	New York City

Since both Mary Jones and Jane Brown have two addresses, there are two records for each of them in the result from this query. As a result, the information from the Customer table is repeated for each City in the CustomerAddress table.

WARNING

Where data from one record is repeated many times in a query's result, Access will not let you update the fields in the query that contain data from the repeated records (the "many" side of the one-to-many relationship).

The Select statement in Exercise 4.8 will join your SimpleCustomer table to your SimpleSalesRep table.

EXERCISE 4.8

Joining Tables

1. In SQL view, enter **Select SimpleCustomer.CustomerName, SalesRegion From SimpleCustomer Inner Join SimpleSalesRep On SimpleCustomer.SalesRep = SimpleSalesRep.SalesRep**.

2. From the Query menu, select Run, or click on the Run button on the toolbar.

3. In the resulting query, change the regions of some of your customers. Then try to change the name of one of your customers.

4. Switch to Query Design view to see your query in a graphical view.

Missing Records

The typical join shows only the records where the Join criteria are met. This query, for instance, will be missing any customer who hasn't been assigned a salesperson or who has a salesperson that isn't in the SalesRep table:

```
Select LastName, FirstName, SalesArea
From Customer Inner Join SalesRep
On Customer.SalesRep = SalesRep.SalesRep
```

There are occasions when you will want to see all of the records from one of the tables in a query—even if some of the records don't have a match in the other table. This is called an *outer join*. The syntax for an outer join is:

```
table1 [Left | Right] Join table2 On joincriteria
```

The Left and Right qualifiers are used to indicate which table is to have all of its records included. A left join causes all of the records in the table on the left side of the Join keyword (the first table mentioned in the join) to appear in the result. A right join causes all the records from the second table (the one to the right of the Join keyword) to be included in the table.

The following query will display all of the records from the table on the left side of the join (the Customer table) even if they don't have a match in the SalesRep table:

```
Select LastName, FirstName, SalesArea
From Customer Left Join SalesRep
On Customer.SalesRep = SalesRep.SalesRep
```

The SalesArea field from the SalesRep table will be Null where there is no matching record in the SalesRep table for the Customer table.

Outer join queries let you find the records in a table that are missing matching records in the joined table. In the previous example, for instance, by checking for Nulls in the SalesRep field from the SalesRep table, you can find any customer who has a salesperson who isn't listed in the SalesRep table. The query to do that would look like this:

```
Select LastName, FirstName, SalesArea
From Customer Left Join SalesRep
On Customer.SalesRep = SalesRep.SalesRep
Where SalesRep.SalesRep Is Null
```

The Select statement in Exercise 4.9 uses an outer join on your Simple-Customer and SimpleSalesRep tables to find customers who don't have SalesReps.

Using an Outer Join

1. In your SimpleCustomer table, add some salespeople who do not have any customers in the Customer table.

2. In SQL view, enter **Select SimpleCustomer.CustomerName, Sales-Region From SimpleCustomer Right Join SimpleSalesRep On SimpleCustomer.SalesRep = SimpleSalesRep.SalesRep**.

3. From the Query menu, select Run, or click on the Run button on the toolbar. Notice that the salespeople with no customers assigned to them have Null in the CustomerName field.

4. Return to Design view and add **Where SimpleCustomer.Customer-Name Is Null** to the end of your query.

5. Rerun your query to find the customers who have no sales rep assigned to them.

Order By

SQL does not return the results of a query in any particular order. If you want to get the results back in some particular order, then you must specify that order using the Order By clause. The following query displays all of the customers, sorted by the LastName field (where two customers have the same last name, they are then sorted by the FirstName field):

```
Select *
From Customers
Order by LastName, FirstName
```

You can follow a field name in the Order By clause with either Asc or Desc to indicate if you want the fields to sort in ascending (Asc) or descending (Desc) order. Since ascending is the default, you only need to specify the order when you are sorting in descending order. The following query sorts customers in descending order by birthdate and, when two customers have the same birthdate, sorts them by name in ascending order:

```
Select *
From Customers
Order by BirthDate Desc, LastName, FirstName
```

Predicates

Normally a Select statement will return, or display, one record for every record that meets the criteria in the Where clause. SQL predicates allow you to control how many lines are returned by the query in order to reduce the number of lines displayed by the Select statement. Access SQL supports the predicates Distinct, DistinctRow, and Top.

Distinct

In some queries, you may not want to see any duplicate records found by the query. This query, for instance, will return one record for each customer:

```
Select City
From Customer
```

Since many customers may live in any particular city, there will be many repeated records in the result. A typical result might be:

New York City

Birmingham

New York City

New York City

Washington

Birmingham

Los Angeles

The Distinct keyword eliminates duplicate lines in the query's result. You insert the Distinct keyword before the field list in the Select statement to indicate that duplicate values are to be suppressed:

```
Select Distinct City
From Customer
```

The results returned by this query would look like this:

Birmingham

Los Angeles

New York City

Washington

DistinctRow

This predicate is used to eliminate duplicate data being displayed when you join two or more tables together but don't display data from all of the tables.

When two tables are joined, data from one table may be repeated if the tables are in a one-to-many relationship. As a result, if your query displays only data from the table that is duplicated you may end up displaying a lot of records that are identical. You might be tempted to add the Distinct predicate to your query in order to eliminate the duplicate data.

Unfortunately, Distinct won't remove duplicate records unless all of the data in the record in the Cartesian product is duplicated. In other words, while the data being displayed is duplicated, the undisplayed data from the another table in the join may not be duplicated. The Distinct keyword won't remove the duplicate records in this situation. To eliminate the repeated rows, you must use the DistinctRow predicate, as it will ignore the undisplayed fields when discarding duplicate data (see Figure 4.12).

F I G U R E 4.12

The Distinct vs.
DistinctRow predicate

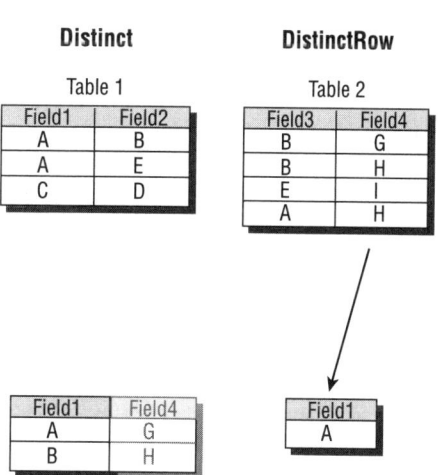

Top

The Top predicate allows you to limit the records returned to a specified number of records. This query, for instance, displays only the first 10 records that meet the criteria:

```
Select Top 10 FirstName, LastName
From Customer
Where City = "New York"
```

The Top predicate can also be used to limit the records displayed to a percentage of the total number of records that meet the criteria. This query returns the first 20 percent of the records that match the criteria:

```
Select Top 20 Percent FirstName, LastName
From Customer
Where City = "New York"
```

When the query contains an Order By clause to sort the records, the Top records are selected after the sort is done. This query, because it is sorted by the TotalPurchases fields, finds the five customers who bought the most in January:

```
Select Top 5 LastName, FirstName
From CustomerPurchase
Where MonthNumber = 1
Order by TotalPurchases
```

In Exercise 4.10 you'll experiment with the Distinct and DistinctRow predicates.

EXERCISE 4.10

Working with Distinct and DistinctRow Predicates

1. In SQL view, enter **Select SalesRegion From SimpleSalesRep Order By SalesRegion**. If you don't have some duplicate records, return to your SalesRep table and assign several salespeople to the same region. Rerun your query.

2. Return to Query Design view, and add **Distinct** after the Select keyword. Rerun your query to see the results.

EXERCISE 4.10 (CONTINUED)

3. Back in SQL view, enter **Select SalesRegion From SimpleCustomer Inner Join SimpleSalesRep On SimpleCustomer.SalesRep = SimpleSalesRep.SalesRep Order By SalesRegion**. This gives you the sales regions for salespeople who have customers. If you don't have any duplicate records, alter your SalesRep table until you do.

4. Change your query by first adding **Distinct** and then **DistinctRow** to your Select statement. Because individual rows do not duplicate in the table, Distinct does not eliminate the duplicates in your result; DistinctRow does.

Using SQL to Summarize Data

In the Sales Order system, it wouldn't be surprising for company management to ask for a report of total sales for each salesperson. Thanks to SQL's Group By clause, you can meet that request with a single query. The Group By clause enables you to summarize your data so that you display one record for each salesperson. You can include a variety of summary information on that salesperson line, including totals, averages, and counts.

Group By

When creating a query to total data in SQL, the best place to begin is with a SQL statement that contains the detail data that you want to summarize. If you wanted to create a query to give you the total amount sold by each sales rep, you should probably begin with the query that lists each SalesRep with the amounts they sold:

```
Select SalesRep, PurchaseAmount
From Customer Inner Join CustomerPurchase
On Customer.LastName = CustomerPurchase.LastName
And Customer.FirstName = CustomerPurchase.FirstName
```

Adding the Group By clause alters this query so that SQL produces a record only when the SalesRep field changes. A Group By clause follows your Where clause (if any) and lists the field (or fields) you want to summarize by. To summarize by the SalesRep field, you would add:

```
Group By SalesRep
```

Since the Group By clause will cause SQL to merge all the records for a SalesRep into a single record, you must also tell SQL how to merge the rest of the fields in the record (in this case, that's just the PurchaseAmount field).

This query uses the SQL Sum function to merge the PurchaseAmount field by totaling up all the PurchaseAmounts for all the records for a SalesRep:

```
Select SalesRep, Sum(PurchaseAmount)
From Customer Inner Join CustomerPurchase
On Customer.LastName = CustomerPurchase.LastName
And Customer.FirstName = CustomerPurchase.FirstName
Group By SalesRep
```

The following query, on the other hand, merges the PurchaseAmount fields for all of the records for a salesperson by averaging the PurchaseAmount field:

```
Select SalesRep, Avg(PurchaseAmount)
From Customer Inner Join CustomerPurchase
On Customer.LastName = CustomerPurchase.LastName
And Customer.FirstName = CustomerPurchase.FirstName
Group By SalesRep
```

The following query merges the records by displaying the largest sale:

```
Select SalesRep, Max(PurchaseAmount)
From Customer Inner Join CustomerPurchase
On Customer.LastName = CustomerPurchase.LastName
And Customer.FirstName = CustomerPurchase.FirstName
Group By SalesRep
```

You can group your output on more than one field by specifying multiple fields in the Group By clause. When you do so, SQL produces a new record every time any one of the fields changes. This query produces a new record every time the SalesRep or the MonthNumber fields change:

```
Select SalesRep, MonthNumber, Sum(PurchaseAmount)
From Customer Inner Join CustomerPurchase
```

```
On Customer.LastName = CustomerPurchase.LastName
And Customer.FirstName = CustomerPurchase.FirstName
Group By SalesRep, MonthNumber
```

You can have as many fields in the Select statement as you want, but each field must either be used in the Group By clause or be summarized in some way.

Totaling Functions

The totaling functions available in Access SQL are:

- **Max, Min:** Selects the largest or smallest value from the field. These functions can be used with fields that don't contain numeric values.

- **First, Last:** Returns the value from the first or last record in the query.

The Access help file documentation on First and Last suggests that the data returned by these functions is arbitrary or affected by the sort order established by the Order By clause. Neither of these statements is true, at least when working with data stored in MDB files.

- **Sum, Avg:** Totals the values in the field or calculates their average.

- **Count:** Tallies the number of records where the field is not null.

- **StDev, StDevP, Var, VarP:** StDev and StDevP calculate the standard deviation for the values in the field. StDev calculates the deviation for a sample drawn from a population, while StDevP calculates the standard deviation for a whole population. Var and VarP calculate the variance.

Having

You can use a Where clause to control which records are totaled. However, if you want to select records based on the results of a totaling operation, you must use a Having clause.

The Having clause follows the Group By clause and looks very much like a Where clause. This query, for instance, retrieves the names of salespeople who have average sales greater than $3,000:

```
Select SalesRep, Max(PurchaseAmount) As AvgAmount
From Customer Inner Join CustomerPurchase
```

```
On Customer.LastName = CustomerPurchase.LastName
And Customer.FirstName = CustomerPurchase.FirstName
Group By SalesRep
HAVING Max(Customer.PurchaseAmount)>3000
```

You'll notice that the preceding query uses the As keyword to assign an alias to the summarized PurchaseAmount field. That's done so that you can refer to the summary field in the Having clause. You don't have to assign the alias yourself, as Access will create one for you made up of the summary function name and the field name (in this case, the Access assigned alias would be MaxOfPurchaseAmount)

NOTE In the Access Query Design window, you generate Group by queries by creating a Totals query.

Union Queries

Microsoft
Exam
Objective

Use union queries.

There are times when you need to extract data from two or more tables but don't need to join the tables. This situation occurs when you extract data with one query and want to append that data to the results of another query (see Figure 4.13). When you want to do this, you need to create a Union query.

A Union query consists of two Select statements combined with the Union keyword. For instance, this query lists all the customers with a particular salesperson:

```
Select *
From Customers
Where SalesRep = "Wilma Deering"
```

This query lists all of the customers who made purchases in the month of January:

```
Select Customer.*
From Customer Inner Join CustomerPurchase
On Customer.LastName = CustomerPurchase.LastName
And Customer.FirstName = CustomerPurchase.FirstName
Where MonthNumber = 1
```

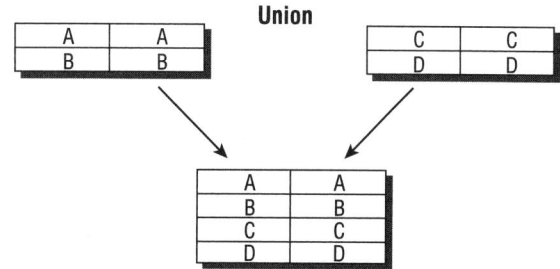

You can create a query that includes the results from both of these queries by joining them together with the Union keyword:

```
Select *
From Customers
Where SalesRep = "Wilma Deering"
Union
From Customer Inner Join CustomerPurchase
On Customer.LastName = CustomerPurchase.LastName
And Customer.FirstName = CustomerPurchase.FirstName
Where MonthNumber = 1
```

You can include as many SQL statements as you want in a Union query.

The Union operation also supports the Table keyword for displaying all the records in a table:

```
Table Customer
Union
Select *
From CustomerPurchase
Union
Table SalesRep
```

There are some restrictions in creating Union queries. Each of the Select statements must have the same number of fields (although they don't have to be the same data type). If you want to control the order in which the records are displayed, you must put the Order By clause in the last of the SQL statements. Finally, SQL takes the names for the columns from the first SQL statement in the Union, so put any aliases (CustomerLastName As LastName) in the first query:

```
Select LastName as Name, City
From CustomerPurchase
Union
Table Customer
Union
Table SalesRep
Order by Name
```

In a Union query, duplicate records are automatically removed from the result. If you want all the records from all of the SQL statements to be displayed, then use Union All instead of just Union.

Exercise 4.11 combines several queries into one result using a Union query.

EXERCISE 4.11

Using a Union Query

1. In SQL view, enter **Select SalesRep from SimpleSalesRep**. Run your query.

2. Start another query and, in SQL view, enter **Select CustomerName from SimpleCustomer**.

3. Finally, create a query that lists all of the salespeople and all of the customers for your company. Enter **Select SalesRep from SimpleSalesRep Union Select CustomerName from SimpleCustomer**.

4. Add a customer with the same name as one of your salespeople and rerun your Union query. The name should only appear once, since Union queries eliminate duplicates.

5. Change the query to **Select SalesRep from SimpleSalesRep Union All Select CustomerName from SimpleCustomer** and rerun the query. Both occurrences of the name should appear.

Changing Data

While being able to retrieve and view your data is very useful, you're also going to need to update your data. SQL provides three keywords to enable you to delete records (Delete), add new records to a table (Insert), and change the value of fields in existing records (Update), each of which has an analog in the Access query design interface (as Delete, Append, and Update queries).

Update

An Update query allows you to specify which fields in which records in which table you want to change. The syntax for the Update statement is:

```
Update tablename
Set fieldname = value [, fieldname = value [,…]]
[Where…]
```

The Update statement begins by specifying which table is to be updated. The Set clause specifies what fields are to be changed (and what they are to be changed to). Finally, a Where clause allows you to select which records you want to update.

Remember that SQL doesn't discriminate between tables and queries. As a result, you can use any of SQL's update statements on a query (provided that the query is updateable).

This statement updates the SalesRep table and gives each salesperson a 10 percent raise:

```
Update SalesRep
Set Salary = Salary * 1.10
```

Of course, you might only want to give a raise to one salesperson:

```
Update SalesRep
Set Salary = Salary * 1.10
Where SalesRep = 'Wilma Deering'
```

You can update several fields in the Set clause by separating them with commas:

```
Update SalesRep
Set Salary = Salary * 1.10,
    CommissionRate = .09
```

In Exercise 4.12 you'll begin updating your database.

Updating Data

1. Change some of your sales regions to **"North East."**

2. In SQL view enter **Update SimpleSalesRep Set SalesRegion = "New England" Where SalesRegion = "North East"**. Run your query. A message box will pop up saying how many records you will be updating and asking if you want to continue. Click on Yes.

3. Check your SalesRep table to see that all of the salespeople in the North East region are now in the New England region.

4. Start a new query and enter **Update SimpleCustomer Inner Join SimpleSalesRep On SimpleCustomer.SalesRep = SimpleSalesRep.SalesRep Set Age = 50 Where SalesRegion = "New England"**. Run your query, and click on the Yes button when asked if you want to continue.

5. Check your customers to see that all of the customers assigned to salespeople in the New England region have had their ages changed.

Insert

The Insert statement is used to add new records to a table. You can either specify a set of values to put in the fields or use a Select statement to extract the data you want from other tables in your database.

The syntax for adding a record when you specify the values is:

```
Insert Into tablename [(field1, field2,…)]
Values (value1, value2, …)
```

An Insert statement to add a new Customer record might look like this:

```
Insert Into Customer (LastName, Firstname, BirthDate, SalesRep)
Values ("Rogers", "Sam", 01/10/56, "Wilma Deering")
```

If you are going to provide values for every field in the database, in the order that the fields are stored, you can omit the field list. This would allow you to write the previous SQL statement like this:

```
Insert Into Customer
Values ("Rogers", "Sam", 01/10/56, "Wilma Deering")
```

It's unusual to use the Values clause, though. More often than not, when you add a record to a table you will do so by extracting data from other tables in the database. The syntax for inserting data from another database is easy to remember—it's a Select statement:

```
Insert Into Customer
Selectstatement
```

If you had a table of new customers and you wanted to add them to your customer table, you might use a SQL statement like this:

```
Insert Into Customer
Select *
From NewCustomer
```

If the two tables don't have exactly the same fields, then you need to supply field lists to ensure that the correct data from the extracted table goes to the correct fields in the inserted table. In this statement, field lists are used in both the Insert statement and the Select statement to ensure that the correct data is going to the correct fields:

```
Insert Into Customer (FirstName, LastName, BirthDate)
Select NewFirst, NewLast, NewBDate
From NewCustomer
```

Any valid Select statement can be used in an Insert statement. This query, for instance, summarizes a table of purchase transactions in order to add the records for December's sales to a table of monthly totals:

```
Insert Into MonthlySummary (SalesRep, Month, TotalPurchased)
Select SalesRep, Month, Sum(TotalPurchased)
From Sales
Where Month = "December"
Group by SalesRep, Month
```

Delete

Finally, there may come a time when you no longer need a record in one of your tables and are ready to delete it. The SQL statement used to delete records is the Delete statement, and its syntax is:

```
Delete *
From joinexpression
Where criteria
```

The Where clause allows you to select which records are to be deleted.

The Delete statement uses the asterisk to indicate that a whole record is to be deleted (you can't delete individual fields). If there is more than one table involved in the Delete, then you must specify from which table records are to be deleted. As an example, the following Delete statement deletes all the customers for the NorthEast sales region. Since the sales region is stored in the SalesRep table, the Delete statement must do a join between the Customer and SalesRep tables to find which customers are to be removed. As a result, the Delete statement uses Customer.* to indicate that it is Customer records that are to be deleted:

```
Delete Customer.*
From Customer Inner Join SalesRep
On Customer.SalesRep = SalesRep.SalesRep
Where SalesRep.Region = "NorthEast"
```

It's important to understand the difference between Delete and Drop Table. A Delete command can remove all of the records from a table, but leaves the table structure intact. A Drop Table statement removes the table (and all of its records) from the database.

In Exercise 4.13 you'll use SQL to delete records from your tables.

EXERCISE 4.13

Deleting Records

1. In SQL view, enter **Delete SimpleCustomer.* From SimpleCustomer Inner Join SimpleSalesRep On SimpleCustomer.SalesRep = Simple-SalesRep.SalesRep Where SalesRegion = "New England"**. Run your query. A message box will pop up saying how many records will be deleted and asking if you want to continue. Click on Yes.

2. Now that the customer records are gone, referential integrity will let you delete the salespeople for that region. Start a new SQL query and enter **Delete * From SimpleSalesRep Where SalesRegion = "New England"**. Again, click on Yes when asked if you want to delete these records.

Summary

This chapter has introduced you to the fundamentals of SQL, the universal database language. Access supports a version of SQL that complies closely with the standards established by ANSI. In Access, you can enter any SQL statement in the SQL view of the Access Query Design window. Most SQL statements can also be viewed in Query Design view, but some statements (including all DDL statements) are only available in SQL view.

SQL contains Data Definition Language (DDL) commands for creating and modifying tables, and Data Manipulation Language (DML) commands for working with the data stored in those tables. Unlike other data manipulation tools, SQL is non-navigational: you can specify which data you want, but not how the data is to be retrieved.

The SQL Create Table command allows you to add new tables to your database (Drop Table removes tables from the database). When a table is created you must specify the name of the table, the fields that make it up (with their data types), and any constraints on those fields. SQL constraints are used to link tables together (Foreign Key…References), to prevent duplicate keys being entered (Unique and Primary Key), and to ensure that no fields contain Nulls (Primary Key). SQL also allows you to create indexes on tables using the Create Index statement to speed data retrieval. Finally, the Alter Table command allows you to add or remove fields and constraints from a table.

The Access DML commands allow you to retrieve (Select), update (Update), add (Insert), and delete (Delete) records. The Select statement is used to retrieve data and has several clauses:

- **From:** Specifies the table that data is to be drawn from

- **Where:** Sets conditions that records must pass to be included in the Select statement's result

- **Order By:** Sorts the records by fields into a set order

- **Group By:** Summarizes data

- **Having:** Selects summarized records based on criteria

In addition, SQL predicates (Distinct, DistinctRow, Top) can be used to reduce the number of rows in the query's result. The Select statement can be included in other DML statements as a subquery.

In the From clause, the Join…On keyword allows you to combine many tables into a single query (Union queries can be used to combine the results of several queries into one result). The default join is the inner join, which only lists records that have matches in the tables they are joined to. You can also create outer joins using the Left or Right keywords. A left join causes all the records from the first table mentioned in the join to be included in the query's result.

The Update, Delete, and Insert commands complete SQL's data manipulation commands. The Insert command comes in two forms—one for adding a single record with specific values and another version for adding all the records from a Select statement. The Update command lets you change the values of fields in a table for selected records, and the Delete command allows you to remove selected records from a table.

Review Questions

Questions 5, 7, 8, 10, 11, and 12 use the in formation in the following tables.

Customer Table Definition	Field	Type	Size	Notes
	CustName	Char	20	Primary Key
	SalesRep	Char	20	
	CreditCardNumber	Integer		
	CustSales	Currency		

SalesRep Table Definition	Field	Type	Size	Notes
	RepName	Char	20	Primary Key
	TotalSales	Currency		

1. SQL consists of:

   A. DML

   B. DDL

   C. Both A and B

   D. Neither A nor B

2. Some typical DML commands are:

   A. Select, Update

   B. Create, Drop

   C. Drop, Update

   D. Select, Alter

3. Which of the following is a valid command to create a table?

   A. Create Table NewTable

   B. CreateTable NewTable (my field VarChar(5))

   C. Create Table NewTable (Myfield String)

   D. Create Table NewTable MyField Integer

4. To create an index that will not permit records with duplicate values or Nulls in the indexed fields, you would use:

   A. Create Index NewIndex On NewTable (NewField) With Unique, Ignore Null

   B. Create Index NewIndex On NewTable With Primary

   C. Create Index NewIndex On NewTable (NewField) With Primary

   D. Create Index NewIndex On NewTable (NewField) With Unique, Disallow Null

5. The SalesRep and Customer tables must reference each other. The Customer table must not have a value in the SalesRep field that is not in the SalesRep table. The appropriate command to create this constraint when creating the Customer table is:

A. Create Table Customer
(CustName Char(20),
SalesRep Char(20) Constraint RefSales References SalesRep)

B. Create Table SalesRep
(RepName Char(20) Constraint RefSales References Customer)

C. Create Table SalesRep
(RepName Char(20) Constraint RefSales References
Customer.SalesRep)

D. Create Table Customer
(CustName Char(20), SalesRep (20) Constraint RefSales
References SalesRep.CustName)

6. You know that creating indexes on fields can speed up queries that join two tables. After creating the Foreign Key in the previous question, in order to speed up joins between the Customer and the SalesRep tables you should:

A. Create an index on the SalesRep field in the Customer table

B. Create an index on the RepName field in the SalesRep table

C. Both A and B

D. Neither A nor B

7. Which of the following statements would speed up a query that listed all customers in order by the SalesRep field and, where a salesperson has more than one customer, list the customers in alphabetical order?

A. Create Index Rep on Customer (CustName,SalesRep)

B. Create Index Rep on Customer (SalesRep, CustName)

C. Create Index Rep on Customer, SalesRep (SalesRep, CustName)

D. None of the above

8. Most customers won't have an entry in the SalesRep field. To speed up a query that finds customers for a specific salesperson, you would use:

A. Create Index FindRep on Customer(RepName) Not Null

B. Create Unique Index FindRep on Customer(RepName)

C. Create Index FindRep on SalesRep(RepName) With Disallow Null

D. Create Index FindRep On Customer (SalesRep) With Ignore Null

9. You need to change the CustomerCreditCard field from numeric to string. To do this you would:

A. Use the Alter command

B. Use the Create Table…Alter command

C. Back up and restore the database

D. Create a new table and copy the data to it

10. The following query, called from a program, fails with a message indicating a parameter was missing.
Select *
From SalesRep
Where RepName = Forms!SalesRep!RepName

The most likely cause is:

A. The SalesRep form is not open.

B. The query parameter is missing.

C. The RepName field is empty.

D. The table has no records in it.

11. Which of the following SQL statements correctly extracts records from the Customer and SalesRep tables?

A. Select *
From Customer Join SalesRep
on RepName = CustName

B. Select *
From Join Customer, SalesRep
On RepName = CustName

C. Select *
From Inner Join On Customer, SalesRep
Where RepName = CustName

D. Select *
From Customer Inner Join SalesRep
On RepName = CustName

12. Prior to applying a Foreign Key constraint, you want to find all of the Customers who have a SalesRep that doesn't appear in the SalesRep table. The syntax for this query is:

A. Select CustName, SalesRep
From Customer
Where SalesRep Is Null

B. Select CustName, SalesRep
From Customer Inner Join SalesRep
Where RepName Is Null

C. Select CustName, SalesRep
From Customer Left Join SalesRep
On SalesRep = RepName
Where RepName Is Null

D. Select CustName, SalesRep
From Customer Right Join SalesRep
On SalesRep = RepName
Where RepName Is Null

13. You have written a query that joined a table of 15 records to another table. You expected to get 15 records back, however, there are only 12 records in the result. The query result includes several duplicated records, which you expected. The most likely cause is:

A. You included Distinct in the query

B. You included DistinctRow in the query

C. You included Unique in the query

D. You must include All in the query

14. Which query will find the five salespeople with the most sales?

A. Select Top 5 RepName
From SalesRep

B. Select Top(5. RepName
From SalesRep

C. Select Top 5 RepName
From SalesRep
Order By RepName

D. Select Top 5 RepName
From SalesRep
Order by TotalSales

15. To total the sales for customers you would use:

A. Select CustName, Sum(CustSales)
From Customer
Group By CustSales

B. Select CustName, Total(CustSales)
From Customer
Group By CustSales

C. Select CustName, Sum(CustSales)
From Customer
Group By CustName

D. Select CustName, Total(CustSales)
From Customer
Group By CustName

16. Some of the salespeople are also customers of the company. To list all of the customers and salespeople, with any records that are in both tables listed twice, you would use:

    A. Select CustName
    From Customer
    Union
    Select RepName
    From SalesRep

    B. Select CustName
    From Customer
    Union All
    Select RepName
    From SalesRep

    C. Union
    Select CustName
    From Customer;
    Select RepName
    From SalesRep

    D. Union All
    Select CustName
    From Customer;
    Select RepName
    From SalesRep

17. To delete all the Customer records where there has never been a value assigned to the SalesRep field, you would use:

    A. Delete *
    From Customer
    Where SalesRep = Null

    B. Delete *
    From Customer
    Where SalesRep Is Null

    C. Delete *
    From Customer
    Where SalesRep = " "

    D. Delete *
    From Customer
    Where SalesRep Is " "

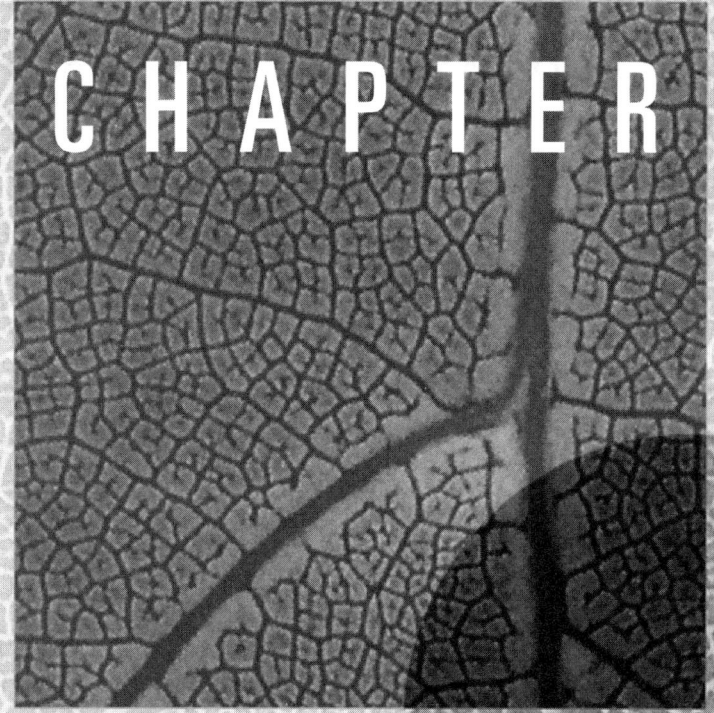

CHAPTER

5

OLE Automation

Microsoft Exam Objectives Covered in This Chapter

- Customize OLE controls.

- Control other applications by using OLE Automation.

- Control Microsoft Access from other applications by using OLE Automation.

Object Linking and Embedding (OLE) is a programming standard developed by Microsoft that allows you to control one application from another. This can be done either from the Access user interface (by using menu commands and mouse movements), or by writing code in VBA.

In this chapter you'll first see how to use OLE from the Access user interface to embed Word documents, Excel spreadsheets, and other objects into your forms and reports. With that under your belt, you'll move on to using Access to take control of another application and use Access to extend your application. Finally, you'll learn how to take control of Access from other applications.

In this chapter, you will learn:

- The best way to move data in Access tables to Excel for analysis.

- How to print a disclaimer document, created in Word, on an Access report.

- About storing bitmap images in an Access database and an Excel spreadsheet. You'll also learn how to display them on forms and print them on reports.

- How to write code in Access to extract data from an Excel worksheet and display it on an Access form. You'll also find out how to write code in Word to extract data from an Access table for use on a Word document.

- How OLE lets you use linked or embedded OLE documents and the costs and benefits of doing so.

- The difference between a bound and an unbound OLE object and whether they work differently on forms and reports.

- About merging name and address data in an Access table to a Word letter.

Using OLE Automation in the User Interface

You can put Excel spreadsheets and Word documents in your Access forms or reports just by using the Access menu options.

In order for you to use an object in an Access form or report, the object's application (Word or Excel, in this case) must be an OLE server. Fortunately, you don't need to wrack your brains or leaf through documentation in order to find out which applications are OLE servers and which are not. The Insert Object dialog box, shown in Exercise 5.1, conveniently lists all the OLE server applications installed and registered on your computer.

Compound Documents

When you insert one object into another, you create a *compound document*. A compound document is a document with inserted OLE objects that display data from another application.

The Access interface provides three different ways to create a compound document:

- Use the Insert Object dialog box by selecting Insert ➤ Object.

- Add an Unbound Object Frame control or a Bound Object Frame control to your form from the Access toolbox.

- Open an OLE server application (Excel, for instance), select some material in the application to be inserted (a range of cells), copy it to the Windows Clipboard, and then use Edit ➤ Paste Special to insert the object into a form or report.

Whichever insertion method you use, you will have a choice between embedding or linking the object.

Linking vs. Embedding

If you choose to *embed* the object, Windows will make a copy of the object you are inserting and Access will store it as part of the Access form or report. This means that your embedded object will not change if the original source document is changed. This also means you don't need to worry about moving or renaming the original document—Access is using the copy it embedded inside your database.

Sometimes you do want an object in an Access form or report to change when the original object is changed; in that case, you should choose to *link* the object.

When a document is inserted as linked, the only thing put in the Access database (MDB file) is a pointer to the file. When a request is made to display the object, Access retrieves the file and displays the object. This means your form or report displays the changes to the original document that have been made by any other application that opened the file.

Using linking will help keep the size of your database down compared to embedding, because the object isn't inserted into your MDB file. There is a downside: if the original document is moved or renamed, the link is broken and has to be fixed in order for the document to display properly. Additionally, forms with linked objects may load more slowly because the files are read from your hard disk.

Embedded Objects

While you can insert into an Access form or report any type of object that shows up in the Insert Object dialog box, some of the selections are pretty obscure (for example, the MIDI sequence selection). The most commonly used objects are images (either Clip Art selections or Paint images), Excel worksheets and charts, and MS Graphs.

When you embed an OLE object in a form, it is disabled by default. If you want to allow users to activate the object and edit it, you must set its Enabled property to Yes in the control's properties sheet.

No matter what method you use for embedding your object in a form or report, Access uses an OLE Frame control to hold the object. You can use either the Bound Object Frame control or the Unbound Object Frame control from your toolbox to embed objects in your form or report.

The Bound Object Frame tool and the Unbound Object Frame tool are on the seventh row of the Access toolbox. Each control displays an OLE object on a form or report; the difference between them is that the Unbound Object Frame control displays an image that is placed on the form itself, and does not change when the user navigates from record to record. The Bound

Object Frame control, on the other hand, displays an image stored in an Access table, which is different in different records of the table.

The Unbound Object Frame

Microsoft
✓ *Exam*
Objective

Customize OLE controls.

You'll notice that the different types of controls behave differently when you bind a form to a table so that you see data from a different row in the table as you navigate from record to record using the form's navigation buttons. In an Unbound Object Frame control, as shown in Exercise 5.1, the image remains the same, while the image in a Bound Object Frame control changes from record to record. See Figure 5.1 for an illustration of such a form.

FIGURE 5.1

A form with Bound and Unbound Object Frame controls

EXERCISE 5.1

Inserting an Unbound OLE Object Frame

This exercise embeds an unbound image into a form.

1. Open a form in Design view.

2. Click the Unbound Object Frame tool on the Access toolbar, or select Insert ➤ Object from the menu.

3. Draw a rectangle on the form (the size can be adjusted later).

4. The Insert Object dialog box opens. Select ClipArt Gallery and click on OK.

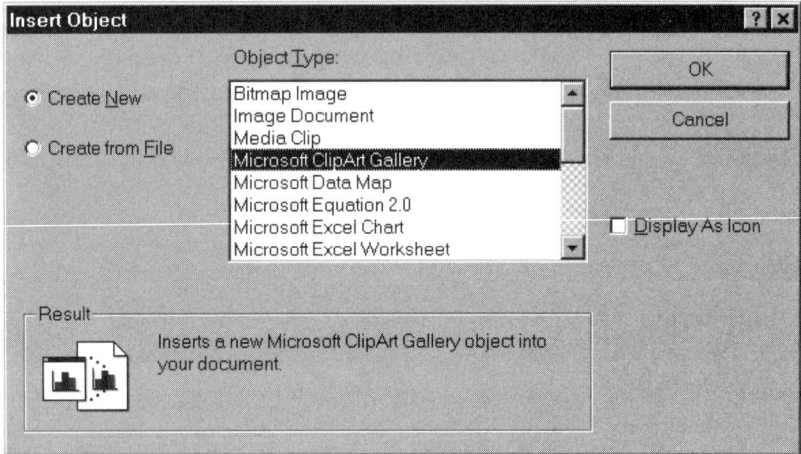

5. The ClipArt Gallery opens. Select a category and a picture.

6. Click on the Insert button to update your form.

The Bound Object Frame

A Bound Object Frame control is tied to data in the record, so its contents will change as you navigate from record to record. A Bound Object Frame control is used to display an image stored in an Access table in an OLE Object field.

A typical example is an image associated with a record, such as an employee picture. See Exercise 5.2 for a description of how to store OLE objects in a table, so they will be available to display in Bound Object Frame controls.

EXERCISE 5.2

Inserting a Bound Object Image

This exercise will show you how to create an OLE field in a table record and bind it to an OLE control on a form.

1. Open the SalesRep table in Design View and add a new field called **SalesRepPhoto**. Set its data type to OLE Object and its Description to SalesRep picture. Close the table, saving your changes.

2. Open a new Access form in Design view. Set its Record Source property to SalesRep.

3. Select the Bound Object Frame and draw it on the form. Set its Control Source property to SalesRepPhoto.

4. Select View ➢ Field List, and drag the SalesRep and SalesRepArea fields onto the form.

5. Switch to Form View and right-click the Bound Object Frame control to open the context menu.

6. Select the Insert Object command from the menu.

7. Select the Create from File option button.

8. Use the Browse button to search for a bitmap image to insert into the OLE Object field.

9. Click on the OK button to update the Bound Object Frame and the field it is bound to.

Repeat as needed for the remaining records in the table.

Once you've put an OLE Object field in your table's record you can use a Bound Object Frame control that's bound to the field on a form.

You can put both bound and unbound controls on the same form. Figure 5.1 shows a form with an unbound image (the light bulb) and a bound image (the employee photo). As you navigate from record to record in the form, the light bulb image will remain unchanged, while the employee photo will be different for every record.

When you insert a bitmap image into a Bound Object Frame control with the Display Type property set to Content, it appears as an image on the form. However, this is not the case with some other graphics types. A Windows Metafile (.WMF) file, for example, appears as an icon. Before creating graphics to insert into Access forms, check that the graphic type will appear as an image.

Inplace OLE Activation

When you double-click on an embedded or linked OLE object whose server application supports inplace editing, the original application's toolbars appear in place of the usual Access toolbars, so you can edit the object by double-clicking on the control. Inplace activation allows you to edit the embedded object without opening it in a separate window. Even with Word activated, though, you still can't move to the second page of a multipage embedded Word document.

The following is a list of requirements for inplace editing:

- The Access form must be in Form view.

- The OLE object's server application must support inplace activation.

- The control's Locked property must be set to True.

- The control's Enabled property must be set to False.

- The control's OLE Type property must be embedded, not linked.

Word Objects

You can't do a whole lot with an embedded Word object. You can embed a Word document on an Access form, but if you can't see the entire page, there is no way to scroll through the document. Nor is there a way to move to another page of a multipage document.

As a workaround for the embedded Word object's limitations, embed your Word document as an icon. When you do this, the Word icon appears on your form instead of the document. When you double-click the icon, the document opens in a separate window with full Word functionality.

Realistically, the best use for an embedded Word document is to display a small amount of text that uses Word features not available in Access. For instance, unlike the Access text box, Word supports multiple fonts, sizes, and colors for text. Word also lets you place text over an image without obscuring the image, which is not possible in Access. If you need these features you can create a formatted Word document and embed it in your form or report.

A Word disclaimer document using several different fonts and colors would be a good choice for embedding on an Access form or report. To print the disclaimer on every page of a report, follow the steps in Exercise 5.3.

EXERCISE 5.3

Inserting a Word Document into a Report Header

This exercise gives you a chance to work with a Word embedded object.

1. Start Word and create a document containing the following text (the font used is Bookman Old Style); color the "All Rights Reserved" phrase red:

This material is copyrighted as of *January 1st, 1997*. **All Rights Reserved.**

2. Save the document as Disclaimer.doc.

3. Open an Access report where you want to embed the Word document in Design view.

4. If the report doesn't have a Page Header section, click View ➤ Page Header/Footer to create Page Header and Footer sections.

5. Move the cursor to the report's Page Header section.

6. Select Insert ➤ Object, and click the Create from File option button.

7. Browse for Disclaimer.doc and select it.

8. Click on the OK button.

9. Resize the OLE object control as needed.

Figure 5.2 shows the Access report with an Unbound OLE Frame control displaying the embedded Word document in Print Preview view.

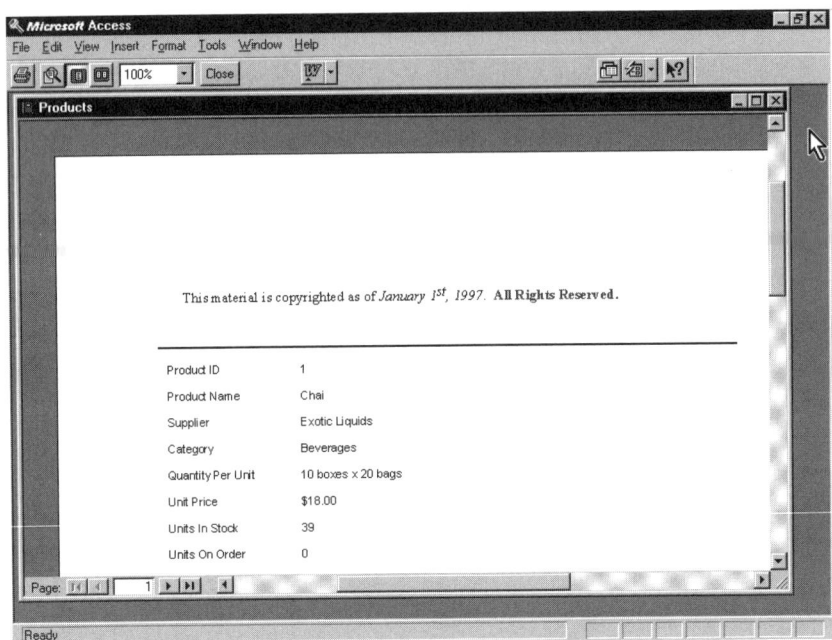

Excel Objects

You can display Excel worksheets or charts on Access forms, or print them on Access reports as embedded or linked OLE objects. For example, you could embed an Excel worksheet containing regional sales data on a form that displays sales results for individuals or groups. Unlike Word, Excel is a fully functional OLE server that supports inplace activation.

When you select an entire Excel workbook to embed on an Access form, the first sheet in the workbook will appear as the embedded object. If that is not the sheet that you want to display, either make the sheet you want the first sheet in the workbook, or insert just the individual sheet from Excel.

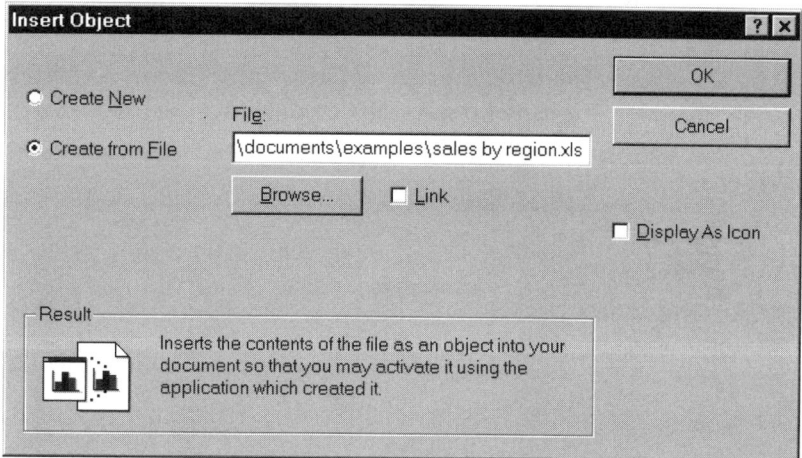

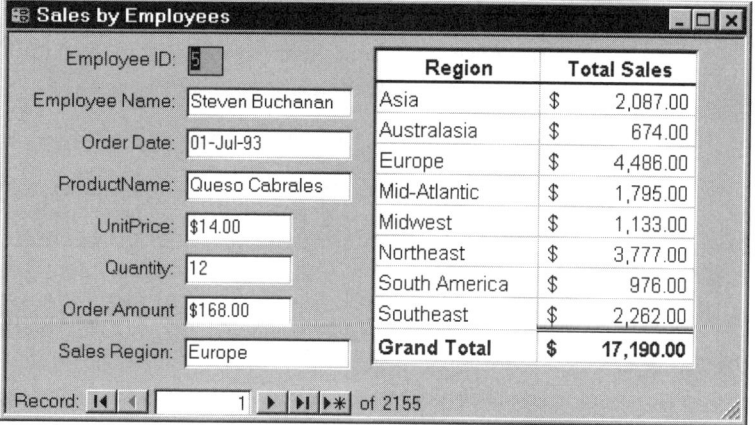

When a worksheet is embedded rather than linked, it remains unchanged as you move through the records on the Access form, and it won't change if you later make changes to the original Excel worksheet. This is appropriate if you want a worksheet representing data at a certain point, such as the end of a quarter.

If you need an Excel worksheet that always reflects current data, link it to the form instead. You can also insert a worksheet into a Bound Object Frame control bound to an OLE Object type field, as with the bound image discussed earlier in Exercise 5.2. This method allows you to view a different worksheet for each record of a table.

Microsoft Graph Objects

If you want to display a graph on an Access form, you don't need to insert an Excel chart—you can use the Microsoft Graph applet. Microsoft Graph is included with Office and allows you to create a graph from Access data on the fly.

Microsoft documentation and help use the terms "graph" and "chart" more or less interchangeably.

If you want to customize your graph, just double-click on it in Design view to open it in Microsoft Graph.

Adding a Chart Button to the Toolbox

The Access toolbox doesn't include the Chart tool by default. Here's how to add it to the toolbox:

1. Open a form in Design view.

2. Right-click on the Toolbox to open its context menu.

3. Choose Customize from the Toolbox context menu.

4. Select Toolbox in the Categories box.

5. Drag the Chart button from the Buttons box to the Toolbox.

6. Close the Customize dialog box.

Linking Objects

You can link an object to your form or report using the Insert Object dialog box—just click the Link option before selecting the file. You can also link objects using the Paste Special menu selection. Exercise 5.4 shows how to insert a linked Excel worksheet object into an OLE control on an Access form.

EXERCISE 5.4

Inserting a Linked Excel Worksheet on an Access Form

1. Open Excel and enter the following information in two columns:

   SalesRep: Clive Jackson, Wanda Deering, and Wilbur James

   Sales for 1997: $15,000, $17,500, and $16,000

2. Highlight the cells to copy, and press Ctrl+C (or select Edit ➢ Copy) to copy the cells to the Clipboard.

3. Switch to Access, and open a new form in Design view.

4. Select Edit ➢ Paste Special from the menu.

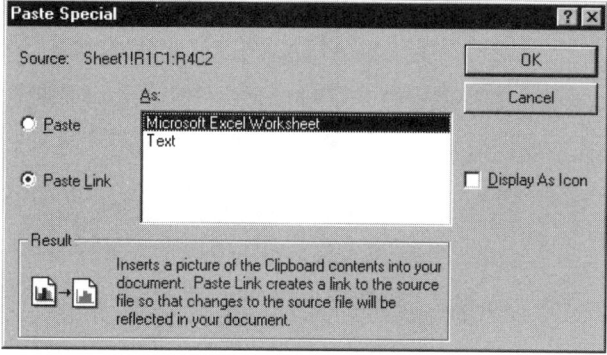

5. Select the Paste Link option button.

6. Select the Microsoft Excel worksheet object type.

7. Click the OK button.

8. Resize the linked worksheet as needed on the Access form.

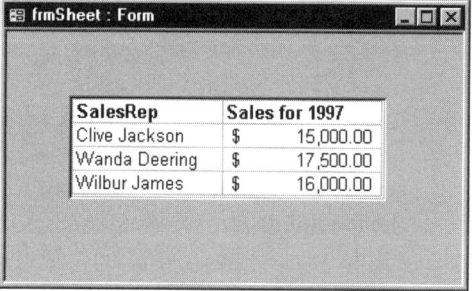

A linked worksheet looks just like an embedded worksheet, but the difference is that it will change if the data in the original worksheet is changed.

If you right-click the Linked Worksheet object just created, you will see that the pop-up menu has a special Linked Worksheet Object menu item. The Linked Worksheet Object menu has a submenu that allows you to edit the worksheet, open it in Excel, or convert it to a static image.

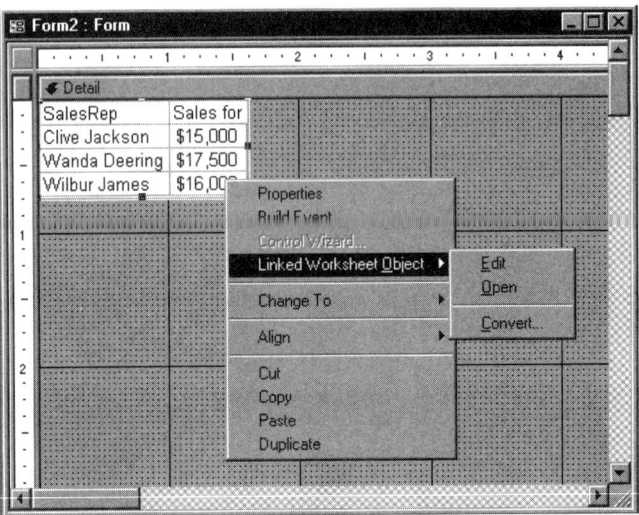

If you select Properties from the pop-up menu, you will discover that the object has been put in an Unbound Object frame (see Figure 5.3). A look at the Data tab of the properties sheet shows that the Source Doc property says "Book1," indicating an unsaved worksheet, since you created the Excel worksheet on the fly (if you had used a previously created worksheet, you would see its name in this property). The Source Item property on the same tab shows the sheet name and range of the linked cells.

Automatic vs. Manual Updating of Linked Objects

There are two different ways that your linked object can be updated with data from the original file: automatically and manually. When you use automatic updating, the file is updated each time the form is loaded. With manual updating, the object is updated only when you specifically ask that it be. Normally, leaving the control's Update Options property set to the default setting of Automatic is the right thing to do. This setting ensures that when the form is displayed, the data in it matches the data in the current version of the file. However, in some cases you may want to set the Update Options property to Manual. If a file is very large, setting the Update Options property to

FIGURE 5.3

The properties sheet
for a linked Excel
worksheet

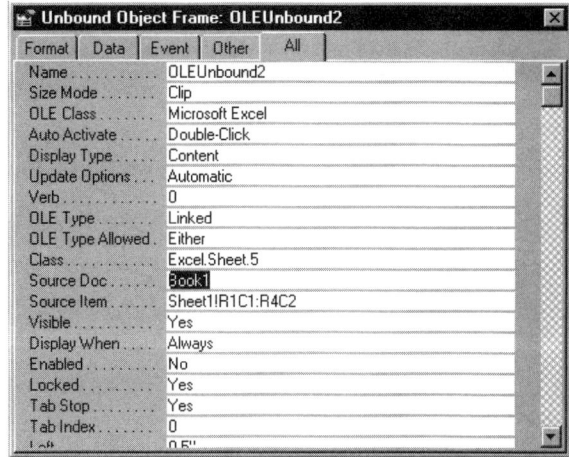

Manual can save time when opening a form; or if the source data doesn't change often, you may not want to update your form every time it is loaded.

In addition to changing the Update Options property on the form, you can change an object from automatic to manual updating, by following the steps in Exercise 5.5.

EXERCISE 5.5

Changing a Linked OLE Object from Automatic to Manual Updating

1. Select the linked object.

2. Select Edit ➤ OLE/DDE Links on the Access menu.

3. Select the link to update.

4. Select the Manual Update option button.

5. Click on the Close button to close the dialog box.

Once you've set an OLE Frame's Updating property to Manual, you'll have to open the OLE/DDE Links dialog box and click the Update Now button to update the object, as shown in Figure 5.4.

FIGURE 5.4

Using the OLE/DDE
Links dialog box

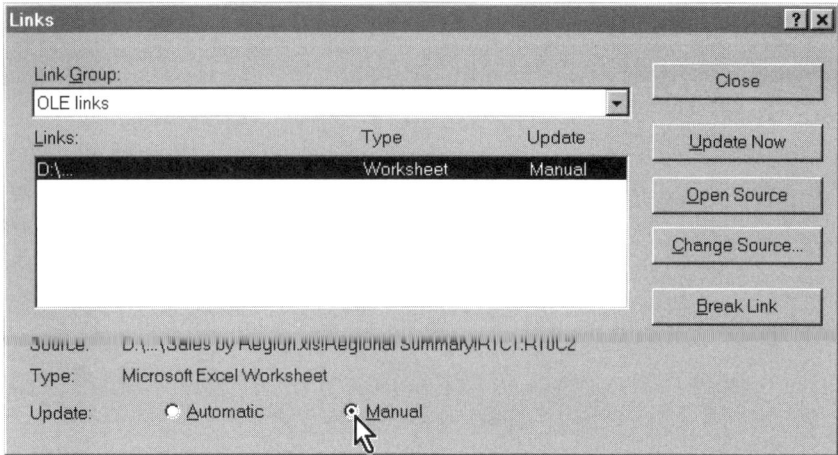

Sometimes you need to make sure that users can't modify the data in an embedded or linked OLE object. Setting the control's Locked property to Yes or its Enabled property to No will keep users from modifying the object's data in Form view. But that's only part of the answer: you'll also have to set security to keep users from switching to Design view and modifying those properties.

Another alternative is to convert an OLE control to an Image control, as in Exercise 5.6 below. This operation converts the OLE object into a static image that can't be modified by the user.

EXERCISE 5.6

Changing an OLE Control to an Image Control

To ensure that the data can't be modified, convert an OLE control into an Image control by following these steps:

1. Open the form with the embedded spreadsheet from Exercise 5.4.

2. Right-click on the control in Design view to open its context menu.

3. Select the Change To command.

4. Select Image Control from the fly-out menu.

As an Image control, a chart, worksheet, or other document can't be opened or changed.

You might think that you could change an embedded OLE control to a linked control, or vice versa, simply by selecting another choice for the control's OLE Type property. This property has a drop-down list offering a choice of Linked, Embedded, or None—but if you select any choice other than Image, you will get an error message telling you that the property is read-only.

Using OLE Automation in Visual Basic for Applications Code

VBA offers a way to integrate Access with other Office applications by using OLE Automation. Earlier in this chapter you learned how to embed or link OLE objects in your Access forms and reports. By writing OLE Automation code with VBA you can control OLE server applications from Access. Other applications that host VBA can also use OLE Automation code to control Access.

OLE Servers and Controllers

In order to support OLE Automation, an application must be an *OLE controller* or an *OLE server* (or it may be both). Excel 95, for example, is both an OLE server and a controller, while Word is only an OLE server.

An OLE server is an application that makes its component objects available for use by another application. An OLE controller is an application that can control an OLE server application. An OLE controller manipulates the component objects exposed by the server to extract data from the server application or, more generally, to use the server for the controller's own purposes. In Microsoft terminology, a server application is said to "expose its objects" to the controller application.

OLE controllers are sometimes referred to as OLE clients or OLE containers.

Office Applications: Which Are OLE Controllers, Which Are Servers?

With each version of Microsoft Office, more of the Office applications become OLE servers or controllers. As usual, Excel led the way by being the first Office application to become both a server and controller (that happened in Office 4.3). With Office 95, both Excel and Access are OLE servers and controllers, but Word lags behind. Word 95 is only an OLE server (and a very limited one at that). (With the release of Office 97, Word has become an OLE server at last.) Tables 5.1 and 5.2 show the OLE status of the two major Office applications for Office 4.3 and Office 95.

T A B L E 5.1 Office 4.3 OLE Status	Application	OLE Controller	OLE Server
	Access 2.0	✓	
	Word 6.0		✓
	Excel 5.0	✓	✓

T A B L E 5.2 Office 95 OLE Status	Application	OLE Controller	OLE Server
	Access 95	✓	✓
	Word 95		✓
	Excel 95	✓	✓

Object Models

Each OLE server application has an *object model*. An object model is a hierarchy of objects that includes all the component objects of the application—or at least the ones that are available for an OLE controller application to use.

Not all of the functionality of an application may be exposed as OLE objects. Word, in particular, has an extremely limited object model (it only exposes one object, representing WordBasic). The Access exposed object model has more objects than Word's but is limited compared to the model available from within Access. From within Access, for instance, you can use the Section object of a report. In the exposed object model, the Section object is missing.

Adding an OLE Server

In order to make use of a server application's objects, you need to check the selection representing the server in the application's References list. This makes the server's *type library* (sometimes called an *object library*) available to Access. A server's type library contains all the information Access needs about the objects that the server exposes for use.

To set up a reference to another application's object library, follow these steps:

1. Open a module window (either code behind forms or a code module).

2. Select Tools ➤ References.

3. Scroll the Available References list until you see the name of the application whose objects you want to use.

4. Click on the application's selection to put a check mark beside it.

5. Close the References dialog box by clicking the OK button.

Now you will be able to reference the objects in this application's object model in your Access VBA code. See Exercise 5.7 for an example of creating and using a reference to a type library.

Access provides a tool called the Object Browser (see Figure 5.5) for reviewing all the objects available to your application. If you press the F2 key from within any module, the Object Browser will appear. You can use the Libraries/Databases drop-down list box at the top of the form to see which servers are available. If you select a server application from the list, the bottom two windows will show you the objects that make up the server's object model along with the methods and properties that each object supports. Figure 5.5 shows Excel objects in the Object Browser.

Exercise 5.7 steps you through setting a reference to the Excel type library and then using the reference in VBA code.

F I G U R E 5.5

The Object Browser
showing Excel objects

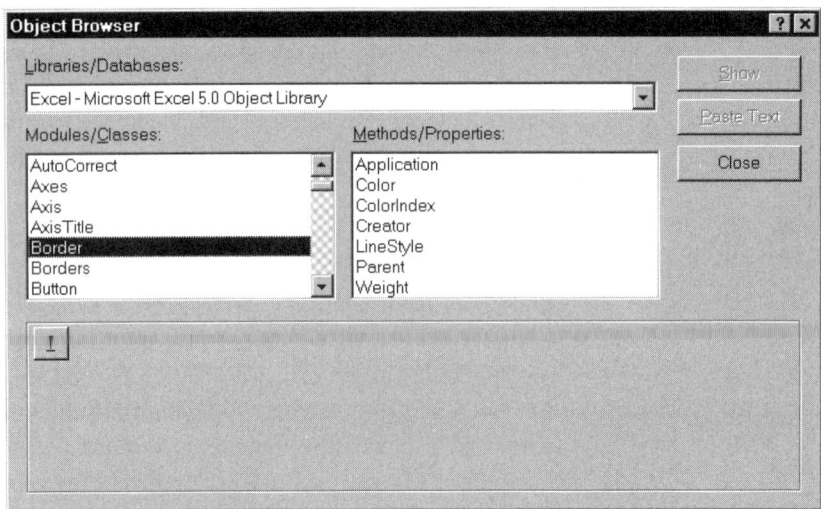

EXERCISE 5.7

Creating a Reference to the Excel Object Library

In this exercise, you'll set a reference to the Excel object library and then create a subroutine to start Excel from Access.

1. Start Access and click on the Modules tab. Click on the New button to start a new module.

2. Select Tools ➤ References to open the References dialog box. Scroll down the Available References list until you see the Microsoft Excel 5.0 object library selection and click on it to place a check in its checkbox.

3. Close the References dialog box by clicking on the OK button.

4. Back in the module window, add the procedure listed below to the module:

```
Sub TestExcel
    Dim xcl as Excel.Application
    Set xcl = New Excel.Application
    xcl.Visible = True
End Sub
```

EXERCISE 5.7 (CONTINUED)

5. In the Immediate Window, type **TestExcel**.

6. Press ↵ to run the TestExcel subroutine. Excel will start up.

7. Switch to Excel and select File ➤ Exit to close the application.

You've now successfully added an OLE Server's objects to the collection of objects available to your program (and started the object up, too).

Since object models aren't upgraded as frequently as applications, the version number of a type library may lag behind the current version of an application. For example, the Excel 5.0 type library matches the Excel 7.0 application.

Using Access as an OLE Controller

Microsoft ✔ *Exam* *Objective* | **Control other applications by using OLE Automation.**

Since Access 95 is now an OLE controller, you can use the power of VBA within Access to take advantage of other applications. You can, for instance, use the superior document formatting properties of Word, or exploit Excel's more extensive analytical and charting capabilities.

Starting an OLE Server

Before using a server object you must create an object variable that will point to, or reference, the server. Creating the object variable is done with the Dim statement, as with any other kind of variable. To get a reference that can be passed to the object variable you can use the New keyword or either the GetObject or CreateObject function.

The New keyword and the two functions all return a reference that points to a server object. That reference can be stored in an object variable which can then be used to access the objects within the server. Once you have an object variable that references the server object, you work with the server using the methods and properties of the various objects it contains. Unlike OLE Controls, though, OLE Automation servers cannot trigger events.

New and CreateObject

Both New and CreateObject do much the same thing: they start a new copy of the requested OLE server and return an object variable that references the object. They both use a class name looked up in the Windows Registry. Once the class name is found, both New and CreateObject use the information in the Registry to determine what program to start to create a new instance of the server.

WARNING   If the Registry entry for an OLE server identifies it as a single-use server, then New and CreateObject won't start a new instance of the server if there's already a copy of the server running. The object variable that is returned by New and CreateObject will, instead, point to the instance of the server that is already running.

However, New and CreateObject do their jobs in slightly different ways. CreateObject does not require you to select the server in the References list. Instead, CreateObject expects the server's class name to be passed to it as a string, like this:

```
Set xcl = CreateObject("Excel.Application")
```

Using the New syntax requires that the class name of the server object (such as Excel.Application) be included in the VBA language. This only happens when you have checked the Server name in the References list. Once you've selected the server in the References list, all of the objects in the server's type library can be used in VBA. Once Excel is checked, for instance, you can use this code:

```
Dim xcl as Excel.Application
Set xcl = New Excel.Application
```

You can use CreateObject both with and without the server selected in the References list. This code, when used with Excel selected in the References list, is perfectly acceptable:

```
Dim xcl as Excel.Application
Set xcl = CreateObject("Excel.Application")
```

Which to Use?

The New keyword is used more frequently than the CreateObject function for two reasons:

- **Performance:** There is a slight performance hit when using Create-Object instead of New. The CreateObject function accepts a string argument and uses that argument at run-time to look up information about the object in the Windows Registry. The New function performs most of that look-up operation at compile time, reducing the number of activities performed at run-time. It's unlikely, though, that you would be able to detect the slight difference in the speed of your program.

- **Usage:** The New keyword can be used in contexts where CreateObject cannot. You can use the New keyword to load a form, for instance:

```
Dim frm as Form
Set frm = New Form_CustomerUpdate
Frm.Visible = True
```

Some developers find that New is more generally useful than CreateObject and use it more often.

CreateObject can do one thing that New can't: you can use CreateObject to start a server that is selected at run-time. This code, for instance, puts an InputBox on the screen for the user to enter the class name for a server to start:

```
Dim obj as Object
Set obj = CreateObject(InputBox("Enter a class name"))
```

Early and Late Binding

When you start your OLE Automation server, you must consider how you will be declaring the object variables that reference it.

You can declare an object variable to reference a specific object, as you did in the exercise that opened the Excel spreadsheet:

```
Dim xcl as Excel.Application
```

You can also declare an object variable to reference any object, regardless of type, as in the last CreateObject example:

```
Dim obj as Object
```

When an object variable is declared as Object, at design time (that is, while working in the Module window) VBA isn't capable of determining what methods and properties are appropriate to the object. This means that when you are compiling a module in the module window, some errors won't be caught. Only at run-time, when the variable is actually pointed at the object, will VBA be able to check whether the methods and properties that you use in your program are valid for the object, and catch any errors in your code. In addition, VBA must do additional checking at run-time to validate the methods and properties used in your program. This approach is called *late binding* because the variable is bound to the object at the last possible moment—just before the variable is used.

When an object is declared as a specific type (such as Excel.Application), VBA can check the methods and properties used in your code at design time. In addition, VBA has to do less error checking at run-time because those checks were done at design time. This results in fewer errors and faster run-times when the program goes into production. This approach is called *early binding* because the variable is bound to the object as early as possible—while the code is being written.

Early binding is only possible if the object has a type library and you have selected the object in the References list. Late binding is only desirable if one object variable may be referencing several different objects in the course of the program.

GetObject

The GetObject function has several features that New and CreateObject don't. Like CreateObject and New, GetObject is used to get a reference to a server object. Unlike CreateObject or New, GetObject's default behavior is to get a reference for an already running copy of the server. You can set an object variable to reference an already running copy of Excel with this code:

```
Set xcl = GetObject(,"Excel.Application")
```

Notice that the server's class name is the second parameter passed to the function.

 **WARNING**   If several copies of the server are running, GetObject will point to one at random.

As its first parameter, GetObject accepts the name of a file. Using this parameter causes the appropriate OLE server for the file to be started and the file to be loaded by the server. (Windows uses the file's extension to determine which OLE server to start.) This code, for instance, starts Microsoft Word because the requested file ends in DOC, the standard Word file extension:

```
Set xcl = GetObject("c:\MyWorkBook.DOC")
```

If you specify a file name that's a zero length string (""), then GetObject functions just like CreateObject. These two lines of code are identical:

```
Set xcl = GetObject("","Excel.Application")
Set xcl = CreateObject("Excel.Application")
```

You can also use GetObject to load the file and reference a specific object in the file. To do that, you append to the file name an exclamation mark followed by the name of the object. This code opens WorkSheet2 in the Excel workbook MyWorkBook.XLS:

```
Set xcl = GetObject("c:\MyWorkBook.XLS!WorkSheet2")
```

You will get an error message if the file doesn't exist or the object doesn't exist in the file.

Closing an OLE Server

When you are finished with an OLE server you should shut it down to free up whatever resources it's using (memory, mostly).

Windows will destroy any object that has no object variables referencing it. Since an object variable declared inside a procedure will be destroyed when the procedure ends, any servers pointed to just by those variables will be destroyed at that time.

If you have been working on OLE code and suspect that you may have extra instances of an OLE server running, pop up the Windows Task List with Ctrl+Alt+Del and check for extra instances. If you find an extra instance, highlight it and delete it by clicking on the End Task button. Repeat as necessary until all the extra instances are closed.

You can also set a variable to the predefined keyword Nothing so that it is no longer pointing to an object. In this code the Word object will be destroyed on the last line of the routine:

```
Dim objWord as Object
Set objWord = CreateObject("Word.Basic")
Set objWord = Nothing
```

Not all object servers follow this convention: Word does, for instance, but Excel does not. Some objects may need to perform special activities before shutting down. If so, they will have a method that you should call to perform those activities. To shut down Excel, for instance, you must use Excel's Quit method to close all open worksheets and then close Excel. It's still a good idea to point the object variable to Nothing after that, though, just to make sure that all the resources used by the object are freed:

```
Dim xcl as Excel.Application
Set xcl = New Excel.Application
xcl.Quit
Set xcl = Nothing
```

Using Automation Servers

When you use Access as an OLE controller, you are controlling OLE servers such as Excel and Word. To use a server, you need to understand which objects it contains and what you can do with them.

Controlling Word

Word has a stunningly simple object model—it consists of a single object, WordBasic. Using the WordBasic object, you can run all the WordBasic commands and use them to create a new document or open an existing document, and then format the document in various ways.

How do you find out about the objects, methods, and properties of the OLE server that you want to use? The Object Browser can be helpful, but the documentation for the application in question is the best guide. The Word Help file, for instance, documents WordBasic commands (see the *WordBasic Reference* Help topic). Additionally, the *Using WordBasic* volume in the Word documentation set is very useful.

As a shortcut to writing VBA code to control Word, first turn on the Word macro recorder and create a Word macro to do what you want to do with the document. Open the new recorded macro in the macro window and use it as a prototype for writing your VBA code in Access. Since WordBasic is a different dialect of VB than VBA, you won't be able to just cut and paste the code into an Access module, but at least you'll know what commands you need to use.

WordBasic vs. VBA Code Syntax

When you write VBA code to manipulate Word via the WordBasic object, you need to use a different syntax for the more complex commands. VBA doesn't recognize the names of WordBasic command arguments (such as .DateTimePic and .InsertAsField in this example), so you have to strip out the named arguments, leaving just the actual text or numeric component, if any. Because you can't use WordBasic named arguments in VBA code, you need to preserve all the commas needed to separate arguments, even when you omit one or more arguments, as VBA only knows what argument you are referencing by its position. These samples illustrate a Word command recorded in Word as a WordBasic macro, and its VBA equivalent, as used in Access VBA code.

The WordBasic macro is as follows:

```
InsertDateTime .DateTimePic = "MMMM d, yyyy",
    .InsertAsField = 0
```

Here's how its Access VBA equivalent looks:

```
objWord.InsertDateTime "MMMM d, yyyy", 0
```

Exercise 5.8 shows how to manipulate Word from Access, using OLE Automation.

EXERCISE 5.8

Creating a New Document from a Word Template

This exercise creates a new document based on a specific Word template, maximizes it, and then runs a Word macro.

1. Create a new module and enter this routine:

```
Private Sub TechReport()

    Dim objWord As Object

    Set objWord = CreateObject("Word.Basic")

    objWord.FileNew "Technical Report"
```

```
        objWord.AppMaximize
        objWord.ToolsMacro "SelectComponents", True


    End Sub
```

2. In the Debug Window enter **TechReport** and press ↵.

3. Word starts, creates a new document, runs the specified macro, and shuts down.

4. Start Word and repeat step 2.

5. Word starts, creates a new document, runs the specified macro, and doesn't shut down.

Stopping and Starting Word

In the first few steps of the previous exercise, Word shut down when its object variable was destroyed at the end of the routine. In most cases, this is not a problem—for example, if you just want to print a Word document.

If you want to leave Word open for editing when the function ends, make sure you have an instance of Word open before you use CreateObject. Since Word is flagged as a single-instance object, CreateObject returns a variable referencing the running copy. As a result, your new Word document will appear as a document window in the existing instance of Word. Then, when your object variable goes out of scope, Word will stay open.

Word stays open because the original reference to it, the one that existed before you ran your program, is still available. If you don't already have Word open, you can use VBA's Shell function to start Word before issuing your CreateObject command. See Exercise 5.9 for an example of working with Word from Access using OLE Automation.

The final code sample in this section outputs a list of addressees, selected in an Access form, to a text file. That text file is then used as the data source for a Word mail-merge document. The code assumes that you have already created a Word mail-merge document template called Merge Letter.dot, and selected the MergeList.txt file as its data source.

Using Word from Access

In this exercise you'll create a simple Word template to generate a letter. Follow these steps:

1. Create an AutoForm based on the Employees table in the Northwind Database (you'll find the table in the My Documents folder where it was installed by Access). Switch to Code view. Select Tools ➤ References, and then check the Word 95 Objects for Access selection. Close the References dialog box.

2. Add a command button to the Detail section of the form and display its properties list. Name the button **cmdLetter**. Set its Caption property to **Create Letter**.

3. Create the following procedure for the button's Click event:

```
Private Sub cmdLetter_Click()

    Dim objWord As Object
    Dim strFirstName As String
    Dim strLastName As String

    Set objWord = CreateObject("Word.Basic")
    strLastName = Me![txtLastName]
    strFirstName = Me![txtFirstName]
    objWord.FileNew "Simple Letter"
    objWord.AppMaximize
    objWord.EditGoTo "LetterDate"
    objWord.InsertDateTime "MMMM d, yyyy", 0
    objWord.EditGoTo "FirstName"
    objWord.Insert strFirstName
    objWord.EditGoTo "LastName"
    objWord.Insert strLastName

End Sub
```

4. Name the FirstName text box **txtFirstName**. Name the LastName text box **txtLastName**. Save the form.

5. Start Word and open a new blank document. Select Edit ➢ Bookmark to create a new Bookmark. Enter **LetterDate** as the name of the Book-mark and click on the Add button. Press ↵ twice to leave a blank line after the date and before the letter's salutation.

6. Enter **Dear** followed by a space to begin your letter. Select Edit ➢ Bookmark to display the Bookmark dialog box. Enter **FirstName** as the Bookmark name and click the Add button. Type a space and then create a LastName Bookmark.

7. Press ↵ twice to start a new line and type the following text:

   Just a note to tell you how much we appreciate your hard work on the project.

8. Select File ➢ Save As. Enter **Simple Letter** as the file name. Select Document Template as the type, and select the default Templates folder as the path. Click the Save button.

9. Close the new template but leave Word open, and return to Access. Switch your form to Form view. Click the Create Letter button for one of the displayed records. A new Word document is created, and Access updates the bookmarks in your letter with data from the form.

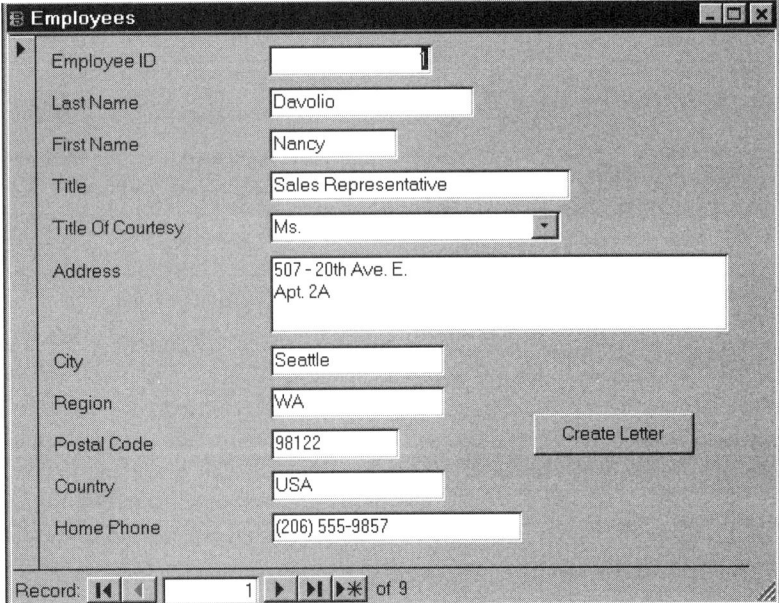

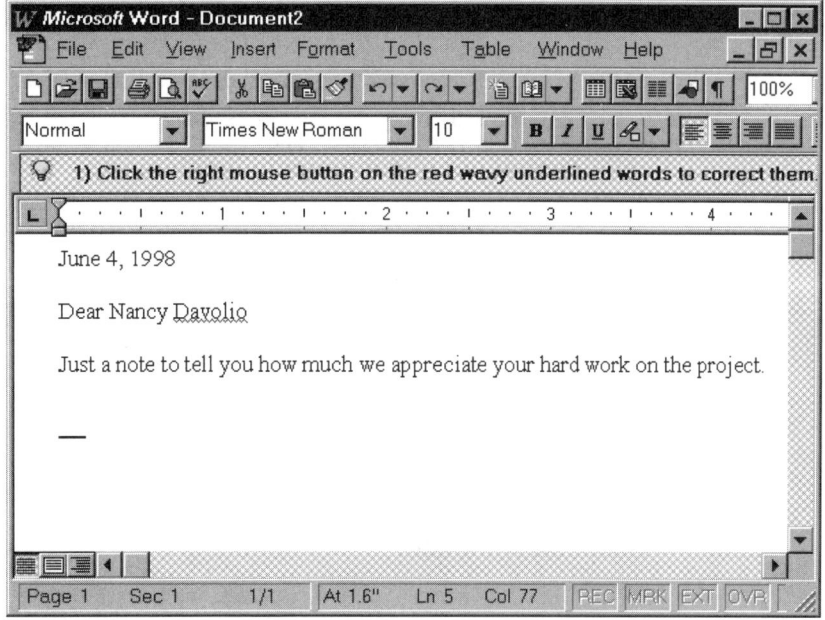

 You can output data from Access to a Word mail-merge document without using this technique. From Access you could use the Merge It command on the OfficeLinks drop-down list. From Word you could attach to an Access data source using the Mail Merge Helper. Both methods are memory intensive if you already have Access open because they open another instance of Access. The method in the code sample avoids this problem, and lets you do mail merges even in limited memory situations.

The procedure below outputs Access data to a text file, which is used as the data source for a Word mail-merge letter. The new Word letter is left open for editing.

```
Private Sub cmdMerge_Click()

    Dim objWord As Object
```

```
      Dim strFileName As String
      Dim strDocsDir As String

      strDocsDir = "D:\Documents\Examples\"
      strFileName = strDocsDir & "MergeList.txt"
      DoCmd.TransferText acExportMerge, , "tblMergeList",
      ➥ strFileName, True

      Set objWord = CreateObject("Word.Basic")
      objWord.FileNew "Merge Letter"
      objWord.EditGoTo "LetterDate"
      objWord.InsertDateTime "MMMM d, yyyy", 0
      objWord.AppMaximize
      objWord.EditGoTo "TextOfLetter"

   End Sub
```

Controlling Excel

You can export a table or query to an Excel worksheet with a single click by using the Analyze It with MS Excel command on the OfficeLinks menu drop-down list. The resulting worksheet will contain only raw data, with no title or formatting, so you must apply any formatting, titles, grouping, and totals manually.

By writing OLE Automation VBA code to create the worksheet, you can apply formatting using components of the Excel object model. The result will be a fully automated process that exports the Access data to Excel and produces a professional-looking spreadsheet as a result.

Excel has an extensive object model (over 130 objects), which allows you great flexibility for manipulating worksheets and charts from VBA code. The code that follows exports an Access query to a worksheet, then opens the new worksheet in Excel and formats it.

```
   Private Sub cmdExport_Click()

      Dim i As Integer
      Dim j As Integer
      Dim strWorksheet As String
      Dim strWorksheetPath As String
```

```
Dim strQueryName As String
Dim objExcel As Object
Dim objSheet As Excel.Worksheet
Dim objBooks As Excel.Workbooks
Dim objRange As Excel.Range
Dim objCell As Object
Dim strRange As String
Dim strStartAddress As String
Dim strFormula As String

strWorksheet = "Orders.xls"
strWorksheetPath = "D:\Documents\Examples\"
strWorksheetPath = strWorksheetPath & strWorksheet
strQueryName = "qryOrders"

'Delete existing worksheet (if there is one)
On Error Resume Next
Kill strWorksheetPath

'Export query data to a new worksheet
DoCmd.TransferSpreadsheet acExport, 5,
➥ tablename:=strQueryName, FileName:=strWorksheetPath,
➥ hasfieldnames:=True

'Open the newly created worksheet and insert title
material
Set objExcel = CreateObject("Excel.Application")
Set objExcel = GetObject(strWorksheetPath)
objExcel.Application.Visible = True
objExcel.Parent.Windows(1).Visible = True

With objExcel
    'Make entire worksheet Arial 9 pt font
    .Range("A:F").Font.Name = "Arial"
    .Range("A:F").Font.Size = 9
```

```
'Apply hairline borders to entire worksheet
.Range("A:F").Borders.LineStyle = xlContinuous
.Range("A:F").Borders.Weight = xlHairline
.Range("A:F").Borders.ColorIndex = xlAutomatic

'Set column widths
.Range("A:A").ColumnWidth = 7
.Range("B:D").ColumnWidth = 9
.Range("E:E").ColumnWidth = 14
.Range("F:F").ColumnWidth = 10

'Insert blank rows at top of worksheet
.Range("1:1").Insert Shift:=xlDown
.Range("1:1").Insert Shift:=xlDown
.Range("1:1").Insert Shift:=xlDown
.Range("1:1").Insert Shift:=xlDown

'Format column headings row
With .Range("5:5")
   .Font.Size = 10
   .Font.Bold = True
   .Borders(xlTop).Weight = xlMedium
   .Borders(xlBottom).Weight = xlMedium
   .Interior.ColorIndex = 15
   .Interior.Pattern = xlSolid
   .Interior.PatternColorIndex = xlAutomatic
   .RowHeight = 30
   .VerticalAlignment = xlBottom
   .HorizontalAlignment = xlCenter
   .WrapText = True
End With

'Insert and format title material
.Range("A1:F1").HorizontalAlignment = xlCenter
.Range("A1:F1").VerticalAlignment = xlBottom
.Range("A1:F1").WrapText = False
.Range("A1:F1").Orientation = 0
```

```
    .Range("A1:F1").Borders(xlLeft).LineStyle = xlNone
    .Range("A1:F1").Borders(xlTop).LineStyle = xlNone
    .Range("A1:F1").Borders(xlBottom).LineStyle = xlNone
    .Range("A1:F1").Borders(xlRight).LineStyle = xlNone
    .Range("A2:F2").HorizontalAlignment = xlCenter
    .Range("A2:F2").VerticalAlignment = xlBottom
    .Range("A2:F2").WrapText = False
    .Range("A2:F2").Orientation = 0
    .Range("A2:F2").Borders(xlLeft).LineStyle = xlNone
    .Range("A2:F2").Borders(xlTop).LineStyle = xlNone
    .Range("A2:F2").Borders(xlBottom).LineStyle = xlNone
    .Range("A2:F2").Borders(xlRight).LineStyle = xlNone
    .Range("A3:F3").HorizontalAlignment = xlCenter
    .Range("A3:F3").VerticalAlignment = xlBottom
    .Range("A3:F3").Orientation = 0
    .Range("A3:F3").Borders(xlLeft).LineStyle = xlNone
    .Range("A3:F3").Borders(xlTop).LineStyle = xlNone
    .Range("A3:F3").Borders(xlBottom).LineStyle = xlNone
    .Range("A3:F3").Borders(xlRight).LineStyle = xlNone
    .Range("A4:F4").Borders(xlLeft).LineStyle = xlNone
    .Range("A4:F4").Borders(xlTop).LineStyle = xlNone
    .Range("A4:F4").Borders(xlRight).LineStyle = xlNone

    'Enter column titles and format them
    .Range("A5").Value = "Order ID"
    .Range("B5").Value = "Order Date"
    .Range("C5").Value = "Required Date"
    .Range("D5").Value = "Shipped Date"
    .Range("E5").Value = "Shipped Via"
    .Range("D1:D4").Font.Size = 14
    .Range("D1:D4").Font.Bold = True
    .Range("D3").Value = "As of " & Date
    .Range("D2").Value = "Northwind Traders"
    .Range("D1").Value = "Orders"
End With

End Sub
```

In contrast with Word, you don't have to have Excel open before running OLE Automation code in order to keep it open after the code has finished running. As long as you don't issue Excel's Quit method, Excel will stay open.

The formatted worksheet is shown in Figure 5.6.

FIGURE 5.6

An Excel Worksheet formatted from Access

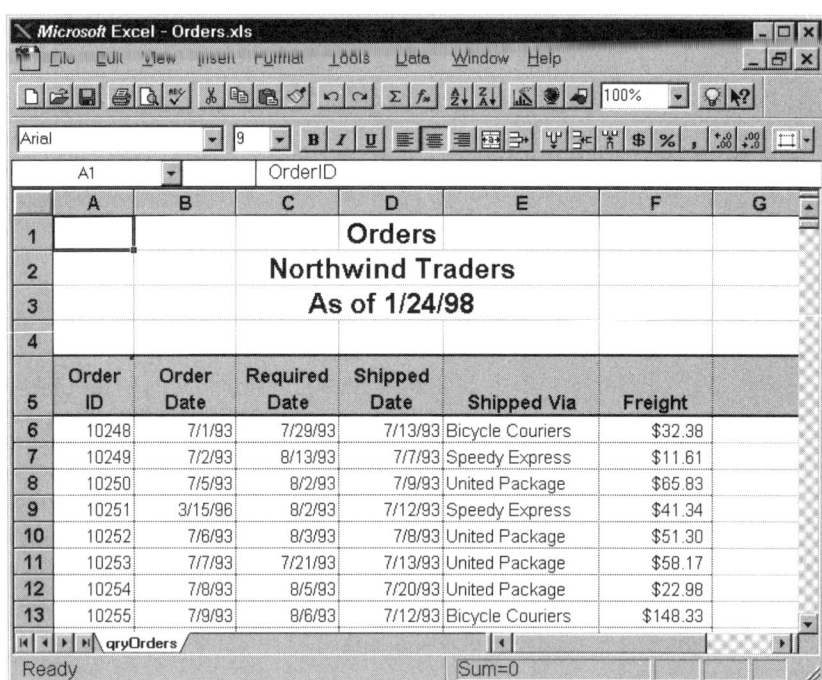

Using Other Office Applications to Control Access as an OLE Server

There are two object models you can use when working with Access databases. If you want to access the data stored in Access database files, use the Data Access Objects (DAO) object model. If you want to control Access itself, use the Access object model, which lets you work with Access-specific components like forms, reports, and macros.

Microsoft *Exam* *Objective*	**Control Microsoft Access from other applications by using OLE Automation.**

Controlling Access from Excel

In order to write Excel VBA code to control Access, you need to make sure that the Access 7.0 type library selection is checked under Tools ➤ References in Excel. If you intend to retrieve data from an Access database, you need to check the DAO 3.0 selection also. Exercise 5.10 illustrates using Access as an OLE server from Excel.

EXERCISE 5.10

Using Access as a Server

This exercise opens the Northwind sample database and displays one of its reports in print preview.

1. Open Excel and start a new module.

2. Enter the following code:

```
Public Function PrintAccessReport()

    Dim objAccess As Object
    Dim strDB As String

    strDB = "C:\Microsoft Office 95\Access\Samples" &
    ➥ & "\Northwind.mdb"
    Set objAccess = CreateObject("Access.Application")
    objAccess.OpenCurrentDatabase strDB
    objAccess.DoCmd.OpenReport ReportName:="Catalog",
    ➥ View:=acPreview
    objAccess.Visible = True

End Function
```

3. In the Immediate window, enter **PrintAccessReport** and press ↵.

4. After a few seconds, Access opens and the Catalog report from the Northwind database is displayed.

As you can see, the methods you use in working with Access from another application are very similar to the methods you use from within Access. You should, for instance, recognize the DoCmd.OpenReport command as the means for printing a report from VBA code in Access.

The one method that may be unfamiliar to you is the OpenCurrentDatabase method. Unlike CurrentDB or OpenDatabase, which provide access to the data in the files through DAO, OpenCurrentDatabase lets you work with the Access objects (forms, reports, and so on) stored in the database.

Summary

Access uses OLE in two different ways. First, Access allows you to add OLE objects into your forms and reports. By creating these compound documents you can extend Access's capabilities by borrowing functionality from some other applications.

Objects can be either linked or embedded. A linked object is a file that exists outside of the Access MDB file. It is accessible to other programs and doesn't add to the size of the Access database. An embedded object is actually placed inside the Access MDB file.

Linked objects can be set to update automatically or manually. When a linked object is updated automatically the file is reloaded each time the form or report it is part of is displayed. If you set the link to manual, the object is updated only when you request it.

You can write OLE Automation code in VBA. OLE Automation controllers can take control of OLE Automation servers and use the objects that make up the servers. Access is both an OLE server and an OLE controller. In this chapter you've seen Access control Word and Excel, and you've seen how Excel can be used to control Access.

When you work with OLE Automation you can use the New keyword or the CreateObject and GetObject functions to get references to object servers. These references are stored in object variables that can be declared generically (late binding) or specifically (early binding). Early binding allows more work to be done by VBA at design time by taking information from the server's type library (which is identified through the References list).

Unless a server is identified as a single-use server, New and CreateObject use a server's class name to start the server and get a reference to a new instance of the object. GetObject, which can accept either a class name or a file name, returns a reference to an already running copy of the server (unless you set its first parameter to "", in which case GetObject functions just like CreateObject).

Review Questions

1. Access users have been opening a linked Excel worksheet and making changes in it, which has led to problems with Excel users who need to maintain control over the data. You want to ensure that Access users can't edit the worksheet. Which of the following is the best method?

   A. Change the control to an Image control by right-clicking it and selecting Change to Image Control from the context menu.

   B. Set the control's Enabled property to False.

   C. Set the control's Locked property to True.

   D. Change the control's OLE Type property to Image.

2. You have a linked OLE worksheet on a form, and you want to freeze it at a certain point in time, so it won't change when the original Excel worksheet is updated. Which of the following methods is the best way to do this?

   A. Change the control's OLE Type property to Embedded.

   B. Delete the control, then insert the object again, this time leaving the Linked check box in the Insert Object dialog box unselected.

   C. You can't change a linked control into an embedded control.

   D. Click the control, select Edit ➤ OLE/DDE Links on the Access menu, then click the Manual Update option button with the link highlighted.

3. You have a table of name and address data in Access, which you need to merge to a Word mail-merge letter from time to time. The computer you are working on has only 12MB of memory. Which of the following methods is the best way to implement this functionality?

   A. Write WordBasic code using the CreateObject function to get the data from Access, using the DAO object model.

   B. Use the Word Mail Merge Helper to link to the Access table.

   C. Write an Access function to export the table to Word Mail Merge format using the TransferText method, and use the resulting text data table as the Word mail-merge document's data source. Run the function from Access when you need to do the mail merge.

   D. Use the Merge It command on the OfficeLinks drop-down list on the Access menu to merge the data to the Word mail-merge letter.

4. You have imported an Excel worksheet into Access, and you have prepared several grouped reports from the data. You would like to be able to print these reports from a command button in Excel. What is the best way to do this?

A. Write Excel VBA code to create an instance of Access using the CreateObject function, and use the OpenReport method of the DoCmd object in the Access object model to print the reports.

B. Write Excel VBA code to create an instance of Access using the CreateObject function, and use the OpenReport method of the DoCmd object in the DAO object model to print the reports.

C. Select the Print from Access command from the OfficeLinks drop-down list on the Excel menu.

D. You can't print an Access report from Excel.

5. Users complain that every time they open a form with a linked Excel chart, there is a long delay while the chart is updated. The chart's data really doesn't need to be updated more than once a month or so. How can you modify the control to prevent these long delays while allowing users to update the chart when needed?

A. Change the linked OLE object control into an Image control by right-clicking it and then selecting Change To Image Control from the context menu.

B. Change the linked OLE object control into an embedded control by changing its OLE Type property to Embedded.

C. Change the linked OLE object control's Update type to Manual by clicking the control, selecting Edit ➢ OLE/DDE Links on the Access menu, and then clicking the Manual Update option button with the link highlighted.

D. Change the Update Type property in the control's properties sheet from Automatic to Manual.

6. Let's say that you write code to create a Word document and insert text into it, and then run the code. But after the code stops, the new Word document is not open. How can you keep the Word document open after the code has run?

A. Put `objWord.Preserve` at the end of the code.

B. Put a Stop command at the end of the code.

C. There is no way to keep a document created by the CreateObject function open after the code finishes running.

D. Open Word before running the code.

7. You should use the _____ function when you want to set a reference to an existing document.

A. GetObject

B. UseObject

C. CreateObject

D. GetFile

8. To free memory used by an Excel OLE Automation session, use the _____ command:

A. objExcel.Quit

B. objExcel.Close

C. objExcel.Exit

D. Set objExcel = Nothing

9. Which of the following are correct ways to declare and set an Excel object (select two)?

A. Dim xcl As Excel.Application
Set xcl = New Excel.Application

B. Dim xcl As New Excel.Application

C. Dim xcl As Object
Set xcl = CreateOject("Excel.Application")

D. Dim xcl As Object
Set xcl = New Excel.Application

10. To create a server entered by the user at run-time, use
_____.

A. GetObject

B. The New keyword

C. CreateObject

D. You can't create a server in this manner.

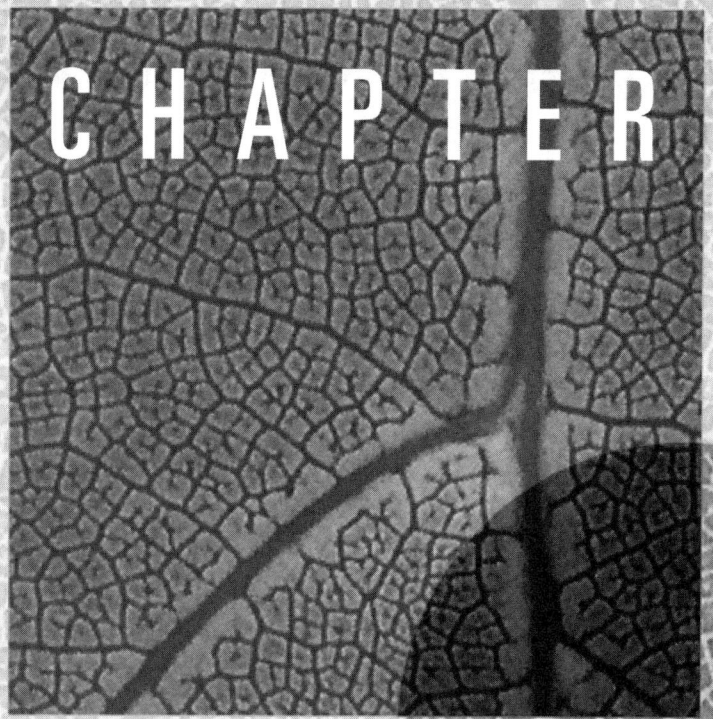

CHAPTER

6

Data Access Objects

- Use Data Access Objects and Microsoft Access objects.

- Given a scenario, determine when to use data access objects.

- Differentiate between objects and collections.

- Select appropriate methods and property settings for use with specified objects.

- Write statements that access and modify database objects.

- Implement transaction processing in a Workspace object.

While SQL is the universal data access language, Access provides a way for you to work with your data using objects. In this chapter and the next, you'll see how to use the methods and properties of the Jet database engine objects to create data structures and manipulate your data.

In this chapter, you will learn:

- What the benefits are in using Data Access Objects.

- How to use SQL to change tables you've created using the Access Table Designer.

- What the DAO object model is and how it works.

- How to create objects in DAO and how to get them to work together.

- How to combine your knowledge of SQL with DAO in an efficient way.

- To tell the difference between Jet and Access and understand how the two work together.

Data through Objects

Microsoft ✓ **Exam** **Objective**

Use data access objects and Microsoft Access objects.

While Access provides you with the ability to use SQL commands to retrieve and manipulate your data, Access also allows you to use objects to work with your data. Though SQL is very powerful and concise, using objects to work with data gives you the benefit of handling data using the methods and properties paradigm that is an integral part of VBA.

Microsoft provides *Data Access Objects (DAO)* as an object-oriented set of tools for manipulating data. DAO lets you create and work with objects that closely model all aspects of a Jet database: tables, queries, users, and so on. Each of these objects has a set of methods and properties that allow you full access to the capabilities of the Jet engine.

WARNING Not every database that Jet can access supports all of the properties and methods of every DAO object, so be careful when working with xBase, Paradox, ODBC, or the other databases that Jet supports.

In this chapter you'll be introduced to the DAO object model and see how it corresponds to the database that your data is stored in. While SQL can be used to create tables and indexes, there are a number of table and index properties that are only available through DAO. You'll learn how to create and manipulate the database itself and the tables that comprise it using the methods and properties of the DAO objects.

DAO and SQL

DAO and SQL work together very well. Several DAO methods let you submit SQL commands, allowing you to do two things:

- Submit SQL update statements to add, change, or delete records

- Use SQL commands to retrieve sets of records which you can then process on a record-by-record basis

In addition, DAO lets you use pre-defined queries containing SQL commands to update your database or retrieve sets of records individually.

The DAO Model

Microsoft ✓ ***Exam*** ***Objective***   **Given a scenario, determine when to use data access objects.**

The DAO object model is a hierarchical collection of objects that model a Jet database. In the same way that Access provides Form objects that can contain TextBox or ListBox objects, DAO gives you database objects that can contain TableDefs and QueryDefs (tables and queries). Figure 6. 1 shows the major components of the DAO object model.

The DAO Database object is an example of a DAO object. The Database object has all of the properties that you might associate with a database (name, version of Access that created it, etc.). The database object has an OpenRecordset method that enables you to retrieve records stored in the database.

The DAO model also contains a Recordset object that represents a set of records retrieved from the database. A Recordset's properties include the data in the current record and the number of records in the set, among others. Recordset methods include the ability to make the next record in the set the current record.

See Chapter 7 for more information on the Recordset object and its uses.

DAO has a hierarchical structure, which means that you can't create DAO objects directly by using either the VBA keyword "New" or the CreateObject method. Two of the DAO objects are available as soon as you start your application (the DBEngine object and a Workspace object). All other objects are created by using methods of these objects, or objects you create from them. For instance, to create a Database object, you must use the OpenDatabase method of the Workspace object. To create a Recordset object you must use the OpenRecordset method of either the Database object or a QueryDef object.

FIGURE 6.1

The DAO object model

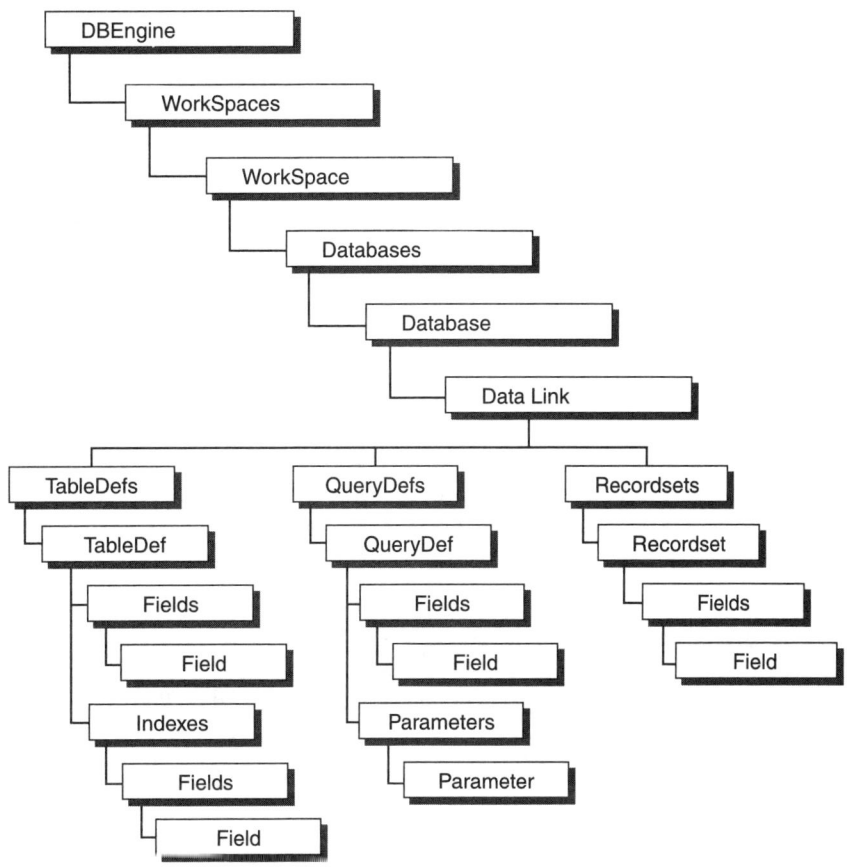

You can inspect the components of the DAO object model in the Access Object Browser by following the steps in Exercise 6.1.

Inspecting the DAO Object Model's Components

1. Open a module window.

2. Select Tools ➢ References from the menu.

3. Check the Microsoft DAO 3.0 Object Library selection, if it is not already checked.

4. Press F2 to open the Object Browser.

5. Select the DAO selection in the Libraries/Databases list box.

6. The DAO objects are displayed in the Modules/Classes list box on the left; the Methods/Properties list box on the right displays the methods and properties of the object selected in the Modules/Classes list box.

7. Select DBEngine in the Modules/Classes list box; the properties and methods of the DBEngine object are displayed in the Methods/Properties list box.

You can paste the correct syntax for a DAO method or property directly from the Object Browser into your code, as shown in Figure 6.2, by selecting the method or property, and clicking the Paste Text button.

F I G U R E 6.2

Pasting a property from the Object Browser into code

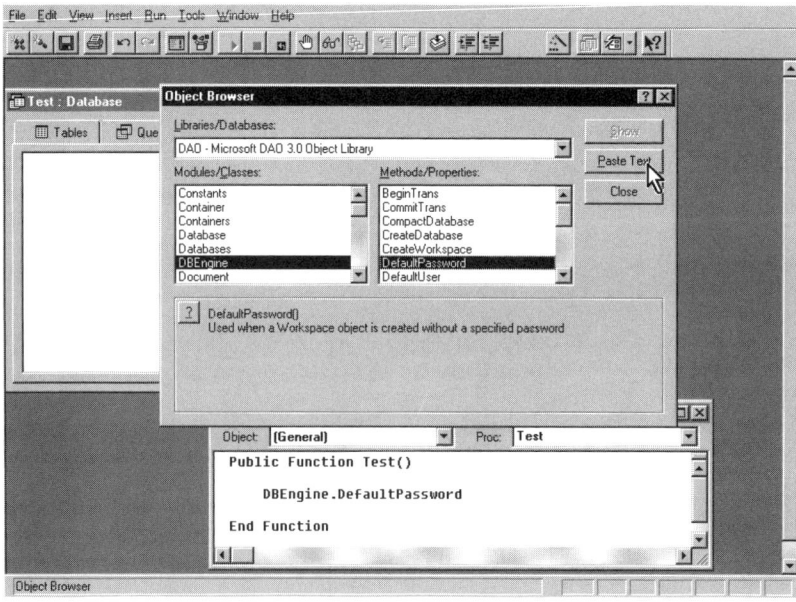

Collections

Microsoft Exam Objective	Differentiate between objects and collections.

Not everything in the DAO model is an object. Some of the elements in the DAO model are *collections*, or sets of objects. A Recordset object, for instance, has a Fields collection which consists of all the Field objects that make up the record. In theory, to work with a single Field object from the Fields collection, you would use the Item method of the Fields collection. If you had created a Recordset object called rst that held records from the Customer database, you could refer to the LastName field like this:

```
rst.Fields.Item("LastName")
```

Since the LastName field is the first field in the record, it is also the first field in the Fields collection. To retrieve the first field in the Fields collection you could refer to the field by its index number 0, like this:

```
rst.Fields.Item(0)
```

However, it would be an unusual program that actually used this syntax. Referencing individual members of collections by index number is risky, as the same number can refer to different members after additions or deletions to the collection. The index number can be useful if you want to iterate through all the members of a collection. The function below iterates through the members of the DBEngine object's Properties collection, listing the name of each property in the Immediate Window:

```
Public Function ListProps()
    Dim i As Integer
    Dim strProps As String
    For i = 0 To DBEngine.Properties.Count - 1
        strProps = "DBEngine Property #" & i & ": " &
        ➥ DBEngine.Properties.Item(i).Name
        Debug.Print strProps
    Next i
End Function
```

Since the Item method is the default method for any collection, if you don't mention what method you are using, DAO will assume that you are using the Item method. Most programmers would retrieve the LastName field like this:

```
rst.Fields("LastName")
rst.Fields(0)
```

Similarly, the Fields collection is the default item for a Recordset object. Most programmers also skip mentioning the Fields collection when working with recordsets and write the two previous lines as follows:

```
rst("LastName")
rst(0)
```

You can also use the ! operator (called the *bang operator*) to indicate a member of a collection, as in the third syntax variant below, which is very commonly used:

```
rst!LastName
```

If the field name contains blanks (such as LastName) then you must enclose the field name in brackets if you are using the ! operator:

```
rst![LastName]
```

DAO contains several collections other than the Fields collection. In order to allow you to work with the structure of the tables in the database, the Database object includes the TableDefs collection. The TableDefs collection has a TableDef object for every table in the database. Each TableDef object allows you to work with the structure of the table it represents. Each TableDef object has a Fields collection of all of the fields that make up the table's structure, so that you can work with the fields that make up a table. Just as you use the Recordset object and its Fields collection to work with the data in the table, you use the TableDef and its Fields collection to work with the structure of the table.

Adding a new item to a collection is a three-step process, as shown in Figure 6.3. In the first step you select or create the object that you want to add the object to. To create a TableDef object, you would use the Create-TableDef method of the Database object:

```
Set tdf = dbs.CreateTableDef("Customer")
```

F I G U R E 6.3

Adding a field to a
TableDef

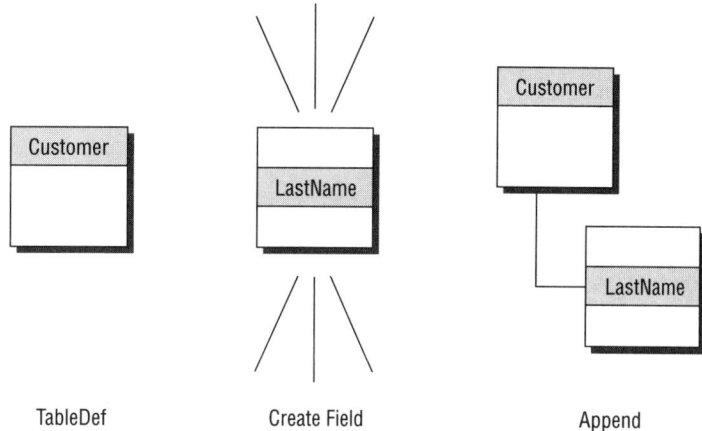

TableDef   Create Field   Append

In the second step you use a method of the object that owns the collection
to create a new object. For instance, to add a new field to a TableDef, you
would use the TableDef's CreateField method to create a new Field object.
The CreateField method requires that you specify the field's name and
data type:

```
Set fld = tdf.CreateField("NumberOfVisits", dbInteger)
```

In the third step, the new object is added to the collection with the Append
method of the collection itself:

```
tdf.Fields.Append fld
```

Again, the Fields collection is the default collection of the TableDef
object, so most programmers would write:

```
tdf.Append fld
```

DBEngine, Workspaces, and Databases

Now that we've introduced the basic concepts of the DAO model, it's
time to look at the objects that make up the model itself.

Microsoft
✓ *Exam*
Objective

Select appropriate methods and property settings for use with specified objects.

Microsoft
✓ *Exam*
Objective

Write statements that access and modify database objects.

The three objects that are at the top of the DAO model are the DBEngine, Workspace, and Database objects. The DBEngine object, in a sense, represents the Jet database engine itself. From it you create workspaces that set the environment in which all other activities take place. From a Workspace object you open or create databases that contain the data you want to update. While you don't use these three objects as much as the other members of the DAO model, it is important to understand the role they play in your database application. You must go through them to get at the more commonly used objects, such as tables and recordsets.

DBEngine Object

The DBEngine object is created automatically by VBA and is available as soon as your code starts executing. The DBEngine object is at the top of the DAO hierarchy, as there is no object with a method that creates a DBEngine object. This means that you cannot create a second DBEngine object.

Properties

Some of the DBEngine properties that you may want to use are:

- **Version:** The version number of the Jet engine that the application is running with. This test checks to see if the Jet engine is version 1.1:

```
If DBEngine.Version = "1.1" Then
```

- **SystemMDB:** This property can be used to establish the System MDB that is to be used to control security for your application. However, you must set this before performing any other DAO activity. Once you've performed some DAO activity, the DBEngine object is initialized and this value cannot be changed. This statement sets the system MDB file to C:\MySys.MDA:

```
DBEngine.SystemDB = "C:\MySys.MDA"
```

Methods

The DBEngine object has the following useful methods:

- **Idle:** When a record is updated (or about to be updated) Access locks the record to prevent others from changing it. Locks aren't freed as long as any other activity (including mouse movement) is taking place. In a single-user environment this won't be an issue (unless you have multiple copies of Access running). However, in a multiuser environment, Jet may not get back to release those locks as promptly as you would like. The Idle method causes all other activity to be suspended and pending locks to be released.

To suspend activity until all the pending locks are released, use the dbFree-Locks parameter: DBEngine.Idle dbFreeLocks.

- **RepairDatabase:** This method performs the same activities as the Repair command from the Access user interface. The RepairDatabase method takes one argument, the name of the database to be repaired (the database must be closed):

```
DBEngine.RepairDatabase "C:\NewDatabase.MDB"
```

- **CompactDatabase:** This method performs the same activities as the Compact command from the Access user interface. Essentially, the CompactDatabase method makes a copy of the original database. The CompactDatabase method accepts a number of arguments that allow you to change the version of the database (from Jet 1.0 to Jet 3.0), the collating order (what order the alphabet sorts in), and whether or not the database is encrypted. If you omit any of these options, the new database will have the same options as the original database. The last parameter for the CompactDatabase method lets you specify a password, useful if the database is protected with password security. This statement compacts Old.MDB (opening it with the password "Sesame") into New.MDB which will be an encrypted Jet 1.1 database using Hungarian collating order:

```
DBEngine.CompactDatabase "C:\Old.MDB" _
    "C:\New.MDB", dbLangHungarian, dbEncrypt and
    ➥ dbVersion11, _
    ";pwd=Sesame"
```

When the new database is created all the data in the tables is defragmented and written out sequentially, and temporary objects are cleared out. As a result, straight reads of the tables run faster and the database itself usually takes up less disk space. It's a good idea to compact your databases on a regular basis.

- **CreateWorkspace:** This method allows you to create additional workspaces. The CreateWorkspace method accepts three parameters: the name that will be used for the workspace, the User associated with the workspace, and the password for the User. To create a new workspace called "SecSpace" with a User of "Peter" and a Password of "Dirt," you would use this:

```
Dim wks As Workspace
Set wks = DBEngine.CreateWorkspace("SecSpace", "Peter", _
    "Dirt")
```

Unlike most members of a collection, a Workspace object does not have to be added to the DBEngine's Workspaces collection in order to be used.

Dealing with Corrupt Databases

If Access is interrupted in the middle of writing a record, the database may be left in an inconsistent state (all of the indexes may not have been updated, for instance). This usually occurs if a network connection is lost or a computer is turned off during an update. However, a database can also be corrupted if it is closed without all open recordsets being closed. In this situation, Windows may not have a chance to make the disk writes that it has been caching.

In repairing a database, Access validates all table structures against the MSys* table information and ensures that the indexes for all tables are created. If data is not complete, it is discarded as part of the repair. If the database cannot be repaired, the RepairDatabase method triggers an error.

In Exercise 6.2 you'll get a chance to display the DAO properties of the DBEngine object.

EXERCISE 6.2

Displaying DBEngine Properties

1. Open the Customer database, click on the Modules tab, and click on the New button.

2. In the code window that's displayed, enter the following routine:

```
Sub PrintDBEngine
Debug.Print DBEngine.Version
Debug.Print DBEngine.LoginTimeout
Debug.Print DBEngine.IniPath
Debug.Print DBEngine.SystemDB
End Sub
```

3. In the Debug window enter **PrintDBEngine** and press ↵ to display the current value of the DBEngine properties.

4. After the routine is finished, close the module, saving it under the name **SampleRoutines**.

Workspace Objects

The DBEngine has a collection of Workspace objects called, not surprisingly, the *Workspaces collection*. When your application starts executing, the first Workspace object is already created and can be referred to using the syntax below:

```
Dim wks As Workspace
Set wks = DBEngine.Workspaces(0)
```

A Workspace object has a number of methods for controlling transactions and establishing security. The Workspace object also has methods for opening existing databases (OpenDatabase) or creating new ones (CreateDatabase). Since a database is created from a Workspace object, the workspace controls the security environment and transaction management for all of the databases created from it.

Generally, in your application, you won't need more than the first workspace that is created for you by Access. In most cases, you will only need multiple workspaces to control transactions and security.

Transactions

Microsoft ✓ **_Exam_** **_Objective_**

Implement transaction processing in a Workspace object.

It's not unusual to have a series of changes made to your database that you want to either succeed or fail in total. The typical example is a transfer of money from one bank account to another. This transaction consists of debiting the balance in the first account and crediting the balance in the second account. In SQL, the two statements to transfer $10.00 from account 12345 to account 67890 would look like this:

```
Update Account
Set Balance = Balance - 10
Where Account = "12345"

Update Account
Set Balance = Balance + 10
Where Account = "67890"
```

It would be unfortunate if the computer failed between the first and the second SQL statement, as the money would be removed from one account but not added to the second. The Workspace object allows you to enclose both of these statements in a transaction, which ensures that either both statements succeed or neither does.

A successful transaction is said to be _committed_, while an unsuccessful transaction is _rolled back_.

If you have two sets of updates happening in your application in parallel, and you want them to be handled as separate transactions, you can create a second workspace and open the databases for one set of updates using the OpenDatabase method of your new Workspace object.

Security

When creating a Workspace object you must specify a user ID and a password. The user and password together establish the identity of the user who opens all the databases opened with the Workspace OpenDatabase method. Any database opened from the workspace will get the security associated with the user and password used to create that Workspace object. For Workspaces(0)—the default workspace—this will be the user "Admin" with a password of "".

If you are opening a database that has been secured, you will need to create a workspace with the appropriate user and password, and open the secured database with that new Workspace's OpenDatabase method (see Figure 6.4). In a situation where a single user does not have the necessary security to update all of the databases involved, you could create multiple Workspace objects. Note that the database that the application is running in has already been opened by the user logging on to it, so you don't need to create a Workspace object to access it.

Other than these two situations, it's unlikely that you will need to create a second workspace in an Access application.

FIGURE 6.4

Two workspaces with different securities for different databases

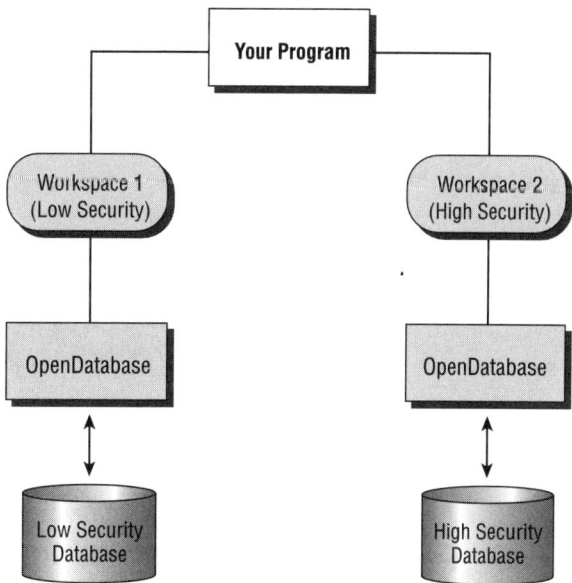

Exercise 6.3 will allow you to see the values of the default workspace and then create a new workspace and display its properties.

EXERCISE 6.3

Working with Workspaces

1. Open the Customer database, click on the Modules tab, and double-click on the SampleRoutines module you created in the last exercise.

2. In the code window that's displayed, enter the following routine:

```
Sub PrintWorkSpaces()
Dim prp As Property
Dim wks As Workspace

Set wks = DBEngine.Workspaces(0)
For Each prp In wks.Properties
    Debug.Print prp.Name, prp.Value
Next
End Sub
```

3. In the Debug window, enter **PrintWorkSpaces** and press ↵ to display the current value of the Workspace properties.

4. Return to the Module window and enter this routine:

```
Sub CreateWorkSpace()
Dim prp As Property
Dim wks As Workspace

Set wks = DBEngine.CreateWorkSpace("NewSpace", "Admin", "")
For Each prp In wks.Properties
    Debug.Print prp.Name, prp.Value
Next

End Sub
```

5. In the Immediate Window, type **CreateWorkSpace** and press ↵ to create a new workspace and print out its properties.

In this exercise you've not only displayed a workspace's properties, you've also created a new workspace.

Methods

The most important methods of the Workspace object are the ones that allow you to create or open databases.

- **CreateDatabase:** This method is used to create a new database; it returns a Database object that you can use to access the database. The Create-Database method accepts three parameters: the name of the database file, the collating order (what order the alphabet sorts in), an Options setting that specifies the version of the Jet database engine to use, and whether or not the database is encrypted. The file name and collating order must be specified. The following code creates a database called Fresh.MDB that uses the Hungarian collating order. Since the final option is omitted, the database will be created with the current version of the Jet engine and will not be encrypted. Once the database is created, the code displays the name property of the database object that was returned:

```
Dim dbs As Database
Set dbs = _
    Workspaces(0).CreateDatabase ("C:\Fresh.MDB", _
        dbLangHungarian)
MsgBox dbs.Name
```

- **OpenDatabase:** This method returns a Database object that refers to an already existing database. The method accepts four parameters that allow you to specify the database name, whether the database is opened read-only (True/False), whether the database can be shared (True/False), and a connect string for opening ODBC databases. This code opens an existing database in read-write, non-shared (exclusive) mode:

```
Dim dbs As Database
Set dbs = Workspaces(0).OpenDatabase _
    ("C:\Fresh.MDB", False, True)
```

The preceding code is more readable if you use named arguments rather than positional notation, as follows:

```
Set dbs = Workspaces(0).OpenDatabase(Database:="C:\Fresh.mdb", _
    exclusive:=True, readonly:=False)
```

Other workspace methods and properties will be discussed in later chapters.

The methods for working with transactions are covered in Chapter 7; security-related properties and methods are covered in Chapter 10.

In Exercise 6.4 you'll create a new database. Once the database is created, you'll access it through the Databases collection of the Workspace object.

EXERCISE 6.4

Displaying DBEngine Properties

1. Open the SampleRoutines module in the Customer database.

2. In the code window that's displayed, enter the following routine:

```
Sub CreateDatabase()
Dim dbs As Database
Dim wks As Workspace

Set wks = DBEngine.Workspaces(0)
Set dbs = wks.CreateDatabase("C:\New.MDB")
Debug.Print dbs.Name
dbs.Close
Set dbs = wks.OpenDatabase("C:\New.MDB")
Debug.Print DBEngine.Workspaces(0).Databases(1).Name
End Sub
```

3. In the Debug Window, enter **CreateDatabase** and press ↵.

4. When the routine finishes running, open Windows Explorer and look for your database in the root directory of your C: drive.

This exercise has allowed you to create a database (which will be used in later exercises) and to access it from your program after it was created.

Database Objects

Because all of the data that you work with is stored in databases, the DAO Database object is one of the most important parts of your application.

A Database object is a member of the Databases collection of the Workspace object from which it was opened or created. Here's an object variable that refers to the first Database object opened in the workspace:

```
Dim dbs As Database
Set dbs = Workspaces(0).Databases(0)
```

The simplest way to get a reference to the database in which your application is executing is to use the CurrentDb() function:

```
Set dbs = CurrentDb()
```

Using the CurrentDb() function allows you to work with a new instance of the current database. Using Workspaces(0).Databases(0) causes you to work with the current database itself. It's generally better to use CurrentDb(). If you use CurrentDb() and then use the Database object's Close method in your code, you will only close your copy of the database. If you use Databases(0) and the Close method, you will close the database itself (see Figure 6.5).

FIGURE 6.5

Using Databases(0) and CurrentDb() to access a database

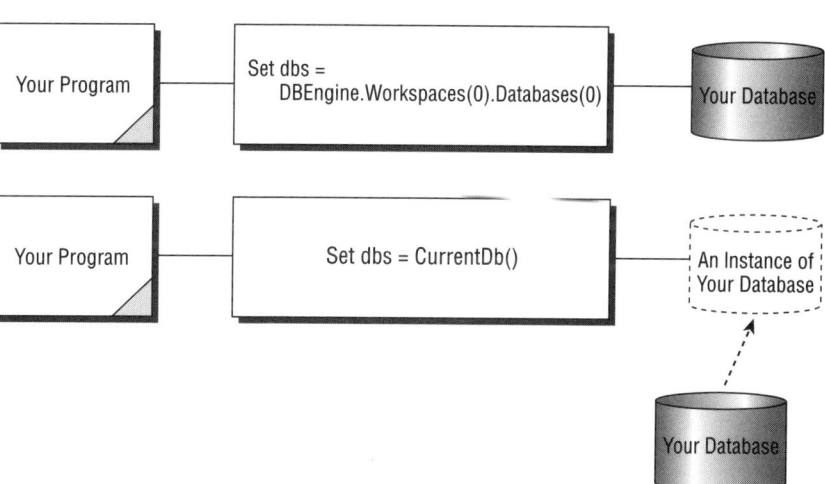

The Database object has a number of useful methods and properties, but its most important feature is its collections. Among other objects, the Database object's collections give you access to the tables in the database, the queries stored in the database, the sets of records that can be created from the database's tables, and the containers holding the Access forms, reports, and macros.

Properties and Methods

Many of the Database object's properties and methods are involved with replication, working with recordsets, or developing client/server database applications; they will be discussed in the chapters that cover those topics. However, there are four properties that you should use to get information about the database that you are working with:

- **Name:** This is the name of the database. For desktop databases (like Jet) this is the fully qualified path name for the file.

Name is a read-only property, so you can't use this property to change the database's name.

- **Updateable:** This property is set to True if you can make changes to the database. If the database was opened in a read-only mode, for instance, this property would be set to False.

- **Transactions:** If you can use the workspaces transaction management methods on the database, this property will be set to True.

- **Version:** As mentioned before, the Version property contains a string that indicates which version of the Jet database engine created this database (not the Access version).

Collections

Since DAO is a hierarchical model, you must use the Database object to gain access to the objects in a database. The Database object organizes these into five collections:

- **TableDefs:** This is a collection of all of the tables in the database. You use the TableDefs collection to work with the structure of these tables, not the data stored in them (to work with the data, you would use a Recordset object). While you can create a recordset using the OpenRecordset method of the TableDef object, you normally use the TableDef object to create, modify, or report on the structure of the table (what fields it contains, what indexes it has, etc.). The following code, for instance, opens the Customer database, finds the tblCustomerAddress table, and then displays the name of the first field in that table:

```
Dim dbs as Database
Dim tbl as TableDef
Dim fld as Field
Set dbs = _
    DBEngine.Workspaces(0).OpenDatabase("C:\Customer.MDB")
Set tbl = dbs.TableDefs("tblCustomerAddress")
Set fld = tbl.Fields(0)
MsgBox fld.Name
```

- **QueryDefs:** The QueryDefs collection gives you access to the queries stored in the database. A query is a SQL statement stored in the database and ready to execute. Like the TableDef object, you use the QueryDef object to create or modify a query. You can also use methods of the QueryDef object to create a recordset or execute the SQL statement stored in the query. This code displays the SQL command stored inside the query qryUpdateCustomer:

```
Dim dbs as Database
Dim qdf as QueryDef
Set dbs = OpenDatabase("C:\Customer.MDB")
Set qdf = dbs.QueryDefs("qryUpdateCustomer")
MsgBox qdf.SQL
```

- **Recordsets:** Unlike the Database object's other object collections, Recordset objects are not stored permanently in the database. Recordsets are collections of records drawn from one or more tables in the database by your applications as you require them. The Recordsets collection gives you access to all the recordsets that you currently have open. This code creates a recordset from a query and then displays the number of records in the recordset by accessing it through the Recordsets collection:

```
Dim dbs as Database
Dim rst as Recordset
Set dbs = OpenDatabase("C:\Customer.MDB")
Set rst = dbs.OpenRecordset("qryGetCustomers")
MsgBox = dbs.Recordsets(0).RecordCount
```

- **Containers:** One of the more innovative features of the Jet database engine is the Container object. Applications can create containers in a Jet database to store non-relational data. Jet will store and retrieve the data in the container for the application. Access uses this feature to store forms, reports, and macros in a Jet database. This code displays the date that the frmCustomer form was created:

```
Dim dbs As Database
Dim doc As Document
Set dbs = OpenDatabase("C:\Customer.MDB")
Set doc = _
   dbs.Containers("Forms").Documents("frmCustomer")
Msgbox Doc.DateCreated
```

- **Relations:** When you create a table with a Foreign Key constraint you are adding a new Relation object to the Relations collection of the database. This code displays the names of the two tables in the tblCustomertblCustomerAddress relation:

```
Dim dbs As Database
Set dbs = OpenDatabase("C:\Customer.MDB")
MsgBox dbs.Relations("tblCustomertblCustomerAddress").Table
MsgBox _
   dbs.Relations("tblCustomertblCustomerAddress").ForeignTable
```

Tables and Fields

The Jet database engine provides a very rich model for the databases it manages. Jet provides tables with a large number of properties that are beyond the capabilities of SQL (or the Access version of SQL, at any rate). For instance, Jet tables can have validation rules applied to the table as a whole or to individual fields. When you attempt to update the table, Jet automatically checks to make sure that the changes you are making do not invalidate the rules defined with the table. If your change does break the rules, Jet will prevent the updates from occurring.

You can use DAO objects and methods to create new tables instead of using SQL. By using DAO objects you will get access to the additional capabilities provided by Jet. In this section you'll learn how to create tables and relations between tables using DAO. You'll also learn how to take advantage of Jet's special features for data objects.

If you don't need the extra power provided by Jet, stick with SQL for creating your tables. Using DAO requires more code than using the SQL Create Table command and runs slower, too.

Creating a Table

Creating a table with DAO requires four steps:

1. Use the CreateTableDef method of the database object to create a TableDef (table definition) object.

2. Set the properties of your newly created TableDef object.

3. Add Field objects to the TableDef.

4. Append the TableDef object to the database's TableDefs collection.

You set the properties of the TableDef object in step 2 because after a TableDef object is added to the TableDefs collection, many of the object's properties cannot be changed.

The syntax for the CreateTableDef method is:

```
Set tbl = dbs.CreateTableDef( [name [, attributes [, source
➥ [, connect]]]])
```

None of the parameters for the CreateTableDef method are required, but all will default to acceptable values except the table name. As a result, a typical routine to create a table called tblCustomer looks like this:

```
Dim dbs As Database
Dim tbl As TableDef
Set dbs = CurrentDb()
Set tbl = dbs.CreateTableDef("tblCustomer")
```

The Attributes parameter is used to set the characteristics of the table that you are creating. The Attributes parameter accepts a number of values:

*   **dbAttachedTable:** Indicates that this is an attached table from a non-ODBC data source.

*   **dbAttachedODBC:** Indicates that is an attached table from an ODBC data source.

- **dbAttachedExclusive:** Attaches a table in exclusive mode so that it cannot be used by any other user.

- **dbAttachSavePWD:** Attaches a table and saves the Password and User so that they do not have to be provided when the table is used.

- **dbSystemObject:** Indicates that the table is to be treated as a system object.

- **dbHiddenObject:** Prevents the table from appearing in the database window.

You can assign multiple attributes to a single table by adding them together using the plus sign (the ampersand won't work). In this example, the code creates a hidden table that is also flagged as a System object:

```
Set tbl = _
    dbs.CreateTableDef("tblCustomerMgmt", dbSystemObject +
    ➡ dbHiddenObject)
```

The Source and Connect parameters are only required if you are creating the table as an attached table from another database. If you are adding an attached table, then set the Source parameter to the name of the table in the other database and set the Connect parameter to the path to the other database (or the ODBC connect string for an ODBC datasource):

```
Set tbl = dbs.CreateTableDef("tblCustomer", dbAttachExclusive,
    ➡"CustTable", ";DATABASE=C:\Old.MDB")
```

Attached tables are one of the most powerful features in Access. An attached table has only its table definition stored in the database. The data is stored in another table in another database. Access, however, treats the attached table as if it were stored in the database with the other tables (see Figure 6.6).

If you don't want to set the parameters in the CreateTableDef method, you can set the equivalent properties after you create the object but before you append it to the TableDefs collection. This code, for instance, creates the TableDef object and then sets the Name and Attributes property of the new object:

```
Set tbl = _
  dbs.CreateTableDef()
tbl.Name = "CustomerMgmt"
tbl.Attributes = dbSystemObject + dbHiddenObject
```

FIGURE 6.6

An attached table

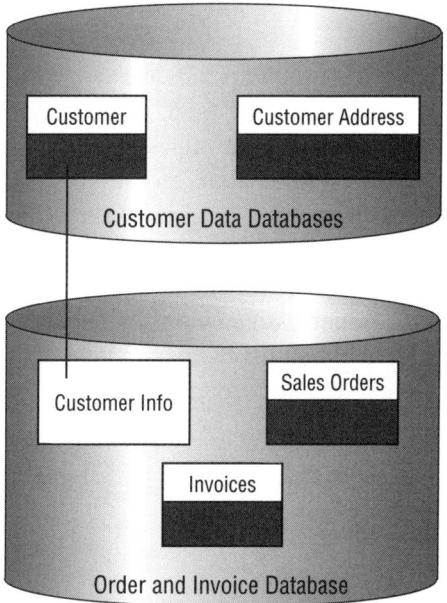

If you create a table from code with the dbHiddenObject attribute, it won't be visible in the Database window, even if you turn on Hidden Objects in the Tools ➢ Options dialog box. (Tables hidden from the interface are visible, but are grayed out.)

Working with Fields

Now that your TableDef object is created, you can create field objects and append them to the TableDef. Field objects are created with the CreateField method of the TableDef object.

There is no relationship between the TableDef object used to create a field and the TableDef object that the field is eventually added to. You can create the field object from any TableDef object and add it to any other TableDef.

The syntax for the CreateField method is:

```
Set fld = tbl.CreateField([name[, type [, size]]])
```

Like the CreateTableDef method, all of the parameters of the CreateField method are optional. However, neither the name nor the type parameters default to valid values, so realistically, you must specify the name and type.

The type parameter must be set to an integer value (or its equivalent named constant) that determines the field's data type. The valid values (which correspond to the SQL data types in Chapter 3) are listed in Table 6.1.

T A B L E 6.1	Data Type Constant	Description
The Data Type Constants	dbBoolean	Boolean
	dbByte	Byte
	dbInteger	Integer
	dbLong	Long Numeric
	dbCurrency	Currency
	dbSingle	Single Numeric
	dbDouble	Double Numeric
	dbDate	Date/Time
	dbText	Text
	dbLongBinary	Long Binary (OLE Object)
	dbMemo	Memo
	dbGUID	GUID (Globally Unique Identifier)

The size parameter is required only if you specify that you are creating a Text field by passing dbText in the type parameter. To create a Customer-Name Text field of 25 characters, you would use:

```
Set fld = tbl.CreateField("CustomerName", dbText, 25)
```

A date field to hold the customer's birth date would be created with:

```
Set fld = tbl.CreateField("CustomerBirthDate", dbDate)
```

As with the CreateTableDef method, you can omit the parameters when you use the method and set the appropriate properties of the field object after it is created. To create the CustomerName field you could write:

```
Set fld = tbl.CreateField()
fld.Name = "CustomerName"
fld.Type = dbText
fld.Size = 25
```

Once a field is created, it must be added to the Fields collection for the TableDef. Every collection in DAO has an Append method just for adding new members. This code uses the Fields collection's Append method to add the CustomerName field to the table's collection:

```
Set fld = tbl.CreateField("CustomerName", dbText, 25)
tbl.Fields.Append fld
```

Putting It All Together

Now that you've seen the code to create a TableDef and a FieldObject, you're ready to put it all together to make a table using DAO. The only new code in this example is the last line, which adds the TableDef object to the database's TableDefs collection. This routine creates a tblCustomer table with three fields: LastName, FirstName, and BirthDate (see Figure 6.7).

```
Dim dbs As Database
Dim Lbl As TableDef
Dim fld As Field

Set dbs = CurrentDb()
Set tbl = dbs.CreateTableDef("tblCustomer")
Set fld = tbl.CreateField("LastName", dbText, 15)
tbl.Fields.Append fld
Set fld = tbl.CreateField("FirstName", dbText, 10)
tbl.Fields.Append fld
Set fld = tbl.CreateField("BirthDate", dbDate)
tbl.Fields.Append fld
dbs.TableDefs.Append tbl
```

In Exercise 6.5 you'll open the database you created in the previous exercise and add a SalesRep table to it.

F I G U R E 6.7

Creating a table
with DAO

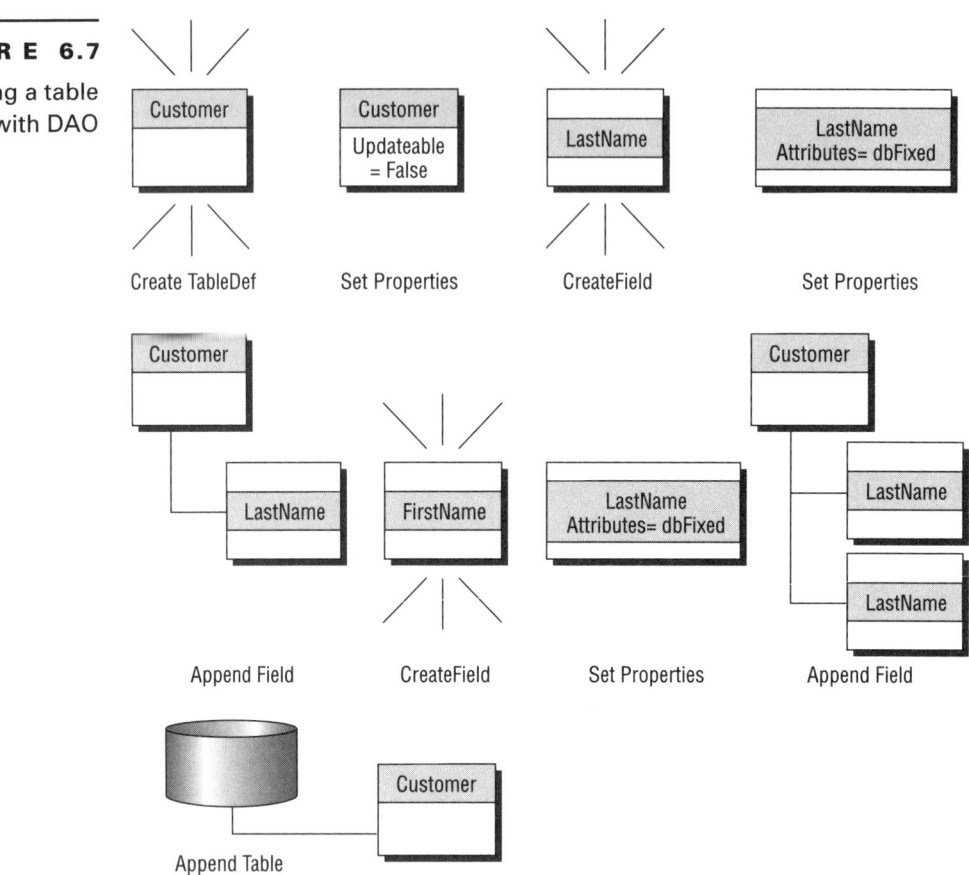

EXERCISE 6.5

Adding a Table to a Database

1. Open the SampleRoutines module in the Customer database.

2. In the code window that's displayed, enter the following routine:

```
Sub CreateTable()
Dim dbs As Database
Dim tbl as TableDef
Dim fld As Field
```

```
Set dbs = OpenDatabase("C:\New.MDB")
Set tbl = dbs.CreateTableDef("SalesRep")

Set fld = tbl.CreateField("RepName", dbText, 15)
Fld.Attributes = dbFixedField
tbl.Fields.Append fld

Set fld = tbl.CreateField("HireDate", dbDate)
tbl.Fields.Append fld

dbs.TableDefs.Append tbl

End Sub
```

3. In the Debug window, enter **CreateTable** and press ↵.

4. When the routine finishes running, close the Customer database and open the C:\New.MDB database using the Access File ➤ Open command. Open the SalesRep table in Design mode to see the results of your routine.

This exercise has given you a chance to create a table in a remote database from another database.

Table Properties

The three properties that are set in the CreateTableDef method are just the minimum set of table properties. A table has about a dozen properties you can use. Some of these properties can be read or written at any time, some can only be changed before the TableDef is added to the database's TableDefs collection.

Not all of the properties that a data access object has are defined by Jet. Jet allows the applications that use it to create their own properties that can be attached to Jet data objects. Access takes advantage of this to add several properties to TableDefs and Fields. In the Access documentation those properties that are defined by Jet are flagged as DAO properties. All the rest are defined by Access.

Access and Jet Properties

As we've said, not all of the properties of DAO objects (like TableDefs and Fields) are defined by Jet. Jet allows the applications that it supports to create their own properties. In the Access documentation, only those properties flagged as "DAO" are native to the Jet database engine. All of the rest of the properties come to you courtesy of Access.

Access doesn't necessarily create all of its properties when you create a TableDef or a Field object. One of the side effects of this is that you may try to read or write a property that Access hasn't created yet. This will raise an error in your program and you'll need to have an error handler in your routine to catch this error.

Later in this chapter, you'll learn how to add your own properties to Jet's objects.

Some of the more interesting properties of the TableDef object are:

- **DateCreated, LastUpdated:** The DateCreated property gives the date that the table was created (unless it is an attached table). If the table is attached, the Date property refers to the date when the table was attached to the database. LastUpdated is the last date that a change was made to the TableDef's structure.

WARNING It's very important that you understand that the LastUpdated property returns the date that the table's structure was changed. It does not refer, in any way, to the last time the data in the table was changed.

- **RecordCount:** For a recordset, the RecordCount property gives the number of records in the recordset. When working with a TableDef (which is only the structure of the table), the RecordCount property is always set to −1.

- **Updateable:** This property is True if you can change the structure of the table. This is always True until the TableDef object is added to the TableDefs collection. The property is always False for an attached table or a table that has been added to the TableDefs collection. In all other situations, the property is governed by the database's security.

- **Validation Rule, ValidationText:** Both Fields and Tables have a validation rule that lets you establish a rule about what records can be allowed in the table. A table's validation rule allows you to establish rules that involve multiple fields in the table. The ValidationText property contains the message that will be displayed when the rule is violated. The following rule, for instance, requires the date of the customer's first purchase to be later than the customer's birth date, and that the customer's gender be either F or M:

```
tbl.ValidationRule = "(PurchaseDate > BirthDate) and
➥ (Gender = 'M' or Gender = 'F')"
tbl.ValidationText = "Not a valid record. Please ensure
➥ that the customer birth date is prior to their first
➥ purchase and that the Gender field is set to M or F"
```

There are serious limitations to what you can use in the ValidationRule property. You can't use user-defined functions or fields from other tables, queries, or forms. The various SQL domain aggregate functions also can't be used (the D* functions like DLookUp, DMax, etc.).

Field Properties

Like the TableDef object, the Field object has a multitude of useful properties:

- **Attributes:** The Field's Attributes property lets you control the Field object by adding together a number of attribute settings. The various settings that you can use are listed in Table 6.2. This constant makes the field fixed-size:

```
fld.Attributes = dbFixedField
```

Many of the Field object properties control what data is (and isn't) allowed in the field. By using these properties in conjunction with the TableDef's Validation rule property, you can eliminate a great deal of VBA code that you would have to write to check for bad data. Instead, the database itself will validate your records. This also ensures that all of the applications using this database have the same rules applied to them.

- **AllowZeroLength:** When this property is set to True, applications will be able to set the field to a zero-length string (" "). When set to False, the field will require that any entry made to it have at least one character in it, even if it's just a space. This property is valid only for Text and Memo fields.

- **DefaultValue:** When a new record is created, the field will automatically be set to the value that you put in here. You can change the value of the field, but this property ensures that the field will never be Null.

As in the case of the TableDef ValidationRule property, there are a lot of things you can't use in the Field object's DefaultValue property: user-defined functions, other fields, queries, forms, or the domain aggregate functions. One special function you can use is GenUniqueId(), which gives you a random number in the range 2 and –2 billion. The only place the GenUniqueId function can be used is in the DefaultValue property of a field.

- **Required:** Setting this property to True means that a value must be supplied for the field before the record is saved. By setting this property to True, you ensure that the field will never be set to Null.

- **ValidateOnSet:** When this property is set to True, the validation rules that you've specified in the other properties are applied as soon as the value in the field is changed. If you set this property to False, then the data in the fields isn't validated until the record is saved.

- **ValidationRule, ValidationText:** These properties are very similar to the ValidationRule and ValidationText properties on the TableDef object. However, you cannot refer to another field in a Field object's ValidationRule. When creating a field level validation rule, you enter a test (or a series of tests joined with the And and Or operators) that can be applied to the field:

```
fld.ValidationRule = "= 'M' Or = 'F'"
fld.ValidationText = "Not a valid record. Please ensure
that the Gender field is set to M or F"
```

T A B L E 6.2: Field Attribute Settings

Attribute Setting	Effect
dbFixedField	The field size is fixed (default for Numeric fields).
dbVariableField	The field size is variable (Text fields only).
dbAutoIncrField	The field value for new records is automatically incremented to a unique Long integer that can't be changed (supported only for Microsoft Jet database tables).
dbUpdatableField	The field value can be changed.
dbDescending	The field is sorted in descending (Z to A or 100 to 0) order (applies only to a Field object in a Fields collection of an Index object). If you omit this constant, the field is sorted in ascending (A to Z or 0 to 100) order (default).
dbSystemField	The field is a replication field (on a TableDef object) used on replicable databases and cannot be deleted.

Properties

You can create new properties and add them to DAO objects. When you create your own properties, you must specify some of the Access properties for these objects before you can use the properties (see Figure 6.8). The TableDef's Description property and the Field's Caption property are examples of these properties.

You must append the TableDef and Field objects to their collections before you attempt to give them new properties.

To add a new property to an object, you must first create the property using the CreateProperty method. Many DAO objects have the CreateProperty method, including the Database, Field, and TableDef objects. The syntax for the CreateProperty method is:

```
Set property = object.CreateProperty([name[, type[, value[,
➥ fDDL]]]])
```

FIGURE 6.8

The Access defined properties for a field are not available until they are created.

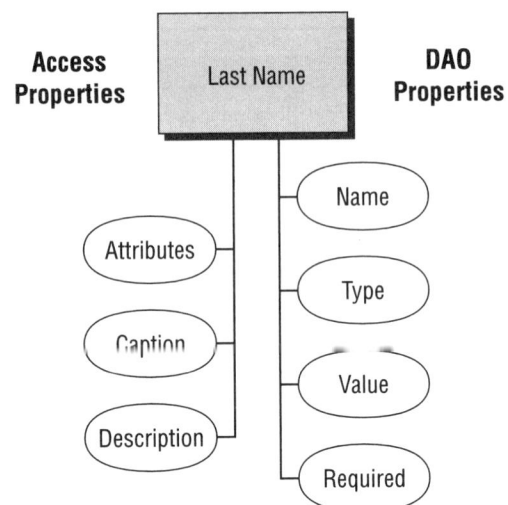

As with the CreateField and CreateTableDef methods, you can create a property without providing any of the parameters, provided you set the appropriate properties of the object afterwards. Only fDDL defaults to a valid value. (fDDL, when True, specifies that this property can only be set by a user with dbSecWriteDef permissions—see Chapter 10 to learn how to assign permissions to users). The Type parameter accepts the same constants as the CreateField method (see Table. 6.1).

You can create a property from any convenient object and apply it to any other object. You can, for instance, use the CreateProperty method of a TableDef object and append the resulting Property object to a Field object.

The Field object in Access has a Caption property which supplies a heading for a field when the field is displayed in a datasheet. Before using the Caption property from your code you must create it. The following code creates the Caption property for a field and appends it to the field's Properties collection:

```
Dim dbs As Database
Dim fld As Field
Dim tbl As TableDef
```

```
Dim prp As Property

Set dbs = CurrentDb()
Set tbl = dbs.CreateTableDef("tblCustomer")
Set fld = tbl.CreateField("LastName", dbText, 15)
tbl.Fields.Append fld
dbs.TableDefs.Append tbl
Set prp = tbl.CreateProperty("Caption", dbText)
prp.Value = "Last Name"
fld.Properties.Append prp
```

WARNING When referring to a non-DAO property, you can't use the dot (.) syntax. Instead you must explicitly use the Properties collection of the object as in fld.Properties("Caption") or the alternate ! syntax fld.Properties!Caption.

Exercise 6.6 will let you work with the fields in the table you created. In this exercise you'll add a property to a field and update a field's attributes.

EXERCISE 6.6

Setting Field Properties

1. Open the New.MDB database that you created, click on the Modules tab, and click on the New button.

2. In the code window that's displayed, enter the following routine:

```
Sub SetField()
Dim dbs As Database
Dim tbl As TableDef
Dim fld As FieldDef
Dim prp As Property

Set dbs = CurrentDB()
Set tbl = dbs.TableDefs("SalesRep")
Set fld = tbl("RepName")

Set prp = fld.CreateProperty("Description", dbText)
```

```
prp.Description.Value = "SalesRep name"
fld.Properties.Append prp

Set fld = tbl("HireDate")
On Error Resume Next
fld.Attributes = dbVariableField
If Err <> 0 Then
    MsgBox "Unable to write to property"
End If
End Sub
```

3. In the Debug window, run the SetField routine.

4. Once the routine has finished running, open the SalesRep table in Design view and look at the Description property of the RepName field.

5. Close the module, saving it under the name **SampleRoutines**.

With this exercise you've added a new property to a field that was part of a table. As you saw, though, the Attributes property of a field cannot be changed once the field is part of a table.

Indexes and Relationships

Like tables, indexes can also be created through DAO. Creating an index is very much like creating a table: you first use the CreateIndex method to create an Index object and then append a set of fields to the index. Once the index is created you append it to the Indexes collection of the TableDef object.

Relationships can also be defined through a similar process by using the CreateRelation method of the Database object. In creating the Relation object you specify the two tables involved and then add the relevant fields to the Relation object.

Creating an Index

When you use the CreateIndex method, the only parameter you provide is the name. Once the Index object is created, you use the object's CreateField method to create fields to be added to the index. The fields that you add to the Index object method must already be defined in the table.

The following code creates an index for the tblCustomer table made up of the table's LastName and FirstName fields:

```
Dim dbs As Database
Dim fld As Field
Dim tbl As TableDef
Dim idx As Index

Set dbs = CurrentDb()
Set tbl = dbs.TableDefs("tblCustomer")

Set idx = tbl.CreateIndex("NameIndex")
Set fld = idx.CreateField("LastName")
idx.Fields.Append fld
Set fld = idx.CreateField("FirstName")
idx.Fields.Append fld

tbl.Indexes.Append idx
```

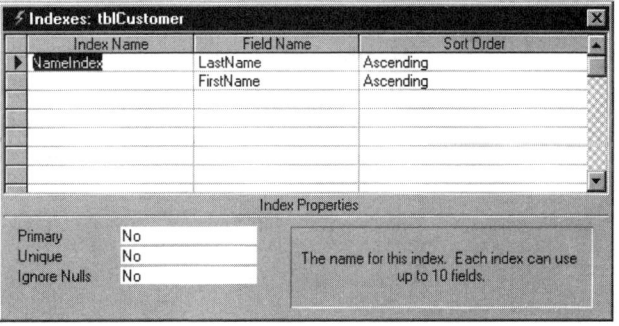

Once the Index object is created you can set the object's properties. The Index object properties include:

- **IgnoreNulls:** If this property is True, then fields with Null values are not added to the index as shown in Figure 6.9. In an index on fields where many records have Nulls in the indexed fields, this can reduce the size of the index and speed searches that use it.

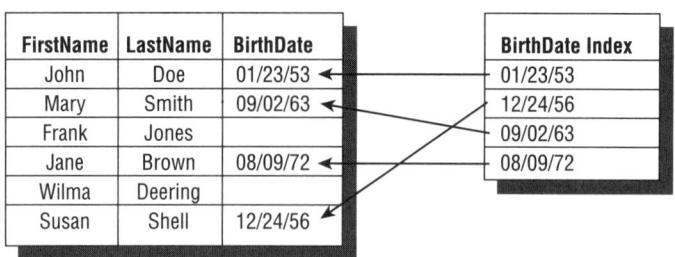

- **Required:** When this property is set to True, the fields in the index are not allowed to have Null values in them.

- **Unique:** Setting this property to True creates a unique index (an index in which no two records are allowed to have duplicate values in the indexed fields).

- **Primary:** Causes the index to be flagged as the primary index of the table (the table's primary key is automatically a primary index for the table). A primary index will also set the Required and Unique properties to True.

- **Foreign:** This property is True if the key was created as part of defining a foreign key for the table.

- **DistinctCount:** This read-only property allows you to determine how many different values are in the index. For instance, an index on a Gender field will have only two values in it (M or F) and so have a DistinctCount of two, no matter how many records there are in the table.

The Field object's Attributes property has one setting (dbDescending) that can only be used on a Field object in an index. Setting the Attributes property to dbDescending causes that field to be sorted in descending order in the index.

Creating a Relationship

The CreateRelation method of the Database object allows you to define a Foreign Key relationship between two tables. Once you've created the Relation object, you append the fields in the relation to it and then append the relation to the database's Relations collection.

The syntax for the CreateRelation method is:

```
Set relation = dbs.CreateRelation ([name [, table [,
➥ foreigntable [, attributes]]]])
```

Again, the optional parameters can be set by using the appropriate properties of the Relation object after the object is created. Only the attributes parameter can be defaulted.

The Attributes parameter allows you to specify the kind of Relation you are creating. If no attributes are set, the Relation will be a one-to-many relationship (for each record in the table there can be many records in the foreign table) with referential integrity enforced. You can set the Attributes parameter to one or more of these values:

- **dbRelationUnique:** For each record in the table there is no more than one record in the foreign table.

- **dbRelationDontEnforce:** No referential integrity is enforced on the tables. As a result, a record in the foreign table may not have a corresponding record in the table.

- **dbRelationUpdateCascade:** If the fields in the relation are changed in the table, the fields in the foreign table will automatically be changed also.

- **dbRelationDeleteCascade:** If the record in the table is deleted, all the related records in the foreign table will also be deleted.

When you use the CreateField method of the Relation object you must (as in the case of the Index object), specify the name of a field already defined in the table. Once the Field object is created you must set its ForeignName property to the name of a field in the ForeignTable.

This code creates a one-to-many relationship between the tblCustomer table and the tblCustomerAddress table with cascading updates and deletes:

```
Dim dbs As Database
Dim fld As Field
Dim rel As Relation

Set dbs = CurrentDb
Set rel = dbs.CreateRelation("Addresses", "tblCustomer", _
"tblCustomerAddress")
rel.Attributes = dbRelationUpdateCascade + _
    dbRelationDeleteCascade

Set fld = rel.CreateField("CustomerLastName")
fld.ForeignName = "CustomerLastName"
```

```
rel.Fields.Append fld
Set fld = rel.CreateField("CustomerFirstName")
fld.ForeignName = "CustomerFirstName"
rel.Fields.Append fld

dbs.Relations.Append rel
```

In Exercise 6.7 you will add an index to the SalesRep table.

EXERCISE 6.7

Adding an Index

1. Open the New.MDB database that you created earlier.

2. Add some records to the SalesRep table giving the salespeople a variety of birth dates (no two salespeople with the same date). Close and re-open the table. Note that the records appear in no particular order.

3. Add the following routine to the module:

```
Sub MakeIndex()
Dim dbs As Database
Dim tbl As TableDef
Dim idx As Index
Dim fld As Field

Set dbs = CurrentDb()
Set tbl = dbs.TableDefs("SalesRep")

Set idx = tbl.CreateIndex("DateIndex")

Debug.Print "Required:", idx.Required
Debug.Print "Unique:", idx.Unique
idx.Primary = True
Debug.Print "Required:", idx.Required
Debug.Print "Unique:", idx.Unique

Set fld = idx.CreateField("HireDate")
fld.Attributes = dbDescending
```

```
idx.Fields.Append fld
tbl.Indexes.Append idx

End Sub
```

4. Run the MakeIndex routine from the Debug window. When the routine is done, open the SalesRep table and note the order of the records (they will be in order by birthdate since you defined the Index as primary).

5. Select View ➤ TableDesign to view the table in Design view. Select View ➤ Indexes to see the indexes on this table.

Compiling the Query

When you pass a SQL statement to the Jet database engine, the statement must go through a process that allows Jet to determine what data you want to have returned to you and how that data is to be retrieved. This process is called *compiling* the query. For complex queries, this process can be time-consuming. Jet allows you to define queries and store them in a Jet database.

When you store the query, Jet will perform all the processing that is required to get the query ready to execute. After that has been done, you can execute that query from your program without having to pay the price of recompiling it.

Creating a Query

To create a query you use the CreateQueryDef method of the Database object. The syntax for the CreateQueryDef method is:

```
Set querydef = dbs.CreateQueryDef([name [, sqltext]])
```

Omitting the Name parameter for the QueryDef object has interesting effects on the behavior of the CreateQueryDef method. If you supply a name for your query, the query is automatically saved in the database. If you omit the name, the QueryDef is not saved, but you can use the QueryDef object repeatedly in your application without the query being recompiled. If you omit the name and then later assign a value to the QueryDef object's Name property, the query will not automatically be saved, but you can append the object to the QueryDefs collection to save it.

The sqltext parameter can be any valid SQL command, including DDL and DML statements. The DML statements can be Select or Update statements. The nature of SQL that you provide has an impact on which methods of the QueryDef object you can use. If the SQL statement is a Select statement, you can use the OpenRecordset method to retrieve the records specified by the statement (see Chapter 7 for information on how to use a recordset). For any other SQL statement (DDL or update statements), you must use the Execute method to have the query carried out.

This code creates a SQL statement that updates the tblSalesRep table:

```
Dim dbs As Database
Dim qdf As QueryDef

Set dbs = CurrentDb()
Set qdf = dbs.CreateQueryDef("qryCustUpdate", _
    "Update tblSalesRep Set Salary = Salary * 1.10")
```

This code uses the query to actually update the tblSalesRep data:

```
Dim dbs As Database
Set dbs = CurrentDb()
dbs.QueryDefs("qryCustUpdate").Execute
```

WARNING CreateQueryDef just creates the query. You must use one of the QueryDef's methods (OpenRecordset or Execute) to actually make Jet execute the SQL statement.

Parameters

Often you will find that you have a query that you want to run multiple times—just changing the criteria in the Where clause each time it is run. These two queries, for instance, are identical except for the level of the salary that they report on:

```
Select *
From SalesRep
Where Salary > 30000

Select *
From SalesRep
Where Salary > 40000
```

If the only change you want to make in a query is the value that a field being tested against, then you can create a *parameterized query* (sometimes known as a *parameter query*). A parameterized query allows you to change the values used by the query each time it is run. Changing the values used by the query does not require that the query be recompiled.

You cannot use parameters to change the fields used in a query or the tests used in the Where clause. A parameterized query only lets you change the value used in a test.

To create a parameterized query, you specify the name of the parameter in the Where clause (the parameter's name can't duplicate a field name in any of the tables used in the query). This query has three parameters, one to test against the Region (RegionName) and two to test against the Salary (High-Salary and LowSalary):

```
Update tblSalesRep
Set Salary = Salary * 1.1
Where Region = RegionName
And Salary Between LowSalary and HighSalary
```

For each parameter in the query, Jet adds a member to the query's Parameters collection. In your code, you must set the value of the parameters before using the query. This code uses the query from the previous example to update sales people who meet two different sets of criteria:

```
Dim dbs As Database
Dim qdf As QueryDef

Set dbs = CurrentDb()
Set qdf = dbs.CreateQueryDef("","Update SalesRep Set Salary
= Salary * 1.1 Where Region = RegionName And Salary Between
LowSalary and HighSalary")

qdf.Parameters("RegionName") = "NorthWest"
qdf.Parameters("LowSalary") = 10000
qdf.Parameters("HighSalary") = 20000
qdf.Execute
```

```
qdf.Parameters("RegionName") = "West Coast"
qdf.Parameters("LowSalary") = 20000
qdf.Parameters("HighSalary") = 40000
qdf.Execute
```

Parameters also have a Type property which allows you to set the data type of the parameter.

You can explicitly create parameters by using the parameters clause. The parameters clause precedes the SQL statement proper and gives the name and data types for the parameters used in the statement. In the example query, the parameters could have been created explicitly with the statement: `Parameters RegionName Text, LowSalary Double, HighSalary Double; Update tblSalesRep Set Salary = Salary * 1.1 Where Region = RegionName And Salary Between LowSalary and HighSalary.`

QueryDef Properties

The QueryDef object has several useful properties. Some of those properties are related to replication or client/server uses of a query and are discussed in the chapters that cover those topics. The ones relevant to the subject of this chapter are:

- **SQL:** The SQL property lets you read or change the query's SQL command.

- **RecordsAffected:** After using the QueryDefs Execute method to carry out an update statement, the RecordsAffected property contains the number of records changed, inserted, or deleted by the query.

- **DateCreated, LastUpdated:** The date when the query was created or the date when it was last changed.

- **Type:** This indicates the kind of SQL command in the query. The valid entries and the corresponding SQL statement type are shown in Table 6.3.

T A B L E 6.3 QueryDef Types	**Property Value**	**SQL Type**
	dbQSelect	Select
	dbQAction	Action

TABLE 6.3 *(cont.)* QueryDef Types	**Property Value**	**SQL Type**
	dbQCrosstab	Crosstab
	dbQDelete	Delete
	dbQUpdate	Update
	dbQAppend	Append
	dbQMakeTable	Make-table
	dbQDDL	Data-definition
	dbQSQLPassThrough	Pass-through
	dbQSetOperation	Union
	dbQSPTBulk	Used with dbQSQLPassThrough to specify a query that doesn't return records

To remove an item from any collection, use the collection's Delete method and pass it the name of the object to be deleted. For instance, to remove the field LastName from the tblCustomer table TableDef you would use dbs.TableDefs("tblCustomer").Fields.Delete "LastName."

Exercise 6.8 will let you work with the fields in the table you created. In this exercise you'll add a property to a field and update a field's attributes.

EXERCISE 6.8

Creating and Running a Parameterized Query

1. Open the SampleRoutine module in the New.MDB database.

2. Add this routine to the module. For the "SelectHireDate" parameters, enter dates for one of the salespeople that you added to the SalesRep table (remember that the dates must be enclosed in #s, like this: #12/15/97#):

```
Sub MakeQueryDef()
Dim dbs As Database
```

```
Dim que As QueryDef

Set dbs = CurrentDB()
Set que = dbs.CreateQueryDef("HireDate", _
  "Delete * From SalesRep Where HireDate = SelectHireDate")
que.Parameters("SelectHireDate") = #enter a date#
que.Execute
MsgBox que.RecordsAffected & " sales people were deleted."

que.Parameters("SelectHireDate") = #enter another date#
que.Execute
MsgBox que.RecordsAffected & " sales people were deleted."

End Sub
```

3. Run the MakeQueryDef routine in the Debug window.

4. When the routine finishes running, switch to the Query tab of the Database window and run the HireDate query from there.

Access and Jet Objects

It is sometimes very difficult to tell where Access ends and Jet starts. Part of the reason for this is that Access stores its objects (Forms, Reports, Macros, and Modules) in Jet databases. In this section we'll look at the Container objects of the Jet database engine that allow the applications that use Jet to store non-relational data in a Jet database.

Jet uses the information stored with the object to control access to the objects depending on the security settings you have created for the database. As a result, there isn't much information stored about any of the objects. Most of the Document properties are related either to security or to replication.

Containers and Documents

The Jet Database object includes a collection called Containers made up of a series of Container objects. Containers provide Jet with a way to organize the different kinds of objects stored in the database.

Jet uses four containers to hold information about its own objects: Databases, Relationships, Tables, and Sysrel. Queries are stored in the Tables container. Sysrel contains relationship-related information. Access uses an additional four containers for its own objects: forms, reports, modules, and scripts. The Script container stores information about macros in the database.

If you wanted to get information on the frmCustomer form, for instance, you would go to the frmCustomer Document in the Forms Container:

```
Dim dbs As Database
Set dbs = CurrentDb()


MsgBox dbs.Containers("Forms").Documents("frmCustomer").
➥LastUpdated
```

This code will loop through all the containers in your database and display the name and the creation date for each Document object in each container:

```
Dim dbs As Database
Dim con As Container
Dim doc As Document

Set dbs = CurrentDb()
For Each con In dbs.Containers
    Debug.Print con.Name
    For Each doc In con.Documents
        Debug.Print , doc.Name, doc.DateCreated
    Next
Next
```

Exercise 6.9 will let you work with the fields in the table you created. In this exercise you'll add a property to a field and update a field's attributes.

EXERCISE 6.9

Displaying Containers and Documents

1. Open the Sample module in New.MDB.

2. Enter the following routine into the module. This code will loop through all the containers in your database and display the name and the creation date for each Document object in each Container.

```
Sub ListDocs()
Dim dbs As Database
Dim con As Container
Dim doc As Document
Set dbs = CurrentDb()
For Each con In dbs.Containers
    Debug.Print con.Name
    For Each doc In con.Documents
        Debug.Print , doc.Name, doc.DateCreated
    Next
Next
End Sub
```

3. In the Debug window, run the ListDocs subroutine. Make the window as large as you can to view the results.

4. Select Tools ➣ Options ➣ View, and check the settings for Hidden Objects and System Objects. If the options are currently selected, de-select them and rerun the ListDocs procedure to see the effect on the results.

Summary

Data Access Objects (DAO) provide a way for you to work with your database using objects, their methods, and their properties. The DAO object model organizes all of the functionality of the Jet database engine into a hierarchical model where the components of one object give you access to objects that are located lower down in the model.

The DAO object model is made up of objects and collections. A collection is a group of objects. For example, the TableDefs collection is a collection of all of the tables in the database. In DAO, a new object is frequently created and added to the database by invoking a method to create the object and then appending it to the appropriate collection.

To use DAO to create a table, you first use the CreateTableDef method of the Database object. Once that's done, you use the CreateField method of the TableDef object to create a Field object and then append that Field object to the Fields collection of the TableDef. To save the table in the database, you append the TableDef object you created to the TableDefs collection of the Database object.

The topmost object in the DAO hierarchy is the DBEngine object, which is created automatically when your application starts. You use the DBEngine object to get information about the Jet engine itself and to gain access to other objects in the DAO hierarchy. There is only one DBEngine object.

The DBEngine object has a collection of workspaces. A default workspace is created when your application begins running. The Workspace object is used to control security and transactions. Each Workspace object has a collection of databases currently open in that workspace. You can create new workspaces by using the CreateWorkspace method of the DBEngine object.

The Database object's most important feature is its collections. These collections give you the ability to work with the tables, stored queries, and other DAO objects stored in the database (but not the Access objects like Forms, Reports, Macros, and Modules).

Within the database, DAO and Access provide capabilities to work with relational objects beyond those provided by SQL. DAO tables have a ValidationRule property, for instance, that tests records and rejects those that do not meet the criteria specified in the rule. You can also use DAO to duplicate the function of SQL's DDL in creating tables and the relationships between them. DAO also lets you create a table by attaching it from another database.

Jet allows the applications that support it to add additional properties to Jet's objects. From DAO you can apply and change a field's Caption or ValidationRule properties, for instance. Many properties in Access are actually provided by Jet. This means that you cannot count on those properties always being present, since Access may not have created them at the time you are working with the object. You can use Jet's CreateProperty method to create Access properties so that you can set their values from within your application.

Indexes and relationships can also be created from DAO. You must use DAO in order to create a relationship that enforces referential integrity with cascading updates and deletes.

While the focus in this chapter has been on creating objects with DAO, all of the properties of these objects are available after the object is created. Many of the properties are read-only after the object has been appended to the appropriate collection but can still be read to determine the status of your database. The DistinctCount property of an Index, for instance, tells you how many different values are stored in the index.

When you submit a query to Jet for processing, it must go through a process called compiling. Rather than pay that price every time you submit the query, you can create a QueryDef in the database which holds the query in a compiled state using the CreateQueryDef method. You can also create parameterized queries that allow you to change a query's Where clause each time the query is run without have to recompile it.

Jet maintains information about the objects stored in a database through a collection of Container and Document objects. These include DAO objects like tables and queries, and also Access objects like Forms and Reports.

Review Questions

1. The DAO object model is hierarchical because:

   A. Some objects inherit properties from other objects.

   B. Some objects are lower in priority than others.

   C. Some objects can only be accessed from other objects.

   D. It represents a hierarchical database structure.

2. In order to determine if you can make updates to the database you should:

    A. Check the Updateable property

    B. Trap for update errors

    C. Check the ReadOnly property

    D. Use the DBStatus method

3. To work with the tblCustomer table in a database you would use:

    A. Set tbl = dbs.Tables("tblCustomer")

    B. Set tbl = dbs. tblCustomer

    C. Set tbl = Tables("tblCustomer")

    D. Set tbl = dbs.TableDefs("tblCustomer")

4. Which of the following objects is created automatically by DAO?

    A. WorkAreas(1)

    B. Workspaces(0)

    C. Workspaces(1)

    D. DBEngine(0)

5. To add a table to a database with DAO you would use:

    A. The CreateTable method of the DBEngine object

    B. The CreateTableDef method of the Database object

    C. The CreateTableDef method of the DBEngine object

    D. The CreateTable method of the Database object

6. To create a table that wouldn't appear in the database window you would use:

    A. tbl.CreateTable(,,False)

    B. tbl.Visible = False

    C. tbl.Hide = True

    D. tbl.Attributes = dbHiddenObject

7. When using the CreateField method you must supply:

   A. No parameters

   B. The name parameter

   C. The name and type parameters

   D. The name, type, and size parameters

8. To create a date field you would use:

   A. tbl.CreateField("Afield",dbDate)

   B. fld.Date = True

   C. tbl.CreateField("Afield,dbDate,8)

   D. fld.Type = Date

9. When creating a field you must provide the size parameter for
   _____ fields.

   A. Integer

   B. OLE

   C. Text

   D. B and C

10. You attempt to read the Caption property of a field property and get
   an error message because:

   A. The Caption property is write-only.

   B. Field objects don't have a Caption property.

   C. You were reading the property into a string variable instead of a
   Text variable.

   D. The Caption property hasn't been created.

11. To determine the last time a table's data was updated, you would check:

A. The LastUpdated property.

B. The results of the LastUpdate method.

C. The DateUpdate property.

D. You cannot check this from DAO.

12. Which of the following code would successfully add a property to a field?

A. Set prp = tbl.CreateProperty("NewProp",dbText,"Avalue")
fld.Properties.Append prp

B. Set prp = fld.CreateProperty("NewProp",dbText,"Avalue")
fld.Properties.Append "NewProp"

C. Set prp = tbl.CreateProperty("NewProp",dbText,"Avalue")
fld.Properties("Avalue").Append

D. Set prp = fld.CreateProperty("NewProp")
fld.Properties.Append prp

13. The steps for adding an index to a table are:

1. Add the index to the indexes collection of the table.

2. Create the index.

3. Add a field to the index.

4. Create a field.

The correct order in which to perform them is:

A. 1, 2, 3, 4

B. 2, 4, 3, 1

C. 4, 3, 1, 2

D. 4, 3, 2, 1

14. Setting an index's Primary property to True has what effect?

   A. The Required property will be set to True.

   B. The Unique property will be set to True.

   C. A and B.

   D. Neither A nor B.

15. Which of the following code snippets will create a relationship between the tblCustomer table and the tblCustomerAddress table where each customer can have several addresses?

   A. dbs.CreateRelation ("ARel", "tblCustomerAddress", "tblCustomer")

   B. dbs.CreateRelation ("ARel", "tblCustomer", "tblCustomerAddress")

   C. dbs.TableDefs("tblCustomer").CreateRelation ("ARel", "tblCustomerAddress")

   D. dbs.CreateRelationship ("ARel", "tblCustomer", "tblCustomerAddress")

16. The primary benefit in creating a QueryDef is:

   A. Improved performance

   B. Smaller query size

   C. Larger recordsets

   D. Ease of use

17. The following code snippet fails because:

```
Set qdf = dbs.CreateQueryDef("","Update tblSalesRep
➥ Set Salary = Salary * 1.1")
Set rst = qdf.OpenRecordset()
```

   A. The query is missing its Where clause.

   B. The query has no name.

   C. CreateQueryDef is a method of the Table object.

   D. The OpenRecordset method shouldn't be used.

18. The GetCustomer QueryDef has a parameter called Customer-
Number. The correct code to set that parameter is:

A. dbs.QueryDefs("CustomerNumber") = "1234"

B. dbs.QueryDefs("GetCustomer").Parameters("CustomerNumber")
= "1234"

C. dbs.Parameters("CustomerNumber").QueryDefs("GetCustomer")
= "1234"

D. dbs.Parameters("CustomerNumber") = "1234"

19. After executing a Delete query you determine the number of records
deleted by checking the _____ property.

A. RecordCount

B. RecordsAffected

C. RecordsDeleted

D. UpdateCount

20. To retrieve the date that the Customer form was created you would use:

A. dbs.Documents("Customer").Containers("Forms")

B. dbs.Documents("Forms").Containers("Customer")

C. dbs.Containers("Forms").Documents("Customer")

D. dbs.Containers("Customer").Documents("Forms")

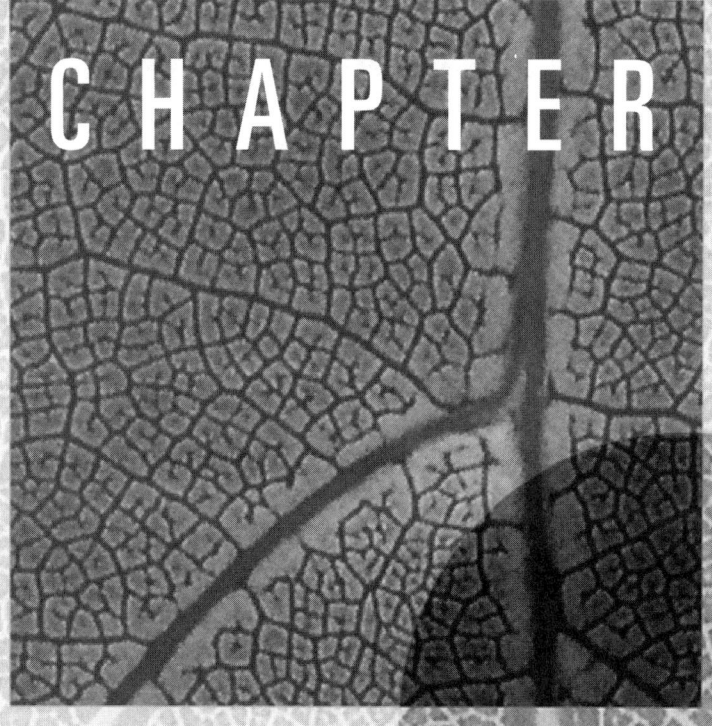

CHAPTER

7

Recordsets

Microsoft Exam Objectives Covered in This Chapter:

- Create Recordset objects.

- Alter an Access SQL statement that is set for an existing QueryDef object.

- Identify the different Recordset object types.

- Differentiate between dynaset-type Recordset objects and snapshot-type Recordset objects.

- Manipulate data by using Recordset objects.

- Use record locking.

- Write procedures that manipulate Recordset objects.

In order to work with Access data, you need to use the DAO object model, and within that object model, recordsets are by far the most useful component. Using DAO recordsets based on native Access tables or tables in non-Microsoft databases, you can add or delete data, filter, sort and update, and work with form and report recordsets.

In this chapter, you will learn:

- What recordsets are and how to use them.

- Whether recordsets are permanent objects in a database or disappear when code finishes running.

- Whether recordsets are updated automatically and what code must be written to keep them up to date.

- Whether records in recordsets have record numbers, as records in dBASE or other database applications do.

- About the limitations on updating records using recordsets.

- Whether recordsets can be used as data sources for forms and reports.

- How to use recordset clones to synchronize a form's record with the user's choice.

Defining a Recordset

In the previous chapter you learned about the DAO object model and the DAO components that are used to create tables, fields, queries, indexes, and relationships. While TableDefs, QueryDefs, and other components of the DAO object model are important, probably the most commonly used DAO component is the Recordset object, as recordsets are used to organize, display, and print data in your Access applications.

A *recordset* is a set of records from one or more tables that behaves as an object. Recordsets created in code let you manipulate temporary collections of records in VBA code without having to create and save a query. The Recordsets collection is at the fourth level of the DAO hierarchy, as shown in Figure 7.1. Because of the hierarchical nature of DAO, this means that in order to use a Recordset object in your code, you need to work down to it through the higher objects, as you will see in the code samples later in this chapter.

FIGURE 7.1

The recordset branch of the DAO object model

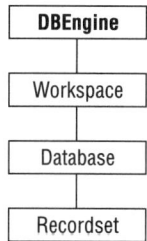

OpenRecordset

Microsoft ✓ *Exam Objective*

Create Recordset objects.

The OpenRecordset method of the Database object is used to create a recordset, as in Exercise 7.1, which creates a recordset from a table.

EXERCISE 7.1

Creating a Recordset from a Table

To create a recordset variable, you have to work down the DAO object model. You don't need to explicitly refer to the DBEngine object (the top level of the DAO hierarchy) when creating a recordset in Access VBA, but you do need to reference a specific database, which can be either the current database or another database.

1. Start by dimensioning variables for the database and recordset:

```
Dim dbs As DATABASE
Dim rst As Recordset
```

2. Then set up a reference to the current database:

```
Set dbs = CurrentDb()
```

3. Finally, you can set up a reference to the recordset, specifying the table it is based on (note that you don't need to use the dbOpenTable constant to specify the recordset type; that selection is the default):

```
Set rst = dbs.OpenRecordset("tblCompanyInfo")
```

Now you can use the rst variable elsewhere in your code to manipulate the table-type recordset created above.

The OpenRecordset method has the following syntax, in two variations:

```
Set variable = database.OpenRecordset(source[, type[, options]])
Set variable = object.OpenRecordset([type[, options]])
```

In the first variant, the Source argument lists the database object (table or query) from which the recordset is created. In the second variant, the Object argument represents a QueryDef, Recordset, or TableDef object used to create the new database; the Source argument is not required.

For both syntax variants, the Type argument accepts three constants representing the different types of recordsets (they will be discussed in more detail in the following sections):

- dbOpenTable
- dbOpenDynaset
- dbOpenSnapshot

The Options argument takes one or more of the following constants (concatenated with a plus sign), specifying various characteristics of the new recordset:

- **dbAppendOnly:** You only append new records (for dynaset-type recordsets only).

- **dbForwardOnly:** The recordset is a forward-only scrolling snapshot. You can't clone these recordsets, and they only support the MoveNext method to move through the records.

- **dbSQLPassThrough:** This option causes the SQL statement to be passed to an ODBC database for processing.

- **dbSeeChanges:** Generates a run-time error if another user changes data you are editing.

- **dbDenyWrite:** Other users can't modify or add records.

- **dbDenyRead:** Other users can't view records (for table-type recordsets only).

- **dbReadOnly:** You can only view records; other users can modify them.

- **dbInconsistent:** Inconsistent updates are allowed (for dynaset-type recordsets only).

- **dbConsistent:** Only consistent updates are allowed (for dynaset-type recordsets only).

Creating Recordsets from QueryDefs

Microsoft ✓ ***Exam*** ***Objective***	**Alter an Access SQL statement that is set for an existing QueryDef object.**

When you create a recordset from a QueryDef, Access executes the SQL statement for that QueryDef in order to create the recordset. Of course, the SQL statement that is contained by the QueryDef must be a valid SQL Select statement.

Using the OpenRecordset method of a QueryDef object to generate your recordset has a significant benefit over using the OpenRecordset method of the database object. Before the Jet database engine can determine which records are to be retrieved, Jet must parse your SQL statement, validate it, and determine the best method to retrieve your data—a process called compiling your query. When you pass a SQL statement to the database object's OpenRecordset method, all of those activities must be performed before your records are retrieved. However, the SQL statement in a QueryDef has already been compiled, and is ready to run. For complicated queries, using an already compiled QueryDef object can save you several seconds over using the database object's OpenRecordset method.

To create a recordset from a QueryDef, you would use code like this routine, which creates a recordset using the QueryDef qryGetGoodCustomers:

```
Dim dbs As DATABASE
Dim rst As Recordset

Set dbs = CurrentDB()
Set rst = dbs.QueryDefs("qryGetGoodCustomers").OpenRecordset
```

You can change the SQL statement associated with a QueryDef object by using the object's SQL property:

```
Dim dbs As DATABASE
Dim rst As Recordset
Dim qdf As QueryDef

Set dbs = CurrentDB()
Set qdf = dbs.QueryDefs("qryGetGoodCustomers")
qdf.SQL = "Select * From Customers;")
Set rst = qdf.OpenRecordset
```

Of course, changing a QueryDef object's SQL statement will force it to be recompiled.

Recordset Types

Microsoft
✓ *Exam*
Objective

Identify the different Recordset object types.

You can create three types of recordsets using the OpenRecordset method. All of them can be used in VBA code to manipulate data in tables, though the three types have different characteristics, as described in the following sections.

Recordset-related Terms

There are several terms that you'll probably come across when working with recordsets. They include:

- **Attached table:** A table in an external database or other supported file format, linked to the current database.

- **Base table:** A saved table in an Access database, as opposed to an attached table.

- **Index:** A list of data in one or more fields in a table, used by Access to speed up searching and sorting of the table.

- **Locking:** Protecting a record being modified by one user from editing by another user.

- **ODBC table:** A table in an external database accessed via the Open Database Connectivity protocol.

Tables

A table-type recordset is created when you set the Type argument for the OpenRecordset method to dbOpenTable, or if you omit this argument and specify a base table for the Source argument. Table-type recordsets represent base tables (to represent an ODBC or attached table, use a dynaset-type recordset). You can use a table-type recordset to add records, delete records, or modify records in a table.

Each table-type recordset represents only one base table, using one or more of the table's indexes. You can select which index to use when sorting data by setting the recordset's Index property to the name of the index. Only the current record is retrieved when its fields are referenced, which results in local memory savings compared to a snapshot-type recordset (described later in this section).

If you create a table-type recordset based on a table that doesn't have any indexes, the data returned may not be in any particular order.

Table-type recordsets are locked during editing and updating, so only one user can update a record at a time. Two types of locking are used: pessimistic and optimistic.

See the *Pessimistic Locking* and *Optimistic Locking* sections later in this chapter for more details on locking in recordsets. Also see Chapter 3 for a discussion of locking as related to forms.

Dynasets

Microsoft ✓ Exam Objective

Differentiate between dynaset-type Recordset objects and snapshot-type Recordset objects.

A dynaset-type recordset is created when you set the recordset's Type argument to dbOpenDynaset. Dynaset-type recordsets (often called *dynasets*) can contain data from one or more base tables or attached tables, or from another recordset, a QueryDef, or a SQL statement (as shown in Exercise 7.2). As with table-type recordsets, only the current record is fetched when its fields are referenced.

EXERCISE 7.2

Using a SQL Statement to Create a Recordset

You can use SQL statements as well as tables or queries to create recordsets. The code sample below illustrates creation of a dynaset from a SQL statement which selects records between two dates, and orders them by one of the fields in the recordset.

1. Start by dimensioning variables for the database, recordset, and a string variable for the SQL statement:

```
Dim dbs As DATABASE
Dim rst As Recordset
Dim strSQL As String
```

2. Next, create the SQL statement. (You can either compose it directly, if you are familiar with SQL syntax, or create a query and then switch to SQL view and copy the SQL code from there:)

```
strSQL = "SELECT * FROM tblInventoryTransactions WHERE
(((TransactionDate) Between #3/1/95# And #12/1/97#)) ORDER
BY PurchaseOrderID;"
```

3. As with any recordset, you need to set a reference to the database to use, in this case the current database:

```
Set dbs = CurrentDb()
```

4. Last, you create the recordset, using the strSQL variable as the source, and the dbOpenDynaset constant to indicate that it is a dynaset-type recordset:

```
Set rst = dbs.OpenRecordset(strSQL, dbOpenDynaset)
```

The entire code segment from Exercise 7.2 is listed below.

Dates in SQL statements are enclosed in hash marks (#); quoted text strings should be enclosed in single quotes, to avoid confusion with the double quotes around the entire SQL statement string. If you copy a SQL statement from a query's SQL window, you may need to convert double quotes in the SQL statement into single quotes.

```
Dim dbs As DATABASE
Dim rst As Recordset
Dim strSQL As String

strSQL = "SELECT * FROM tblInventoryTransactions WHERE
(((TransactionDate) Between #3/1/95# And #12/1/97#)) ORDER BY
PurchaseOrderID;"
Set dbs = CurrentDb()
Set rst = dbs.OpenRecordset(strSQL, dbOpenDynaset)
```

Similar to table-type recordsets, dynasets are locked during editing, either pessimistically or optimistically. Dynasets may be updatable or non-updatable, depending on various factors. A dynaset is locked if:

- An ODBC or Paradox table doesn't have a unique index.

- A table is locked by another user.

- A record was changed since you last read it.

- The user doesn't have permission.

- One or more tables or fields are read-only.

- The database was opened read-only.

- The dynaset was created from multiple tables lacking a JOIN statement, or the query is too complex.

Capitalization of SQL keywords is by nature inconsistent. SQL keywords (such as JOIN and WHERE) are usually printed in all caps in code, and if you create a query and view its SQL equivalent, the keywords will be in all caps. But they work just as well in mixed case, so this is not a syntactical requirement. It is more of a convention, to indicate which words in the SQL statement are keywords.

You can determine whether a dynaset is updatable by checking its Updatable property.

Snapshots

Snapshot-type recordsets (also known as *snapshots*) are read-only, static representations of records, which you can use to inspect data in a table or tables. You can't update snapshots. Snapshots use less system resources than dynasets, because the entire record is downloaded to local memory. The code below opens a snapshot-type recordset:

```
Dim dbs As DATABASE
Dim rst As Recordset

Set dbs = CurrentDb()
Set rst = dbs.OpenRecordset("tblEmployees", dbOpenSnapshot)
```

Working with Recordsets

Once you have created a recordset, you can work with it in VBA code, using its methods and properties. The most commonly used methods and properties are described in the following sections.

Methods

The Recordset object has about 20 methods, but the ones that are most frequently used are the ones that control movement among records: adding, deleting, and updating records. These methods are described in the following sections.

AddNew

The AddNew method is used to add a new editable record to a table-type or dynaset-type recordset. With dynasets, new records are inserted at the end of the recordset. With table-type recordsets, if the Index property is set, records are placed in indexed order; otherwise, they are placed at the end of the recordset.

When writing VBA code to manipulate recordsets, use the dot (.) operator for methods and properties, and the bang (!) operator for fields to ensure that your code will run properly. Also, if field names include spaces, enclose them with square brackets([]).

When you use AddNew to add a new record, initially all the record's fields are filled with Nulls (or default field values). In order to save any changes you make to the new record, you must use the Update method after the AddNew method in your code, as in Exercise 7.3.

EXERCISE 7.3

Adding a New Record to a Recordset

1. First, dimension variables for the database and recordset:

```
Dim dbs As DATABASE
Dim rst As Recordset
```

EXERCISE 7.3 (CONTINUED)

2. Set the dbs variable equal to the current database:

```
Set dbs = CurrentDb()
```

3. Next, open a table-type recordset for the tblShippingMethods table:

```
Set rst = dbs.OpenRecordset("tblShippingMethods")
```

4. Start a With…End With construct to perform a number of actions with the recordset:

```
With rst
```

5. Use the AddNew method to add a new record:

```
.AddNew
```

6. Assign a value to one of the fields in the new record:

```
!ShippingMethod = "Flying Packets"
```

7. Update the new record:

```
.UPDATE
```

8. Close the recordset:

```
.Close
```

9. End the With…End construct:

```
End With
```

Note that you use the bang operator (!) for the ShippingMethod field in Exercise 7.3, since it is a member of the recordset, but the dot operator (.) for the methods. The field does not need to be enclosed in square brackets (though that syntax can be used, if desired) because it does not contain a space.

Figure 7.2 shows the tblShippingMethods table with the new record added by the AddNew method in the above code. Note that the Shipping

Method ID column has a new entry which was not added in the code—it was automatically created as an AutoNumber field.

FIGURE 7.2

A table with a new row created by the AddNew method

Don't confuse AddNew with Append. In other database applications, Append adds a new record to a recordset (equivalent to AddNew in DAO). The Append method in DAO belongs to the Collection object; it adds a new object to a collection, such as adding a field to a table. See Chapter 6 for more information on the Append method.

Delete

The Delete method (as its name implies) deletes a record from a recordset, and from its underlying table record as well. In some situations, records in other tables may be deleted as well, in particular when you delete a record from the table representing the "one" side in a one-to-many relationship with Cascade Deletes set to Yes; in that case the related records in the "many" side of the relationship will also be deleted.

You don't need to use the Update method after using Delete.

You must have a current record when using the Delete method; otherwise, an error will occur. If you have used one of the Move* methods, or have done a successful Find, you will usually have a current record. To make absolutely sure that you have a current record before performing an action, you can check whether rst.EOF or rst.BOF is true; if either one is true, you don't have a current record, as shown in Exercise 7.4.

The following code goes to the last record of a recordset and deletes it:

```
Dim dbs As DATABASE
Dim rst As Recordset

Set dbs = CurrentDb()
Set rst = dbs.OpenRecordset("tblShippingMethods")
rst.MoveLast
rst.Delete
```

EXERCISE 7.4

Checking for a Current Record with EOF

1. Create a table called **tblContacts** with two fields: **LastName** and **FirstName**.

2. Enter two records in the table, and then close the table.

3. Create the following function in a code module:

```
Public Function TestEOF()

    Dim dbs As Database
    Dim rst As Recordset
    Dim strSearch As String

    Set dbs = CurrentDb
    Set rst = dbs.OpenRecordset("tblContacts", dbOpenDynaset)

    With rst
      .MoveFirst
      Debug.Print "First record last name: " & !LastName
      .MoveNext
      Debug.Print "Second record last name: " & !LastName
      .MoveNext
      Debug.Print "Third record last name: " & !LastName
      .Close
    End With

End Function
```

4. Create a macro called **mcrTestEOF** with a RunCode action to call the TestEOF function.

5. Open the Debug Window with Ctrl+G.

6. Run the mcrTestEOF macro.

7. The first and second record last names print in the Debug Window, then the code stops with a runtime error 3021 (No current record). Click on the End button to close the error message, and then on the Halt button on the Action Failed dialog box from the macro. The 3021 error message indicates that you don't have a current record after the third MoveNext statement, because there are only two records in this table.

8. To fix the problem, add the following lines of code after the third MoveNext statement in the TestEOF function:

```
If rst.EOF = True Then
    Debug.Print "No more records; exiting"
    Exit Function
End If
```

9. Close the module and run the macro again; now the Debug Window lists the last names from the first two records, and then the "No more records; exiting" message, and finally exits the function.

If you want to be able to undo a deletion, you should use transactions and set up your code so you can roll back a transaction. (See Chapter 6 for more information on transactions.)

Edit

The Edit method lets you make changes to a record. Technically, it copies the current record from a dynaset or table-type recordset to the copy buffer, where you can edit the record. After editing, use the Update method to save the edited record to the recordset. The code below moves to the last record, puts it into Edit mode, makes a change to a field, and then updates the record:

```
Dim dbs As DATABASE
Dim rst As Recordset

Set dbs = CurrentDb()
Set rst = dbs.OpenRecordset("tblShippingMethods")
With rst
    .MoveLast
    .Edit
    !ShippingMethod = "Fast Deliveries"
    .UPDATE
    .Close
End With
```

WARNING If you edit a record and then move to another record without saving the record with Update, your changes will be lost.

If any of the following conditions is present, you won't be able to edit a record:

- There is no current record.
- The database (or recordset) is read-only.
- None of the record's fields are updatable.
- The database or recordset was opened exclusively by another user.
- Another user has locked the record.

Find*

As their names imply, the FindFirst, FindLast, FindNext, and FindPrevious methods move to the first, last, next, or previous record in the recordset, as ordered by the selected index or ORDER BY clause of a SQL statement, making it the current record for further operations. An optional Criteria argument can be used to select a record meeting certain conditions, as in the code sample below, which finds the first record meeting the criteria, and then modifies that record:

```
dbs As DATABASE
Dim rst As Recordset
```

```
Dim strFind As String

strFind = "[ShippingMethod] = 'Fast Deliveries'"

Set dbs = CurrentDb()
Set rst = dbs.OpenRecordset("tblShippingMethods", dbOpenDynaset)
With rst
    .FindNext strFind
    .Edit
    !ShippingMethod = "Faster Deliveries"
    .UPDATE
    .Close
End With
```

When using one of the Find* methods, it is advisable to check whether a matching record was found before continuing, because if no match was found there won't be a current record and the next line of code may generate an error. Exercise 7.5 gives an example of checking for a current record using EOF.

See the Bookmark section for an example of using the NoMatch method with a bookmark.

Move*

The MoveFirst, MoveLast, MoveNext and MovePrevious methods move to the first, last, next, or previous record (without any conditions) and make it the current record. These methods are very useful when iterating through a recordset to make changes to all records, as you'll see in Exercise 7.5.

EXERCISE 7.5

Using the MoveNext Method to Iterate through a Recordset

1. Dimension variables for the database and recordset:

   ```
   Dim dbs As DATABASE
   Dim rst As Recordset
   ```

2. Set the dbs variable to the current database:

   ```
   Set dbs = CurrentDb
   ```

3. Set the rst variable to open tblSalesRep as a dynaset:

```
Set rst = dbs.OpenRecordset("tblSalesRep", dbOpenDynaset)
```

4. Start a With…End With construct to loop through the recordset:

```
With rst
```

5. Start a nested Do While…Loop construct using EOF to loop through the recordset and perform certain actions while not at the end of the recordset:

```
Do While Not .EOF
```

6. Enter four rows to put the record in Edit mode, increase the Salary field by 10%, update the record, and move to the next record:

```
.Edit
!Salary = !Salary * 1.1
.Update
.MoveNext
```

7. End the Do loop, and then end the With construct:

```
Loop
End With
```

8. Close the recordset:

```
rst.Close
```

See the BOF/EOF section for a discussion of the interaction between the Move* methods and those properties.

Seek

The Seek method locates a record in an indexed table-type recordset that matches the specified criteria. Once the record is located, it becomes the current record. The Seek method uses the following syntax, where *table* represents the table-type recordset, *comparison* represents the comparison operator (<, <=, =, >=, or >), and the *Key1, Key2…* arguments represent one or more fields in the recordset's current index (as specified by its Index property setting):

```
table.Seek comparison, key1, key2...
```

The values specified for the Key1 argument must be of the same data type as the index field it matches. As with the Find* methods, it is advisable to check whether a matching record was found before continuing, because if no match was found there won't be a current record and the next line of code may generate an error.

The code below seeks a match in the Primary Key index, and prints one of the record's fields, if found; otherwise, it exits the function.

```
Dim dbs As DATABASE
Dim rst As Recordset

Set dbs = CurrentDb()
Set rst = dbs.OpenRecordset("tblShippingMethods", dbOpenTable)
With rst
    .INDEX = "PrimaryKey"
    .Seek "=", 8
    If .NoMatch Then Exit Function
    Debug.Print !ShippingMethod
    .Close
End With
```

Update

The Update method saves a record modified after using the Edit method. See the Find method example for an example of the usage of Update. If any of the following conditions occur, you will lose changes to the current record:

- You use the Edit or AddNew method, and then move to another record without first using Update.

- You use Edit or AddNew, and then use Edit or AddNew again without first using Update.

- You set the Bookmark property to another record.

- You close the recordset without first using Update.

- You cancel the Edit.

- You move off the record.

Properties

Microsoft ✓ ***Exam*** ***Objective***	**Manipulate data by using Recordset objects.**

The Recordset object has about 25 properties, which are used to manipulate recordsets in VBA code. Understanding these properties lets you search in recordsets, add new records, delete records, and edit records. The most commonly used recordset properties are described in the following sections.

BOF/EOF

The BOF (Beginning of File) and EOF (End of File) properties are of great use when looping through recordsets. The BOF property is True (–1) when the pointer is before the first record in a recordset, while the EOF property is True when the pointer is after the last record in the recordset. The code below illustrates looping through a recordset all the way to the end, using the EOF property:

```
Dim dbs As DATABASE
Dim rst As Recordset

Set dbs = CurrentDb()
Set rst = dbs.OpenRecordset("tblShippingMethods", dbOpenDynaset)

With rst
    Do While Not .EOF
        Debug.Print "Shipping method: " & !ShippingMethod
        rst.MoveNext
    Loop
End With

End Function
```

The pointer in a recordset is an imaginary cursor moving through the records.

Bookmark

The Bookmark property is a variant array of Byte data that uniquely identifies the current record in a Recordset object; it can also be used to set the current record to a valid bookmark. Bookmarks are strange things. You can't print them or view them; their only use is as markers to allow you to readily move back to a record you were on previously.

The Byte data type holds small positive integers from 0 to 255.

A bookmark is not a record number (such as the dBASE record number). Access does not have a real record number property.

The code below uses a bookmark to return to a previous record in case the Seek method fails:

```
Dim dbs As DATABASE
Dim rst As Recordset
Dim varBookmark As Variant

Set dbs = CurrentDb()
Set rst = dbs.OpenRecordset("tblShippingMethods", dbOpenTable)
With rst
    varBookmark = .Bookmark
    .INDEX = "PrimaryKey"
    .Seek "=", 2
    If .NoMatch Then .Bookmark = varBookmark
    Debug.Print !ShippingMethod
    .Close
End With
```

DateCreated, LastUpdated

The DateCreated property returns the date (and time) the recordset was created (or the base table, for a table-type recordset). The LastUpdated property returns the date (and time) the table's structure was last modified. You can see these dates in the table properties sheet in the Access interface.

LastUpdated does not represent the date when the data was last modified— use the LastModified property to locate the most recently changed record.

Filter

The Filter property is a String expression that contains the WHERE clause of a SQL statement (without the word "WHERE"). Applying a filter restricts the records in a dynaset- or snapshot-type recordset. The code sample below restricts records to those located in the UK:

```
Dim dbs As DATABASE
Dim rst As Recordset
Dim rstUK As Recordset

Set dbs = CurrentDb()
Set rst = dbs.OpenRecordset("tblCompanyInfo", dbOpenDynaset)
rst.Filter = "Country = 'UK'"
Set rstUK = rst.OpenRecordset

With rstUK
    Do Until .EOF
        Debug.Print "Country: " & !Country
        .MoveNext
    Loop
End With
```

After applying the Filter property to a recordset, to see the results you must open another recordset from the filtered original recordset.

It is often more efficient to apply a filter to a recordset and open it in one step, using a SQL statement with a WHERE clause.

Index

The Index property is used with the Seek method to specify the index used while seeking. See the *Seek* section for an example of a use of this property.

LastModified

This property returns a bookmark that indicates the record in a recordset whose data has been changed most recently. The following code goes to the most recently modified record in a recordset and displays the company name from that record in a message box:

```
Dim dbs As DATABASE
Dim rst As Recordset

Set dbs = CurrentDb()
Set rst = dbs.OpenRecordset("tblShippingMethods", dbOpenDynaset)
rst.Bookmark = rst.LastModified
MsgBox "Shipping Method: " & rst!ShippingMethod
```

RecordCount

The RecordCount property gives you a count of the records in a recordset. When used on a dynaset- or snapshot-type recordset, the count is not accurate until all records in the recordset have been accessed, usually by means of the MoveLast method, as in the code below:

```
Dim dbs As DATABASE
Dim rst As Recordset

Set dbs = CurrentDb()
Set rst = dbs.OpenRecordset("tblShippingMethods")
rst.MoveLast
MsgBox "Number of records: " & rst.RecordCount
```

Updatable

The Updatable property indicates whether a recordset can be updated. It is a good idea to check this property before trying to edit a recordset, particularly if you are working in a multiuser environment where the recordset might be locked by another user. The Updatable property is True if the recordset can be updated, and False otherwise.

The code sample below checks whether a recordset is updatable, and makes a change if it is; otherwise it exits the function.

```
Dim dbs As DATABASE
Dim rst As Recordset

Set dbs = CurrentDb()
Set rst = dbs.OpenRecordset("tblShippingMethods", dbOpenDynaset)
With rst
    If .Updatable = False Then
        Exit Function
    Else
        .MoveLast
        .Edit
        !ShippingMethod = "Quick Deliveries"
        .UPDATE
        .Close
    End If
End With
```

Locking in Recordsets

When a record is locked, it is unavailable for editing by other users. Table- and dynaset-type recordsets can be locked in several ways, depending on the setting of their LockEdits property. If the LockEdits property is set to True, pessimistic locking is in effect; if this property is set to False, optimistic locking is in effect. The two types of locking are described below.

Microsoft ✓ *Exam* *Objective*   **Use record locking.**

Pessimistic Locking

With pessimistic locking, the page containing the record being edited is unavailable to other users while you are using the Edit method, and it remains unavailable until you use the Update method to end the editing session and save the record. This method is more effective than optimistic locking at preventing two users from simultaneously working on a record, so that one user's changes might wipe out the other users' changes, but it may cause delays while records are unnecessarily locked. True is the default setting for the LockEdits property, and it implements pessimistic locking.

Optimistic Locking

With optimistic locking, a record you are editing is available for use by other users after you have used the Update method; it is only unavailable briefly while you are using the Update method. This method is riskier than pessimistic locking, as it leaves open the possibility of simultaneous editing of a record by two users.

Form and Report Recordsets

Microsoft ✓ *Exam* *Objective*	**Write procedures that manipulate Recordset objects.**

In addition to creating recordsets from tables, queries, and SQL statements, you can manipulate the recordsets representing the data sources of Access forms and reports. One of handiest uses of form recordsets is for synchronizing a form's record with one chosen by the user, usually from a combo box, as described in Exercise 7.6.

RecordsetClone

The RecordsetClone property of a form recordset is a copy of the form's recordset; you can search in it without leaving the form's current record. The code in Exercise 7.6 lets the user go to the desired record on a form by just selecting an item from a combo box.

As an alternative to using nested single quotes, you can use Chr$(34) (the ANSI number for the single quote character) in SQL statements and other expressions in VBA code.

EXERCISE 7.6

Using a RecordsetClone to Simplify Record Navigation on a Form

1. Add a few more records to tblContacts (which you created earlier in Exercise 7.4).

2. Create an AutoForm based on tblContacts.

3. Create an unbound combo box called **cboSearch** in the form's header.

4. Select Table/Query as the Row Source Type for the combo box.

5. Enter the following SQL statement as the Row Source:

   SELECT tblContacts.LastName FROM tblContacts ORDER BY tblContacts.LastName;

6. In Design view, open the combo box's properties sheet and select Event Procedure from the After Update property's drop-down list.

7. Click the Build button to open the event procedure code stub, and fill it in with the following code:

```
Private Sub cboSearch_AfterUpdate()
   Dim strSearch As String

   strSearch = "[LastName] = " & Chr$(34) & Me![cboSearch]
➥ & Chr$(34)
   Me.RecordsetClone.FindFirst strSearch
   Me.Bookmark = Me.RecordsetClone.Bookmark

End Sub
```

8. Switch to Form view and select a last name in the combo box to move to that person's record.

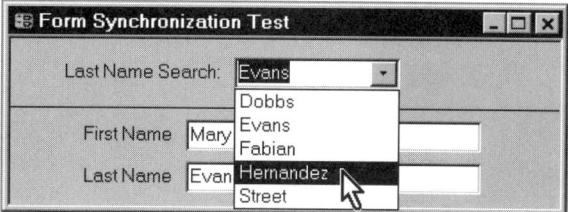

The code sets up a recordset clone, then searches for the user's selection in the recordset clone, and finally sets the form's recordset (represented by the Me keyword) to match the record in the recordset clone, using the Bookmark property.

Summary

Recordsets are probably the most widely used component of the DAO object model. The Recordset object is directly under the Database object in the DAO hierarchy, and is accessed via the Database object in code. Recordsets are used to access data in base tables, attached Access tables, and ODBC and other non-Microsoft database tables.

Recordsets may be table-type, dynaset-type, or snapshot-type. Table-type recordsets represent Access base tables, and can be used to add, delete, or modify records. Dynaset-type recordsets can represent base tables, attached tables, and non-Access tables, and may be updatable, depending on the nature of the links and possible locks. Snapshot-type dynasets are not updatable.

Using methods, you work with recordsets to add, delete, move through, filter, locate, and update the records, using properties such as BOF/EOF, bookmarks, and others having to do with filtering and indexing, and the dates when the recordset was created or last updated.

Recordsets can be locked in two ways: pessimistically, where a record is locked to other users while one user is editing it; and optimistically, where a record is only locked while it is being updated.

You can use the RecordsetClone property of a form to work with a copy of a form or report's recordset.

Review Questions

1. You need to find the record in a recordset that was last changed. Which of the following is the right way to do this?

   A. Use the LastModified property.

   B. Use the LastUpdated property.

   C. Use the MoveLast method on an indexed recordset.

   D. Use the EOF property.

2. Which of the following code samples will ensure that you get an accurate count of records in a dynaset?

   A. rst.RecordCount

   B. rst.EOF
   rst.RecordCount

   C. rst.MoveLast
   rst.RecordCount

   D. rst.Count

3. Assuming that the recordset and relevant field are both updatable, which two of these code samples would update the record?

   A.
   ```
   Dim dbs As DATABASE
   Dim rst As Recordset

   Set dbs = CurrentDb()
   Set rst = dbs.OpenRecordset("tblShippingMethods")
   With rst
       .AddNew
       !ShippingMethod = "Flying Packets"
       .UPDATE
       .Close
   End With
   ```

B.
```
Dim dbs As DATABASE
Dim rst As Recordset

Set dbs = CurrentDb()
Set rst = dbs.OpenRecordset("tblShippingMethods")
rst.MoveLast
rst.Delete
```

C.
```
Dim dbs As DATABASE
Dim rst As Recordset

Set dbs = CurrentDb()
Set rst = dbs.OpenRecordset("tblShippingMethods")
With rst
    .MoveLast
    .Edit
    !ShippingMethod = "Fast Deliveries"
    .Close
End With
```

D.
```
Dim dbs As DATABASE
Dim rst As Recordset
Dim strFind As String

strFind - "[ShippingMethod] - 'Fast Deliveries'"

Set dbs = CurrentDb()
Set rst = dbs.OpenRecordset("tblShippingMethods",
dbOpenDynaset)
With rst
    .FindNext strFind
    !ShippingMethod = "Faster Deliveries"
    .UPDATE
    .Close
End With
```

4. Which property should you check to determine whether a record was found before trying to edit a record?

  A. Found

  B. NotFound

  C. Match

  D. NoMatch

5. Use the _____ method to add a new record to a recordset.

  A. Add

  B. Append

  C. AddNew

  D. NewRecord

6. You need to be able to return to the record you were on if a Find* method fails. Which of the following would work?

  A.
```
Dim dbs As DATABASE
Dim rst As Recordset
Dim varBookmark As Variant

Set dbs = CurrentDb()
Set rst = dbs.OpenRecordset("tblShippingMethods",
dbOpenTable)
With rst
    varBookmark = .Bookmark
    .INDEX = "PrimaryKey"
    .Seek "=", 2
    If .NoMatch Then .Bookmark = varBookmark
    Debug.Print !ShippingMethod
    .Close
End With
```

  B.
```
Dim dbs As DATABASE
Dim rst As Recordset
```

```
    Dim strBookmark As String

    Set dbs = CurrentDb()
    Set rst = dbs.OpenRecordset("tblShippingMethods",
    dbOpenTable)
    With rst
        strBookmark = .Bookmark
        .INDEX = "PrimaryKey"
        .Seek "=", 2
        If .NoMatch Then .Bookmark = strBookmark
        Debug.Print !ShippingMethod
        .Close
    End With
```

C.
```
    Dim dbs As DATABASE
    Dim rst As Recordset

    Set dbs = CurrentDb()
    Set rst = dbs.OpenRecordset("tblShippingMethods",
    dbOpenTable)
    With rst
        .INDEX = "PrimaryKey"
        .Seek "=", 2
        If .NoMatch Then .Bookmark
        Debug.Print !ShippingMethod
        .Close
    End With
```

D.
```
    Dim dbs As DATABASE
    Dim rst As Recordset
    Dim varBookmark As Variant

    Set dbs = CurrentDb()
    Set rst = dbs.OpenRecordset("tblShippingMethods",
    dbOpenTable)
    varBookmark = .Bookmark
    With rst
        .INDEX = "PrimaryKey"
```

```
        .Seek "=", 2
        If .NoMatch Then .Bookmark = varBookmark
        Debug.Print !ShippingMethod
        .Close
    End With
```

7. Which two of the following code samples will iterate through all the records in a table-type recordset?

A.
```
Dim dbs As Database
Dim rst As Recordset

Set dbs = CurrentDb
Set rst = dbs.OpenRecordset("tblContacts")

Do While Not rst.EOF
    Debug.Print rst![LastName]
Loop
```

B.
```
Dim dbs As Database
Dim rst As Recordset

Set dbs = CurrentDb
Set rst = dbs.OpenRecordset("tblContacts")

Do While Not rst.EOF
    Debug.Print rst![LastName]
    rst.MoveNext
Loop
```

C.
```
Dim dbs As Database
Dim rst As Recordset

Set dbs = CurrentDb
Set rst = dbs.OpenRecordset("tblContacts")

For Each fld In rst
    Debug.Print rst![Last Name]
Next fld
```

D.
```
Dim dbs As Database
    Dim rst As Recordset

    Set dbs = CurrentDb
    Set rst = dbs.OpenRecordset("tblContacts")

    Do Until rst.EOF
        Debug.Print rst![LastName]
        rst.MoveNext
    Loop
```

8. You write the code below to open a recordset clone, based on a form's recordset, and move to a new record in the recordset clone. After running the code, which record are you on in the form's recordset?

```
Private Sub cboSearch_AfterUpdate()

    Dim strSearch As String

    strSearch = "[LastName] = " & Chr$(34) & Me!
    ➥ [cboSearch] & Chr$(34)
    Me.RecordsetClone.FindFirst strSearch

End Sub
```

A. The same record as the recordset clone

B. The first record

C. The same record as the form

D. At the beginning of the file (BOF is True)

9. When you add new records to a table-type recordset with its Index property set to a valid index, the new records are placed:

A. At the end of the recordset

B. In indexed order

C. At the beginning of the recordset

D. In a random location

10. If a recordset's LockEdits property is set to True, _____ locking is in effect for the recordset.

   A. Optimistic

   B. Pessimistic

   C. Read-only

   D. Write-only

CHAPTER

8

Advanced Coding

Microsoft Exam Objectives Covered in This Chapter:

- Define and create form and report modules.

- Given sample code, identify the scope of a form or report module.

- Declare symbolic constants, and make them available locally or publicly.

- Use common built-in functions.

- Create user-defined functions.

- Declare and use object variables and collections, and use their associated properties and methods.

- Write an error handler.

- Use the Errors collection and the Error object to trap errors.

- Use debugging tools to suspend program execution, and to examine, step through, and reset execution of code.

- Debug given code samples.

- Use the Debug window to monitor variable values.

- Properly declare Windows API functions.

- Use the ByVal and ByRef keywords.

In Chapter 2, we introduced Access VBA coding; this chapter deals with advanced coding techniques which you will need to create complex applications in Access.

In this chapter, you will learn:

- How to make and use your own functions.

- How to process all elements of a collection without having to count them.

- The difference between a subroutine and a function.

- How to use functions in Code Behind Forms (CBF).

- How to fix problems with upgrading an Access 2.0 application to Access 95, when you get error messages referring to 16-bit DLLs.

- How to handle errors in a standard fashion.

- How to get information about elements of the Windows interface that aren't available from within Access VBA.

- The various sorts of errors that can occur in Access code.

- About the tools Access VBA provides to help you debug your code.

Managing Complexity: Designing for Maintenance

Microsoft ✓ *Exam* *Objective*

Define and create form and report modules.

If you write procedures to support the functionality you need on forms and reports—storing them in Code Behind Forms (CBF) modules—you may find yourself needlessly duplicating functionality in different procedures. If you understand how to write subs and functions that can be used on more than one object, and how to store them in standard modules, you can use the same procedure in many different places and make your application more efficient and easier to maintain.

This chapter will show you how to move from writing functions in CBF modules to writing functions in standard modules, and how to call them from event procedures in your forms and reports, using more efficient programming techniques to avoid unnecessary duplication of code.

If you need to make changes to many controls on a form such as the one shown in Figure 8.1, and you write a function or sub in the form's CBF module to change each control separately, you will quickly tire of writing repetitive code. If you need to make a change, you will have to go through all the lines of code referencing the controls separately, making the same change in each one (see the code sample later in this section).

Demystifying Modules

Modules come in two flavors: *class modules* and *standard modules.* Form and report modules (also known as Code Behind Forms, or CBF modules) are class modules, while the modules you see in the Module window are standard modules. They differ in the following ways:

- Class modules contain event procedures for their form or report, private subs and functions, and public procedures that define custom methods and properties for the form or report.

- Standard modules contain private functions and subs that can be used in that module only, or public functions and subs that can be used anywhere in the application.

The error trapping used in the following code samples will be explained in more detail in the *Handling Errors* section later in this chapter.

F I G U R E 8.1

The Change Product Prices form

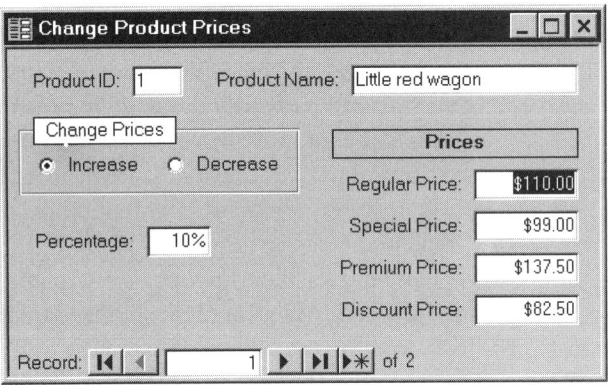

The first code listing below is run directly from the After Update event of a text box (txtPercentage) on a form. Because the sub is run from a form, it uses the Me keyword to reference the form itself. The code starts by picking up the value of an option group (fraChange), which indicates whether to increase or decrease the price in txtPercentage, then runs a Select Case statement—one case for increasing, and one for decreasing prices.

Under each case in the Select Case statement, there are four sets of value assignments, in which the modified price is calculated and is then assigned to a specific control on the form (the four Currency controls).

```
Private Sub txtPercentage_AfterUpdate()

On Error GoTo txtPercentage_AfterUpdateError

    Dim intChange As Integer
    Dim dblChange As Double
    Dim curPrice As Currency

    intChange = Me! [fraChange]
    dblChange = Nz(Me![txtPercentage])

    If dblChange = 0 Then Exit Sub

    Select Case intChange

        Case 1
            'Increase prices
            curPrice = CCur(Me![txtRegularPrice])
            curPrice = curPrice + (curPrice * dblChange)
            'Copy increased price to current price control
            Me![txtRegularPrice] = curPrice
            curPrice = CCur(Me![txtSpecialPrice])
            curPrice = curPrice + (curPrice * dblChange)
            Me![txtSpecialPrice] = curPrice
            curPrice = CCur(Me![txtPremiumPrice])
            curPrice = curPrice + (curPrice * dblChange)
            Me![txtPremiumPrice] = curPrice
            curPrice = CCur(Me![txtDiscountPrice])
            curPrice = curPrice + (curPrice * dblChange)
            Me![txtDiscountPrice] = curPrice

        Case 2
            'Decrease prices
            curPrice = CCur(Me![txtRegularPrice])
```

```
                         curPrice = curPrice - (curPrice * dblChange)
                         'Copy decreased price to current price control
                         Me![txtRegularPrice] = curPrice
                         curPrice = CCur(Me![txtSpecialPrice])
                         curPrice = curPrice - (curPrice * dblChange)
                         Me![txtSpecialPrice] = curPrice
                         curPrice = CCur(Me![txtPremiumPrice])
                         curPrice = curPrice - (curPrice * dblChange)
                         Me![txtPremiumPrice] = curPrice
                         curPrice = CCur(Me![txtDiscountPrice])
                         curPrice = curPrice - (curPrice * dblChange)
                         Me![txtDiscountPrice] = curPrice

             End Select

      txtPercentage_AfterUpdateExit:
          Exit Sub

      txtPercentage_AfterUpdateError:
          MsgBox Error.Description
          Resume txtPercentage_AfterUpdateExit

      End Sub
```

You could simplify this code considerably by writing a function in the form's
CBF module to increase or decease the price, and running it from each control's AfterUpdate event. The modified function is shown here:

```
      Public Function ChangePrice(ctl As Control, _
          intChange As Integer, dblChange As Double) As Integer

      On Error GoTo ChangePriceError

          Dim curPrice As Currency

          'Increase prices
          curPrice = CCur(ctl)
```

```
    Select Case intChange
        Case 1
            curPrice = curPrice + (curPrice * dblChange)
        Case 2
            curPrice = curPrice - (curPrice * dblChange)
    End Select

    'Copy changed price to current price control
    ctl.Value = curPrice

ChangePriceExit:
    Exit Function

ChangePriceError:
    MsgBox Error.Description
    Resume ChangePriceExit

End Function
```

The function is called from the AfterUpdate event procedure as follows:

```
Private Sub txtPercentage_AfterUpdate()

On Error GoTo txtPercentage_AfterUpdateError

    Dim intChange As Integer
    Dim dblChange As Double
    Dim curPrice As Currency
    Dim i As Integer

    intChange = Me![fraChange]
    dblChange = Nz(Me![txtPercentage])

    If dblChange = 0 Then Exit Sub

    i = ChangePrice(Me![txtRegularPrice], intChange, dblChange)
    i = ChangePrice(Me![txtSpecialPrice], intChange, dblChange)
```

```
    i = ChangePrice(Me![txtPremiumPrice], intChange, dblChange)
    i = ChangePrice(Me![txtDiscountPrice], intChange, dblChange)

txtPercentage_AfterUpdateExit:
    Exit Sub

txtPercentage_AfterUpdateError:
    MsgBox Error.Description
    Resume txtPercentage_AfterUpdateExit

End Sub
```

This function called from the event procedure is more efficient, but it still has to deal with each control separately by name. What if you want to allow for the possibility of adding more price controls to the form, and want the code to be able to automatically deal with them all? This further refinement of the code will be described in the section on *Using Collections* later in this chapter.

Scope and Lifetime of Variables

Microsoft ✓ *Exam* *Objective*	**Given sample code, identify the scope of a form or report module.**

The procedures, variables, and constants you create are available in various parts of your applications (this is called their *scope*), and have varying *lifetimes*, depending on how and where they are declared. You can declare variables or constants in the Declarations section of a module (*module-level* declaration) or in a Sub or Function procedure in the main section of a module (*procedure-level* declaration).You can also use the Sub, Function, Private, Public, Dim, Static, and Const keywords when declaring procedures, variables, and constants, with varying results for their scope and lifetimes, as shown in Table 8.1.

T A B L E   8.1:   Scope and Visibility of Procedures, Variables, and Constants

Keyword Combinations	Declaration Level	Scope and Lifetime of Variables
Public Sub	Module-level	Available to all modules in all projects
Public Function	Module-level	Available to all modules in all projects
Public Sub	Procedure-level	N/A
Public Function	Procedure-level	N/A
Private Sub	Module-level	Only available in the module in which it appears
Private Function	Module-level	Only available in the module in which it appears
Dim *variable* Private *variable*	Module-level	Only available in the module in which it is declared; exists as long as the procedure is running
Static *variable*	Module-level	N/A
Public *variable*	Module-level	Available to all procedures in all modules
Dim *variable*	Procedure-level	Only available in the procedure in which it is declared; exists as long as the procedure is running
Public *variable*	Procedure-level	N/A
Static *variable*	Procedure-level	Only available in the procedure in which it is declared; exists as long as the application is running
Const *constant*	Module-level	Only available in the module in which it is declared
Public Const *constant*	Module-level (standard modules only)	Available to all procedures in all modules
Const *constant*	Procedure-level	Only available in the procedure in which it is declared

Procedures are Public by default; variables and constants are Private by default.

If you give the same name to variables with different scope (say, one declared with Dim in a procedure, and the other declared as Public in the declarations section of a module), the more local variable will be used in preference to the less local one of the same name. You can avoid confusion when referencing variables in other modules by storing all the variables you want to use throughout your application in one or more standard modules, and using an extra *g* prefix for these global variables (for example, gstrOffice instead of strOffice for a String variable).

If you need to occasionally use a public variable from another form or report module, preface the variable name with the form or report name, as in the code sample:

```
Forms!frmOrders.intCharge
```

To avoid confusion, don't give variables the same names as fields or controls.

Constants

You can use two types of constants in Access: intrinsic constants, which are predefined by various applications and can be used without declaration throughout your code; and user-defined constants, which you declare with the Const keyword.

Intrinsic Constants

There are three groups of intrinsic constants which are very useful in Access code: those provided by Access, Visual Basic for Applications (VBA), and Data Access Objects (DAO). These constants are listed in the Constants selection in the Modules/Classes pane of the Object Browser. Figure 8.2 shows the Access constants.

Intrinsic constants are sometimes referred to as predefined constants or named constants.

Intrinsic constants are frequently used as arguments for functions and methods, as in the code sample that follows, which uses two Access intrinsic

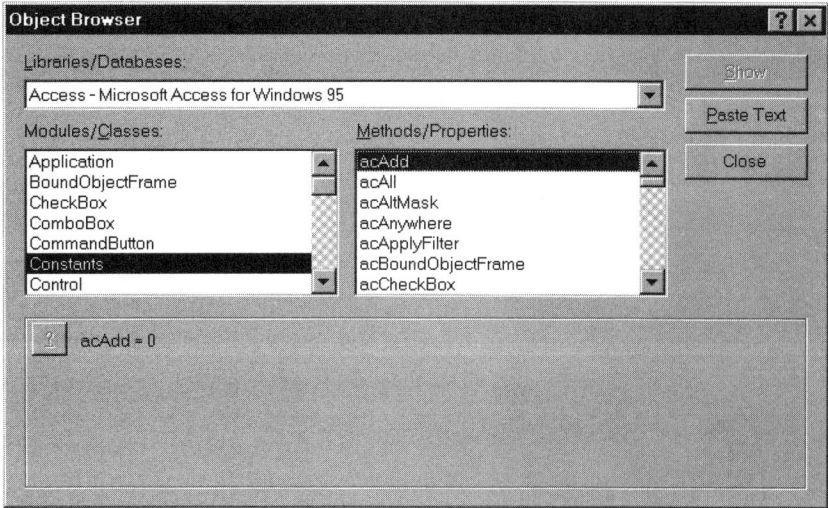

FIGURE 8.2

The Access intrinsic
constants in the
Object Browser

constants as values for the Objecttype and Save arguments of the
DoCmd.Close method:

```
DoCmd.Close acForm, strFormName, acSaveYes
```

Check a function or method's Access Help topic for a table of the intrinsic
constants its arguments accept.

Access intrinsic constants are prefixed by ac, VBA constants by vb, and
DAO constants by db.

Declaring Your Own Constants

Microsoft
✓ *Exam*
Objective

**Declare symbolic constants, and make them available locally
or publicly.**

When you need to frequently refer to a value that does not change, and perhaps is arbitrary and difficult to remember, you can declare that value as a

constant. As the name implies, constants can't be changed, and they maintain the same value throughout your code. Declaring Pi as a constant with the declaration:

```
Const conPi = 3.14159265358979
```

will save a good deal of time you would spend retyping the value of Pi, if you needed to use it throughout a module. If you place the declaration in the Declarations section of a standard module, and preface it with Public:

```
Public Const conPi = 3.14159265358979
```

it will be available throughout the entire application.

See Table 8.1 earlier in the chapter for more details on how declaring constants affects their scope and lifetime.

Functions and Subroutines

Functions are procedures that return a value (as opposed to subroutines, commonly called *subs*, which don't return a value). You can write your own functions and subs, or make use of a large set of built-in functions provided by Access.

Built-in Functions

Microsoft ✓ *Exam Objective*   **Use common built-in functions.**

To select a built-in Access function for use in your code, click on the Build button on the Module Design toolbar in a standard or CBF module to open the Expression Builder.

In the Expression Builder, double-click on the Functions folder to open its two branches: the Access Built-in Functions and a folder containing the current database's functions. To select a built-in function, you can either locate it in the alphabetic list of all functions (the default <All> selection), or select a function category and browse within the category. Once you have located the function you want to use, click on the Paste button to paste the function into the Expression pane, with placeholders for its arguments, as shown in Figure 8.3.

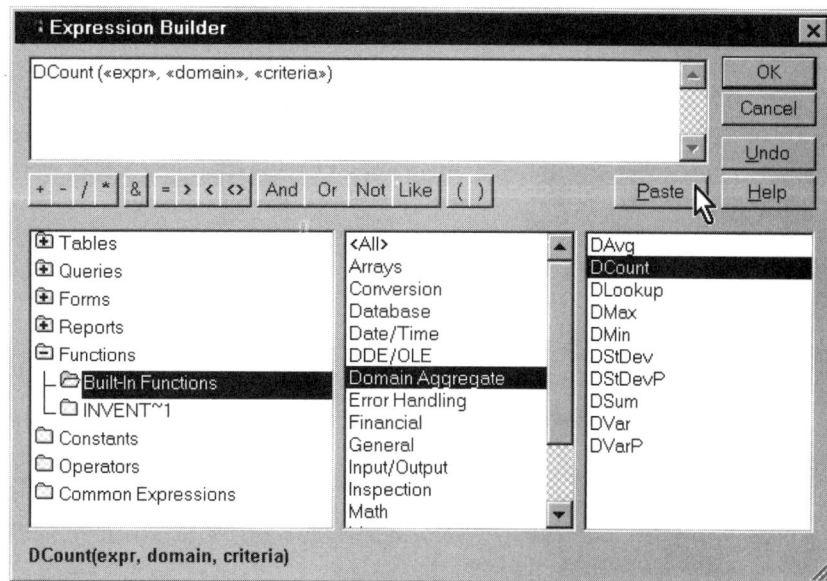

Creating Your Own Functions and Subs

Microsoft
Exam
Objective

Create user-defined functions.

If you frequently perform a certain set of actions in an application, you can save time by encapsulating them in a function or sub, and then calling the procedure wherever it is needed in your application. For example, the function listed below strips certain nonalphanumeric characters from strings, to prevent problems when using strings for control names or in other places where special characters could be a problem. Since the purpose of this procedure is to return a cleaned-up string, a function is required.

If you need to return a value, make a function. If you just need to perform some actions, but don't need to return a value, make a sub.

The code listing that follows processes two non-alphanumeric characters, and, if found, strips them from a text string. Each target character is processed in its own section of the function. The code listing illustrates stripping characters 32 (the space character) and 33 (the exclamation point) from text strings. You would want to remove spaces, for example, if you were creating a control name (control names can't contain spaces), and to strip out exclamation points, as they are used for a specific purpose in Access VBA—indicating membership in a collection.

The full function includes many more characters, up to character 126 (the tilde); it is included in the Smart Access March 1998 download file, which accompanies the article *Applying a Naming Convention to a Legacy Application*.

For each target character, the code sets up a Do loop, and seeks the target character in the input text string. If it is found, the character is removed from the string, and the loop is restarted (because the same character could occur multiple times in a text string). When the target character is no longer found in the string, the loop exits, and the function proceeds to the next label, to process a new target character. At the end of the code, the cleaned-up text string is assigned as the function's output value:

```
Public Function StripNonAlphaNumericChars(strText As String)
➥ As String

On Error GoTo StripNonAlphaNumericCharsError

    Dim strChar As String
    Dim lngFound As Long

Seek32:
    'Strip space character
    strChar = Chr$(32)
    lngFound = 1
```

```
    Do Until lngFound = 0
       lngFound = InStr(strText, strChar)
       If lngFound = 0 Then GoTo Seek33
       strText = left(strText, lngFound - 1) & Mid(strText,
       ➥ lngFound + 1)
    Loop

Seek33:
    'Strip exclamation character
    strChar = Chr$(33)
    lngFound = 1
    Do Until lngFound = 0
       lngFound = InStr(strText, strChar)
       If lngFound = 0 Then GoTo Seek34
       strText = left(strText, lngFound - 1) & Mid(strText,
       ➥ lngFound + 1)
    Loop

Done:
    StripNonAlphaNumericChars = strText

StripNonAlphaNumericCharsExit:
    Exit Function

StripNonAlphaNumericCharsError:
    MsgBox Error.Description
    Resume StripNonAlphaNumericCharsExit

End Function
```

This function can be called in code or used as the row source of a TextBox control, anywhere you need to remove extraneous non-alphanumeric characters from text. Using the function as follows:

```
StripNonAlphaNumericChars("Call me!")
```

yields the cleaned-up string Callme.

Organizing Your Program

You can create a workable application just by writing event procedures and a few subs or functions in CBF modules for forms and reports, but that is not the most efficient way to design an application. Event procedures are fine for simple actions such as closing a form, but if you need more complex procedures, it is generally better to create them as procedures that can be applied to different objects as needed, and store them in modules organized by subject.

Instead of writing code that references specific form and control objects by name, or using the Me and Parent keywords to reference the current object or its parent object, you can rewrite your code as functions that accept form and control arguments. The successive variations of the ChangePrice function in the *Using Collections* section of this chapter show how to convert an event procedure referencing specific controls on a specific form into a general-purpose function that can process all controls on all forms.

Using Collections

<table>
<tr><td>*Microsoft* ✓ *Exam* *Objective*</td><td>**Declare and use object variables and collections, and use their associated properties and methods.**</td></tr>
</table>

The Access object model contains a number of collections of objects, such as Forms, Reports, and Controls; and the DAO object model contains other data-related collections, such as Tables, Queries, and Indexes. Each collection contains one or more items of the same type, and you can perform operations on all members of a collection by using the For Each...Next construct (this is new to Access 95).

The syntax for referencing members of collections has three variants:

```
Forms!frmEmployees
Forms("frmEmployees")
Forms(0)
```

The first variant is the most commonly used, but the second also has its uses, especially when you need to use a String variable to reference a form.

```
Forms(strFormName)
```

will work, where

```
Forms!strFormName
```

won't. The third variant is of little use for referencing individual forms, since the index numbers assigned to forms (and other members of collections) are not stable identifiers; they are reassigned every time you open a collection. Since the Forms and Reports collections in Access include only the currently open forms or reports, the index number for a particular form or report is likely to be different every time you use the Forms or Reports collection. The one situation where collection index numbers are useful is when you are iterating through a collection, as in the code samples that follow.

The code sample in the *Managing Complexity: Designing for Maintenance* section earlier in the chapter applied a custom function to each of four price controls on a form. Since the controls on a particular form are a collection, you can use the form's Controls collection to iterate through all of its controls and to run certain actions on controls that meet the criteria you specify.

In this case, the code loops through the Controls collection, using the convenient For Each…Next construct (which does not require you to know the number of members in the collection) to determine which controls are Currency controls, and to run the ChangePrice function only on those controls.

The TypeOf construct used in this code is used only with controls; it is used to determine which type they are. It is equivalent to the commented-out line of code underneath it, which checks the control's ControlType property, and uses a VB intrinsic constant to represent the TextBox control.

The TypeOf construct can't be used in a Select Case statement. To use a Select Case statement to take different actions for many types of controls, use the ControlType property instead.

The next version of the price modification code uses the Controls collection of the current form (the form is referenced by the Me keyword) to process all the controls on the form. Using a For Each…Next loop, the code examines each control. If it is a text box control with the Currency format, the Change Price function is called, with the control name, the Increase/Decrease choice, and the change amount as its arguments. Controls that aren't Currency formatted text boxes are skipped.

```
Private Sub txtPercentage_AfterUpdate()

On Error GoTo txtPercentage_AfterUpdateError

    Dim intChange As Integer
    Dim dblChange As Double
    Dim curPrice As Currency
    Dim i As Integer
    Dim ctl As Control

    intChange = Me![fraChange]
    dblChange = Nz(Me![txtPercentage])

    If dblChange = 0 Then Exit Sub

    For Each ctl In Me.Controls
        If TypeOf ctl Is TextBox Then
        'If ctl.ControlType = acTextBox Then
            Debug.Print "Name: " & ctl.Name & vbTab & _
            ➥ "Format: " & Nz(ctl.Format)
            If ctl.Format = "Currency" Then
                i = ChangePrice(ctl, intChange, dblChange)
            End If
        End If
    Next ctl

txtPercentage_AfterUpdateExit:
    Exit Sub

txtPercentage_AfterUpdateError:
    MsgBox Error.Description
    Resume txtPercentage_AfterUpdateExit

End Sub
```

You can make the ChangePrice function available to all forms with price controls that need changing by moving the function to a standard module, declaring it as Public, and then calling the function from the txtPercentage text box's AfterUpdate event on all the forms with currency controls that need updating. This means that it will be available to all forms, regardless of which other forms are open (a public function in a CBF module is only available when that form is open).

A dialog form is a form whose Popup and Modal properties are set to Yes (or True, from VBA). Such a form works much like a dialog box created from code, but a dialog form gives you a lot more flexibility, as you can place a variety of controls on it, not just a label and a few command buttons.

You can streamline price changes even more by creating a dialog form with the Increase/Decrease option group and a text box for entering the change percentage. The ChangePrices function in a standard module is called from the AfterUpdate event procedure of the txtPercentage TextBox control on the dialog form. In this case, the ChangePrices function is modified to iterate through the Forms collection, and to first check that each form in the collection is a standard form (not a dialog form or subform) by checking that its name starts with frm, and if it meets that test, then the code iterates through the controls in that form's Controls collection. Figure 8.4 shows the dialog form, and the code sample that follows lists the next version of the ChangePrices function.

FIGURE 8.4

The dialog form for changing prices on all open forms

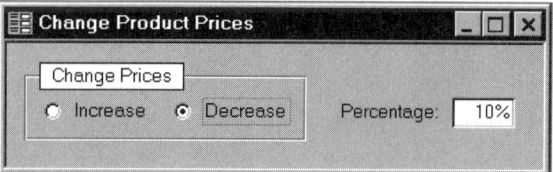

This version of the code picks up the Increase/Decrease choice and change amount from the dialog form, then uses the Forms collection to cycle through all currently open forms, on each form cycling through the form's controls as in the last version of the code. Basically, the code simply wraps the Controls collection processing inside a Forms collection processing loop, and picks up the values used to change the prices from a dialog form, instead of from controls on each form, thus making the function totally generic.

You can add new forms as needed, without having to modify them in any special way. The function will process them, changing prices in any Currency-formatted text boxes on the forms.

```
Public Function ChangePrices() As Integer

'Changes prices on all open forms

On Error GoTo ChangePricesError

    Dim frm As Form
    Dim intChange As Integer
    Dim dblChange As Double
    Dim curPrice As Currency
    Dim i As Integer
    Dim ctl As Control

    intChange = Forms![fdlgProductPrices]![fraChange]
    dblChange = Nz(Forms![fdlgProductPrices]![txtPercentage])

    If dblChange = 0 Then Exit Function

    For Each frm In Forms
        If Left(frm.Name, 3) = "frm" Then
            Debug.Print "Processing " & frm.Name
            For Each ctl In frm.Controls
                If TypeOf ctl Is TextBox Then
                    Debug.Print "Name: " & ctl.Name & vbTab & _
                    ➥ "Format: " & Nz(ctl.Format)
                    If ctl.Format = "Currency" Then
                        curPrice = CCur(ctl)
                        Select Case intChange
                            Case 1
                                curPrice = curPrice + _
                                ➥ (curPrice * dblChange)
                            Case 2
```

```
                                curPrice = curPrice -
                              ➥ (curPrice * dblChange)
                    End Select
                    ctl.Value = curPrice
                End If
            End If
        Next ctl
    End If
  Next frm

ChangePricesExit:
  Exit Function

ChangePricesError:
  MsgBox Error.Description
  Resume ChangePricesExit

End Function_
```

The Forms collection represents all the open forms in an Access database, so the ChangePrices function only changes prices on open forms. If you need to process all the forms in a database—not just the open forms—you can use the MSysObjects system table to retrieve the names of all the forms in the database, then open each form in turn and process its Controls collection. Figure 8.5 shows the MSysObjects table, with form names displayed in its Name column.

LvProp	Name	Owner	Type
	fmnuSwitchboard	II	-32768
	frmProducts	II	-32768
	fsubProducts	II	-32768
	frmPurchaseOrders	II	-32768
	fsubPurchaseOrders	II	-32768
	frmEmployees	II	-32768
	frmSuppliers	II	-32768
	frmCategories	II	-32768
	frmCompanyInfo	II	-32768
	frmShippingMethods	II	-32768
	frmDateRange	II	-32768
	rptProductCostComparisons	II	-32764

MSysObjects : Table

Record: 26 of 75

The ChangeAllPrices function, listed in the code sample below, uses a recordset to retrieve the form names from the MSysObjects table. This version of the function also prints information about the price changes to the Debug Window, so you can see exactly what changes were made to each control on each form processed.

Press Ctrl+G to open the Debug Window before running the code, so you can see the changes being made to prices.

The final version of the code adds one further refinement. To overcome the limitation with the Forms collection (it only processes currently open forms), the function retrieves the names of all the forms in the database (whether open or closed) from MSysObjects table, using a table-type recordset based on this system table. Since the For Each...Next construct can't be used in a recordset (it only works for collections), the code uses a Do loop instead to process all the records in the recordset.

The ChangeAllForms function depends on consistent use of a naming convention to identify the forms to process. If you want to process forms that aren't named in accordance with a naming convention, you need to add another check for Type = -32768, as that is how forms are identified in the MSysObjects table.

If the Name field in the recordset starts with frm, the object is a form; and the code opens the form, and then proceeds to process the controls in the form, as in the earlier versions of the code. This version of the code also uses Debug.Print statements to print information to the Debug Window to document the function's processing of forms and controls:

```
Public Function ChangeAllPrices() As Integer

'Changes prices on all forms in the database,
'whether they are open or closed

On Error GoTo ChangeAllPricesError
```

```
Dim dbs As DATABASE
Dim rst As Recordset
Dim frm As Form
Dim intChange As Integer
Dim dblChange As Double
Dim curPrice As Currency
Dim i As Integer
Dim ctl As Control
Dim strFormName As String
Dim strMessage As String

intChange = Forms![fdlgProductPrices]![fraChange]
dblChange = Nz(Forms![fdlgProductPrices]![txtPercentage])

If dblChange = 0 Then Exit Function

Set dbs = CurrentDb
Set rst = dbs.OpenRecordset("MSysObjects")
Do Until rst.EOF
    strFormName = rst!Name
    If Left(strFormName, 3) = "frm" Then
        DoCmd.OpenForm strFormName, acNormal
        Debug.Print "Processing " & strFormName
        Set frm = Forms(strFormName)
        For Each ctl In frm.Controls
            If TypeOf ctl Is TextBox Then
                Debug.Print "Name: " & ctl.Name & vbTab
                ➥ & "Format: " & Nz(ctl.Format)
                If ctl.Format = "Currency" Then
                    curPrice = CCur(ctl.Value)
                    Debug.Print "Original price: " &
                    ➥ Format(curPrice, "$0.00")
                    Select Case intChange
                        Case 1
                            curPrice = curPrice +
                            ➥ (curPrice * dblChange)
```

```
                                    Case 2
                                        curPrice = curPrice -
                                        ➥ (curPrice * dblChange)
                                End Select
                                ctl.Value = curPrice
                                strMessage = "Price " &
                                ➥ Switch(intChange = 1, _
                                "increased by ", intChange = 2,
                                ➥ "decreased by ")
                                strMessage = strMessage &
                                ➥ Format(dblChange, "0%") & " to "
                                strMessage = strMessage &
                                ➥ Format(curPrice, "$0.00")
                                Debug.Print strMessage
                            End If
                        End If
                    Next ctl
                    DoCmd.Close acForm, strFormName, acSaveYes
                Else
                    Debug.Print "Skipping " & strFormName
                End If
                Debug.Print vbCrLf
            rst.MoveNext
            Loop
            rst.Close
            MsgBox "All forms processed!"

    ChangeAllPricesExit:
        Exit Function

    ChangeAllPricesError:
        MsgBox Error.Description
        Resume ChangeAllPricesExit

    End Function
```

See Chapter 7 for more information on recordsets and the MSysObjects table.

Handling Errors

There are several types of errors that can occur when compiling or running an Access application. Some errors are the result of carelessness in typing text into the module; others result from the code trying to do something that can't be done; and yet others are the result of not thinking through what the application is supposed to do (the code is syntactically correct, but doesn't do what you had in mind). These errors are described in the sections that follow.

Compile Errors

Compile errors result from mistyping a keyword, leaving out punctuation, or having similar syntax errors in code. VBA detects and reports on these errors when you compile or run the code.

Putting an Option Explicit statement in the Declarations section of each module guarantees that VB generates an error when it encounters an undeclared variable. This prevents errors caused by mistyping a variable. Without the Option Explicit statement, VB will assume you are creating a new variable on the fly, and your program won't work as expected.

To avoid syntax errors, use the Object Browser to paste a method and its arguments into your code, as shown in Figure 8.6. This technique has the advantage of pasting in all the named arguments, so you can just cut out the arguments you don't need, without having to keep all the separating commas. Additionally, you can use the Expression Builder to paste in form and control references with correct syntax. This is particularly helpful when referencing controls on subforms, as their syntax is quite complex.

See the *Functions and Subroutines* section earlier in this chapter for a discussion of the Expression Builder.

FIGURE 8.6

Using the Object
Browser to paste a
method and its
arguments into code

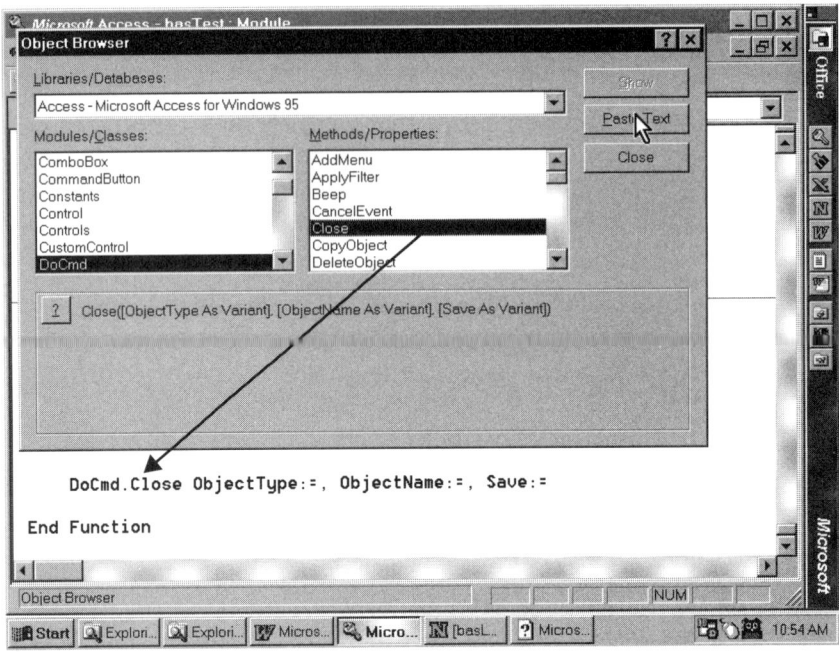

FIGURE 8.6

Using the Object
Browser to paste a
method and its
arguments into code

Run-Time Errors

Run-time errors occur when a statement tries to do something impossible,
such as dividing by zero or assigning a Null value to a variable that will only
take an Integer value. Exercise 8.1 shows the causes of certain common run-
time errors and how to prevent them from stopping your code.

EXERCISE 8.1

Handling Run-Time Errors

1. Create a form with two unbound text boxes, one for a date and the
   other for text, and do not apply any particular format to the text boxes.

2. Place a command button on the form, and run this sub from its Click
   event to assign text entered into the two text box controls to a Date
   and String variable respectively:

```
Public Sub TestVars1()
```

```
        Dim dteMeetingDate As Date
        Dim strMeetingPlace As String

        dteMeetingDate = Me![txtMeetingDate]
        strMeetingPlace = Me![txtMeetingPlace]
        MsgBox "The meeting will be at " & strMeetingPlace _
            & " on " & dteMeetingDate

    End Sub
```

3. To see what happens when you assign the wrong type of information to a Date variable, type **tomorrow** into the Meeting Date text box, then click the TestVars command button. The Access "Type Mismatch" error message pops up.

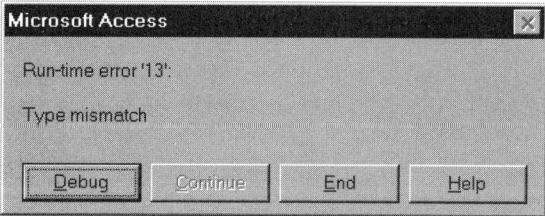

4. To see what happens when you assign a Null to a String variable, enter **2/2/98** into the Meeting Date text box, and then click the command button without entering anything in the Meeting Place text box. The Access "Invalid Use of Null" error message appears.

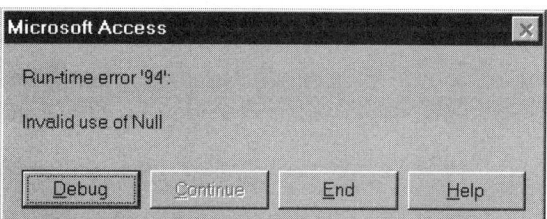

5. A run-time error stops your code. The message is usually cryptic and often leaves users unclear as to what action they should take to correct the problem. The best way to deal with these errors is to prevent them, either by screening values before passing them as arguments, or by trapping the error and showing the user a more meaningful message.

6. Modify the TestVars function as shown below to use the Number property of the Access Err object to respond to a particular error. (The Access Err object contains Access run-time errors. To trap DAO errors, use the Errors collection of the DBEngine object, discussed in *The Errors Collection* section later in this chapter.)

```
Public Function TestVars2()

On Error GoTo TestVars2Error

    Dim dteMeetingDate As Date
    Dim strMeetingPlace As String

    dteMeetingDate = Me![txtMeetingDate]
    strMeetingPlace = Me![txtMeetingPlace]
    MsgBox "The meeting will be at " & strMeetingPlace _
        & " on " & dteMeetingDate


TestVars2Exit:
    Exit Function


TestVars2Error:
    If Err.Number = 13 Then
        MsgBox "You entered text in the date field; please
        ➥ reenter the date"
    ElseIf Err.Number = 94 Then
        MsgBox "The meeting place is blank; please enter a
        ➥ meeting place"
    Else
```

```
        MsgBox Err.Description
    End If


    Resume TestVars2Exit


End Function
```

7. A more meaningful error message is displayed when the Type Mismatch error is detected:

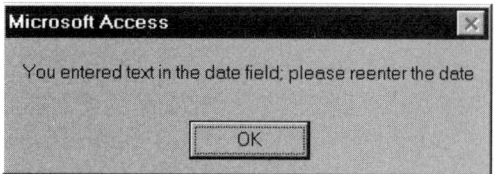

8. To prevent the error from occurring in the first place, test that the value in the Meeting Date text box contains a date by using the IsDate function; similarly, test whether the value from the Meeting Place text box is Null by using the Is Null function, or whether it is a zero-length string by testing whether it equals "", as in the following code. (The <> "" expression is the way Access tests for something being equal to an empty string. <> is read "not equal to".)

```
Public Function TestVars3()


On Error GoTo TestVars3Error


    Dim dteMeetingDate As Date
    Dim strMeetingPlace As String


    If IsDate(Me![txtMeetingDate]) Then
        dteMeetingDate = Me![txtMeetingDate]
    Else
        MsgBox "You entered text in the date field; please
        ➥ reenter the date"
        Exit Function
    End If
```

```
        If IsNull(Me![txtMeetingPlace]) _
            = False And Me![txtMeetingPlace] <> "" Then
            strMeetingPlace = Me![txtMeetingPlace]
        Else
            MsgBox "The meeting place is blank; please enter a
            ➥ meeting place"
            Exit Function
        End If

        MsgBox "The meeting will be at " & strMeetingPlace _
            & " on " & dteMeetingDate

    TestVars3Exit:
        Exit Function

    TestVars3Error:
        If Err.Number = 13 Then
            MsgBox "You entered text in the date field; please
            ➥ reenter the date"
        ElseIf Err.Number = 94 Then
            MsgBox "The meeting place is blank; please enter a
            ➥ meeting place"
        Else
            MsgBox Err.Description
        End If

        Resume TestVars3Exit

    End Function
```

9. After the entered values pass their tests and are assigned to the variables, an informative message box appears:

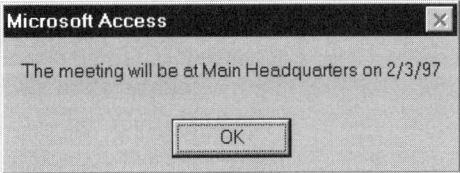

Program Logic Errors

Program logic errors are the result of poor design or a lack of understanding of the business process being coded. The code may be syntactically correct, and may not try to do anything impossible, but nevertheless it may not yield the desired results. For example, on the form shown in Figure 8.7 there is an unformatted text box where users can enter a percentage amount, another text box where they can enter an amount, and a third text box to accept the result of calculating the percentage (using the code statement below on the command button's Click event):

```
Me![txtResult] = Me![txtPercent] * Me![txtNumber]
```

FIGURE 8.7

An incorrect calculation caused by a program logic error

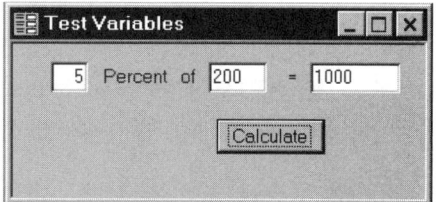

However, when the code is run, instead of yielding the desired results—5 percent of 200, or 10—the Results box contains 1000. This is because 10 percent is really .10 (10/100), not 10. To correct this program error, you could apply the Percent format to the text box. After formatting the text box with the Percent format, when the user types 5 into the box, it appears as 500; the user needs to type .05 into the text box so that it will display as 5% after exiting the control. The modified form with the Percent format applied to the first text box is shown in Figure 8.8.

FIGURE 8.8

The calculation after correcting the program logic error

This is undoubtedly the cleanest method for the programmer to use, but users may not appreciate having to mentally divide by 100 when entering percentage numbers on the form; you can get the original form to work without using the Percent format by modifying your code as follows:

```
Me![txtResult] = Me![txtPercent] / 100 * Me![txtNumber]
```

Error Traps

Microsoft ✓ *Exam* *Objective*

Write an error handler.

Several of the code samples in the last section made use of *error traps* (also called *error handlers*). They are logical structures intended to deal with possible run-time errors by presenting the user with an informative message and then exiting the procedure without hanging up the code and dumping the user into the code module (or freezing up completely, in case it is a run-time application). There are two statements you can use in creating error traps: On Error GoTo and On Error Resume Next.

On Error GoTo

The On Error GoTo statement, used in conjunction with a label, takes the user to a special section at the end of a procedure where errors can be processed. The following code sample is an error handling template that you can use in any sub procedure by replacing the *XXX*s with the procedure name:

```
On Error GoTo XXXError



XXXExit:
    Exit Sub

XXXError:
    MsgBox Error.Description
    Resume XXXExit
```

This error handling template just displays the default Access error message (if any), and exits the procedure; if you want more sophisticated error handling you can set up an If…Then…Else…End If statement, or a Select Case statement, to handle different errors that you anticipate might occur in a procedure. See the earlier TestVars3 function code sample for an example of such an error handler.

On Error Resume Next

The On Error Resume Next statement handles an error without taking you to another location in the procedure. It is handy for cases where you want the code to continue running if there is an error on a single line. If you have a Kill statement in your code that would delete a file on the computer's hard disk, but you don't know whether such a file exists, use On Error Resume Next before the Kill statement to prevent an error from occurring if there is no text file to delete. The code fragment below will delete TestFile.txt if it exists, and go on to the next statement otherwise:

```
On Error Resume Next
Kill "D:\Documents\TestFile.txt"
```

Error Handling Strategies

In addition to handling errors within procedures, you can use database libraries to implement generic error handling.

See Chapter 12 for an example of using a library database for error handling.

The Errors Collection

Use the Errors collection and the Error object to trap errors.

The DBEngine object in the DAO object model includes the Errors collection, which is a collection of stored Error objects generated by DAO operations. When you need to trap DAO errors, you will need to use the Errors collection (for Access run-time errors, the Access Err object is used).

The DAO Errors collection contains all the stored Error objects for a single DAO operation. If an error occurs when your code is using DAO objects, an Error object is placed in the Errors collection for that operation. Every new DAO operation clears the previous Errors collection and starts a new one. The code sample below illustrates using the Errors collection to present a specific error message when a particular DAO error occurs:

```
Public Function DAOErrorTest()

On Error GoTo DAOErrorTestError

    Dim dbs As DATABASE
    Dim strError As String
    Dim err As Error
    Dim strDBName As String

    strDBName = "XYZ.mdb"
    'Try to set the dbs variable to a non-existent database to
    'generate a DAO error
    Set dbs = OpenDatabase(strDBName)

DAOErrorTestExit:
    Exit Function

DAOErrorTestError:

    For Each err In Errors
        With err
            Select Case err.Number
                Case 3024
                    MsgBox "Could not find the database " &
                    ➥ strDBName
                Case Else
                    MsgBox err.Description
            End Select
        End With
    Next
    Resume Next

End Function
```

Debugging Your Code

Debugging is the process of locating and fixing errors in your code. The Access development environment has a number of tools to help you find out what went wrong and caused an error.

The Debug Window

The Debug Window (also called the *Immediate window*) can be used in several ways. You can use it to display information printed from your code, as in some of the code samples earlier in this chapter, or you can use it to examine the values of variables or to test statements directly. To open the Debug Window, press Ctrl+G while in a module window.

You can't minimize the Debug Window. When you close it, the values in the Immediate pane are retained and will reappear when you reopen it (until you highlight and delete them).

The Debug Window has two panes: the Watch pane (the upper pane), which shows the values of variables or expressions as they change when the code runs; and the Immediate pane, where you can enter statements to test, or see text written from your code with the Debug.Print statement.

In order to test a function in the Debug Window, you type a question mark followed by the function name and supply any arguments it needs. In Exercise 8.2 you'll test a function directly in the Debug Window (this is a test of the StripNonAlphaNumericChars function created above).

EXERCISE 8.2

Testing a Line of Code in the Debug Window

1. Press Ctrl+G while in a module window to open the Debug Window.

2. Enter the following line in the Immediate pane:

   ```
   ? StripNonAlphaNumericChars("Big Sale!")
   ```

3. As soon as you press ↵, the result of the function appears on the next line:

   ```
   BigSale
   ```

Some functions won't run correctly in the Debug Window because they reference objects that aren't open at the time (although they would be open when the function is run from its normal location), or they use the Me or Parent keywords.

If you don't need the Watch pane, you can use the slider on the horizontal scrollbar to shrink it down to nothing, so the Immediate pane can use all the space in the Debug Window (or vice versa).

Setting Breakpoints and Stepping through Code

Microsoft ✓ *Exam* *Objective*	**Use debugging tools to suspend program execution, and to examine, step through, and reset execution of code.**

If you are experiencing run-time errors, you can set a *breakpoint* in your code by pressing F9 on the line where you want to stop the code. The line of code with the breakpoint is highlighted dark red in the module window, so you can see which it is. As the code executes (when it reaches the line with the breakpoint) it stops, so you can execute the remaining code line by line by pressing F8 or clicking the Step Into button on the toolbar (at any point, you can resume continuous execution by pressing F5).

Stepping through code allows you to determine exactly which line caused the error, and you may be able to tell what the problem is by observing, for example, that the code is entering or skipping a loop inappropriately.

When you are done with examining the code, you can click on the Reset button, press Shift+F5, or select Run ➢ Reset to reset your code, so you can modify it as needed.

WARNING   If you switch to other objects in the application without resetting stopped code in the module window, the other objects may behave strangely, and the application may freeze. If this happens, try resetting with Shift+F5. If that doesn't work, close the database and reopen it to reset the halted code.

Setting Watches

Microsoft ✓ *Exam* *Objective*

Debug given code samples.

As a further aid to debugging your code, you can use the Watch pane of the Debug Window to examine the values of selected variables or expressions. This is particularly useful when you suspect that a problem is caused by an inappropriate value in a variable. To set a watch for a variable, follow the steps in Exercise 8.3.

EXERCISE 8.3

Setting a Watch for a Variable in the Debug Window

1. Open the Debug Window by pressing Ctrl+G.

2. Open the module containing the procedure, and place your cursor on any line of code containing the variable you want to watch.

3. Switch to the Debug Window.

4. Place your cursor in the Watch (upper) pane and right-click to open the context menu.

5. Select the Add Watch command.

6. In the Add Watch dialog box, the Expression text box shows the variable on the highlighted line and tells you its procedure and module.

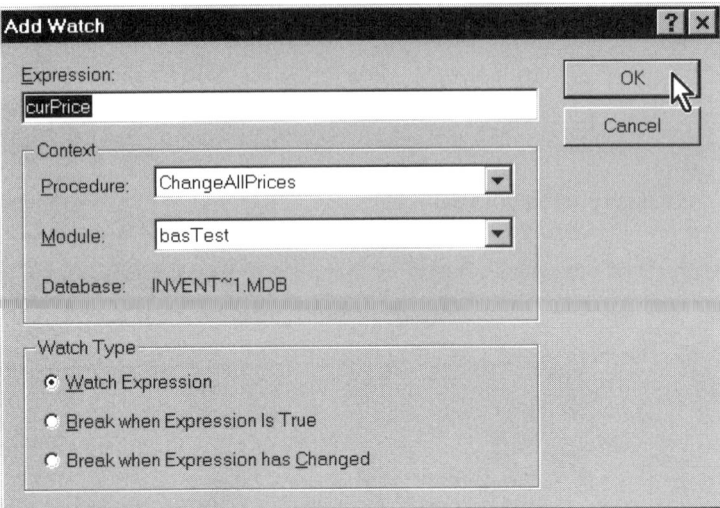

7. Select the appropriate Watch Type option (normally, the default Watch Expression selection is appropriate, but you can select Break When Expression Is True or Break When Expression Has Changed in special cases).

8. Click on the OK button to set the watch for the variable.

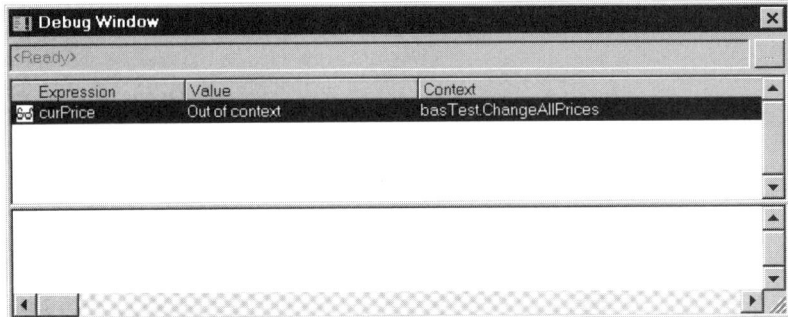

9. The new variable name appears in the Watch pane of the Debug Window.

10. Repeat as needed for any other variables you want to watch.

If you declare all your variables at the beginning of each procedure, you can set watches on the ones that need them without having to search them out as they occur later in the procedure.

Examining and Changing Variables

Microsoft
✔ Exam
Objective

Use the Debug window to monitor variable values.

After setting watches on the variables you want to examine, when you step through code you can see the values of the variables changing. To see how variables change in the Watch pane, follow the steps in Exercise 8.4.

EXERCISE 8.4

Watching Variables in the Watch Pane of the Debug Window

1. Open the module containing the ChangeAllPrices function described earlier in the chapter.

2. Set watches on the intChange, dblChange, and curPrice variables, using the technique in Exercise 8.3.

3. Press F9 to set a breakpoint on the line of code shown below—the beginning of the loop that processes Currency formatted controls.

4. Run the ChangeAllPrices function (in this example you do so by entering a new value in the Percent text box on the fdlgChangePrices form).

5. The module window opens and the line with the breakpoint is highlighted with a dotted box. You can see the current values of the three variables in the Watch pane of the Debug Window, and some informative text written by Debug.Print statements in the Immediate pane.

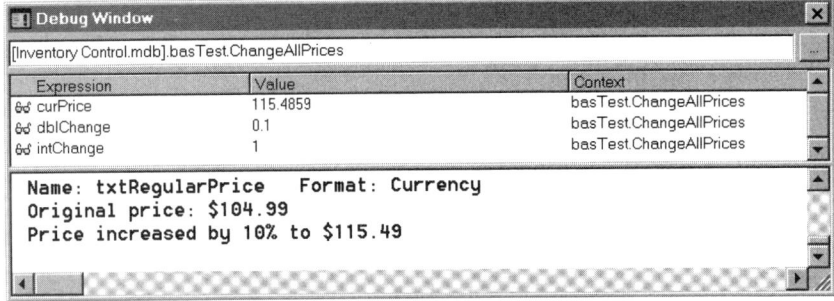

6. Since no prices have been changed yet, curPrice is at its initial value of 0.

7. Press F8 to start stepping through the code, and note how the variables change as you proceed; in particular, curPrice will change every time the amount in a Currency control is increased by the specified percentage.

Controlling Flow

In addition to setting breakpoints and stepping through code line by line, Access offers several other techniques for controlling the execution of code. If you call other procedures in a sub or function, you may not want to step through their code (especially if it has already been thoroughly debugged); press the Step Over button in that case. The Step Over button treats the entire called procedure as a unit and doesn't go into it and step through its code.

The Step Into and Step Over buttons are disabled except when you are actually running code.

If you are having problems with a particular section of code, you can skip over it by placing your cursor on the line of code where you want to resume executing the code, and selecting Run ➤ Set Next Statement. (You must have suspended execution of the code, typically by setting a breakpoint, in order to use this command.)

Similarly, you can execute code only up to a certain point by selecting Run ➤ Step to Cursor with your cursor on the line of code where you want execution to stop.

You can set a permanent breakpoint in your code by inserting the Stop command on a line by itself. (Breakpoints are cleared automatically when you close the database.)

The Calls Window

There is one more tool you can use to aid in advanced debugging of complex code: the Calls window, which shows a list of all active procedure calls (calls that have been started, but not completed). The Calls window is especially useful for tracking down problems with nested procedures. Follow the steps in Exercise 8.5 to open the Calls window and display a list of active procedures started from the Open event of a form.

EXERCISE 8.5

Tracing Nested Procedures in the Calls Window

1. Create a new form called **frmTestCalls**.

2. Create an event procedure for its Open event, containing the following code:

```
Private Sub Form_Open(Cancel As Integer)

    MsgBox "The Open event fired"
    CalledProc

End Sub
```

3. Create two subs in a standard module as follows:

```
Public Sub CalledProc()

    MsgBox "First called procedure"
    CalledProc2

End Sub

Public Sub CalledProc2()

    MsgBox "Second called procedure"

End Sub
```

4. Place a breakpoint on the MsgBox line in the form's Open event procedure, using the F9 key.

5. Switch the frmTestCalls form to Form view. The code module opens, with the breakpoint line indicated by a dotted line.

6. Press F8 to step through the code until you are on the MsgBox line of the CalledProc2 sub.

 7. Click on the Calls button to open the Calls window.

8. The Calls window displays a list of the procedures that have been called. If you place your cursor on another procedure in the list and click on the Show button, you will be taken to that procedure in its module.

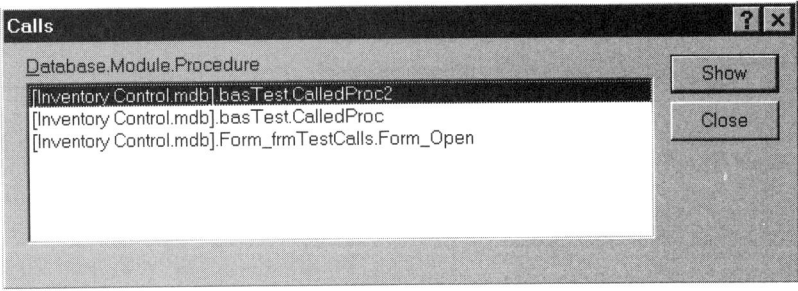

Dynamic Link Libraries

Dynamic link libraries (DLLs) are libraries of procedures that applications can link to dynamically at run-time as the procedures are needed (in contrast to procedures that are compiled into the application, and remain static). DLLs can be updated independently of the applications they support and can be shared by multiple applications.

Windows 95 itself consists of several DLLs containing information that all Windows applications use to perform activities such as displaying windows and graphics, memory management, and other common activities.

The Windows API

Sometimes you need to get information about elements of the Windows interface that are not under the control of Access or VBA, but are accessible only through the Windows Application Programming Interface (API). The Windows API is a set of DLLs which contain system-related procedures used to create Windows 95 applications. Access VBA allows you to manipulate the Windows API by making API calls in code modules to use the components of the User32.dll, Kernel32.dll, and GDI32.dll DLLs.

Declaring a DLL

Microsoft ✓ *Exam* *Objective* | **Properly declare Windows API functions.**

In order to use a DLL function or sub from the Windows API in your code, you must first declare it in the Declarations section of a module. The syntax for declaring a Windows DLL procedure is as follows:

Syntax 1:

```
[Public | Private ] Declare Sub name [CDecl] Lib "libname"
[Alias "aliasname" ][([arglist])]
```

Syntax 2:

```
[Public | Private ] Declare Function name [CDecl] Lib
"libname" [Alias "aliasname" ] [([arglist])][As type]
```

The components of the Declare statement are listed in Table 8.2.

Component	Description
Public	Declares procedures that are available to all other procedures in all modules.
Private	Declares procedures that are available only within the module where the declaration is made.
Sub	The procedure doesn't return a value.
Function	The procedure returns a value that can be used in an expression.
Cdecl	The procedure uses C language argument order, naming conventions, and calling conventions (applies only to Macintosh).
Lib	A DLL or code resource contains the procedure being declared. The Lib clause is required for all declarations.
libname	Name of the DLL or code resource that contains the declared procedure.
Alias	The procedure being called has another name in the DLL; useful when the external procedure name is the same as a keyword, a public variable or constant, or another procedure in the same scope.
aliasname	Name of the procedure in the DLL or code resource.
arglist	A list of variables representing arguments that are passed to the procedure when it is called.
type	Data type of the value returned by a Function procedure; it may be Byte, Boolean, Integer, Long, Currency, Single, Double, Date, String (variable length only), Object, Variant, a user-defined type, or an object type.

The syntax for the *arglist* argument is as follows:

```
[Optional][ByVal | ByRef][ParamArray] varname[( )][As type]
```

Table 8.3 has a description of the *arglist* components. The arglist components are the heart of an API call: they are the values passed to, or returned from, the call. You need to feed the correct values to the function in the Windows API in order to get back the information you need in your code.

Microsoft	**Use the ByVal and ByRef keywords.**
✓ *Exam*	
Objective	

T A B L E 8.3	Component	Description
The Components of the Arglist Argument	Optional	The argument is not required. If used, all subsequent arguments in *arglist* must also be optional and declared using the Optional keyword. All Optional arguments must be Variant. Optional can't be used for any argument if ParamArray is used.
	ByVal	The argument is passed by value.
	ByRef	The argument is passed by reference.
	ParamArray	Used only as the last argument in *arglist* to indicate that the final argument is an Optional array of Variant elements. The ParamArray keyword allows you to provide an arbitrary number of arguments. May not be used with ByVal, ByRef, or Optional.
	varname	The name of the variable representing the argument being passed to the procedure.
	type	The data type of the argument passed to the procedure; it may be Byte, Boolean, Integer, Long, Currency, Single, Double, Date, String (variable length only), Object, Variant, a user-defined type, or an object type.

WARNING When you pass an argument by reference, using the ByRef keyword (the default), VB passes a 32-bit address where the value is stored instead of passing the actual value of the argument. When you pass the argument by value, using the ByVal keyword, the actual value of the argument is passed. If you try to pass an argument by reference to a procedure that needs an argument passed by value, the procedure won't operate properly.

The syntax for declaring DLLs is formidable, but fortunately you don't need to figure it out from scratch for each procedure you need to use; the Access Distribution Kit includes several text and database files listing the Windows 95 API declarations, and it has a handy Win32 API Viewer so you can easily select the one you need. Exercise 8.6 shows how to use the API Viewer to select an API declaration and paste it into a code module.

EXERCISE 8.6

Pasting an API Declaration into Your Code from the API Viewer

1. Create a new code module. Your cursor will be in the Declarations section of the new module.

2. Open the Win32 API Viewer from the Microsoft ADT program group.

3. Select File ➢ Load Database File.

4. In the Select a Jet Database dialog box, select the Win32api.mdb file.

5. Highlight the procedure you want to use and click on the Add button to add the procedure to the Selected Items box.

6. Next, click on the Copy button to copy the selected procedure to the Windows Clipboard.

7. Switch to the module window, and press Ctrl+V (or select Edit ➢ Paste) to paste the procedure into the module.

EXERCISE 8.6 (CONTINUED)

8. Windows API declarations tend to be very long, so you may want to use the Space+Underscore continuation character to break up the declaration into several lines for readability.

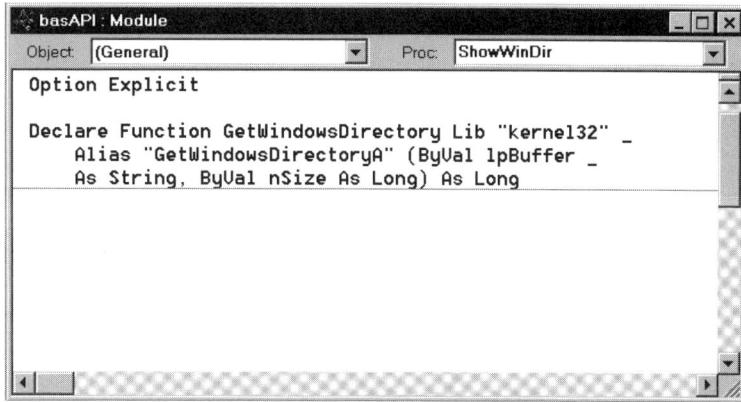

```
basAPI : Module                                          _ □ ×
Object: (General)          ▼      Proc: ShowWinDir              ▼

Option Explicit

Declare Function GetWindowsDirectory Lib "kernel32" _
    Alias "GetWindowsDirectoryA" (ByVal lpBuffer _
    As String, ByVal nSize As Long) As Long
```

Calling a DLL

If you declare a DLL procedure in a public module, you can call it from code anywhere in your application; if you declare it in a form or report module without using the Private keyword, you can call it from elsewhere in the application if the form or report is open.

Once you have declared a DLL procedure with the appropriate scope, you can call it from your procedures and use it to retrieve information about the Windows environment or modify elements of the Windows environment. The following procedure uses the GetWindowsDirectory API call to retrieve the Windows directory and display it in a message box:

```
Public Function ShowWinDir()

    Dim lngReturn As Long
    Dim i As Integer
    Dim strReturn As String
    Dim strWinPath As String
```

```
strReturn = String$(255, 0)
lngReturn = GetWindowsDirectory(strReturn, 255)
MsgBox "Windows Path: " & strReturn

End Function
```

Summary

In this chapter we've covered ways you can make your code more efficient by redesigning procedures that refer to specific objects so they can be run on multiple objects, and by moving code from CBF modules to standard modules to make it available throughout your application. Depending on how and where you declare them, variables have different scopes and lifetimes. You can use the built-in constants in Access, or you can create your own constants.

Procedures can be functions, which return a value, or subs, which don't. There are two types of modules: class (or CBF) and standard. You can manipulate objects of the same type stored in collections by using the For Each…Next construct.

There are three types of code errors: compile errors, run-time errors, and program logic errors. You can trap errors using the On Error GoTo and On Error Resume Next statements, and debug your code with the aid of breakpoints, the Step Into and Step Over buttons, and the Debug Window and Calls window.

The Access Err object is used to trap Access run-time errors, and the DAO Errors collection is used to trap DAO errors.

You can use API calls to call functions in the DLLs comprising the Windows API in your applications.

Review Questions

1. You need to use a variable (intChoice) declared as Public in the frmOrders form's CBF module. Which syntax is correct?

    A. You can't reference a variable located in another form's module.

    B. Forms!frmOrders.intChoice

    C. frmOrders.intChoice

    D. frmOrders!intChoice

2. You create the following function and run it three times, with the argument 5. What is the number in the message box on the third time the function is run?

```
Public Function RunningCount(ByVal intInput As Integer) As
➥ Integer

    Static intCount As Integer

    intCount = intCount + intInput
    RunningCount = intCount

    MsgBox "Running Count: " & intCount

End Function
```

    A. 5

    B. 0

    C. 15

    D. 10

3. You close the module containing the function in question 2 and run the function again. What is the count in the message box?

    A. 0

    B. 15

    C. 10

    D. 20

4. You close the entire application, then reopen it and run the function in question 2 again. What is the count in the message box?

   A. 5

   B. 10

   C. 15

   D. 20

5. You are having problems with code failing at a certain point when you run it. Which two of these strategies would be helpful in debugging the code?

   A. Set a breakpoint in the code, highlight the line of code before the problem area, and select Run ➤ Set Next Statement.

   B. Set a breakpoint in the code, highlight the line of code before the problem area, and select Run ➤ Set To Cursor.

   C. Set watches on the variables used in the problem area of code, set a breakpoint in the code before the problem area, and step through it, observing the values of variables as they change in the Debug Window.

   D. Set a breakpoint in the code, highlight the line of code after the problem area, and select Run ➤ Set Next Statement.

6. You have a procedure that calls a number of other procedures, all of which have been debugged. Your procedure has problems and needs debugging. Which of the following tools should you use in this case (assuming you have set a breakpoint in your code before the problem area)?

   A. The Step Into button on the VB toolbar

   B. The F8 function key

   C. The F5 function key

   D. The Step Over button on the VB toolbar

7. You write a function to make certain changes to data on forms, using the Forms collection in your code. After running the function with no error messages, you open a form and find that its data has not been changed. What is the most likely reason?

A. There is an error in the code.

B. The form whose data wasn't changed was closed when the function was run.

C. The For Each...Next construct doesn't work with collections.

D. All forms have to be closed for the code to work.

8. You write a function in a CBF module, using the Me keyword to reference a control on a subform's main form, then move the function to a standard module. When you run the function, you get an "Invalid use of Me keyword" compile error. How can you fix this problem?

A. Change the Me keyword into a specific form reference, such as Forms![frmAuthors].

B. Call the function from an event procedure on the form.

C. Change "Me" to "Forms".

D. Change the reference to Forms![frmAuthors]!Me.

9. You need to manipulate the Access window in a way that can't be done with Access VBA. What tool would be helpful here?

A. The Windows API

B. The Office API

C. Assembly language

D. C++

10. An "Invalid Use of Null" error message when running a function most likely results from:

A. Trying to assign a Null to a variable whose data type can't accept Nulls

B. Trying to assign an empty string to a variable whose data type can't accept Nulls

C. Trying to save a record with no value in a field whose Required property is set to Yes

D. Trying to save a record with no value in a field whose Allow Zero Length property is set to No

CHAPTER

9

Client/Server Issues

Microsoft Exam Objectives Covered in This Chapter:

- Given a scenario, decide whether to use SQL pass-through queries or Microsoft Access queries.
- Access external data by using ODBC.
- Trap errors that are generated by the server.
- Optimize connections.
- Optimize performance for client/server applications.
- Optimize performance for a given client/server application.

As networking and the use of the Internet have become more prevalent, the line has been blurred between mobile and office-based personnel. When the workplace moves to the workgroup, things become much more complicated. Fortunately, there are ways to migrate databases to work well in a multi-user environment. This chapter discusses the concepts behind the client/server paradigm.

There are many things to consider when creating or moving an existing solution to a network-based workgroup. Those topics, including ODBC, SQL pass-through, and optimizing the result, are covered in detail here.

In this chapter, you will learn:

- The difference between single and multi-tier database applications and how to choose the right one for the problem you are trying to solve
- How to work with Open Database Connectivity (ODBC) and a SQL Server back-end
- How to create outer joins for use in a multi-user environment
- How to manage, optimize, and error-proof your applications
- How to define indexes to speed up user access to your databases
- What you need to know to make your application run as smoothly as possible
- About multi-tier applications

Access in the Client/Server Environment

Not so long ago, a single-tier or monolithic application was the only solution available for even the largest of companies. Since there was no database management and no platform capable of handling the interface and logic chores, complete applications were served entirely by a single computer, often called a main- or mini-frame computer. This computer would perform all application duties, including database management, business logic, database access, and data storage. Dumb terminals, simple ASCII-based units, merely echoed the actions of the user to the server and back to the user.

Serving applications in this manner was very burdensome—fraught with problems to which there were no simple or speedy solutions. Since each terminal relied on the mainframe to supply the application, logic, and data, hurdles had to be overcome (such as how to separate the application from the data and how to give users faster access to the data). The solutions to these problems brought about two-tier solutions and beyond.

Two- and multi-tier applications bring several benefits to the table (no pun intended). The classic single-tier application has a number of drawbacks. Since the data, management code, and interface code are located in a single, monolithic application, any changes will be complicated and time-consuming. Also, since the processing is data-centric, a great amount of network bandwidth is dedicated to moving potentially extraneous information around—not a particularly attractive side-effect.

How Many Tiers Make an Application?

You'll often encounter the terms *single-tier* and *multi-tier* as you work with client/server applications. Here's a quick rundown of what they mean:

- **Single-tier application:** A database application that contains all data, management, and logic in a single system. Dumb terminals are fed their interface, connectivity, and logic from a central location or server.

- **Multi-tier application:** A derivation of the above that separates data, management, and logic into various operative groups that can be arranged in the most efficient fashion, typically relying on workstations.

Single-Tier Applications

Though basic, the single- or one-tier solution can be a reasonable choice for small environments that do not demand high traffic and a lot of speed. A small law office can successfully use a single-tier solution for file management, messaging, client billing, and time keeping. On the other hand, if that law firm were to grow to have 50 partners, the system would become unworkable and require replacement. Fortunately, Access is scalable in this sense, allowing the system to be split, improved, and optimized for serving.

In the above case, there is no client in the strictest sense. The client would be a *dumb terminal* that merely submits to the wishes of the server. By its very nature, a single-tier application does not utilize the querying tools normally used in a front-end application. A single-tier application simply provides the data, management, logic, and interface to all end-users—all of which provides the means and way for end-users to query the database. In this case, there is no client, as the application server tackles all chores independently of any workstation.

As you can see from Figure 9.1, a workstation provides little more than a way to interface with the remote server that is most likely stuffed in a closet somewhere. Fortunately, there are very few of these types of installations around these days (outside of government agencies and large insurance companies). A user would most likely be using Access on the desktop for personal data archiving, maintenance of a list of business and industry contacts, or local storage of a company's replicated database for faster access.

F I G U R E 9.1

A simple single-tier application

Terminal   Server

Obviously, there are no client/server issues involved in this type of arrangement, barring the occasional remote user requiring a recent synchronization. The user would instead make queries to the database as described in Chapter 4. The user needs to query a remote application only when synchronizing a replicated database. That brings us to multi-tiered applications, primarily the Access two-tier solution.

Multi-Tier Applications

Looking back at the history of databases, the first solution to break out of the monolithic database application design was the two-tier application model. A two-tier model moves the interface and application logic portion of the database, more commonly referred to as a *client*, to the terminal, as shown in Figure 9.2. The terminal becomes a standalone computer, able to run the client application (typically a Pentium-based system running some flavor of Windows). Under this scenario, the mainframe's only job is to process, manage, and serve the data, and thus it is called a *server*. Once the duties were divided between the server and the client, the data became smaller and users could perform similar actions in less time, which led to increased productivity.

FIGURE 9.2

A two-tier application

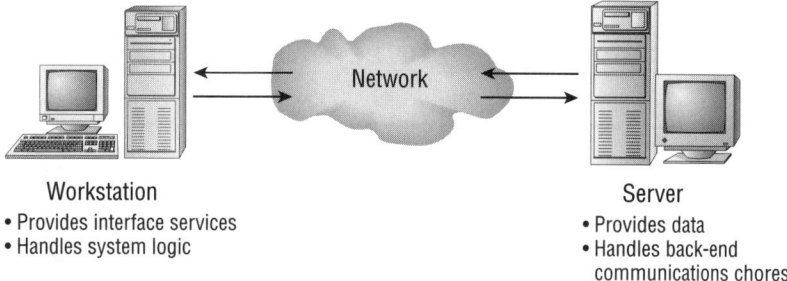

Workstation
• Provides interface services
• Handles system logic

Server
• Provides data
• Handles back-end communications chores

There are many benefits to the two-tier application model, not the least of which are small size, speed, and ease of development. For example, a small art department in a large corporation requires a workgroup environment so artists can share work on a complex project involving a number of artists. A simple workgroup environment can be developed with Access that allows the artists and project managers to have immediate access to all the work completed at any given time. The database wouldn't have to be very complex (small size), would only have to serve a known number of users (speed), and could be developed in a short time by a developer working for the department (ease of development).

Of course, this can present problems when either the business logic or interface needs to be scaled or modified, since they are part and parcel of the "fat" client package used by the workstations. The solution to this problem paved the way for multi-tier solutions, the most common of which is called the "thin" client solution. Database developers found that separating the logic from the interface code and moving it to another server would make things more modular, and easier to maintain and scale. Some variants of this approach package the logic and data server operations in the same code base, but the most popular keep the data and logic in separate code bases, thereby increasing the modularity.

A three-tier application is exponentially more complex due to the many variants on the form and the technology required to make it work. The most common form removes the application code, or logic, from the interface code—resulting in a thin client—and moves it back to the server. This solution benefits database application developers in that it keeps interface and logic code separate, allowing for greater ease in maintenance and scaling.

Of course, now the problem becomes deciding how the client should communicate with the server, and vice versa. We'll cover that in the following sections.

Communication between Client and Server

Microsoft Exam Objective	Given a scenario, decide whether to use SQL pass-through queries or Microsoft Access queries.

There are a few ways to get a query from the client application to a database back-end. In a typical Access environment, the common solution uses Access as both the front-end and the back-end. Microsoft's Jet Engine is used to facilitate communication between the Access MDB file on the server and the Access client front-end. This model, however, is limited by the ability of Access to use ODBC and its various database drivers. Let's examine the possibilities—but first, we'll look at the root of all database communications.

The Database Query

The query is the single most important end-user action performed in database settings. It could even be argued that queries drive the entire database, data mining, and data archival industries. All database activity is focused around defining, modifying, delivering, and interpreting queries. In this section we'll focus on the delivery of those queries and the many ways to get them from the user to the database and back again.

The Total Access Model

Don't confuse the Total Access model discussed in this section with the Total Access line of Access add-ons from FMS, Inc.

In the Total Access model, Access can be used as both the front-end and the back-end application for complete data sharing and management in a small- to medium-sized workgroup setting. Access acts as the front-end, providing all the interface and logic for the workgroup, and uses Jet to communicate with the back-end, which in this case is an Access MDB file, as shown in Figure 9.3.

FIGURE 9.3

The Total Access model

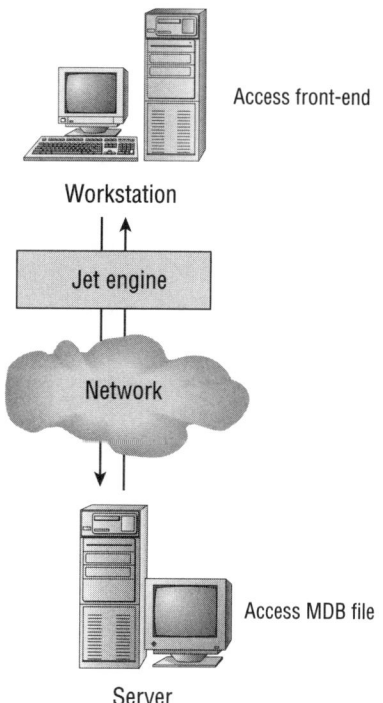

The ODBC Access Model

While Access can make a great front-end and a valuable back-end, it's not perfect for all solutions. Many companies that rely on fast and accurate data retrieval use a SQL Server as a back-end. SQL (Structured Query Language) is not an available query output of Access, which uses Access SQL instead. Since the Access version of SQL varies from other SQL implementations in some details, the SQL statements require some translation.

For more about using Access SQL, see Chapter 4.

The mechanism for translating Access SQL is called ODBC (Open Database Connectivity) We'll cover ODBC in more detail a bit later in this chapter. The general idea, as illustrated in Figure 9.4, is to pass the query to Jet. Jet translates the Access SQL query into an ODBC SQL query and then contacts the ODBC Manager to request the correct SQL driver. If the ODBC Manager finds the specified driver, it hands the query off to the driver. When it's finished the query is sent to the SQL Server, which asks the database for the queried information. This is a simplified description of a rather complicated process; we'll get into more detail about it later in the chapter.

FIGURE 9.4

The path of a Jet query slated for a SQL database

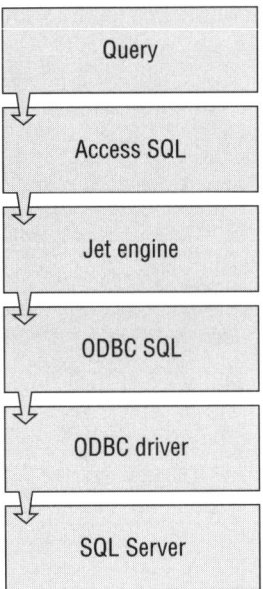

Obviously, this is not the preferred way to handle time-critical database queries for a large number of end-users. This is due to the lag-time involved in Jet translating the Access SQL query into an ODBC SQL query. There are, however, some ways in which this usage will be beneficial, which we will cover in examples later on. Before we cover more of the details of ODBC, let's take a look at another model that can make more sense in a data-intensive environment, the SQL pass-through model.

The SQL Pass-Through Model

The Access > Jet > ODBC > SQL translation path is rather long and complicated. Fortunately, there is a way to get around this. It is called *SQL pass-through*. There are many reasons to consider pass-through, not the least of which are its bandwidth-saving characteristics. Some other reasons are:

- The solution calls for a process to be handled by the back-end.

- Access SQL does not support an operation that is supported by the back-end.

- The translated query is not optimized for the back-end, a problem with Jet or ODBC's translation capabilities.

In order to use a pass-through query you need to code the query in the language of the back-end server. When the query is sent it passes through Jet (hence the name), the ODBC Manager, and the ODBC Driver to go directly to the database. The Jet, ODBC Manager, and Driver are not removed from the process; they merely act as non-interfering agents to transmit the query directly to the back-end without translation. Let's look at it in more detail.

More on SQL Pass-Through

Jet, though great for connecting Access to an MDB back-end, lacks certain finesse when asked to perform more complicated external access duties. Part of the blame lies with Access itself and its rather lackluster implementation of SQL, called Access SQL. As mentioned before, Access passes off its SQL to Jet, which, under the auspices of ODBC, converts the query into a format the back-end can comprehend. This is not always the most accurate solution, but it does come through in a pinch.

Considering the number of times the query must be wrung through a filter, that's a lot more time than most network administrators would like to have spent on such things. Ideally, the network administrator and user would like to be able to access their data as quickly as possible. Unfortunately, in a multi-user environment, there are real-world loads on the networks that must carry this data back and forth. From this we can gather that the most efficient method of getting data is for the query to go through untouched by translating hands, which is why SQL pass-through was developed.

Access defaults to Jet for its SQL query needs, but Jet can be bypassed using the pass-through method, which sends preformatted queries (written in the native language of the back-end) directly to the database. This has some great advantages, which are listed in the previous section as reasons why you would use pass-through. However, in examining pass-through and its benefits, we must also examine the negative side to this solution.

The largest hurdle to leap when implementing pass-through is that the data returned from the query is not updateable. To work around this problem you would create SQL statements to Insert, Delete, and Update the data on the server as needed. Though not altogether impossible, it would make migrating to a new back-end very time-consuming. Another drawback is that SQL statements disallow ASCII data of greater than 32KB in size and allow absolutely no binary data. Though not a common point of conflict—since 32KB is more than enough in most cases and binary data is rarely used in queries—some solutions will suffer from the loss.

Also, Jet does not check the syntax of pass-through queries, but this is not unexpected since Jet is merely the conduit for the query. Now that we understand all the factors involved in using SQL pass-through, Exercise 9.1 shows how to make one using Access 95.

EXERCISE 9.1

Creating a SQL Pass-Through Query

1. Open the database to which you want to add the pass-through query.

2. Select the Queries tab in the Database window and click on New.

3. Choose Design view.

4. Dismiss the next two dialog boxes.

5. Go to Query ➢ SQL Specific ➢ Pass-through, which opens the Design window.

6. Enter the statement in the syntax of your back-end.

There! You're all done. Though the process of defining a pass-through query is simple, the management and use of it can be complex. Make sure to spend time examining your proposed client/server model so you can determine where you will need pass-through and eliminate the extraneous.

Make sure you visit the properties for the query you have just composed. You need to enter data appropriate to your back-end into the ODBC Connect Str field. A typical string looks like this:

    ODBC;DSN=???;UID=???;PWD=???;

(The question marks should be replaced by the required data for your back-end.) The next two fields, Return Records and Log Messages, should be modified as needed. The Description and ODBC Timeout fields are optional.

NOTE   For more information on connect strings for your specific back-end solution, refer to the manual or request assistance from the vendor.

Accessing External Data with ODBC

Microsoft ✓ Exam Objective   **Access external data by using ODBC.**

The Open Database Connectivity protocol mentioned earlier, commonly referred to as ODBC, was made a standard in 1994. It was created to allow users of the myriad different proprietary database formats to access other proprietary database formats. The goal was to make multi-system connectivity simple, something ODBC does quite well, as long as all the applications that are used support the ODBC protocol.

ODBC makes it easy to connect various users, in various locations, to various database back-ends. There's little muss, little fuss. ODBC allows a department or section to use exactly what it needs in order to be most productive and efficient. (In some cases this means making the most of the legacy application the department is forced to use until funds are available for upgrading). Of course, there are also problems.

The Problem with Multiple Back-Ends

With each back-end database application system in use, like Access, File-Maker Pro, SQL Server, or Sybase, among others, the complexity of the system grows immensely. To keep this complexity to a minimum, it is best to limit the number of back-ends you will use to the most critical ones. A SQL Server back-end combined with an Access front-end is the most common choice and is an excellent combination for many purposes. Access provides many powerful features that can solve most problems for the small work-group, and SQL Server is very scalable.

Of course, it's not always possible to use a single back-end. For example, if a small company that began operation with Access (in the Total Access model) decides to expand its scope of services and add another server, typi-cally a SQL Server, it adds complexity to the upgrade. Some rewriting of que-ries would be required, as Access SQL does not handle all SQL operations, and ODBC would have to be implemented, due to the incompatibility between Access and SQL. But the effort would mean a more robust environ-ment that is easily scalable for a growing company.

The ODBC Solution

ODBC brings many cards to the connectivity table, not the least of which is com-patibility. Microsoft Access 95 is one of hundreds of products that fully support the ODBC protocol. This compatibility is a great boon to solution developers who are contracted to upgrade existing database solutions or create new mul-tiple back-end solutions. The basic concept is to translate a front-end query into a format that an incompatible back-end can recognize. As we said earlier, there are many different ways to get this information to the back-end, most of which require some sort of translation. ODBC handles this quite well.

The ODBC Administrator

As with most enhancements to the Windows system, ODBC is controlled by a Control Panel applet (this one is called 32-bit ODBC), although it may also be installed as a standalone application. You'll need to add the files to your system, if ODBC was not included when you installed Access 95 (ODBC is installed as the result of choosing the Typical Install, but the installation may have been performed by a network administrator who eliminated seemingly needless extras). You'll find the options for installing ODBC under the Custom Install button in the installer. When you have installed ODBC, you're ready to get connected. Once you have the ODBC Administrator installed, you have complete access to all of its features.

If you have to install ODBC from the CD you need to be careful which options you leave checked in the Custom Installation. If you don't make any changes to the default options, you may add files that you don't need or replace files that you have already modified. Carefully go through each option before committing to an install.

ODBC Drivers

ODBC uses drivers to perform its small miracles. Each driver allows ODBC to access a specific solution. Some of the drivers that come with Access 95 are for dBase, Paradox, and Publisher. Other drivers that are included are for Excel, FoxPro, and Access 7.0. There is a Text Files driver that often turns out to be convenient. Each of these drivers allows Access to communicate with various back-ends.

Some commercial vendors also have ODBC drivers for their database systems, but not all are free for the taking. Some charge a single fee for their drivers while others require a "per seat license" to be purchased based on projected usage. Inquire with the vendor of the back-end you wish to implement to see if there are fees for using the ODBC driver you'll need.

ODBC drivers are similar in nature to Web browser plug-ins, in that you can simply drop one into My Computer\C:\Windows\System and the new driver is available. Whenever you need to provide additional connectivity, you simply add a driver. The driver adds all appropriate translation and communication capabilities to the Access front-end.

Drivers for ODBC 2.5 and 3.0 are available only in 32-bit versions, and Windows 95 is restricted to 32-bit drivers. Windows NT 3.51 and greater can use 16-bit drivers, but not many are available. The majority of back-ends have been migrated to 32-bit. There are, however, 16-bit drivers available for legacy systems, as long as they are served and queried with Windows NT 3.51 or better.

Data Sources

A *data source name* (DSN) is a name assigned to a remote database that contains all the information required to access that data. A user defines that name using the ODBC Administrator, the nifty control panel/applet mentioned earlier. When all the data is correct and the workstation is connected to a network that contains the specified database, the links will be made. Once these links are made the user has access to the remote tables. Any queries made using Access will be routed through the ODBC filter indicated in the link settings and sent to the database.

Defining a Data Source

Fortunately, defining a data source is easy. You first determine which option you chose when installing ODBC, either the Control Panel or the standalone application, so you can locate it on your hard drive. Your best bet is to look in the Control Panel for an item called 32-bit ODBC, as it is the default installation. Double-click the icon to open the ODBC Administrator, shown in Figure 9.5.

FIGURE 9.5

The ODBC Administrator applet's main dialog box (called Data Sources)

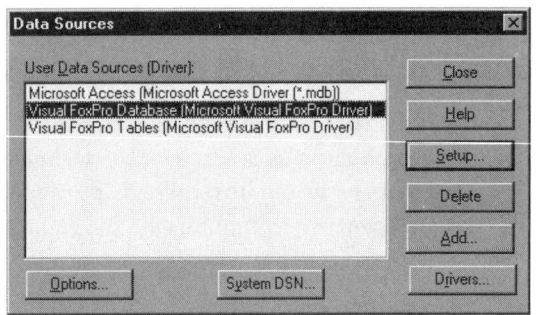

In Exercise 9.2, you'll create a new Data Source.

EXERCISE 9.2

Creating a New Data Source

1. Open 32-bit ODBC.

2. Click on the Add button.

3. Select a driver from the list of available drivers. For this example, we'll use the Visual FoxPro driver, one of the drivers that comes with ODBC.

EXERCISE 9.2 (CONTINUED)

4. Click on OK to accept the driver selection.

5. Enter a descriptive name for your new Data Source. It should clearly indicate the purpose and, if possible, the properties of the source file.

6. Enter a short, but concise, description of the defined driver's job. This does not appear in the main driver list of the ODBC Administrator, but the Data Source Name does. Here, you can add more helpful information if the name is not enough.

7. Next, select the directory that the source will be available in. The Use Current Directory checkbox is on by default.

Remember, a good database name is one that you don't have to decipher.

This defines a new ODBC Data Source. However, there are a few options that are available. If you need to define more options, click on the Options button, which displays the Options panel (see Figure 9.6). Each driver has its own set of options and information that needs to be entered in order for the driver to translate queries properly with Access and the back-end.

FIGURE 9.6

Entering an informative name into the ODBC Text Setup dialog box. Note that the Options panel is open and the Options button is disabled.

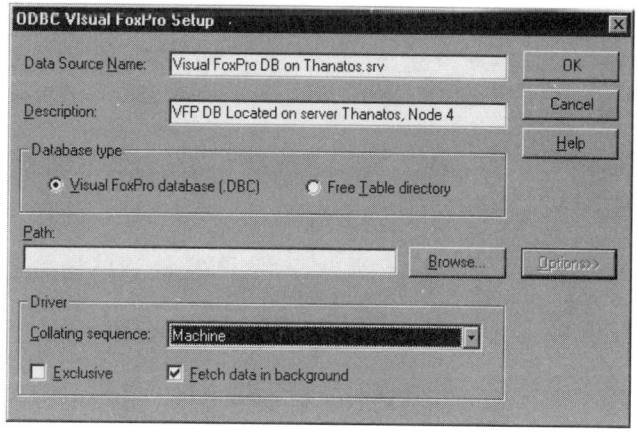

Creating Outer Joins

As we discussed in Chapter 1, relationships have quite a bit to do with creating an effective Access database. When working in the client/server environment, relationships become almost crucial to maintaining an efficient workgroup setting. We've discussed some examples of how this works. In this section we provide a brief refresher course on the topic of relationships and discuss how they relate to joins in a multi-user workgroup.

Relationships and Workgroups

If there were no relationships in a database, data could be stored willy-nilly and without a care to organization and efficiency. This is obviously very ineffective and an unlikely outcome of a custom Access database design study. It's something that we estimate happens to about one in every 20 newcomers to the field of database design. The basic idea of relationships is to group and prioritize record sets (often referred to as parents and children) so they receive, store, and return the data as they were meant to in the appropriate context.

It is unlikely that a one- to three-user office would ever lose anything saved into a flat-file database, though it might be misplaced for a while. However, when you have a dozen or so people responsible for handling thousands of technical service calls per week, a flat-file system with no capability for establishing relationships would result in nothing short of chaos, and very possibly would lead to complete ruin for the corporation. This is why relational database systems were developed. The result of defining relationships across several relatively related tables is called *referential integrity*. This process can prevent the loss of critical data.

For a detailed look at how referential integrity works, see Chapter 1.

Let's look at an example of how a company might make efficient use of referential integrity.

Heath Sideburn Replacement Corp. ships, receives, and repairs over 10,000 replacement sideburn systems a month. The company has 40 executive staffers (along with junior members and secretaries), 30 customer service representatives, 30 technical support staffers, 30 factory staffers, and 40 sales representatives. They are all connected via a five-node FDDI Token Ring topology, the fifth node of which supports a 30-terabyte data warehousing archive.

The front-end is Access. It communicates via SQL pass-through for common queries and with Jet to pass uncommon Access SQL queries to a SQL Server back-end. The server data is replicated to a backup server and a node server, one of which resides on each node. The system supports a large number of related tables, not the least of which is a comprehensive replacement sideburn model table and detailed customer table. Other tables are for manufacturing, technical support responses, availability, ordering, and shipping.

The general idea is that at least one field from each table has a relationship with a field in another table. For example, a salesperson gets a call from an eager sideburn replacement system buyer for a Model A1 Classic Brown. The salesperson uses Access to get information from the Model table to make sure that's the right product for the customer. The form that the salesperson uses contains queries that have relationships to the Model field of the Models table, the In Stock field in the Availability table, and the Currently Shipping field of the Shipping table, among others.

This arrangement allows the salesperson to see the model, how many are in the warehouse, and how many of those are being shipped today. The salesperson sees that there are plenty in stock, and the customer is more than willing to part with some cash to get the sideburns in the mail the next day. A week after the customer receives his new sideburns he detects a slight itching sensation in his left replacement sideburn and calls technical support. The technician queries the system for similar occurrences and finds 17 in the last month.

Since this was a recurring problem, it has been flagged with a note to manufacturing, which discovered that some joke itch powder from an executive's son was accidentally spilled into the mat glue of 30 units. Manufacturing identified the units and contacted shipping, which pulled the offending products from the shipping queue, preventing a disaster. Since all this information is available to the technician, he is confident in his decision to offer a free sideburn replacement system to the customer, and even tacks on free overnight shipping.

As you can see, if the tables had not all been related to each other, the result would have most likely been an absolute nightmare, and the customer would have gone to another supplier. All of the people involved with this single customer were privy to important information that allowed them to keep their new client happy, and they would most likely never even meet face-to-face on a daily basis.

So, how does this relate to client/server issues? Each of the department- and task-specific tables holds information that relates to another table or many other tables. In this example a number of different representatives were able to easily locate information regarding a single customer because all of the information was tied together by a small group of critical joins.

The Actual Join

We can see from the previous example that defining relationships is critical for a multi-user environment. Joins, and the way they handle complex data groups, are also critical. Generally speaking, outer, or *heterogeneous*, joins allow records from one table to be added to a dynaset, regardless of whether or not they contain the query criteria. A complete join occurs only when both sets match the query criteria absolutely. As we've seen in Chapter 4, this can be quite useful.

Complicated Joins Don't Have to Be Complicated

The discussion of joins can get quite complicated and more than a bit confusing. Joins are a complex issue that deals with relationships, queries, and form design—and not always in that order. To help understand this complex issue we provide an example.

This example focuses on two tables in the Heath Sideburn Replacement Corp. stable: Customers and Orders. The Customers table includes information on the customer ID number, name, phone, address, typical payment type, previous model ordered, and so on. The Orders table holds data on the model number, item color, shipping type, customer ID number, and a couple of lookups related to that customer ID.

Here's how it works. In most cases, a user would query the database to find all instances of customers that have ordered before. This would be helpful in many cases. Unfortunately, there is no way to find out which customers have orders with this type of join. This is where the outer join comes in handy.

In this case, the outer join would return all orders that are open (by that we mean orders that have not shipped or are in transit). By requesting a list of customer names from the outer join, which targets open orders in the Orders table, the user will receive a list of customer names that have open orders.

Unless the database developer had actually entered a field into the Customers table that indicated whether the customer had an active order, the outer join would be the only easy way to get the information. Of course, adding that field to the Customer database would needlessly complicate the available data that could be had elsewhere and in other ways. In the final analysis, this is the reason for using joins—and for using outer joins in particular.

There are three types of outer joins: full, right, and left. These procedures are defined by a set of table relationships (see Chapter 1 for a more complete description of relationships). A left outer join populates a dynaset with data from all left outer rows; matching output is set to Null. A right outer join performs the opposite operation. The full outer join culls the corresponding data from either side and sets the data that is duplicated to Null.

Linking or Importing Tables

Using our Sideburn Corp. example and an understanding of how joins and relationships work together, we can now gain a greater appreciation for the all-powerful link. Linking tables allows the user direct access to the original data. When the user's Access client is linked to one or more external data sources, that user is able to access that data via ODBC translation. In a multi-user environment, this allows many people to access, add to, and modify the same data.

WARNING   Modifying the structure of the linked database is not possible unless you are working with a native Access MDB file. External data sources are typically of another database format, such as Oracle, SQL Server, or FoxPro—not Access MDB.

Because linking or importing is an important topic that is very relevant to client/server issues, let's examine it further.

Linking

As we said earlier, linking is a live event. When the user is allowed to make modifications to a linked table, those changes will appear in that table (depending on a few variables defined by the system administrator). All of the data in the linked table remains in its original format, be it dBase, FoxPro, or what have you. All translations are handled by ODBC, unless the table or tables are native to Access (in other words, to an Access back-end).

HSR Corp. would use linking to maintain live connections to all tables so that all departments would be aware of new purchases, recent shipping activity, new stock in the warehouse, or technical support issues. All of these departments require the latest information regarding their products so they can stay profitable. This is typical of most companies that are involved in retail, resale, marketing, or support of their products.

There is only one rule for deciding whether to use linking. Linking is an appropriate solution when users must either have access to the most recent news/information/status or must update news/information/status on a regular basis.

Importing

You may have imported a text document or a graphics file from one program to another. Say you receive a Lotus Word Pro document from a colleague and you use only Microsoft Word 97. You can *import* that file into Word, which has the appropriate translators for Word Pro. This is exactly the way importing into Access works; but we're on the subject of client/server issues, so we won't cover the actual importing process here, just the multi-user aspects.

When a user imports a file into Access, the data from the incompatible application is converted into data Access can understand and display. Let's say that HSR Corp. was using a dBase IV system prior to migrating to Access and SQL Server. They had accumulated a great deal of customer information and were unwilling to lose it all. Since Access 95 supports dBase IV format database files, the old data was imported relatively well.

Always expect some reformatting and coding when importing an older database into Access. Most of the older systems used proprietary languages and coding techniques, which are difficult for even the most talented filter to understand. Memo fields and binary data are particularly likely to be lost or corrupted during conversion.

Once that data is imported it becomes part of an Access database. Unlike linking, the data brought in is static and will stay that way until modified by an administrator or someone granted access by the administrator. Good candidates for importing are news and informational archives, dictionaries and encyclopedias, and historical data.

As in linking, there is only one real rule for importing over linking. If the data is intended as a resource that will not be changed, modified, or otherwise altered (with the exception of the occasional addition of material), it is a candidate for importing.

Multiple Database Queries

Access is not limited to simple, single criterion queries. In fact, Access can deal with large and complex query trees that might bring any database to its digital knees. Unfortunately, they might bring Access down as well, but it can execute them. A multiple database query requests a number of returns (data sent back to the requesting client that meets the query criteria) from a database.

Say, for instance, that you want to find all instances of a customer requesting a catalog with their order of the Heath Replacement Sideburn System. You would structure a query that would ask for all the table fields that contain the specified data and it would return a list containing that information. Let's look at this a little more closely.

Sales receives a call from a previous customer to order a new Sideburn Replacement System. During the call, the customer, already identified by the representative, requests that a catalog be sent to his home. A simple glance at the representative's workstation reveals that only the customer's work address is available. The representative is thus prompted to ask for an additional mailing address, if any is needed.

The point is that the representative was able to query the Customer database for the customer's existing information. Figure 9.7 shows some of the contents of the customer's database entry.

As we can see from the figure, the representative has all the pertinent information immediately available, including the customer's previous order. This data is requested using a query that is predefined for this very task, which makes the job of the salespeople easier. Since this query required more information than is available in one table, several tables were queried and results were returned and compiled into one form for display.

F I G U R E   9.7

Part of the contents of the customer's database entry. Note the reference to a previous order.

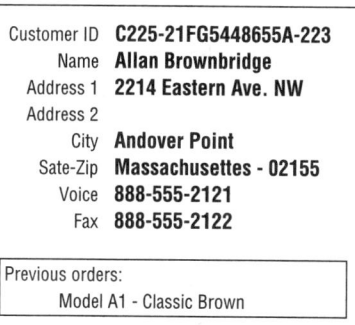

Customer ID	**C225-21FG5448655A-223**
Name	**Allan Brownbridge**
Address 1	**2214 Eastern Ave. NW**
Address 2	
City	**Andover Point**
Sate-Zip	**Massachusettes - 02155**
Voice	**888-555-2121**
Fax	**888-555-2122**

Previous orders:
    Model A1 - Classic Brown

Working with the Server

As we said at the beginning of this chapter, the server is the computer that you use to "serve" data to your users. A server can be connected to workstations using a number of different networking protocols, such as Ethernet, Fiber, or even the Internet with a bit of effort. (The use of Internet protocols has become common these days for remote users, though admittedly this is much easier with Access 97 than Access 95.)

Trapping Errors

Microsoft Exam Objective	**Trap errors that are generated by the server.**

There is no doubt that the activity a database designer likes least is locating, identifying, and eradicating bugs. Nevertheless, it is an important part of the design process. Often, when a user detects an error they are faced with an application that "just sits there" and does not give any warning that a problem has occurred. Or the user receives a cryptic error code that reveals little to nothing about the actual problem. These cryptic responses often leave the user, and at times the developer, wondering what happened.

Though it is much less entertaining, writing traps for your database's errors is much kinder than leaving your users staring at a cryptic error message. It is time consuming, but you can rest easier knowing that when a user experiences an error, it will be well explained. This will also benefit you, especially when you get that call at 3 A.M., by giving you the information you need to solve the user's problem.

Though macros are not nearly as robust as Visual Basic for Applications (VBA), developing a prototype of your error trap as a macro script can often be helpful. It can help you organize your thoughts and needs before you actually write the VBA code. However, we would never suggest that you use a macro-based error trap in a real solution, because of the limitations of macros in run-time applications.

With this goal in mind, let's examine a general purpose trap written in Visual Basic:

```
Sub GenErrSub()
    Dim strSubName As String
    strSubName = "GenErrSub"
    On Error Goto GenErrSub_Err

    MsgBox "Your application returned an error of type "
    Err.Raise 11

    Exit Sub

GenErrSub_Err:
    Dim intAction As Integer
    intAction = ErrHndlr(IntErrNum:=Err.Num, _
            strErrDescr:=Err.Descr, _
            strModName:=mstrModName, _
            strRoutnName:=strSubName)
    Select Case intAction
        Case Err_Cont
            Resume Next
        Case Err_Entry
            Resume
        Case Err_Exit
            Exit Sub
        Case Err_Quit
            Quit
    End Select
End Sub
```

This code segment creates an Integer variable that returns the value sent by the error system. IntAction holds the appropriate response to the error code generated. When the routine calls ErrHndlr, it passes the number generated by Err.Num, the dialog text from Err.Descr, and the name of the code that returned the error. This is not overly complicated.

From this you can write a simple function that handles the data the subroutine requires to be complete.

Managing Databases and Connections

There is nothing more important than taking care of your database. Keeping it in shape, using the various utilities available to you in Access and ODBC, is only part of what you can do to ensure its continued usefulness. If you are using ODBC, you can repair and compact your database from buttons in the DSN setup dialog box.

Compacting is useful to reduce the database's size—databases become bloated over time, as temporary objects are created. Some database corruption can be fixed by repairing a database. To compact or repair an Access database, first close the database, leaving the main Access window open, and select Tools ➢ Database Utilities. Then choose either Compact or Repair Database from the fly-out menu.

Replicating a Database

Very often in a multi-user environment there is a need to have more than one floor, server, or network segment. These logical, and sometimes literal, separations can make it impossible to share a single database for an entire operation. Someone was thinking overtime when they came up with replication.

The concept and, not surprisingly, the reality are actually amazingly simple. Replication merely involves copying an entire database, its operations, and the collection of structured data into a duplicate. This duplicate becomes a fully functional *replica* of the original database. Functionally, no user would be able to tell the difference between a *Design Master* and one of its replicas, unless they knew what to look for and were looking for it. Only the data can be updated in the replicas; design changes can only be made in the Design Master.

The Design Master is the original file from which a copy has been made. The Design Master and its replicas share a special relationship, as they are the only files that can be synchronized with each other. The Design Master is covered in detail in Chapter 11.

Replication can be very helpful for a salesperson on the road who does not have a permanent connection, remote offices that have limited connectivity options that restrict their connection speed, or even data archiving departments that do not have a need for more than a "snapshot" of a database at a particular point in time, among others. Let's take a quick look at how to create a replica.

See Chapter 11 for a more detailed discussion of replication. We cover the basics here for the purpose of illustration.

Before you begin:

- You need to remove any password protection that you may have used to secure the database.

- You need to have the Windows 95 Briefcase and Access Briefcase Replication installed. If you don't, you'll get an error. To install/reinstall the files, open the Control Panel and run Add/Remove Programs.

Access will now take a few moments to create your replica. Take the time to open it and make sure all the data was re-created exactly. This is a good time to make a backup of your Design Master. Remember that the Design Master and its replicas are the only files that can be synchronized with each other.

To update a replica, open the database in the Briefcase and choose Update Selection from the Briefcase menu. This will synchronize the changes in all replicas that are available at the time of updating. To perform the same actions in Access, do the following:

1. Open the database, and go to Tools ➤ Replication ➤ Synchronize Now.

2. Choose the Design Master or replica, and click on OK.

3. Close the database when prompted.

Fine-Tuning the Database

Microsoft ✓ Exam Objective

Optimize connections.

No database is ever finished until it has been tested and fine-tuned. There are a great number of hurdles to leap to implement a database application, but they are often easier to surmount than you might think. This section includes information about tuning your system, server, and application to work their best.

Keep in mind, however, that no guide is ever complete. Each developer must write their own. You will find that it comes easier with time.

Using Indexes

Tuning your database for optimal operation is critical when people need information—and need it fast. One way to improve overall application speed is by indexing certain fields to improve sorting and searching speed. However, excessive indexing can slow down your database, as it has to update each index as it is modified. The key is to index only those fields that will actually improve system performance and employee productivity.

Not all fields can be indexed, however. Check the Indexed property in the General field properties tab to determine whether a field can be indexed. Each table can have up to 32 indexes and five multi-field indexes.

Single-Field Indexes

To create an index on a single field, do the following:

1. Switch to Design view for a table and highlight the field you want to index.

2. Click on the General tab on the properties field and check the last entry.

3. Select the index that makes the most sense for your database. (Note: Choose No Duplicates only if you want to prevent duplicate values for that field in the table.)

Setting the field to No will delete the index.

Multiple-Field Indexes

To create a multi-field index, do the following:

1. Switch to Design view of the table you want to add indexes to.

2. Click on the Indexes button on the Toolbar, or go to View ➣ Indexes to open the Indexes window.

3. Name the Index in the Index Name field.

4. Enter the names of the fields to be indexed in the Field Name column and set its sort order. Continue adding field names and setting sort order until you have finished with all of the fields. Leave the Index Name field empty unless you are starting a new Index.

Optimizing Your Environment

Microsoft ✓ *Exam* *Objective*	**Optimize performance for a given client/server application.**

Microsoft ✓ *Exam* *Objective*	**Optimize performance for client/server applications.**

There are lots of directions to take when making your system, and subsequently your database, run as smoothly and quickly as possible. Many of these have little to with actual, direct client/server activity, but the modifications made to client systems and servers can make a difference in end-user satisfaction, productivity, and server robustness. We'll cover optimizing both the systems and the database applications. Here's a rundown of the most basic tweaks for your systems.

Buying More RAM

The cheapest and speediest way of giving a speed boost to your server is to add RAM, unless it already has more than 32MB. Unfortunately, anything over 32MB will do nothing more than allow you to run more applications than before. To move from 8 to 16MB will grant you a 20–30 percent speed increase. Moving up to 32MB of RAM will garner a mere 10–15 percent. Going to 64MB of RAM yields only a 5 percent performance gain. If you run all the applications you need and have plenty of RAM, you are safe.

Access eats RAM, so you may wish to evaluate the number of expected users. If you expect a moderate number of users then 32–64MB of RAM will most likely be fine. If the number of users will be great or the type of data being served is complex or sizeable, consider anywhere from 64MB all the way up to 512MB.

Tweaking Windows

Quit and remove from automatic startup any applications that are not specifically needed for serving. Disable any TSRs (uncommon these days) and virus-checking utilities that are not specifically needed for serving your database. Open the System applet in the Control Panel and click on the File System button located at the bottom of the Performance tab. Choose Network Server from the drop-down list. Windows defaults to Full Read-Ahead Optimization so you shouldn't have to change this setting.

Defragment your hard drive. Do this regularly, using either the Windows Defrag utility or a third-party utility. Contrary to what you may have heard, defragmentation does *not* damage your hard drive; although, if your drives have been formatted in FAT32 and you use a third-party defrag utility, it would be prudent to check and see if they have any updates to fully support FAT32. Compact your databases often, as this will make them run more smoothly, as well as shrinking their size considerably. Don't use wallpaper, since it requires a good amount of precious RAM.

If you are really low on memory, there are a few more ways to save RAM. If you have the Plus Pack, and have installed a theme, turn off Themes and remove all sound alerts. They also take up RAM. Though you will be sacrificing some convenience, as a last resort you can turn off the Office shortcut bar, which is a real RAM hog!

Optimizing Your Memory Settings

Windows memory management has come a long, long way, and most users will find that the automatic memory management of Windows 95 works just fine. There are a few things you can do to improve your RAM position, though. Open the System control panel and click on the Performance tab. Click on the Virtual Memory button at the bottom of the window. Select the Customize option (actually it's labeled "Let me specify my own Virtual

Memory settings." A mouthful, eh?) and choose a fast drive, but only if it's connected directly to the server. Do not choose a remote drive since this will just slow things down again.

Now, set the minimum to 5MB of RAM. This may seem arbitrary, but the default for Windows is 0, and you will need a minimum of 5 just for serving. Set the maximum to three times your RAM. Say you have 32, you would set the maximum to 96, 64 would mean 196, and 128 would mean 384, etc. Of course, most servers don't need more than 32 to 64MB anyway. Also make sure you have enough hard drive space.

Using the Performance Analyzer

Access comes with a little utility called the Performance Analyzer that can tell you how well, or how poorly, your system is working. Go to Tools ➤ Analyze ➤ Performance to open it. Select the items you want to analyze among the tabs and click on OK.

Choose the All tab in the Performance Analyzer to analyze your entire database.

Analyzer will scan your database and return a report that covers all aspects of your application. Examine these suggested modifications in detail before making them. When the report appears, click on an item and the lower pane will reveal more information on what you can do to improve speed. Uncompiled databases will always return a suggestion to compile the database, and so on.

Optimizing Your Application

We've examined what we can do to make that old workhorse on the desktop perform like a thoroughbred, now let's examine how to squeeze the last bit of go juice out of the application itself.

Speeding Up Databases

As we've seen throughout this book, the database itself is a hugely complex and detailed collection of information, data, code, queries, and forms, among other things. Here are a few basic tips to keep your database down to a lean and mean fighting weight—especially important for distributed applications:

- **For an unreplicated database, split your database.** Separate the interface and data from each other. The data goes on the server and the interface is run on the workstation. The application will run faster, and this method allows for smoother and easier scaling. Replicated databases can also benefit from splitting. Investigate the needs of the workgroup to define a more comprehensive and efficient solution.

- **Use graphics sparingly.** Sure, they look nice, but they take up space and RAM.

- **Don't repeat yourself.** The point of using a relational database is to optimize the storage of information. Repeating fields in a number of tables defeats this purpose. Don't do it. See Chapter 1 for more details on creating a normalized database.

- **Make code portable.** If you plan on coding your database in VBA, make your code clean and object-oriented. Blocks of reusable code can also be improved easily, making interface scaling a relatively simple chore. This also applies to queries. Keep them as simple as possible, as long as they meet the requirements for the job.

- **Keep your display trim and timely.** Don't show every field in every form every time, unless they are critical to the performance of the job. Make forms spare, easy to read, and useful for the specified task. If you must use graphics, make them nice, small, unobtrusive, and uncomplicated. A 2.5MB background of Mount Rushmore may look "neato" but is hardly appropriate—unless it is important enough to the client to make the drop in performance acceptable. The Standard pattern in the Form Wizard uses no graphics, so it is the most sparing of system resources.

- **In relation to the above, put base forms on queries and not on tables.** You will appreciate the greater control you have over the presentation of data and the smaller hit on the network as a result.

- **Use the correct data types for fields.** Examine the data you will be storing in the field and determine the appropriate data type for it. The use of incorrect types will needlessly decrease your application's performance.

- **Use indexes—sparingly.** Defining indexes for commonly accessed data can greatly improve performance, but indexing an entire table would be a mistake. Indexes require large amounts of space and reduce performance when adding or deleting fields.

Let's examine some more specific ways to optimize your application.

Queries

Since queries are the most active components of your applications, it stands to reason they would benefit from tweaking. Let's examine some basic rules for optimizing queries. But keep in mind that no book can replace actual experience. Practice will help you improve your query design skills.

- **Compile your queries.** Open the query in a Datasheet view and close it. This will compile the query, unlike simply saving it.

- **Limit your use of complex expressions.** Every complex expression you include in your queries is a boon to the Slow Network Goblin. Instead, take the time to include those expressions in your forms and reports, as this will improve network performance.

- **Limit the number of columns that will be included in the results.** The more columns, the more processing time, the less system performance.

Code

The code in your application is complex and takes up a great deal of room, making it difficult to parse through when optimizing. This fact makes it all the more important to take certain factors into consideration when developing the database in the first place. Keep the following in mind:

- **Limit the number of call-outs an application will make.** This will go a long way in increasing overall database performance in itself. Each time VB needs to go looking for an external procedure, time is wasted that could have been spent processing user queries.

- **Limit the use of Variants and define your data types specifically.** Defining your variables without specifying a type results in a Variant being declared. Examine your needs and declare variables using the smallest data type for the job.

- **Clean out your code closet.** During the development stage of any application you are bound to declare and abandon variables, write and eliminate subroutines, and code functions that you will never use. All this orphaned code takes up memory, so you need to eliminate it. Careful documentation of your code, though time consuming, is the best friend in the world when your application reaches 30,000 lines of code.

Don't just delete all old, unused code. Examine your subroutines and functions to see if they have any possible future as code fragments for projects to come. Code recycling can save you endless hours of development time.

- **Deliver your solutions pre-compiled.** Open the Modules window, select Run ➤ Compile All Modules, and then choose Save All Modules from the File menu. If you plan on modifying your application be aware that opening your database decompiles it. You will have to re-compile it and re-distribute—a rather complicated process, but worth it.

Forms

Since forms are the interface of your application, it is important to make them as efficient as possible, while providing a useful balance of information that does not rely on excessive queries to the server. As always, though, practice makes perfect. This section will *not* make you a forms guru, only practice can do that. If you follow a few simple steps during the creation process, you will be rewarded with improved efficiency:

- **Limit the use of controls.** The more controls in a form, the more processing time involved. It is best to develop forms with a task-based orientation.

- **Make your forms query-based.** This goes the farthest to eliminate the chaff from the wheat. The point is to make the forms data-centric, providing only the data needed by the people that need it. Don't supply manufacturing data for the sales personnel, and vice versa.

- **Try not to use resource-hogging features.** Including subforms and OLE objects is an enormous draw. A subform is exactly the same as a form in terms of resource use. Try to include the controls from the subform on the main form. OLE objects also require a great deal of resources. Unless the object, say a BMP picture, is functionally integral to the form, convert it to an image.

- **Try not to modify objects from their default style.** Access does not store object definitions for default objects, so there is less network time. Also, keep all objects, with the exception of data, of course, local to the user. This eliminates the needless passing of object definitions with queries.

Summary

In this chapter we've covered a number of things, not the least of which is what makes a single- or a multi-tier database right for a multi-user environment. A database system with a few tables, ODBC connectivity, and Access for a front-end does not a client/server solution make. More to the point, we have learned that a good client/server solution involves examining a number of variables. These variable include expected/projected users, the benefits and pitfalls of various front-end and back-end factors, and the efficient use of existing and new data. With this in mind, you have learned that there are many challenges to creating a multi-user solution that is elegant, effective, and efficient.

You've also learned how to use ODBC for network connectivity between incompatible database systems, without which a solution would not be possible. We've examined the concepts behind how to join databases for more complete data sharing and effective querying. We've also examined procedures for how to manage and tweak a server and your application for improved performance, and how to make errors more informative using Visual Basic code.

We've learned how to define indexes for common fields for increased system performance. And, finally, we have discussed in more detail multi-tier applications and how they can improve a multi-user environment.

Review Questions

1. What is the difference between a single- and a multi-tiered application?

   A. The total number of tables equals or exceeds five.

   B. Queries are sent to the back-end using ODBC SQL.

   C. All joins are of the left outer variety.

   D. In a multi-tier application the interface code can be located on the workstation.

2. What is the most effective use of a multi-tiered application?

   A. To increase productivity in a small workgroup

   B. To increase activity in a small workgroup

   C. To improve access speed in a large workgroup

   D. To separate the front-end from the back-end

3. Which of the following are possible applications of the Total Access model?

   A. A small office with few workstations and no major traffic requirements

   B. A data warehousing facility

   C. A high volume sales environment with 150 salespersons

   D. A law firm where the system is used to store and retrieve client information

4. Which front-end/back-end combination works best with ODBC? (Select two.)

   A. Access/Access

   B. Access/FoxPro

   C. Access/SQL Server

   D. Access/Text File

5. What are the three types of outer join?

   A. Left, right, and obtuse

   B. Far, near, and center

   C. Left, right, and full

   D. There are only two: left and right

6. What does separating the interface from the system logic accomplish?

   A. Gives you a thinner application

   B. Increases modularity

   C. Streamlines the data

   D. Streamlines the codebase

7. What are the benefits of using SQL Server as a back-end? (Select two.)

   A. Simpler indexing

   B. Less code

   C. Scalability

   D. Better network performance

8. Under what circumstances would you use linking rather than importing?

   A. As a way of making the incoming data native, which improves data warehousing.

   B. Linking is required if the solution calls for ODBC.

   C. The solution calls for immediate access to the latest data.

   D. As a much more efficient way of handling archived data.

9. What is the best reason for trapping your application's errors?

    A. It benefits the end-user and the developer because it allows them to understand more clearly what the problem is.

    B. It lowers support costs.

    C. It prevents the error from occurring in the first place.

    D. It promotes end-user troubleshooting techniques.

10. Which of these are ways a system administrator can care for a database? (Select two.)

    A. Compact the database to improve speed and eliminate unused space.

    B. Use Norton Utilities to identify and replace corrupted objects.

    C. Repair the database for improved overall performance.

    D. Add RAM to the server.

11. Which of the following are ways to optimize a server for best operation?

    A. Defragment your hard drive regularly.

    B. Don't use wallpaper or desktop themes.

    C. Eliminate the Office shortcut bar.

    D. All of the above.

12. Which of the following are ways to speed up the back-end? (Select two.)

    A. Split your database.

    B. Eliminate unnecessary graphics.

    C. Utilize ODBC connectivity for all queries.

    D. Make use of SQL pass-through.

CHAPTER

10

Access Security

Access security has often been described as difficult and complex to master. In addition, it has been poorly documented in the Microsoft manuals and online help. The learning curve is steep, but it's worth the climb when you need to secure your Access database. We'll cover security concepts and the steps you need to take in order to avoid some of the pitfalls that can occur.

In this chapter, you will learn:

- How to secure your Access application.

- The difference between the two different kinds of Access security: user-level and share-level. You'll also learn which is right for you.

- The best method for distributing a Microsoft Access library database as shareware without allowing users to view the code.

- How to secure an application you have inherited that was supposed to have been secured. (People are able to get into the application just by copying the database onto their own PCs and opening it.) You'll learn what went wrong and how you fix it.

- About distributing your application using the runtime version of Access and how to manage groups, users, and permissions in code when the built-in security menu commands aren't available.

The Access/Jet Security Model

What we think of as Access security is actually a function of the Jet database engine, not Access itself. Jet provides the security for all the objects in the Containers and Documents collections of your database, and Access stores the components of your application.

Microsoft ✓ *Exam* *Objective*

Analyze a scenario, and recommend an appropriate type of security.

Jet provides you with two different flavors of security: share-level and user-level. You can pick which level you want to use based on how much security you need and how much time and effort you want to invest in setting up and managing your application's security.

Levels of Security

Share-level refers to the level of security you get when you set a database password on your database. Share-level security is easy to implement and simple to manage but is relatively unsophisticated compared to user-level security. With share-level security, whoever knows the password can open the database. Once the database is open, the user has access to all of the objects in the database.

User-level security is more complex; it involves setting up separate user and group accounts. However, user-level security is essential when you need multiple levels of access to the objects in your database. If, for instance, you have sensitive data that some of the application's users must work with, but that you do not want other users to see, you need to implement user-level security.

Share-Level Security (a.k.a. Database Password)

Share-level security was introduced in Access 95 and is called the "database password feature" in the Access documentation. This is the simplest form of security and consists of simply setting a password on a database. Every user shares the same password, and, if you know the password, you can get into the database. All users have all rights to all objects—there is no concept of separate users or different levels of access.

Setting the Password

In order to set the database password, you need to open the database exclusively by checking the Exclusive checkbox in the File ➢ Open dialog box. Then select Tools ➢ Security ➢ Set Database Password, as shown in Figure 10.1.

FIGURE 10.1

Setting the database password

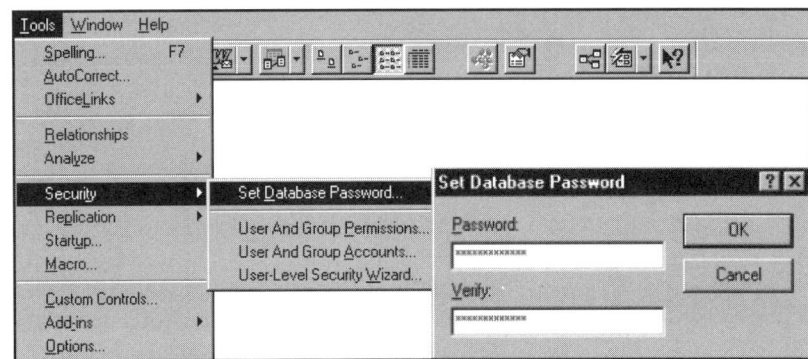

 The default setting in Access 95/97 is to open the database in shared mode, which occurs when you double-click on a database from an Explorer window or select it from your most recently used file list. If you don't wish to use the default setting, you must open the database using the File ➢ Open dialog box in Access. You can change the default by selecting Tools ➢ Options ➢ Advanced from the menu and selecting either Shared or Exclusive as the Default Open Mode setting.

The database password is case-sensitive, which means that if you enter it as a combination of upper- and lowercase letters, your users must enter it with the same combination of upper- and lowercase letters (for example, "KingKong" will not open a database whose password is "kingkong"). The password can be almost any combination of letters that you want—up to 14 characters in length (see the *Password Gotchas* sidebar for some characters to stay away from).

> **Password Gotchas**
>
> There are two bugs you need to be aware of with the database password:
>
> - If you type a space in the database password and then compact your database, your password will be truncated to the portion before the first space. So, for example, "My Password" becomes just "My" after compacting. So don't use spaces!
>
> - If you use a backslash (\) in your password, you won't be able to use it to open your database. Instead, to open your database, you would need to type two backslashes where you entered only one. So if you enter your password as "My\Password," you'll need to type "My\\Password" to get in.

Share-Level Dangers

The database password feature was intended to give a minimal level of security to your database and assumes that you don't need the multilevel features of user-level security (see Exercise 10.1). However, it is not very secure—browsing the Internet will yield several Web sites offering to crack your database password for a nominal fee. That turns out to be fortunate because, in addition to being relatively easy to break, share-level security is also easy to invoke.

Share-level security is dangerous for the same reason that it is attractive: it is so easy to set. Share-level security can be set by anyone who can open an Access database exclusively. So, anyone can set or reset the password—and then forget it. When that happens, everyone will be locked out of the database. If you want to prevent your users from setting or resetting the database password, you need to implement user-level security and remove your users' permission to open the database exclusively.

You should only use share-level security when you want to apply a minimal level of security without much effort. Share-level security should only be used when you are willing to give all of your users complete access to your database once they have opened it. To put it another way: share-level security should be used only when you are not really concerned about security, and when you have taken the necessary precautions to prevent users setting and forgetting the database password.

EXERCISE 10.1

Setting and Changing a Database Password

In this exercise you'll set, test, and change the database password.

1. Start Access and open the Northwind database (C:\MSOFFICE\ACCESS\ SAMPAPPS\NWIND.MDB) exclusively by selecting File ➢ Open and making sure the Exclusive option is selected in the Open dialog box.

2. Choose Tools ➢ Security ➢ Set Database Password… and type in a password up to 14 characters long. Repeat the password in the Verify box and click on OK.

3. The database password is now set. Close the database.

4. Reopen the database. You will be prompted for a password. Type in the password.

5. Close and reopen the database, making sure to check the Exclusive checkbox in the Open File dialog box. To clear the password, choose Tools ➢ Security ➢ Unset Database Password… and type in the password. Click on OK. The password will now be cleared.

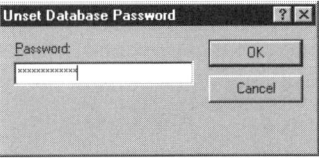

User-Level Security

If you need more robust security—or want to provide different levels of access for different users—then you will need to implement user-level security. In user-level security, each user is assigned a user ID and password. When a user logs on, their user ID/password combination is validated against their workgroup file. Once a user opens a database, their access to each object is determined based on a combination of explicit permissions assigned to that user plus permissions inherited from any groups to which they belong.

You can assign permissions to specific users or to groups of users. Assigning permissions to groups is far simpler to administer than assigning permissions to individual users, even if you have only two or three users. You can define as many of your own custom groups as you need, set each group's security, and then, by making users members of specific groups, assign those group permissions to users.

By using groups you can also ensure that permissions are assigned uniformly, since everyone in the group will have exactly the same permissions. You can also remove a complete set of permissions from a user just by removing the user from a group with those permissions.

Users always have the permissions assigned directly to them plus any permissions inherited from groups they are a member of. Where permissions conflict, the user actually has permissions based on the *least restrictive rule.* With the least restrictive rule, a user is assigned the permission that lets them do the most, in other words, is the least restrictive of the conflicting permissions. You might assign Terry only Read Data permissions on the Customers table. But you also put Terry in the Developers group, which has full Administer permissions on the Customers table. According to the least restrictive rule, Terry will then have both the Read Data and the Administer permissions. Removing Terry from the Developers group will remove his Administer permissions and leave him with just Read Data.

If you are planning on replicating your secured database, you must use user-level security. You cannot set a database password on a replicated database, nor can you replicate a password-protected database.

How User-Level Security Works

When a user logs on, their ID and password combination is validated against the workgroup file (also called the *system database*). A default workgroup file, System.mdw, is created automatically when you install Access. Even in an unsecured application, the workgroup file is used to validate user IDs. In an unsecured database everyone is silently logged on as the Admin user, with no password.

Once the user has been validated, Access finishes loading and the user can attempt to open a database. Whether or not the user can do so is determined by the permissions that have been set on that database for that user (either directly or through the groups that they belong to). The permissions used are the ones saved in the database being opened, and they are used to determine the user's level of access to objects in the database.

Permissions and AllPermissions

Permissions in Access are properties of Container and Document objects, which are assigned to specific User and Group objects. The Permissions property stores its data internally as a Long Integer number. This number can be used with the logical AND, OR, and NOT operators in conjunction with the predefined security constants available in VBA, in order to retrieve or manipulate the specific permissions you are interested in.

The Permissions property of an object is used in conjunction with that object's UserName property to retrieve or set permissions that the user has been assigned directly.

The AllPermissions property of an object returns the sum of a user's permissions—both those directly assigned to the user and those inherited by membership in a group. It is read-only.

The Built-In Accounts

As noted earlier, in an unsecured application everyone is silently logged in as the Admin user. Admin is the built-in user account that ships with Access. Table 10.1 shows all of the built-in accounts and groups and describes their properties.

	Account	Description
T A B L E 10.1 The Built-In Accounts and Groups	Admin user	The default user account installed with Access. The Admin user account has no special powers or properties of its own. However, Admin is installed as a member of the Admins group, and so inherits the administer permissions all members of Admins possess. You can remove Admin from the Admins group once you have created another user account to take its place.
	Admins group	The administrative group, which does have special, irrevocable powers to administer security. Members of Admins can create new users and groups, assign and clear passwords, and set permissions on database objects. You cannot remove administer permissions from the Admins group.
	Users group	The default group that all users must belong to, no matter what other groups they may belong to. The Users group has no special powers.

You can't delete any of these built-in accounts and you probably won't want to use them, either.

To begin with, the members of the Admins group have far more power than you want your users to have. Admins members can perform any action on any object in the database, including setting permissions and administering user and group accounts. Admins group members are so powerful that one of the first steps you will perform in setting up security is to remove the default user account—Admin—from the Admins group. You don't want the Admin user account to have all the power of the Admins group, because everyone in the world with a copy of Access can log on as Admin. Since you can't remove or restrict the powers of the Admins group, you must remove Admin from it.

On the other hand, you can restrict the permissions assigned to the Users group. Unfortunately, the Users group is too broadly defined for most purposes, since everyone who uses Access must belong to it.

So this really leaves you with no viable options for securing your application using the built-in accounts. You must create your own custom groups and users to successfully secure your application and also allow users to work with it.

There are two other built-in accounts, Engine and Creator, that are used internally by Access. You will see them if you poke around Access's internal collections in code. You can't change, delete, or use them yourself, so just ignore them.

Owners

Another aspect of Access security you need to consider is the concept of ownership. The owner of an object is the user who created the object, and the owner has irrevocable Administer permissions on that object. That means that owners can assign or revoke permissions for themselves and others on their objects. In an unsecured application, the Admin user owns everything.

So what does this all mean when it comes time to implement user-level security on your database? You need to:

- Remove direct permissions assigned to the Admin user since, otherwise, Admin is too powerful.

- Remove the group permissions assigned to the Users group, since Users includes too many users.

- Remove Admin from the Admins group to further restrict the permissions associated with the Access default logon ID.

- Make sure the Admin user doesn't own anything since the default is that Admin owns (and so can administer) everything.

- Create your own custom groups and users, and assign them permissions to use your secured application.

In the next section you'll see how to make these changes. Exercise 10.2, which covers exploring the built-in accounts, demonstrates why you'll want to create new users and groups.

EXERCISE 10.2

Examining the Built-In Accounts

1. Open the Northwind database.

2. Select Tools ➤ Security ➤ User and Group Accounts… from the menu. As you can see, there are two available groups, Admins and Users, and Admin is a member of both. You can use this dialog box to create or delete users (although you can't delete the Admin user). You can also clear passwords of other users if you are a member of Admins.

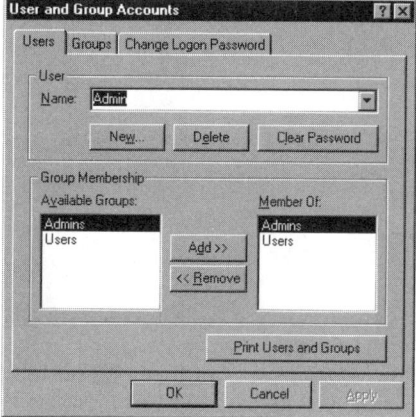

3. Click on the Groups tab. This is where you create new groups or delete groups that you created and no longer need. You can't delete the built-in groups, but you can delete groups you create yourself.

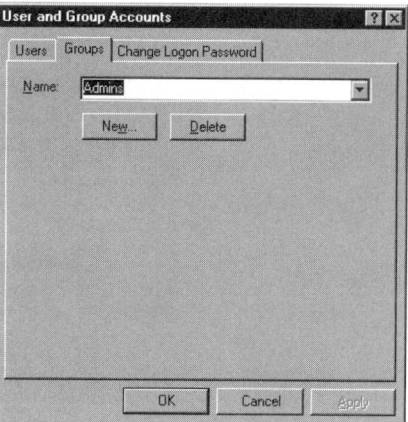

4. Click the Change Logon Password tab. This is where you change your own password. Note that you need to supply the old password in order to do so. Pressing the Cancel button will close this dialog box.

5. Now select Tools ➢ Security ➢ User and Group Permissions from the menu. The default view shows the Admin user and displays the permissions set for Admin on the Categories table in Northwind.

6. Click on the Groups option button (you can find it below the User Group/Name box) to display the Admins and Users groups. Note that the Admins group has no permissions listed even though, in fact, it has administer permissions on all objects. Click on the Users group. As you can see, in an unsecured application, the Users group has full permissions on all of the database objects.

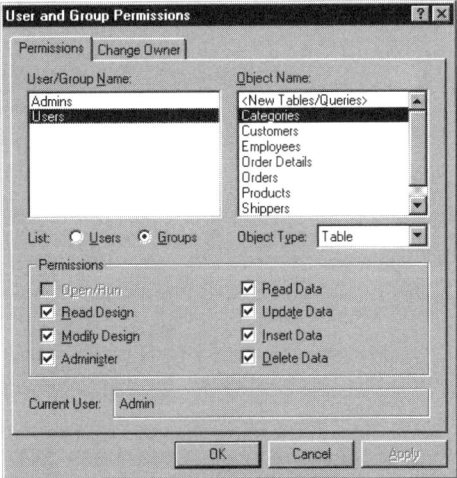

7. Now click on the Change Owner tab. Note that the Admin user is the owner of everything in sight. This is always the case in any unsecured application.

You also have the option of making a group the owner of an object—the owner doesn't have to be a user.

Implementing Access Security

Microsoft ✓ *Exam* *Objective*	**Explain the steps for implementing security.**

Access 95 ships with a Security Wizard that will help you to set up your security. But the Security Wizard won't perform the entire task of securing your application for you—there are some crucial steps that you need to take first. If you omit any of these steps, security will not work the way you expect and your application will be vulnerable.

The Workgroup File

The very first step you need to take in the process of securing your application is to create a new workgroup file.

You might wonder why this step is necessary—wouldn't it just be easier to use the built-in System.mdw file and have done with it? Why not just go ahead and create the necessary custom groups and users in the existing workgroup file? Well, you could—the problem is that your application wouldn't be secure.

When Access is installed, it creates the System.mdw workgroup file and asks you for your name and company. Access uses the information that you type in for your name and company to create a workgroup ID (or WID). The WID is important because the Admins group is uniquely identified through it.

The WID makes the Admins group unique to each workgroup file. The Users group and the Admin user, on the other hand, are the same across all installations of Access.

Since anyone can see your name and company settings by choosing Help ➢ About Microsoft Access ➢ Microsoft Access, anyone can re-create your workgroup file by reentering your name and company information. Once that's done, your database can be taken over by creating a new account and adding it to the Admins group.

Creating a Workgroup File

To create a new workgroup file, you need to use the Workgroup Administrator, which is a standalone applet and not part of Access itself. (See Exercise 10.3.) In addition to creating workgroup files, the Workgroup Administrator allows you to switch between workgroup files if you need to work with secured and unsecured databases.

If a shortcut to the Workgroup Administrator hasn't been installed, you can locate it by searching for the file name Wrkgadm.exe.

In Access 2.0 and Access 95, the Workgroup Administrator is installed in the Access directory. In Access 97, it is installed in the Windows directory.

A workgroup file is identified by its Workgroup Identifier (WID). This WID is created out of the strings you type in the Name, Organization, and Workgroup ID textboxes, so you should write your entries down and save them in a secure location. If your workgroup file is ever lost or corrupted, and you don't have a backup, you could be locked out of your own application. By saving the settings you used initially, you can re-create your workgroup file.

EXERCISE 10.3

Using Workgroup Administrator to Create a Workgroup File

In this exercise we will use the Workgroup Administrator to create a new workgroup file.

1. Close down any open sessions of Access.

2. Locate the Workgroup Administrator icon and double-click on it to load the application. It will show you your name, company, and the path and file name of the currently active workgroup file.

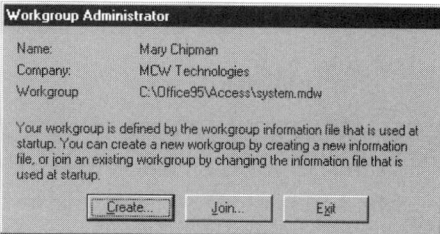

3. Click on the Create... button to create a new workgroup file.

4. Type in the name, company, and Workgroup ID. Make sure to write down the strings you used, especially for the Workgroup ID. Unlike the default workgroup file, these strings will not be visible from Help ➢ About Microsoft Access dialog box.

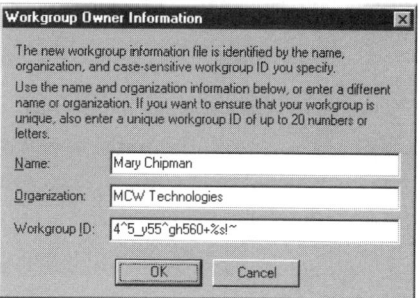

5. Click on the OK button. You will then be prompted to save the new workgroup file. Do not overwrite your existing System.mdw file. Chances are you will be working with both secured and unsecured applications, and will want to have both workgroup files on hand.

Steps to Secure Your Database

Once you have created your workgroup file, you are ready to continue with the next steps in securing your database.

Since you are going to remove the Admin user from the Admins group, you need to create a new user account to replace the Admin user. Access prevents you from shooting yourself in the foot and having a database with no administrator by requiring that there always be at least one member in the Admins group. As a result, you need to create a new Admins account, as shown in Exercise 10.4, before you remove the Admin user from the Admins group.

Because the Admin user is the owner of any unsecured database, you also need to make sure that Admin does not own the secured database or any of the objects in it.

WARNING Although you can't delete all the members of the Admins group through the Access user interface, you can use code to delete all members of the Admins group. If you've done this in error, you'll have no means of creating new users and groups, clearing passwords, or performing other administrative tasks. These are tasks that only members of Admins can perform. In such a case, you'd need to restore a backup version of your workgroup file that still contains a user in the Admins group.

EXERCISE 10.4

Adding a New Account to the Admins Group

1. Log on to Access using the workgroup file you created in the previous exercise. Note that you will be logging on as the Admin user. Open any database (the Access security menus are not available unless a database is loaded).

2. Select Tools ➢ Security ➢ User and Group Accounts from the menu, and click on the New button on the Users tab.

3. Type in a name and Personal ID (or PID) for the new user. The PID can be from 4–20 alphanumeric characters. The strings used for the name and the PID will be encrypted to form a SID, or *System Identifier,* which is what Access uses to identify the new user.

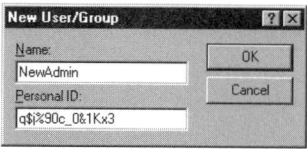

4. Write down the strings you used for the name and PID. If you ever need to re-create your workgroup file, you will need to re-create this account as well. Click on OK.

5. Now click on the Add button to add the new user to the Admins group.

6. Since we have a new account in the Admins group, it is now OK to remove the Admin user from the Admins group. From the User Name drop-down list box, select the Admin user. Select Admins in the Member Of list box, and then click on the Remove button.

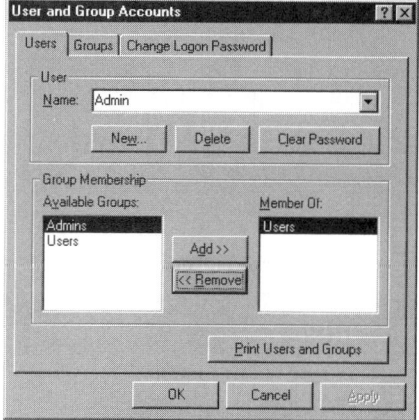

7. The next step is to activate the login dialog box when Access starts. You do this by setting a password for the Admin user. (Note that you are still logged on as the Admin user.) Select the Change Logon Password tab from the Tools ➢ Security ➢ User and Group Accounts dialog box. Since the Admin user does not currently have a password, leave the Old Password text box blank. Type in a new password in the New Password and Verify text boxes, and click on OK.

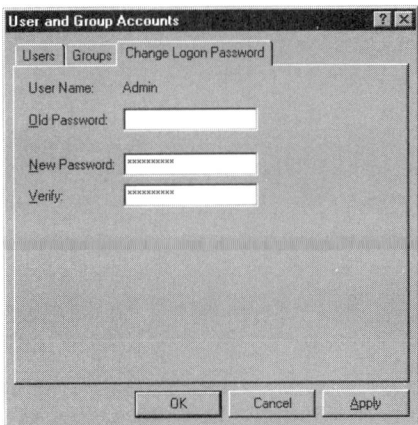

8. Close down Access. The next step in securing your database is running the Security Wizard.

Running the Security Wizard

The Security Wizard assists you in the task of transferring ownership of your database from the Admin user to the new user you have just created. The Change Owner option in the Security dialog box can't change ownership of the database itself, so the wizard creates a new database and imports all of the objects you select into it. In addition, it removes all permissions from the Admin user and the Users group, grants full permissions to the Admins group, and encrypts the new database. Your original, unsecured database is not altered in any way and your new database has you, rather than Admin, as its owner. We'll run the Security Wizard in Exercise 10.5.

One permission the Security Wizard does not remove is the Open/Run permission on the databse itself from the Users group. If you don't want users who are not in your secured workgroup file to open the database, you need to remove this permission manually after the Security Wizard has run.

The Security Wizard also encrypts your database. Encryption is designed to prevent users from accessing the data in a secured database using a program other than Access (like a text editor). An encrypted database adds about 15 percent to the application's processing time. If you decide you do not wish to have the additional overhead and are not worried about strings in your database being read by someone using a file editor, you can decrypt the database. To do that, select Tools ➢ Security ➢ Encrypt/Decrypt from the menu after the Wizard has run.

EXERCISE 10.5

Running the Security Wizard

1. If you did not close down Access after the last exercise, do so now. Open Access again and log on as the new user you created in the previous exercise. You have not set a password for this user yet, so leave the Password text box blank.

2. Open the database you wish to secure and choose Tools ➢ Security ➢ User-level Security Wizard from the menu.

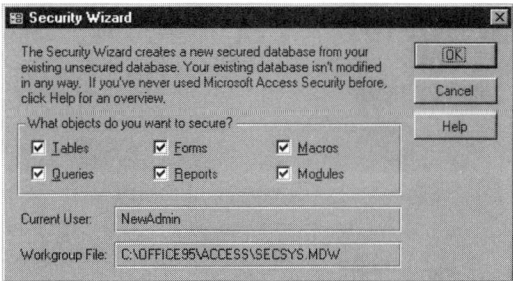

3. Leave all of the items selected and click on OK. You will then be prompted for a new name and destination folder for the secured database. Type in a new name for the database and click on OK. You will then see one last dialog box from the Security Wizard informing you that your database has been secured and that the original, unsecured database has not been altered.

When Security Doesn't Work...

If you think you have secured your database but users who should not have permissions are still getting in, it's most likely *not* a bug with Access security—you probably left out a step somewhere. Make sure that you have performed all the necessary steps. Here's a brief summary of what you should have done:

1. Created a new workgroup file.
2. Created a new user and added the user to Admins group.
3. Removed the Admin user from the Admins group.
4. Set a password for the Admin user.
5. Logged on as the new user and run the Security Wizard.
6. Removed Open/Run permissions for the database from the Users group.
7. Assigned permissions to your own custom groups and created new user accounts.

Creating Groups and Users and Assigning Permissions

Once you've run the Security Wizard, you will have a new, secured database. However, if you've done things correctly and followed all of the steps, your new Admins account user/owner is the only one who can use the database. While this is very secure, it's also very limiting.

At this point you need to create new users and groups, and assign permissions for the different database objects you want them to use, as shown in Exercise 10.6. It helps to map out on paper which permissions the various users and groups are supposed to have before you begin the task. This will give you a clear plan to implement when you start making changes in the database.

Remember: assign permissions to groups, not users. Using groups makes sense even if you only have one user in a particular group. When that user leaves the firm and you need to replace them with another user, you don't need to reassign a complicated set of permissions. All you need to do is delete the user account for the person who is leaving, create a fresh user account for the new person, and add the new account to the group.

Assigning Permissions to a Group

1. Open the secured database and choose Tools ➤ Security ➤ User and Group Accounts from the menu.

2. Click on the Groups tab and click on New. Type in a name for the new group and a Personal ID. Remember that the PID is not a password—groups can't log on and don't have passwords anyway.

Always write down the exact names and PIDs of the groups and users you create. Then store them in a safe place. Groups and users can be re-created by using the same strings used to create the originals.

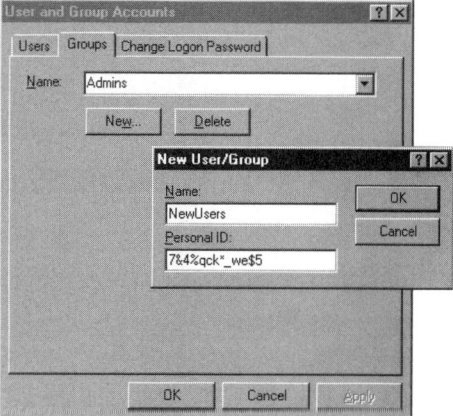

3. Click the Users tab and create a new user, repeating steps 3 and 4 in Exercise 10.4. Note that Access automatically adds the new user to the Users group. Click on the Add button to add the new user to the group you have just created. Click on OK to close the dialog box.

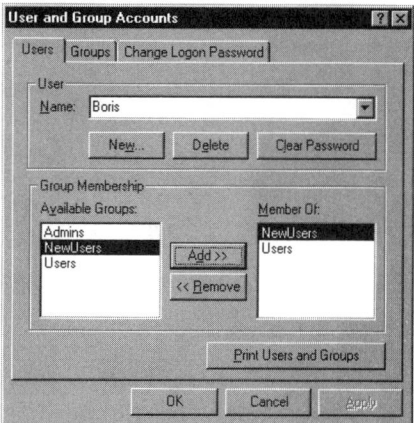

EXERCISE 10.6 (CONTINUED)

4. To set permissions for the new group, choose Tools ➢ Security ➢ User and Group Permissions from the menu.

5. You don't want the default option for this dialog box—Users. So click on the Groups option button next to List to display permissions for groups.

6. Select the objects you want to grant permissions to in the Object Name list box. (You can select multiple objects by holding down the Shift key.) When you select the <New Tables/Queries> option, you are setting default permissions for any new object that you create in the future. Continue with the remaining objects in the database.

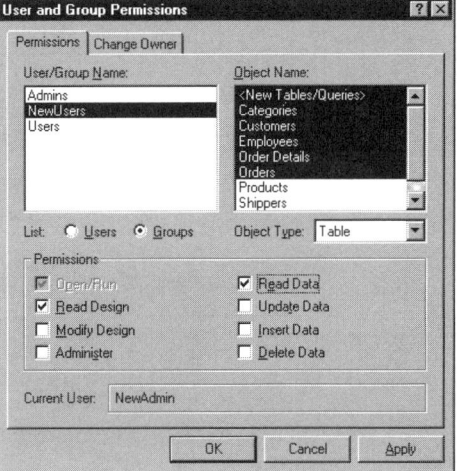

 When you set Read Data permissions on a table, Read Design is also automatically selected. Access needs to read the definition of the table (such as validation rules and formatting) in order to display the data for the user. If the user didn't have Read Design along with Read Data permissions, Access couldn't display the data.

Managing Access Security

Securing your application is only the beginning—now you have to actually make your security plan work in the real world. The following is a list of some of the security challenges that you may face:

- You want to be able to restrict users from viewing certain rows or columns in a table.

- You want to distribute your application as a library database. You will need to secure and distribute it without having the users log on.

- Your application will be distributed to remote sites where you are not available to perform administrative tasks (such as adding new users and groups). You will need to set up an on-site administrator who doesn't have the ability to mess up the existing permissions you've set.

- You are distributing your application using the runtime version of Access where the built-in security menus are not available. You're going to need to work with security using VBA code.

- You have an application where the tables are in a separate database from the application database. What permissions do the users need in order to be able to relink the tables?

Setting Row- and Column-Level Permissions on Tables

When you set permissions on a table, you can grant permissions only on the entire table. So what do you do if you have a Salary column in the Payroll table that you don't want certain users to be able to see? Or perhaps you want to restrict users from seeing the Salary column for their supervisors.

To set security on part of a table, you begin by removing all permissions from the Payroll table. Then create a query that selects just the rows and columns you want your users to view, and set the Run Permissions to Owner's (instead of the default—User's). Setting the Run Permissions to Owner's lets the query run with your permissions (since you created the query, you are the owner), as shown in Figure 10.2.

Once you have created the query, grant Open/Run permissions on it to the users who you would like to be able to see the data. The query will run with your permissions (the Owner's permissions) applied to the underlying tables instead of your users' permissions. This is essential, since you removed your

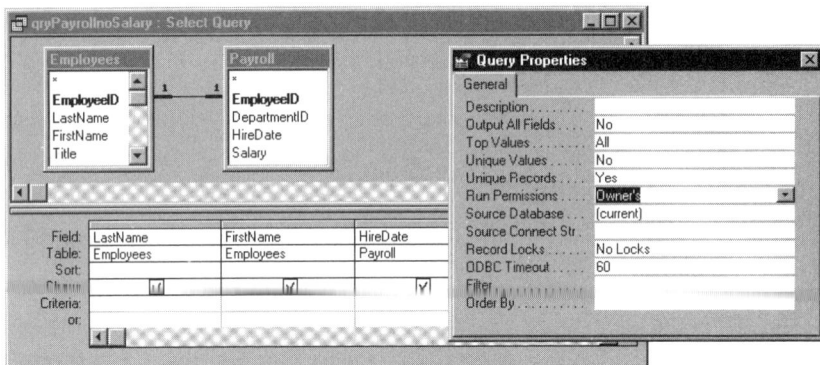

users' permissions for the table! The users will only be able to see the columns
or rows defined in the query and won't be able to open the tables directly.

The reason this works is that the owner of an object can administer that
object and grant or revoke permissions for other users to use it. Also, since
you were able to design the query, you must have the necessary permissions
on the underlying tables. By setting the query's Run Permissions property to
Owner's, as shown in Exercise 10.7, you are telling Access, "Run this query
with my permissions, not the permissions of the user actually running it."

EXERCISE 10.7

Changing Run Permissions on a Saved Query

1. Open an existing Select query or create a new one in your secured
   database.

2. In Design view, select Query Properties and set the Run Permissions
   option to Owner's.

3. Open the query in SQL view. Note that when you chose the option in
   the last step, the line WITH OWNERACCESS OPTION was added at the end
   of the SQL statement.

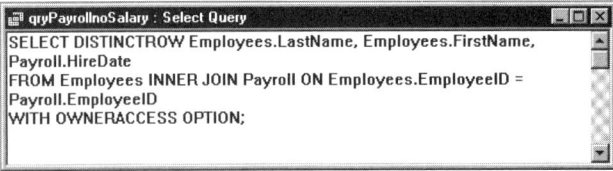

Setting the Run permissions to Owner's only works on saved queries. It doesn't work on SQL statements created on the fly in code, SQL in the RecordSource for a form or report, or SQL used for the RowSource for a combo box.

Securing a Library Database

If you are writing an add-in or library database, and you want to secure your code, you need to take the same steps to secure it as you would for a regular database. That means that you need to create a new workgroup file, create a new Admins user/owner, and run the Security Wizard on the database. However, with a library, you're only interested in securing your code and don't want to force your users to have to log on to it in order to use it.

So, after you take the normal steps to secure the library, you won't be creating any new users or groups. You do need to grant Open/Run permissions to the Users group on the database itself and any forms it may have. In this situation, the fact that the Users group includes every Access user is actually an advantage.

Next, make sure that there are no Read Design permissions set for the Admin user or the Users group on any of the library's forms or modules. Distribute your add-in, but don't distribute your workgroup file. Your users will be working with their default workgroup file (System.mdw), and it won't have permission to view your code.

If you are debugging code that calls a secured library database and you do not have permission to view the code, you must use the Step Over option (Shift + F8) to run the code without stepping through it.

Managing Security at Remote Sites

If your application will be distributed to remote sites where you are not available to perform administrative tasks (such as adding new users and groups), you need to set up an on-site administrator who can perform these chores. Normally you would simply create an account and add it to the Admins group. Then you would hope that your new Admins user can be trusted.

If there isn't anyone at the remote site who is knowledgeable about Access, you stand a good chance of compromising security on the entire application. Fortunately there is a workaround for this problem. All you need to do is create two separate workgroup files, the first for you to create and secure the application with, and a second to distribute with the application. In the workgroup file that you will be distributing, create an administrator account with no power to alter the permissions on your database. Here are the steps:

1. Secure your database normally, going through all of the steps in Exercises 10.4 and 10.5.

2. Using your secured development workgroup file, create custom groups, and assign permissions to all database objects to those groups. Make sure to write down the exact strings used when creating the groups.

3. Create a new workgroup file, using different strings for the Workgroup ID. This will be your distribution workgroup file.

4. Create a new user account and add it to the Admins group of the distribution workgroup. Don't use the same name and PID as the owner/administrator account in the development workgroup file.

5. In the distribution workgroup file, create groups with the exact same name and PID settings as the groups in the workgroup file with which you secured the database.

6. Distribute this workgroup file with the application. Users created in the distribution workgroup file will inherit their permissions from the groups you have created, which are identical to the groups in the development workgroup.

While the new Admins user account will be able to create new users, clear passwords, and add/remove users from groups, it won't be able to alter permissions in the database. Only the Admins user account in the workgroup file you used to secure the database will be able to do that—so make sure you hang on to it against the day when the database needs to be revised.

Writing Code to Manage Security

<table>
<tr><td>*Microsoft* ✓ *Exam* *Objective*</td><td>**Write code to implement security options.**</td></tr>
</table>

Microsoft ✓ *Exam* *Objective*

Analyze code to ensure that it sets security options.

If you are using the run-time version of Access to distribute your application, the built-in security menus will not be available. You will need to build your own forms to manage basic security tasks. Even if you are not planning on using the run-time version of Access, you may wish to use your own forms instead of the built-in menus. By using your own forms you can perform additional validation or other tasks not available on the menus.

Permission to Run Code

Many procedures that involve working with security (such as creating users and groups, manipulating passwords, and setting permissions) require the user who is running the code to be a member of the Admins group.

To handle this without adding a new permanent member to the Admins group, you can, in your code, log the user on to a second workspace as a member of the Admins group. After logging in as a member of the Admins group, the code the user is running can perform operations that the user would otherwise not have permissions to perform. You should recognize that this technique will compromise security for your entire application, since it embeds a valid Admins account ID and password in your code:

```
Dim wsNew as Workspace
Set wsNew = DBEngine.CreateWorkspace("NewWS", "NewAdmins",_
➡"ValidPassword")
```

Even securing your module code and removing all Read Design permissions is no guarantee, since security holes involving module and form code exist in all versions of Access.

Creating and Deleting Users in Code

You may find that you need to use code to create users or groups, as shown in Exercise 10.8. In fact, using code to create users is actually more efficient than going through the Access user interface, since you can assign a password at the same time. If you create a new user in the UI, adding a password is a separate step, which requires logging on as the new user.

EXERCISE 10.8

Adding a User to the Users Group

In this exercise, you will write a procedure to create a user and add them to the Users group. You will then delete the user.

1. Create a new module in your secured database. Create a subprocedure named CreateNewUser, with three arguments: strUser As String, strPID As String, and strPwd As String.

2. Declare 3 local variables: ws As Workspace, grp as Group, and usr As User.

3. Use the CreateUser method of the workspace object to create the new user, passing it the strUser, strPID, and strPwd arguments.

4. Then add the user to the Users group. Omitting this step will cause your new account to be crippled—they won't be able to open Access. The completed code should look like this:

```
Public Sub CreateNewUser(strUser As String, _
    strPID As String, strPwd As String)

    Dim ws As Workspace
    Dim usr As User
    Dim grp As GROUP

    Set ws = DBEngine(0)
    Set usr = ws.CreateUser(strUser, strPID, strPwd)
    ws.Users.Append usr
    ws.Users.Refresh
```

```
                    'Add user to Users group
                    Set grp = ws.Groups("Users")
                    Set usr = grp.CreateUser(strUser)
                    grp.Users.Append usr
                    grp.Users.Refresh


             End Sub
```

5. Compile and run the code. You can call it from the Debug Window using the following syntax:

```
CreateNewUser "Rocky", "Q3$x;^)df", "NewPwd"
```

The second parameter to this routine (the Q3$x;^)df) is the Personal Identifier for this user and can be any arbitrary string of characters you choose.

To delete a user, use the Delete method of the workspace's Users collection.

6. Create a new procedure named DeleteAUser with one argument, `strUserName As String`.

7. Declare a local workspace variable.

8. Set the workspace variable to the default workspace and use the Delete method on `strUser` as a member of the workspace's Users collection. The completed code should look like the following:

```
Public Sub DeleteAUser(strUser As String)
    Dim ws As Workspace

    Set ws = DBEngine(0)
    ws.Users.Delete strUser
End Sub
```

9. Compile and run the code. You can call it from the Debug Window using the following syntax:

```
DeleteAUser "Rocky"
```

Working with Passwords in Code

One of the things users seem to be particularly good at is forgetting their passwords. Any member of the Admins group can reset or clear a user's password, as shown in Exercise 10.9, without having to know the old one. However, if you are trying to reset your own password, you'll have to supply the old password.

EXERCISE 10.9

Creating a Utility to Reset or Clear a Password

1. Create a new procedure named ResetUserPassword with three arguments: strUser As String, strOldPassword as String, and strNewPassword as String.

2. Declare a local Workspace variable and a local User variable. Set the Workspace variable to the default workspace and the User variable to strUser.

3. Use the NewPassword method on the User object. The completed code should look like:

```
Public Sub ResetUserPassword(strUser As String, _
   strOldPassword As String, strNewPassword As String)


   Dim ws As Workspace
   Dim usr As User


   Set ws = DBEngine(0)
   Set usr = ws.Users(strUser)
   usr.NewPassword strOldPassword, strNewPassword
End Sub
```

4. Compile and save the procedure. You can call it from the Debug Window with the syntax that follows. Pass an empty string ("") for the strOldPassword argument if you are changing another user's password.

```
ResetUserPassword "Natasha", "", "NewPwd"
```

To reset or clear a database password, use the NewPassword method on a Database object. You must supply the old password—you can't use an empty string if you've forgotten the old password.

Disabling the Shift Key at Startup

In earlier versions of Access there was no way to prevent users from holding down the Shift key when opening your application, thus preventing your AutoExec macro from running (or your Startup Options in Access 95 and 97). One solution to this is to distribute your application using the run-time version which always ignores the Shift key at startup.

Access 95 introduced the AllowByPass property in order to allow you to control how the full version of Access deals with the Shift key at startup. (See Exercise 10.10.) You can't work with the AllowByPass from the Access user interface. Initially, the property isn't even present for a database and code must be used to add it. Once the property is added to a database and set to False, Access will ignore the Shift key when the database is opened.

EXERCISE 10.10

Setting and Removing the AllowByPassKey Property

1. Create a new procedure named SetAllowByPassKeyProperty.

2. Declare two local variables, db As Database and prp As Property.

3. Set the Database variable to the current database and set the Property variable to create the AllowByPassKey property. Then append the property to the database's Properties collection. The completed code should look like this:

```
Public Sub SetAllowByPassKeyProperty()
    Dim db As DATABASE
    Dim prp As Property

    Set db = CurrentDb
  Set prp = db.CreateProperty("AllowByPassKey", _
    dbBoolean, False)
    db.Properties.Append prp
End Sub
```

4. Compile and save the code. Run the procedure from the Debug Window to set the property.

5. To remove the AllowByPassKey property, create another procedure named RemoveAllowByPassKeyProperty.

6. Declare a local Database variable and set it to the current database.

7. Use the Delete method to remove the property from the database Properties collection. The completed code should look like this:

```
Public Sub RemoveAllowByPassKeyProperty()
    Dim db As DATABASE

    Set db = CurrentDb
    db.Properties.Delete "AllowByPassKey"
    db.Properties.Refresh
End Sub
```

8. Compile and save the code. Run the procedure from the Debug Window to remove the property.

Adding and Removing Permissions in Code

The Permissions and AllPermissions properties of the Containers and Document objects contain bit masks that hold the current users' permissions for the object. You can use logical And, Or, and Not operators with the built-in security constants in order to manipulate the Permissions and AllPermissions properties. By manipulating these two properties you can set permissions for users, or groups for various database objects. Table 10.2 lists the available constants.

T A B L E 10.2	Permission	Constant
The Access Security Constants	**All Container/Document Objects**	
	No permissions	dbSecNoAccess
	Full permissions	dbSecFullAccess

	Permission	Constant
T A B L E 10.2 *(cont.)* The Access Security Constants	**All Container/Document Objects**	
	Can delete	dbSecDelete
	Can read security-related information	dbSecReadSec
	Can edit permissions	dbSecWriteSec
	Can change the Owner property	dbSecWriteOwner
	Table Container/Document Objects	
	Can create new tables and queries	dbSecCreate
	Can read table definitions	dbSecReadDef
	Can modify table definitions	dbSecWriteDef
	Can read records	dbSecRetrieveData
	Can add records	dbSecInsertData
	Can edit records	dbSecReplaceData
	Can delete records	dbSecDeleteData
	Database Container	
	Create new databases (valid only on Database Container in the workgroup file)	dbSecDBCreate
	Can replicate or set password on a database	dbSecDBAdmin
	Can open the database	dbSecDBOpen
	Can open the database exclusively	dbSecDBExclusive

T A B L E 10.2 *(cont.)*	Permission	Constant
The Access Security Constants	**Form/Report/Macro/Module Objects**	
	Can open a form or report	`acSecFrmRptExecute`
	Can read the design of a form or report	`acSecFrmRptReadDef`
	Can edit the form or report definition	`acSecFrmRptWriteDef`
	Can execute a macro	`acSecMacExecute`
	Can read the macro definition	`acSecMacReadDef`
	Can edit a macro	`acSecMacWriteDef`
	Can read the module definition	`acSecModReadDef`
	Can edit a module	`acSecModWriteDef`

Permissions can be set on either the Container object or the Document object. Permissions set on Container objects form the default permissions for new objects created in that container. Permissions set on a Document object control what actions can be performed on the object by which users.

To set a single permission, you can just assign it directly for that person or group. First you must set the UserName property to the user ID of the user whose permissions you want to check or set:

```
Set con = db.Containers("Tables")
Set doc = con.Documents("Payroll")
doc.UserName = "Rocky"
doc.Permissions = dbSecRetrieveData
```

If you want to grant full permissions, you can use the dbSecFullAccess constant:

```
doc.Permissions = dbSecFullAccess
```

If you want to remove all permissions, you can use the dbSecNoAccess constant:

```
doc.Permissions = dbSecNoAccess
```

To set a specific permission without altering any other permissions that the user might already possess, use the Or operator with the Permissions property to pick up the existing value of the property:

```
doc.Permissions = doc.Permissions Or dbSecInsertData
```

To remove a specific permission without altering any other permissions, use the And Not operators with the Permissions property:

```
doc.Permissions = doc.Permissions And Not dbSecInsertData
```

(For more on setting and removing permissions, see Exercise 10.11.)

If you want to see if a user has any permissions on an object, you can check the Permissions property. If the user has permissions, the property will have a non-zero value:

```
lngPermissions = doc.Permissions
```

But this doesn't tell you which permissions the user actually possesses. If you want to check to see if a user has a particular permission on a particular object, use the logical And operator to check against that permission:

```
fCanRead = ((doc.Permissions And dbSecRetrieveData) _
  = dbSecRetrieveData)
```

In this code, the variable fCanRead will be True if the permission to read data exists, and False if it does not.

The Permissions property provides information on the permissions for a single user, and the AllPermissions property provides information on the users' implicit permissions (permissions inherited from the groups the user belongs to). In this code, fCanRead will be set to True if the user has permission to read the object because of the group she belongs to:

```
fCanRead = ((doc.AllPermissions And dbSecRetrieveData) _
  = dbSecRetrieveData)
```

NOTE Unlike the Permissions property, the AllPermissions property is read-only; it can only be used to retrieve permissions, not to set them.

In Exercise 10.11 you will set, retrieve, and remove permissions in code.

EXERCISE 10.11

Setting, Retrieving, and Removing Permissions in Code

1. Create a new procedure and name it SetReadDataOnTable with two arguments, strTable As String and strUser as String.

2. Declare local Database, Container, and Document variables. Set them to the current database, the Tables Container, and strTable respectively.

3. Use the dbSecRetrieveData intrinsic constant along with the Or operator to set Read Data permissions on the table. The completed code should look like this:

```
Public Sub SetReadDataOnTable(strTable As String, _
   strUser As String)

   Dim db As DATABASE
   Dim con As Container
   Dim doc As Document

   Set db = CurrentDb
   Set con = db.Containers("Tables")
   Set doc = con.Documents(strTable)
   doc.UserName = strUser
   doc.Permissions = doc.Permissions Or _
      dbSecRetrieveData

End Sub
```

4. Compile and save the procedure. Test it from the Debug Window:

```
SetReadDataOnTable "Payroll", "Natasha"
```

5. To remove Read Data permissions, create a new procedure named RemoveReadDataOnTable with two arguments: strTable As String and strUser as String.

6. Declare three local variables: db As Database, con As Container, and doc as Document, and set them to the current database, the Tables container, and strTable, respectively.

7. Use the dbSecRetrieveData intrinsic constant along with the And Not operators to remove Read Data permissions on the table. The completed code should look like this:

```
Public Sub RemoveReadDataOnTable(strTable As String, _
   strUser As String)

      Dim db As DATABASE
      Dim con As Container
      Dim doc As Document

      Set db = CurrentDb
      Set con = db.Containers("Tables")
      Set doc = con.Documents(strTable)
      doc.UserName = strUser
      doc.Permissions = doc.Permissions And Not _
         dbSecRetrieveData

   End Sub
```

8. Compile and save the procedure. Run it from the Debug Window using the following syntax:

```
RemoveReadDataOnTable "Payroll", "Natasha"
```

9. To check to see if a user has Read Data permissions on a table, create a new procedure called CheckForReadData with two arguments, strTable As String and strUser as String.

10. Declare three local variables, db As Database, con As Container, and doc as Document and set them to the current database, the Tables container, and strTable, respectively. Declare a fourth variable: fFound as Boolean.

11. Use the dbSecRetrieveData intrinsic constant and the And operator against the Permissions property of the table to see if the permission exists. The completed code should look like this:

```
Public Sub CheckForReadData(strTable As String, _
```

```
    strUser As String)

        Dim db As DATABASE
        Dim con As Container
        Dim doc As Document
        Dim fFound As Boolean

        Set db = CurrentDb
        Set con = db.Containers("Tables")
        Set doc = con.Documents(strTable)
        doc.UserName = strUser
        fFound = ((doc.Permissions And dbSecRetrieveData) _
          = dbSecRetrieveData)

        Debug.Print fFound

    End Sub
```

12. Compile and save the procedure. Run it from the Debug Window using the following syntax:

```
CheckForReadData "Payroll", "Boris"
```

Managing Secured, Linked Tables

Most Access applications consist of at least two databases: one MDB containing all the tables and another, the application database, containing all the forms, modules, reports, and other components. The procedure for securing all the databases that make up your application is straightforward: secure each database with tables separately and then link the tables to the application MDB.

You may also elect to remove all permissions to the tables and use queries with the Run Permissions property set to Owners so that access to the data is strictly controlled.

Linked tables in Access 95 are the same as attached tables in Access 2.0. The terminology has changed, but the way they work has not. The link information for each table is stored as hard-coded strings stored in the table's Connect and SourceTableName properties. Unlike OLE or DDE links in other Office applications, these links do not update automatically when you move the source database to another location.

With this method your users will not have sufficient permissions to relink the tables to the application database. If you install your application yourself and the table database is never moved to a new location, you shouldn't have any problems because your users will never need to relink tables.

But if your users need to link your tables as part of the setup procedure, or if the table database is ever moved to a new location, this process won't work. The reason is simple: your users will not have sufficient permissions to relink the tables to the application database either manually or by using the Tools ➤ Add-ins ➤ Linked Table Manager. Unlike OLE or DDE links, Access table links are not dynamic, and are not adjusted as part of the procedure of moving a database. If the table database is moved, the application will fail until your users relink the tables—which they don't have the permissions to do.

There are actually two sets of permissions that you need to consider with linked tables: the permissions set in the table database and the permissions set in the application database. If you remove all permissions in the source table database, you can safely grant full permissions on the links in the destination database. Users won't be able to view the data in the tables if they try to open the table database directly but will be able to work with the links in the application database.

Modify Design is the absolute minimum in terms of the permissions you need to grant the users in the application database in order for them to be able to relink tables. Your users won't actually be able to modify the design of the tables, but this permission allows the linking process to work. Although Modify Design is the minimum that you must grant, in the long run it's easier just to grant full permissions on the links.

Permissions set on tables in the database in which they reside cannot be overridden. These permissions will be strictly enforced by Jet, regardless of whether you are using Access, Visual Basic, or Automation from some other application in order to access the data.

Table 10.3 describes the available methods for relinking tables and the permissions needed on the source table database (remember, it's safe to grant full permissions on the links in the destination database as long as the source table permissions are correct). No matter which of the methods in Table 10.3 you use, you need to grant Open/Run on the source table database itself—you can't get to the candy counter if the store is closed.

T A B L E 10.3 Methods for Relinking Tables	Method	Permissions Required in Source Table Database
	RefreshLink	Read Data permissions on the tables
	TransferDatabase	Read Design permissions on the tables
	The Connect property	None!

Obviously, the third choice, using the Connect property, is the preferred option in a secured application where you wish to remove all permissions to the underlying tables. When you use the Connect property in code, an error is returned, but if you use a Resume Next error handler in your procedure, as shown in Exercise 10.12, you can safely ignore the error and the table will be relinked.

EXERCISE 10.12

Relinking a Table with the Connect Property

1. Create a new procedure (name it RelinkUsingConnect) with two arguments: strTable As String and strDatabase As String. These two variables represent the name of the table being relinked and the fully-qualified path and file name of the source table database. The routine assumes that the table name is the same in both the source and destination databases.

2. Declare two local variables: db As Database and tdf As TableDef. Set the database variable to the current database.

3. Implement inline error handling with On Error Resume Next and delete the table (strTable) from the current database.

EXERCISE 10.12 (CONTINUED)

4. Create a new TableDef object of the same name and set its Connect property to strDatabase. Append to the TableDefs collection. The completed code should look like the following:

```
Public Sub RelinkUsingConnect(strTable As String, _
    strDatabase As String)

    Dim db As Database
    Dim tdf As TableDef

    Set db = CurrentDb

    On Error Resume Next
    db.TableDefs.Delete strTable

    Set tdf = db.CreateTableDef(strTable)
    tdf.SourceTableName = strTable
    tdf.Connect = ";DATABASE=" & strDatabase
    db.TableDefs.Append tdf
    db.TableDefs.Refresh
End Sub
```

5. Compile and save the procedure. Test it by logging on to your secured application as a user who does not have any permissions on tables in the source database. Call the routines from the Debug Window using the following syntax:

```
RelinkUsingConnect "Payroll", "C:\Office\Access\Secured.mdb"
```

Summary

Access security is complex and demanding to implement. If you leave out a step while implementing it, you may leave your application unsecured without meaning to.

There are two types of security in Access: share-level security (the Database Password) and user-level security. The Database Password is easiest to use, since you set a single password for everyone on an individual database, but it isn't very secure or very safe. User-level security is much more complex, but is the best choice for when you need to assign multiple levels of permissions on various database objects or when you need more robust security than that offered by the Database Password feature.

Access security works by storing user and group information in the workgroup file and the actual permissions for each user and object in the database file. When a user logs on to Access, their user ID and password are validated by the workgroup file. When they open a database and use the objects in it, their permissions are verified against those assigned to them in the database. Permissions can be assigned either directly to users or to groups. When permissions are assigned to groups, the user inherits those permissions through membership in the group.

You can manage security either through the Access menu commands or by using code. Code gives you more flexibility and allows you to do things that are not on the Security menus.

Review Questions

1. Why should you set permissions in a secured database for Groups rather than for Users?

    A. To make it easier to administer.

    B. There is no such thing.

    C. So that the database will compile.

    D. You can't assign permissions directly to Users anyway.

2. If your database is replicated, you can:

    A. Use the database password feature to implement share-level security.

    B. Use the database password feature to implement user-level security.

    C. Implement security using share-level security.

    D. Implement security using user-level security.

3. Which query property and setting allows you to create row-level or column-level security on your tables?

   A. The Caption set to User's.

   B. The Description set to Owner's.

   C. Run Permissions set to Owner's.

   D. Access does not support row-level or column-level security.

4. How do you distribute a secured library database without requiring your users to log on?

   A. Secure the library database normally, assigning permissions to custom groups. Remove the password from the Admin user and distribute the workgroup file used to secure the database.

   B. Secure the library database normally. Remove the Admin account from the Admins group and revoke all permissions from the Users group to view the code in the library database. Do not distribute the workgroup file with the database.

   C. Simply remove the Admin account from the Admins group and clear the password for the Admin account.

   D. Secure the library database normally. Delete the Admins group so it will not have administer permissions on the library database. Do not distribute the workgroup file with the database.

5. Which database property can you set to prevent users from being able to hold down the Shift key and bypass your Startup options or AutoExec macro when opening a database?

   A. AutoShiftOff

   B. AutoShiftOn

   C. AllowBypassKey

   D. BypassStartup

6. Which two properties of a Document or Container object can you check in code to see if a user has permissions set for a given object? Which logical operator do you use?

   A. The Permissions property and the AllPermissions property along with the logical AND operator.

   B. The Permissions property and the AllPermissions property along with the logical OR operator.

   C. The Permissions property and the AllPermissions property along with the logical AND NOT operator.

   D. The DocPermissions and ConPermissions properties along with the logical OR operator.

7. Which logical operator(s) do you use to set specific permissions on an object without affecting the user's existing permissions?

   A. XOR

   B. AND

   C. OR

   D. IIF

8. Which logical operator(s) do you use to remove permissions on an object without affecting the user's existing permissions?

   A. XOR

   B. AND NOT

   C. OR NOT

   D. IF NOT

9. Which is the best method to use when relinking tables and what permissions do you need to set for users in the source table database in order for them to use this method?

   A. The .Connect property. No permissions are needed on the underlying tables.

   B. The TransferDatabase action. No permissions are needed on the underlying tables.

   C. The .RefreshLink method. No permissions are needed on the underlying tables.

   D. The .AttachTable method. No permissions are needed on the underlying tables.

10. When you create a new user in code using the CreateUser method, what additional step do you need to take?

   A. None. The CreateUser method alone is sufficient.

   B. Add the new user to the Admins group.

   C. Add the new user to the Users group.

   D. Create a new custom group for the new user.

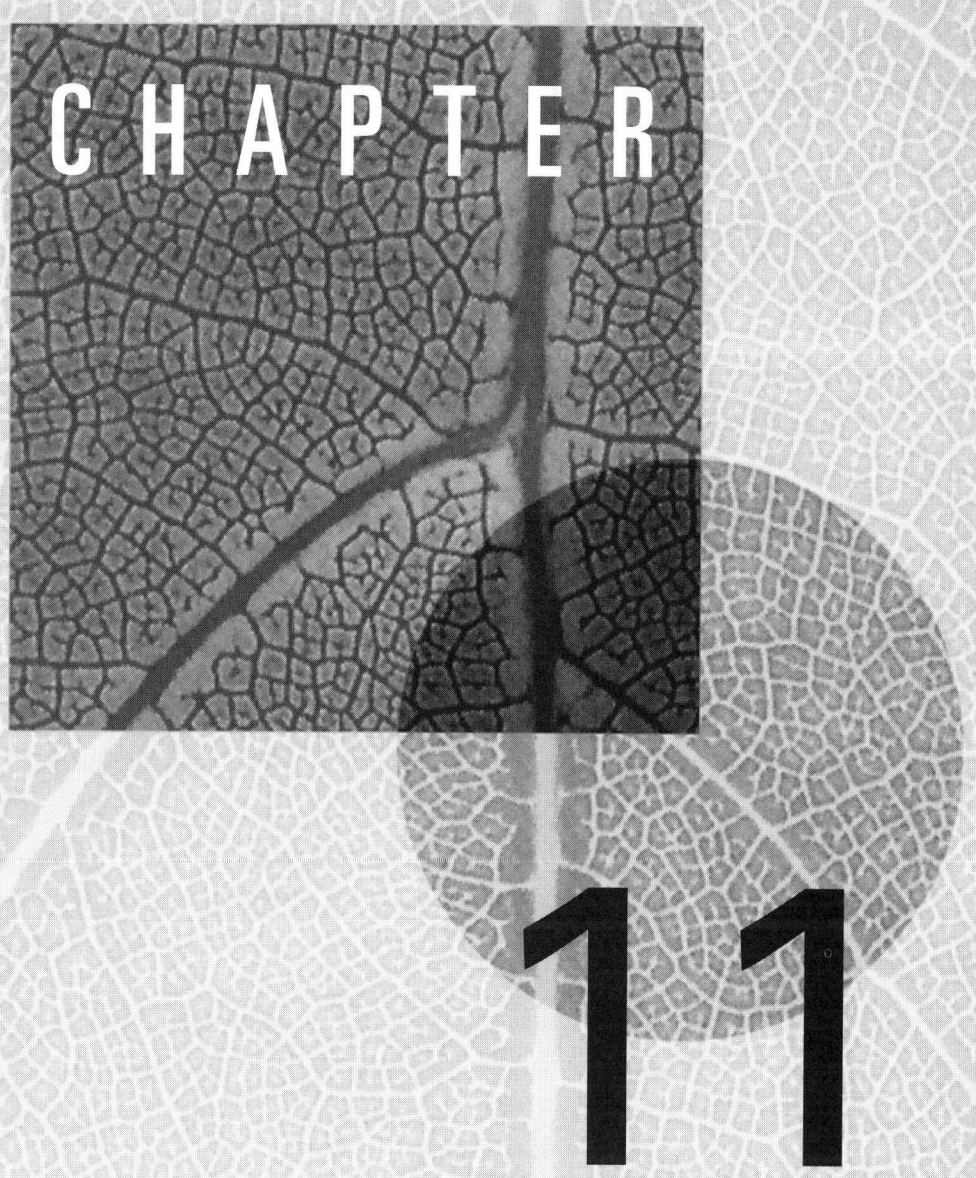

CHAPTER

11

Implementing Replication

Microsoft Exam Objectives Covered in This Chapter:

- Use Visual Basic for Applications, Microsoft Access, Briefcase, or Replication Manager to make a database replicable.

- Use Replication Manager to view a synchronization schedule.

- Explain the purpose of the Replication ID.

- Explain how Replication Manager resolves synchronization conflicts.

- Identify the advantages of using replication for synchronization.

- Identify the changes that the Microsoft Jet database engine makes when it converts a nonreplicable database into a replicable database.

Access replication was introduced in Access 95. It is a powerful new feature that allows you to keep multiple copies of the same database updated without having to copy the entire database file. It is flexible enough so that you can configure it to communicate over a LAN, a WAN, or a dial-up connection. You can work with Access replication using the Windows Briefcase, Access built-in menus, Visual Basic for Applications code (VBA), and the Replication Manager.

In this chapter you will learn:

- How to distribute multiple copies of your database to different locations and keep each copy current.

- How to replicate a database.

- The different parts of replication.

- How to synchronize changes.

- How to resolve replication conflicts.

What Is Replication?

Access replication lets you update data by keeping two or more copies of a single database synchronized so that every copy contains the same information. Only the information that has been changed is exchanged between the copies—*not* the entire database. Each copy of the original database (known as the *Design Master*) is called a *replica*, and a group of replicas is called a *replica set*. Replicas share the same objects, such as tables, queries, forms, reports, macros, or modules. You don't need to share all the objects—any of the replicas can also have local objects that are not replicated. You can make design changes to replicated objects only in the Design Master. Design changes as well as data changes can be propagated to the replicas in the replica set.

The process of communicating the changed information between replicas is called *synchronization*. During synchronization, only the changes from the replicable objects participate. For example, if you change a single record in a table, only that record gets synchronized with the other replicas; the entire table does not.

WARNING Each replica set can have only one Design Master. However, if the Design Master in a replica set gets corrupted or deleted, any remaining replica can then be designated as the new Design Master. You should never attempt to restore a Design Master from a backup—doing so could result in data loss.

You can locate replicas on a network, multiple networks, different computers, or any combination of computers or networks. This configuration of replicas is known as the *replication topology*. In addition, you can configure replication to synchronize data one way only (import or export), or bi-directionally (both import and export at the same time).

The most common replication topology is the star: a single replica sits at the center, or hub, and controls synchronizations to the replicas located at the spokes, or points.

Synchronizing only the changes in replicated databases is far more efficient than copying entire objects. If you use a telephone connection, this means less time and lower phone charges. On a network or WAN, synchronizing changes can mean reduced network traffic. Any conflicts (such as the same record being changed in more than one location) are logged into tables, and no data is lost. Access includes a Conflict Resolution Wizard to assist you in handling conflicts.

You can use the Access menus, Visual Basic for Applications code, the Windows Briefcase, or the Replication Manager (which ships with the Office Developers Toolkit) to work with replication.

If you do not install Access with Briefcase Replication installed, the Briefcase will work only at the file level, performing simple date/time comparisons to keep the most recent version of a file. It will not create a replicated Access database; it will only overwrite an earlier version. This can cause problems in Access, since merely opening the database changes the file date/time stamp. In other words, the database with the most recent date/time stamp might not be the one that contains the most up-to-date data.

In Exercise 11.1 you will create a replica of Northwind.mdb using the Windows Briefcase. To complete this exercise, you must have first installed Access with the Briefcase Replication option.

EXERCISE 11.1

Creating a Replica Using the Windows Briefcase

1. Open the Windows Explorer and locate the folder where the Northwind.mdb database is installed. It is normally located in the \Access\Samples folder.

2. Select Northwind.mdb by clicking on it with the left mouse button, and drag and drop it onto the Briefcase icon on your Desktop.

3. This will start the Briefcase Replication Wizard, which will step you through making a replica. Follow all of the steps and make sure to create a backup copy of Northwind.mdb when prompted.

4. When the Wizard is finished, explore the options available to you on the Briefcase menu and toolbar.

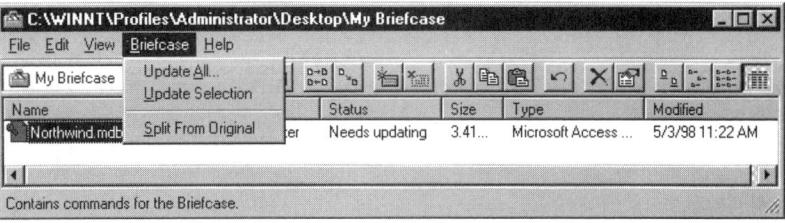

 Because of its limited functionality, Briefcase replication is not recommended for distributed database solutions. You can't program it, automate it, or use it with existing applications. It works best for a single user.

Replication Scenarios

Microsoft ✓ ***Exam*** ***Objective***	**Identify the advantages of using replication for synchronization.**

Replication is a powerful new feature in Access 95 that is useful in many different situations. Replication allows you to easily:

- Share data with remote offices via WAN or dialup.

- Share data with users who are not always connected to the network, such as users working on the road who need either to post data or to update existing data from the main office.

- Distribute processing by off-loading expensive queries. A query running on a local replica will save processing on an overloaded server.

- Improve server performance by load balancing with replicas on multiple servers. The replicas can synchronize only changed data with each other.

- Partition applications between data entry and decision-support.

- Make warm, or incremental, backups of your database throughout the day without having to require that your users log off. Users can continue to use a replica while it is being synchronized. This gives you more flexibility than a normal backup. A replica used as a backup can be quickly brought online if the original is lost or destroyed.

As wonderful as replication is, it is not suitable for all applications. It works best in situations where you don't need the most up-to-date data at all times. There are some situations where replication is not suitable:

- Applications requiring transactions across multiple databases, such as banking, credit and debit transactions, and some kinds of order entry databases.

- Applications where data consistency is critical, such as ticket sales, where you need to know instantly whether a seat is available or not.

- Real-time applications, such as trading, tracking, or currency exchange.

- Applications with high-volume updates at multiple sites.

- Applications where users are modifying the same records in different replicas, and so are generating a lot of conflicts during synchronization.

Is Replication Right for Your Application?

Successfully implementing replication takes a lot of careful planning—it's not something you just slap on at the end of the development cycle and hope will work out okay—it probably won't. In addition to the different types of database applications that are unsuitable for replication, there are other considerations you need to take into account:

- Are the same records being updated in multiple locations? If so, there may be a natural way to partition data so that conflicts do not occur. For example, an orders table may be implicitly partitioned into territories so that each salesperson is updating records in only one territory and there is no overlap with other salespeople's records. If there is no natural partition, you may need to physically break up tables in order to avoid conflicts.

- Is your application complete? If you were thinking of using replication as a means of distributing application updates, think again. It's supposed to work, but most problems reported with replication involve attempts to replicate design changes.

- Will there be a high volume of data participating in synchronizations? A classic client/server configuration can be more efficient than replication in some cases.

- Is the physical connection between the replicas robust? If your replicas are synchronizing via a direct dial-up connection which is interrupted, one or both replicas can become corrupted.

- How many replicas do you anticipate participating in your replication topology? It can take multiple synchronization passes for the data to be consistent across an entire replica set.

- Can your users live with data that is likely to be inconsistent? No two replicas are guaranteed to have the same data at the same time, although they may eventually synchronize to a consistent state. If data concurrency is important, then replication is not a good solution.

- Will you have people competent to support replication? In addition to resolving conflicts, you also have to consider maintenance issues. Replicated databases need to be frequently compacted, can become corrupted more easily, and generally need more attention from technical support people.

Implementing Replication

You can create replicas from the Access menus or from code. When you convert an ordinary database to a replica, it becomes the Design Master. Design changes can only be made in the Design Master. If you use the Access menus, an additional replica will be created in addition to the Design Master. You can locate the replicas in the same folder or create a separate folder.

When replicating a database in Access, always choose to make a backup copy when prompted by the wizard. If you change your mind and want to return to your database in an unreplicated state, all you need to do is delete the replica and rename the backup copy (it will have the same name with a .BAK filename extension).

In Exercise 11.2 we're going to make a replica from the Northwind.mdb database using the Access menus. Before you start, create separate folders and place a copy of the Northwind.mdb database in one of them.

EXERCISE 11.2

Creating a Replica Using the Access Menus

1. Open Northwind, and choose Tools ➢ Replication ➢ Create Replica… from the menu. You will be prompted to close the database to continue running the wizard. Click on Yes.

2. The next dialog box asks if you want to make a backup of the database. Click on Yes.

3. You will then be prompted for the location of the new replica, as shown here. The Design Master will be named Northwind.mdb, and the default name suggested for this replica is "Replica of Northwind.mdb." You can either accept this name or type in another name. You can also elect to locate the replica in another folder at this time.

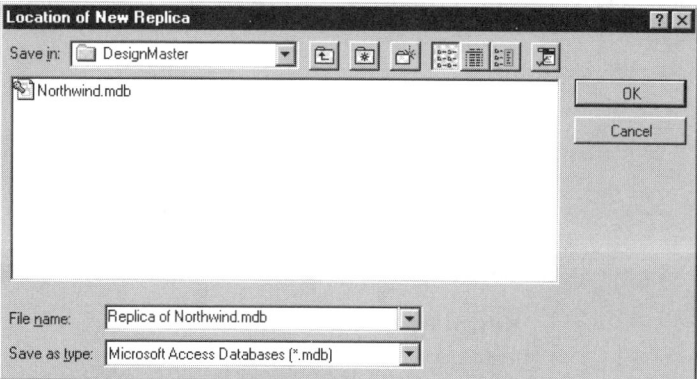

4. The wizard will then display the new Design Master and a message confirming the name and location of the replica you have created.

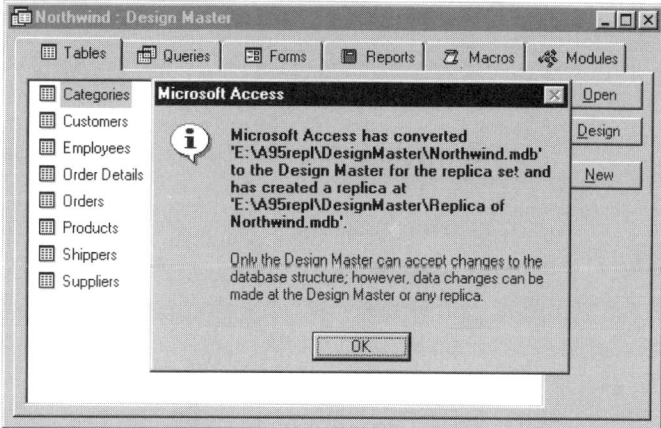

When you replicate a database, you are not required to make all of the objects replicable—you can elect to have local database objects that do not participate in replication. However, local tables can't have relationships with replicated tables if referential integrity is enforced. To experiment with making a table local, make a copy of the Categories table in the Northwind database and name it LocalTable.

See Chapter 1 for an explanation of how referential integrity works.

In Exercise 11.3, you're going to create a procedure in the Northwind database to keep the LocalTable table local by setting its KeepLocal property to the text value "T."

EXERCISE 11.3

Keeping Objects Local

1. Open a fresh copy of Northwind.mdb that has not been replicated.

2. Copy the Categories table and name it LocalTable.

3. Create a new procedure (either in an existing module or in a new module) and name it **KeepTableLocal**.

4. Create a Database variable, a Property variable, and a Document variable.

5. Set the Database variable equal to the current database. Set the document variable to the LocalTable document in the Tables container.

6. Create the KeepLocal property, set its value to "T", and append it to the Document's Properties collection. The completed code should look like this:

```
Sub KeepTableLocal()
    Dim db As Database
    Dim doc As Document
    Dim prp As Property
    Set db = CurrentDb
    Set doc =
db.Containers("Tables").Documents("LocalTable")
    Set prp = doc.CreateProperty("KeepLocal", dbText, "T")
    doc.Properties.Append prp
End Sub
```

Now when you convert this copy of the Northwind database to a Design Master, LocalTable will not be replicated.

In Exercise 11.4, you'll create a new Design Master from the same copy of the Northwind.mdb database used in Exercise 11.3. This involves setting the database's Replicable property to "T". In addition, you'll designate it as the new Design Master.

EXERCISE 11.4

Converting a Regular Database into a Design Master from Code

1. You can't convert the database where the code is running to a replica, so create a new, empty database, and create a new module in the database.

2. Name the procedure **MakeDesignMaster** with a parameter of strDB as String. You will need a workspace, database, and property variable.

3. Set a reference to the default workspace and use the OpenDatabase method to open the copy of the Northwind.mdb database exclusively.

4. Create the Replicable property and set it to the text value "T". Append it to the database's Properties collection.

5. Set the database's DesignMasterID property equal to the database's ReplicaID property. The completed code listing should look like this:

```
Sub MakeDesignMaster(strDB As String)
    Dim ws As Workspace
    Dim db As Database
    Dim prp As Property
    Set ws = DBEngine.Workspaces(0)
    Set db = ws.OpenDatabase(strDB, Exclusive:=True)
    Set prp = db.CreateProperty("Replicable", dbText, "T")
    db.Properties.Append prp
    db.DesignMasterID = db.ReplicaID
End Sub
```

6. To run the procedure, you will need to pass it the fully qualified path and filename of the database you wish to replicate, as follows:

```
Call MakeDesignMaster("E:\Replicas\Northwind.mdb")
```

Database Changes

Microsoft ✓ ***Exam Objective***	**Identify the changes that the Microsoft Jet database engine makes when it converts a nonreplicable database into a replicable database.**

Microsoft ✓ ***Exam Objective***	**Explain the purpose of the Replication ID.**

When you replicate a database, new tables, fields, and properties are added. To view the new tables and fields that are added, select Tools ➤ Options ➤ View and check the Hidden Objects and System Objects checkboxes. As you can see by comparing Figure 11.1 with Figure 11.2, many new systems tables have been added to the replicated version of the Northwind database. These are used by Jet to track synchronizations, errors, locking conflicts during synchronization, location of other replicas in the replica set, changes made to individual records, deleted records, and many other pieces of information needed to keep replication running smoothly.

F I G U R E   11.1

The Northwind database tables container before replication

F I G U R E   11.2

The Northwind data-
base tables container
after replication

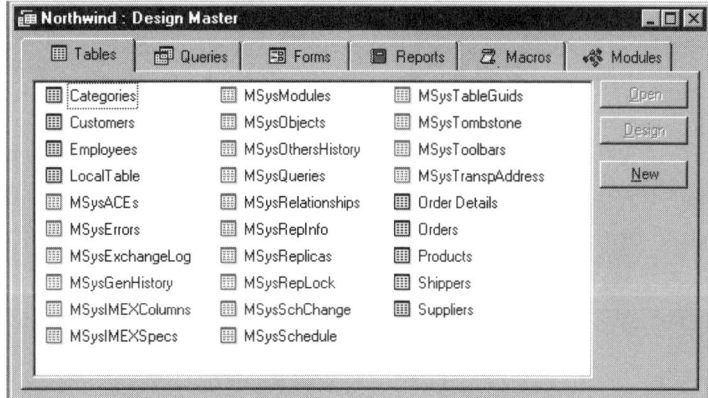

The Northwind data-
base tables container
after replication

You can't manipulate the replication systems tables, either in code or in the
Access user interface.

In addition, replication adds new fields to existing tables and can change
the New Values property of existing AutoNumber fields from Increment to
Random. This is to prevent conflicts caused by users adding new records in
multiple replicas and generating duplicate values.

In Exercise 11.5, you'll examine some of the new fields added to the
Northwind database replicated in Exercise 11.4.

EXERCISE 11.5

Examining Changes Made to the Replicated Northwind Database

1. Open the replicated version of Northwind.mdb. The title bar should
   say "Northwind: Design Master."

2. Display the systems tables by choosing Tools ➢ Options ➢ View from
   the menu, and check the Hidden Objects and System Objects checkboxes. All the new replication systems tables should be visible in the
   database container.

3. Open the Categories table in Datasheet view. You should see the additional fields that have been added to track replication.

4. Attempt to enter a new category by typing in the Category Name field.
   Note that the behavior of the CategoryID AutoNumber field has been
   changed from increment to random.

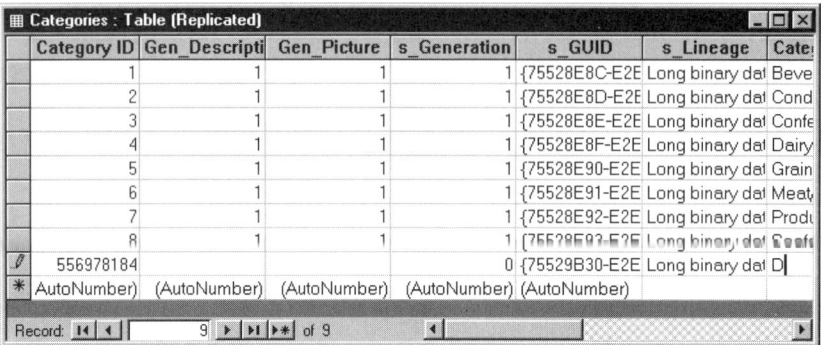

5. Cancel the change and open the Category Name field in Design view. Note that the CategoryID field's New Values property has been changed to Random, as shown.

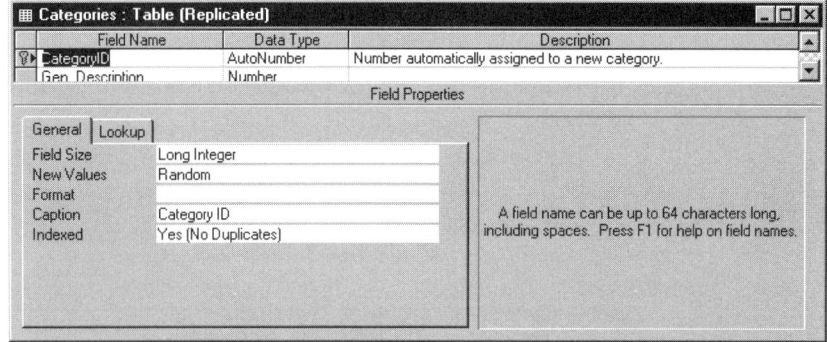

6. Close the Categories table and open LocalTable in Design view. Note that none of the replication fields have been added to this table, since it was flagged as a local object. The behavior of the CategoryID field is still set to increment.

The most important of the new fields is the *Unique Identifier*, or *GUID*. The GUID uniquely identifies each record in a replica set, whereas the Auto-Number field for a specific record is identical across all replicas. This unique value is stored in the s_GUID field and cannot be changed or deleted.

Table 11.1 lists some of the properties added to a replicated database.

	Property	Description
T A B L E 11.1 Replication Properties	ReplicaID	Uniquely identifies each replica in a replica set.
	Replication ID	The GUID added to each row of a replicated table that uniquely identifies that row.
	DesignMasterID	Setting the DesignMasterID to the ReplicaID will designate a replica as the new Design Master.

Replication and Security

You can secure a replicated database using user-level security. Share-level security (the Database Password feature) is not available. Permissions are stored in the database itself and can be altered only in the Design Master. They will be replicated during synchronization.

In addition, you can't replicate your workgroup file (or System.mdw). You need to have your replicas connect to a centrally located workgroup file or else you need to distribute copies to remote users. This poses a problem when you need to add or remove user accounts, since it is difficult to control multiple copies of the workgroup file to ensure that your replicas are all using the most current version.

For more information on how security works, see Chapter 10.

Conflicts and Errors

Microsoft
✓ Exam
Objective
Explain how Replication Manager resolves synchronization conflicts.

You can synchronize data between replicas from the Access menus by choosing Tools ➤ Replication ➤ Synchronize Now… or from code using the Synchronize method of the database object:

```
CurrentDb.Synchronize "E:\Repl\OtherReplica.mdb"
➥ dbRepImpExpChanges
```

When synchronizing in code, you can choose between the following intrinsic constants to control whether data is imported, exported, or both:

- dbRepImpExpChanges, which is a two-way bi-directional exchange (the default)

- dbRepExportChanges, which exports changes only

- dbRepImportChanges, which imports changes only

You can only specify an import-only or export-only synchronization from code. This option is not available from the Access menus or the Replication Manager.

Make sure to compact your database twice before synchronizing design changes. Failure to do so can result in database objects not propagating properly during synchronizations. You need to compact twice because a compact occurs in two phases: on the first pass Jet consolidates and recovers disk space, and on the second pass it goes through and marks the objects slated for deletion. The second compact will actually recover the space from the deleted objects left over from the first compact.

Never repair a database before compacting—this can cause your database to become corrupted. Repairing and then compacting was a recommended procedure in Access 2.0, but not in Access 95. Only repair an Access 95 database if you receive a message telling you to do so.

If the same record has been modified in more than one replica, a *conflict* will arise. Access then chooses one record to be the winner based on the following rules:

- The record with the most changes wins.

- In case of a tie (the record was changed an equal number of times in both replicas), the replica which has the lowest ReplicaID wins.

- If the same change is made in both replicas (for example, both replicas change the value of the Category Name field to "Fruit" in the same record), there is no conflict. Access is smart enough to detect that the records are identical and does not generate a conflict table.

The ReplicaID is assigned at the time the replica is created and cannot be modified.

Access does not consider whether changes were made to multiple fields when determining whether a conflict exists—the finest level of granularity is at the record level. If the Last Name field is modified in one replica, and the First Name field is modified on the same record in another replica, then a conflict is created even though different fields were involved.

The losing record is saved in a conflict table (named *tablename*_Conflict). You can edit the conflict table manually, use the Conflict Resolution Wizard, or write code to handle conflicts.

You can also trigger data errors by creating duplicate keys, violating validation rules, violating referential integrity, or attempting to write to locked records. Data errors are saved in the MSysErrors table. Design errors can occur when an object is created in the Design Master with the same name as a local object in a replica, causing synchronization to fail. Data and design errors can be complex and difficult to resolve.

In Exercise 11.6, you're going to deliberately create a conflict between two replicas, examine the conflict table, and resolve the conflict.

EXERCISE 11.6

Handling Conflicts Using the Conflict Resolution Wizard

1. Open the replica of Northwind.mdb that you created in Exercise 11.2 (the one created using the Access menu commands).

2. Open the Categories table and change the Category Name of the first record from "Beverages" to "Drinks." Save the record and close the database.

3. Now open the Replica of Northwind.mdb and open the Categories table. Change the Description field of the first record to read "Soft drinks, coffees, teas, and spirits." Save the record and close the table.

4. Choose Tools ➢ Replication ➢ Synchronize Now… from the menu. You will be prompted for confirmation of the name and location of the other replica. Click on OK.

5. You will then see a dialog box telling you that the synchronization was successfully completed and notifying you that all the changes won't be visible until the database is closed and reopened. Click on Yes to close and reopen the database.

6. You will then see a dialog box explaining that this member of the replica set has conflicts and asking if you want to resolve the conflicts now. Click on No.

7. Click on the Tables tab of the replica's Database Explorer window. Note that there is a new table named Categories_Conflict. Open the table in Datasheet view. This is the losing record—the winning record appears in the Categories table. Close the Categories_Conflict table.

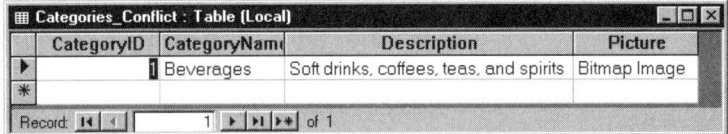

8. Choose Tools ➢ Replication ➢ Resolve Conflicts… from the menu. You will see the tables listed that have conflicts. Click on the Resolve Conflicts button to load the Conflict Resolution Wizard.

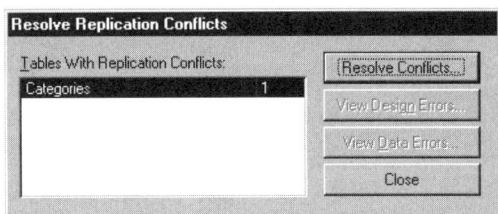

9. The existing record and the conflict, or losing record, are shown here side by side. You can edit the fields manually and select the option either to keep the existing record, or to overwrite with the conflict record. Click on the Overwrite with Conflict Record button. Click on Yes when asked to confirm.

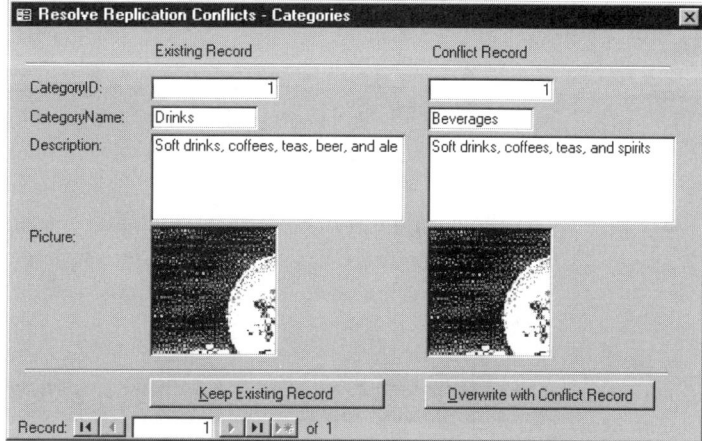

10. Close any remaining dialog boxes and note that the Categories_Conflict table was automatically deleted. Open the Categories table in Datasheet view and note that the record was overwritten with the data in the conflict table. Close the replica.

11. Open Northwind.mdb and open the Categories table in Datasheet view. Note that the data between the two replicas is now inconsistent. Close the table.

12. Choose Tools ➤ Replication ➤ Synchronize Now... from the menu and synchronize with the replica. This is the final step you need to take for all of the conflicts to be resolved and for the data to be consistent.

13. Open the Categories table in Datasheet view. It now matches the record in the replica. There was no conflict this time, and the winning record from the first synchronization has now been overwritten.

Replication Manager

Microsoft
Exam
Objective

Use Replication Manager to view a synchronization schedule.

The Replication Manager is a standalone application designed to manage replicas distributed across multiple computers in diverse locations. It is distributed as part of the Office Developers Toolkit in Access 95 and provides a graphical user interface, making it easy to create synchronization schedules and perform other replication maintenance tasks.

In Exercise 11.7, you'll configure the Replication Manager, if you have not yet installed it. If you have previously installed the Replication Manager, skip this exercise.

EXERCISE 11.7

Configuring the Replication Manager

1. From your Windows Start menu, choose Programs ➤ Microsoft ADT ➤ Microsoft Replication Manager, and click on the Configure... button. Click on Next after reading the contents of the introductory dialog box.

2. The next dialog box asks you which folders you would like managed. Click on the Add... button to designate any additional folders.

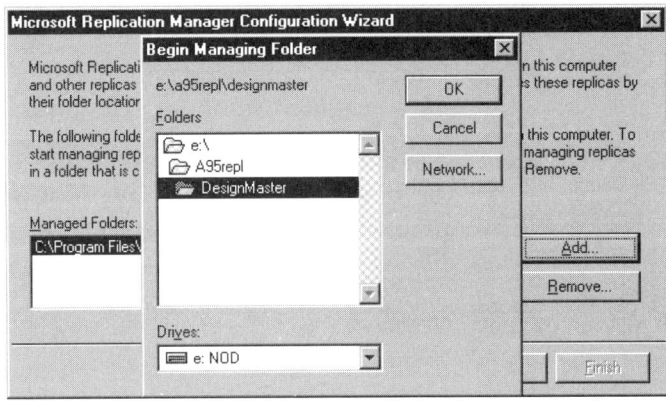

3. You will then be prompted to specify the location of the Transporter folder. The Transporter is the underlying mechanism, which does all the work (such as handling synchronizations) for the Replication Manager.

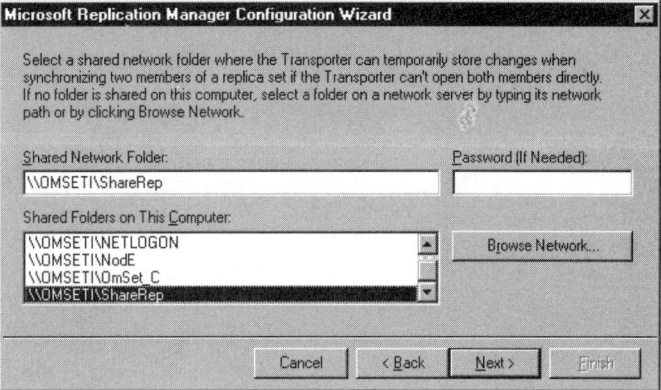

4. The final screen asks you to name the icon for the Transporter that is managing the replica set. The default is the machine name. You can also specify that the Transporter be loaded each time you start Windows. Click on Finish to complete the Replication Manager setup process.

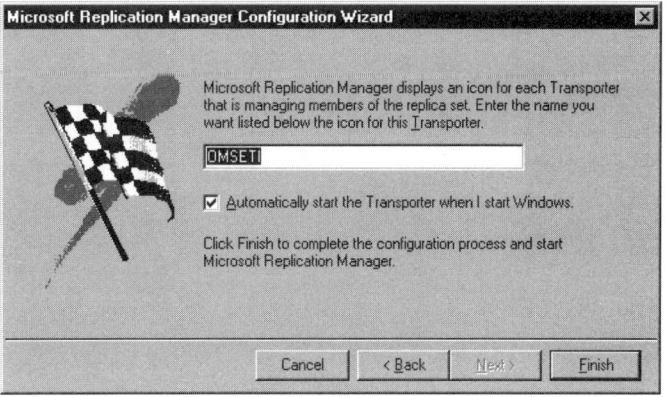

TIP If the Transporter is not running, scheduled synchronizations will not take place.

In Exercise 11.8, we'll explore the Replication Manager and set up a schedule to synchronize replicas.

EXERCISE 11.8

Scheduling Synchronizations with the Replication Manager

1. Open the Replication Manager and examine the menu structure. Note that under the File menu you can convert, create, and move replicas; manage folders; stop the Transporter; and exit. The View menu lets you view the Legend and various properties. The Tools menu has selections for synchronizing, scheduling, editing databases, managing the Design Master, starting and stopping the Transporter, and configuring the Replication Manager.

2. Right-click on various objects to view the context-sensitive menus available. Drag the mouse slowly across the toolbar buttons to display the ToolTip text identifying each one.

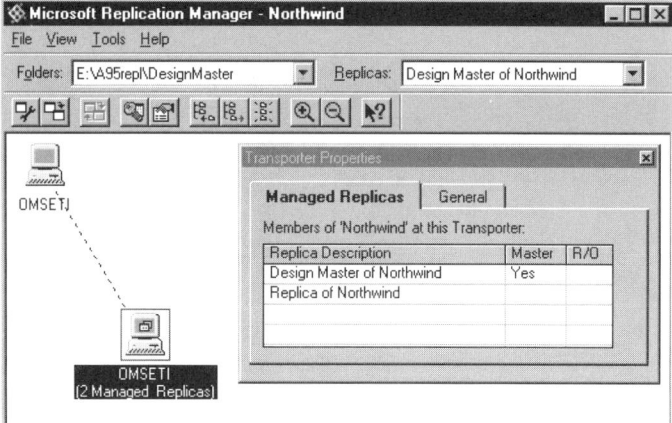

EXERCISE 11.8 (CONTINUED)

3. Choose Tools ➤ Edit Schedule... from the menu. This will open the scheduler. Select the times and days you would like to schedule synchronizations for your replica set.

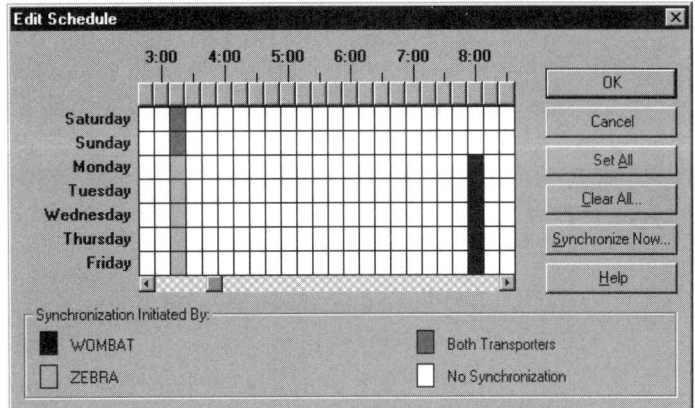

Summary

Replication is a powerful new feature in Access 95. You can use it to:

- Distribute multiple copies of your database to different locations and keep each copy current by synchronizing only the changed data.

- Create warm backups.

- Offload expensive queries to ease the load on a server.

A database can be replicated and managed several different ways:

- Through Briefcase Replication, which is good for single-user scenarios.

- Through the Access menu commands, which allow you to create replicas, synchronize, resolve conflicts, and recover a lost Design Master.

- Through VBA code, which you can use to create replicas, perform synchronizations (including one-way synchronizations), and set replication properties.

- Through the Replication Manager, which allows you access to a user interface for managing and scheduling replicas.

Replication is an advanced feature that needs to be planned for in the early stages of database development. You need to understand the tradeoffs involved with the various methods of handling replication.

Review Questions

1. Which of the following methods will enable a regular Access database for replication?

   A. Drag a copy of the database and drop it onto the Windows Briefcase icon.

   B. Drag a copy of the database and drop it onto a shared network folder.

   C. Write code to set the database's Replicable property to "Synchronize."

   D. Use the built-in Access menu commands.

2. When you create a replica in code, how do you make it the Design Master?

   A. Set its Replicable property to Design Master.

   B. You don't need to do anything. A Design Master is created automatically if none exists.

   C. Set its DesignMasterID equal to its ReplicaID.

   D. Set its DesignMasterID property to True.

3. How can you schedule synchronizations for users at different locations over a WAN?

A. Drag everyone's replica into the Windows Briefcase located on a central server.

B. Use the scheduling services available in the Replication Manager.

C. Write code to copy the replica to the different locations.

D. Use the built-in Access menus.

4. How is each record in a replicated table distinguished from the same record in other replicas?

A. Each record is identified by its ReplicaID, or GUID.

B. Each record is identified by its Replication ID, or GUID.

C. Each record is identified by its AutoNumber field set to Random instead of increment.

D. Each record is identified by its AutoNumber field set to a GUID.

5. How is each replica in a Replica Set distinguished from the other replicas?

A. By its unique Replication ID

B. By its Replicable property

C. By its name

D. By its unique ReplicaID

6. If there is a conflict during synchronization, how does Access determine the winning record?

A. The record with the most changes wins.

B. The most recently changed record wins.

C. The record with the fewest changes wins.

D. Neither record wins. Both are written to the conflict table so you can choose later.

7. What happens to the losing record in a synchronization conflict?

   A. It is deleted.

   B. It is saved in a conflict table in the winning replica.

   C. It is saved in a conflict table in the losing replica.

   D. The system administrator is notified by e-mail.

8. Jackie is editing a record in one replica and changes the Last Name field. Pat is editing the same record in another replica and changes the First Name field. The record was edited only once in each replica since the last synchronization. What happens when the two replicas are next synchronized?

   A. Both replicas reflect the changes to the Last Name and First Name fields.

   B. Both replicas end up with a conflict table showing the field that was different from the one saved in the current replica.

   C. The replica with the lowest ReplicaID wins, and the losing record is written to the Conflict table in the winning replica.

   D. The replica with the lowest ReplicaID wins, and the losing record is written to the Conflict table in the losing replica.

9. Which of the following applications would be a good candidate for replication?

   A. An order entry system where salespeople are out on the road taking orders on their laptop computers

   B. A ticket selling operation with multiple branches in the same city

   C. A banking application with a high volume of transactions

   D. An online trading system for an investment bank

10. Identify some of the changes the Jet database engine makes to a replicated database:

    A. New tables, fields, and database properties are added. Queries now run across multiple replicas.

    B. New tables, fields, and database properties are added. These are stored in the Replication Manager for future reference.

    C. New tables, fields, and database properties are added. The behavior of AutoNumber fields is changed from Increment to Random.

    D. New tables, fields, and database properties are added. The data type of all AutoNumber fields is changed from Long Integer to GUID.

11. How do you keep an object from being replicated?

    A. Write code to set its Synchronization property to False before replicating the database.

    B. Write code to set its KeepLocal property to "T" before replicating the database.

    C. Write code to set its Replicable property to False before replicating the database.

    D. Write code to set its Replication ID property to Null before replicating the database.

12. Jackie is editing a record in one replica and changes the Last Name field to Cartman. Pat is editing the same record in another replica and also changes the Last Name field to Cartman. The record was edited only once in each replica since the last synchronization. What happens when the two replicas are next synchronized?

    A. Both replicas have the same value in the LastName field. No conflict is recorded.

    B. Both replicas end up with a conflict table showing the field was changed. The old value is kept in each replica.

    C. The replica with the lowest ReplicaID wins, and the losing record is written to the Conflict table in the winning replica.

    D. The replica with the lowest ReplicaID wins, and the losing record is written to the Conflict table in the losing replica.

CHAPTER

12

Distributing Applications

Microsoft Exam Objectives Covered in This Chapter:

- Test and debug library databases.

- Implement error handling in add-ins.

- Describe the purpose of the USysRegInfo table.

- Provide online help in a Microsoft Access application.

- Prepare an application for distribution using the Setup Wizard.

- Choose the best way to distribute a client/server application.

- Distribute OLE custom controls with an application.

- Optimize performance in distributed applications.

Creating your Access application is only half the battle—now you've got to get it into the hands of your users. Access provides a number of ways of doing this. With Access you can deliver full-blown applications—or just wizards and add-ons to enhance Access functionality for all applications. Best of all, your users don't even have to have Access installed on their computers.

In this chapter, you will learn:

- The differences between regular Access and the run-time version.

- How to distribute an Access application to users who don't have Access installed on their computers.

- How to make sure that end users don't modify your application's design or introduce errors into the code.

- How to create your own Access Wizards, Builders, and Add-ins.

- How to enhance your application's functionality with OLE custom controls.

- About which OLE custom controls work in Access 95.

- How to distribute an OLE control in your application with the run-time version of the application.

Regular Access vs. Run-Time

When you use Access as a developer, you are using the full version of Access, which lets you create and modify objects, as well as enter data. When you distribute an application to end users, it is generally preferable to distribute it as a run-time application, which lets users enter and modify data (using security to restrict access as discussed in Chapter 10), but does not allow them to view code or modify the design of database objects.

However, there are some situations where distributing applications that use the full version of Access is an excellent choice.

Using the Full Version

The full (or regular) version of Access is the one you get when you purchase Access, either as a standalone application or as part of Office 95. When you develop an application in Access, you can make any changes you want to database objects. Unfortunately, so can any users who run your application with the full version of Access, unless the application has been secured to prevent it.

In some cases, this may be desirable. If, for example, your application is intended for use by workers who are knowledgeable Access users and will need to create new forms, reports, and queries on the fly, this is the only choice you have. Of course, these users must be willing to put up with any errors they may introduce into the application as a trade-off for the convenience of being able to make their own modifications.

Indeed, the ease of use provided by Access, coupled with the ability to let users do their own enhancements, is one of the advantages that Access has over other products in the market. Other programs require a trained developer to make even minor modifications to an application's interface or functionality. In many cases, having a developer prepare a foundation application, and then turning it over to knowledgeable users for fine-tuning, is an excellent choice.

But this is not always so—far more often, end users are not knowledgeable Access users or the management does not want users creating their own forms, reports, or queries (or modifying existing ones). The quick and easy way to make sure that an application stays "as delivered" (except for data entry) is to prepare the application as a run-time application, using the Setup Wizard. This means that your users will need the run-time version of Access covered in the *Access Developers Toolkit* section later in this chapter.

WARNING   A run-time application is not a secured application. See Chapter 10 for information about securing an application.

Access Libraries

An Access Library is just an Access database. Conventionally, libraries have the MDA extension, but this is not mandatory. An Access library is not used directly; instead it is installed as an add-in so that you can use its procedures and database objects from other Access databases. Libraries are often used to make code collections available for all your Access applications. Access comes with a utility library, a system library, and a set of libraries that support various wizards.

A number of Access add-ins use libraries. You can also create your own libraries to use in your applications, as described in the following sections. Access libraries can be used either with the run-time or the full version of Access, and they provide an excellent way to distribute functionality without having to build a complete application. To use an Access library it must be added to the list of references in your database (Figure 12.1).

F I G U R E 12.1

An Access database references list

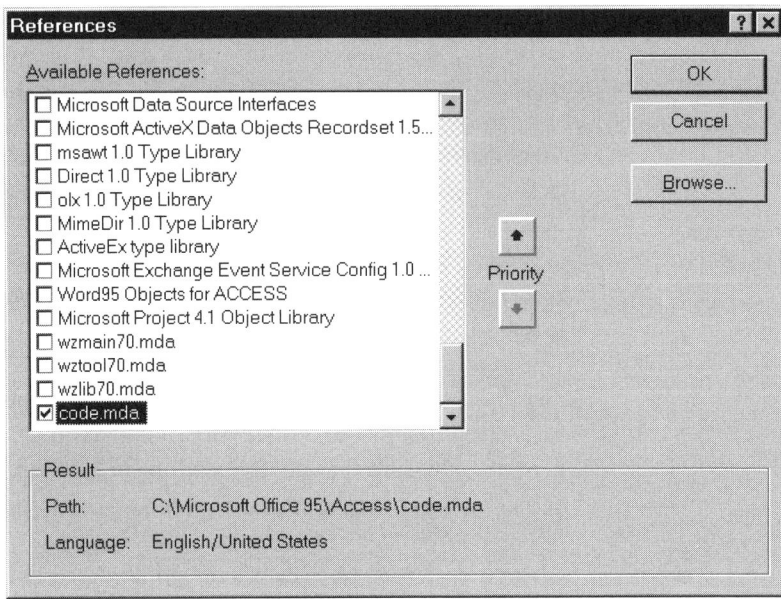

Creating a Library

Follow the steps in Exercise 12.1 to create a library database containing functions you would like to make available to all your Access applications.

Creating a Simple Library

1. Create a new Access database and save it in the main Access folder (normally C:\MSOffice\Access) as Code.mda. Make sure that you set the Save As Type to Add-Ins (*.mda) before you save your database.

2. Create one or more code modules in the library database, and write some simple procedures for them (or import modules from other Access applications). Here's a procedure that simply displays the traditional greeting for a new program:

```
Sub HelloWorld()
    MsgBox "Hello, World"
End Sub
```

3. Compile the database, then close it.

4. Open an Access application, and open any module (standard or CBF).

5. Select Tools ➤ References from the menu.

6. In the References dialog box, click on the Browse button.

7. In the Add Reference dialog box, select Databases (*.mdb, *.mda) in the Files of Type list box.

8. Locate Code.mda in the Access folder, and click on the OK button to add the library to the References dialog box.

9. Back in the References dialog box, Code.mda appears at the bottom of the Available References list, checked. Click on OK to close the dialog box.

Now you can use any functions in Code.mda when writing expressions in code or as row sources. To test your add-in, open the Customer database, open a new module and, in the Debug Window, type **HelloWorld** and press ↵. The message box you added in step 2 will display.

Unfortunately, libraries you create do not appear in the Expression Builder; you have to type library procedure names manually when you use them in code or expressions.

When you set up a reference to a library, the full path to the library database is stored with the reference. So if you move the library, or if it is in a different path on the user's computer, an error will occur. When distributing libraries, be sure to include error-handling code to deal with this situation.

Testing and Debugging Libraries

Microsoft
✓ *Exam*
Objective

Test and debug library databases.

Even if you have debugged and compiled a library database before setting a reference to it, errors may arise when using code or objects from the library in another database. If you have problems when using library procedures or objects in another database, you don't have to close the current database to fix the problem in your library. Instead, from an Access module, press the F2 key to display the Access Object Browser (shown in Figure 12.2). From the list at the top of the dialog box, select your library and click on the Show button. A module window opens to let you work on your library code.

Even if you add the libraries that Microsoft ships with Access to the References list, they won't show up in the Object Browser. If you want to see the code in Wzmain70.mda or the other Access libraries, you'll have to download them from Microsoft's Web site.

Methods (like OpenForm and OpenReport) that reference specific objects for performing an action can cause problems with library databases. When

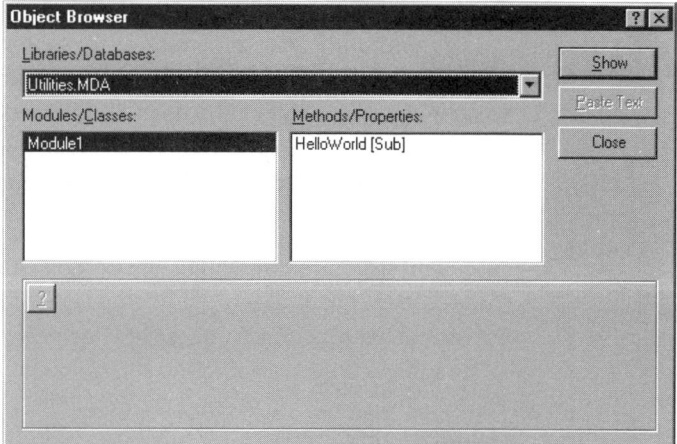

FIGURE 12.2

The Access Object
Browser

such a method is run from a library database, Access looks for the named
object in the library database first, and executes it there if the object is found.
Otherwise, it looks for the object in the current database, and then executes
the action there.

It is best to avoid using macros in library databases. Macros don't have
VBA error-trapping, so you can't trap run-time errors that a library data-
base macro might generate. If you need to use macro actions, use the
DoCmd object in VBA, with the method corresponding to the macro action.

Using a Library to Handle Errors

Microsoft
Exam
Objective

Implement error handling in add-ins.

You can use a library database to provide standardized error handling to all
your Access applications. For example, you could display custom messages
for the errors most likely to occur in your applications instead of the sometimes cryptic Access error messages.

To create a handy error code reference, search for Trappable Errors in the Help index, open the Determining the Error Codes Reserved by Visual Basic Help topic, and cut and paste the procedure from the Help topic into a module. Run the procedure to create an Access table containing all the current VBA error codes and their descriptions.

In Exercise 12.2 you will create an error-handling function in a library that will generate a user-friendly message when the user tries to write to Drive A. This function handles these drive- and disk-related problems:

- Device I/O
- Disk Full
- Device Unavailable
- Path/File Access
- Path Not Found
- Disk Not Ready

As part of this exercise you'll create the form that you see in Figure 12.3 to test your new add-in.

FIGURE 12.3

A form to generate errors to test your add-in

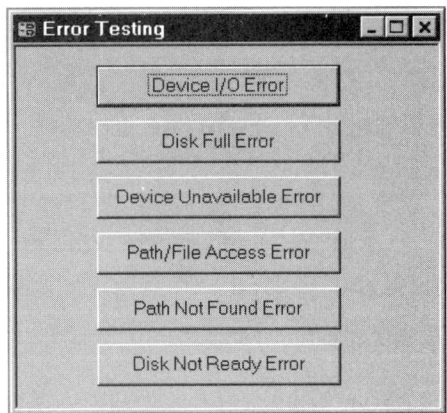

EXERCISE 12.2

Writing an Error Handler to Run from a Library Database

1. Open the Code.mda library created in Exercise 12.1.

2. Create a new function, with the code listed below, to display specific error messages for particular errors.

```
Public Function ErrorHandler(ErrCode As Integer)


    Select Case ErrCode


        Case 57
            MsgBox "From library module:  There is a problem
            ➥ with outputting the file"
            Exit Function


        Case 61
            MsgBox "From library module:  The destination
            ➥ disk in Drive A is full"
            Exit Function


        Case 68
            MsgBox "From library module:  Drive A is
            ➥ unavailable"


        Case 71
            MsgBox "From library module:  The disk in Drive A
            ➥ is not ready"


        Case 75
            MsgBox "From library module:  There is a problem
            ➥ with the file path"
            Exit Function


        Case 76
            MsgBox "From library module:  The specified path
            ➥ on Drive A was not found"
```

```
        Exit Function

    Case Else
        MsgBox "From library module:  " & Err.Description

    End Select

End Function
```

3. In another Access database, create a form with a command button for each error to test, with code on the Click event using the Raise method to generate errors. The code below lists one such procedure, to raise the Disk Full error (#61).

```
Private Sub cmdDiskFull_Click()

On Error GoTo cmdDiskFullError

    Dim intError As Integer

    intError = 61
    Err.Raise intError

cmdDiskFullExit:
    Exit Sub

cmdDiskFullError:
    MsgBox "From CBF procedure:  Error No.: " & Err.Number & _
        "; Description: " & Err.Description
    ErrorHandler (intError)
    Resume cmdDiskFullExit

End Sub
```

4. Click on the Disk Full Error command button to generate a Disk Full error. You will first see a message from the procedure's own error handling routine that lists the standard Microsoft error description. Then you will get the custom message from your library module.

With this exercise you've created a standard error-handling module that you can use in any of your Access applications.

You need to set a reference to your library database separately in each Access database from which you want to use it.

If a library database is open in another copy of Access, you won't be able to use any of its procedures, even if the specific procedure you want to use is closed.

Working with Add-Ins

There are three different types of Access add-ins: Wizards, Builders, and Menu add-ins. If you need an add-in that is called when the user creates a new database object (a table, query, form, report, or control), then you'll create a Wizard or Builder. An add-in that is not context-specific is a Menu add-in. Access will call your Wizards and Builders the way it calls the Wizards and Builders that are delivered with Access. However, menu add-ins are only accessible to your users via the Tools ➤ Add-ins submenu.

Each add-in category has its own type of interface and functionality, as described in the following sections.

Wizards

Wizards are used to handle complex operations, such as creating a form or control. Wizards guide the reader through a series of screens where options are made available in a user-friendly and familiar interface. When you create a Wizard for an object, it will be invoked when you create a new object of that type, just like the built-in Access Wizards.

Access provides four types of Wizards:

- Table and Query Wizards
- Form and Report Wizards
- Property Wizards
- Control Wizards

To make your add-ins user-friendly, you should model their appearance after the built-in Access add-ins. Some of the interface elements you can use to make your add-ins look like the familiar ones used in Access are listed below:

- Set the forms' AutoCenter property to Yes.

- Turn record selectors off.

- Set scrollbars to Neither.

- Turn navigation buttons off.

- If you use several forms, make sure that controls used on more than one form in a series of Wizard screens appear in the same place on each form.

- Make all forms dialog boxes by setting their Modal property to Yes, PopUp to Yes, and BorderStyle to Dialog, so that the user can't move to the next box until the current one has been filled in.

Control Wizards

Control Wizards pop up when you place a new control on a form; they allow you to select various attributes for the new control. Access provides several built-in Control Wizards:

- Combo Box Wizard

- Command Button Wizard

- List Box Wizard

- Option Group Wizard

- Subform/Subreport Wizard

You can create your own Control Wizards to apply formatting of your choice to controls.

Exercises 12.3 and 12.4 walk you through the creation of a Text Box Wizard. This Wizard lets you format a newly inserted text box and its attached label so that it matches one of four styles featured in the built-in Form Wizards.

EXERCISE 12.3

Creating a USysRegInfo Table for a Text Box Wizard

1. Create a new library database, called Addins.mda.

2. Open the new Addins.mda database.

3. Select Tools ➢ Options, check the System Objects checkbox, and close the Options dialog box.

4. Select File ➢ Get External Data ➢ Import, and select the Wztool70.mda library database.

5. Select the USysRegInfo table to import into Addins.mda. (All add-ins must have a USysRegInfo table. For more extensive information about the USysRegInfo table, see the section later in this chapter.)

6. Close the Options dialog box. You should now see a system table called USysRegInfo. This table is used to store information needed to register add-ins.

7. Enter the records in Table 12.1 into the USysRegInfo table to provide the information needed to register your Text Box Wizard.

T A B L E 12.1:   USysRegInfo Entries

Subkey	Type	ValName	Value
HKEY_LOCAL_MACHINE\Wizards\Control Wizards\TextBox*Design Wizard*	0		
HKEY_LOCAL_MACHINE\Wizards\Control Wizards\TextBox*Design Wizard*	1	Description	Text Box Design Wizard
HKEY_LOCAL_MACHINE\Wizards\Control Wizards\TextBox*Design Wizard*	4	Can Edit	0
HKEY_LOCAL_MACHINE\Wizards\Control Wizards\TextBox*Design Wizard*	1	Library	|ACCDIR*addins.mda*
HKEY_LOCAL_MACHINE\Wizards\Control Wizards\TextBox*Design Wizard*	1	Function	TextBoxDesignWizard

Most of the entries in the table don't vary from Wizard to Wizard. The four italicized entries in Table 12.1 are different for each Wizard. They are:

- The last portion of the Subkey (Design Wizard) is the name of the TextBox Wizard Registry key.

- The Value (Text Box Design Wizard): the Value stored in the Registry corresponding for the Description ValName.

- The Add-in database name (add-ins.mda): the right side of the Value corresponding to the Library ValName entry.

- The name of the function that implements the Wizard's functionality (TextBoxDesignWizard), corresponding to the Function ValName entry.

In Exercise 12.4, you'll finish creating the interface for the Text Box Wizard.

EXERCISE 12.4

Creating the Text Box Wizard's Interface

1. Create a form to serve as the Wizard's interface, following the guide-lines above so it will have the familiar Access Wizard look. The form illustrated here has four option buttons with sample sets of text boxes and labels. Each sample is displayed on a background matching the form backgrounds of some of the standard Form Wizard selections. The user selects an option button, then clicks on the Apply command button to close the form and apply the chosen attributes to the text box with the attached label.

2. The form has code in the option group's AfterUpdate event to save the selected text box and label's attributes to global variables. There is also code on the form's Open event to initialize the first option's prop-erties, in case the user just accepts the default option. (The code for the form's module is listed at the end of this exercise.)

3. The function referenced in the USysRegInfo table is located in the bas-Addins module. This function will be called by Access whenever a text box is added to the form. This function has two required arguments, which represent the object that the control is placed on (a form or a report) and the control to be modified. The function assigns the values stored in global variables (picked up from the Wizard dialog box form) to the new text box and its label. The relevant portions of the Decla-rations section and the function are listed at the end of the section that follows this exercise.

4. After creating the form and code for the Wizard, compile Addins.mda by selecting Run ➣ Compile All Modules from the module menu. If any errors are found, fix the problem and compile the database again. Repeat until the modules compile successfully.

5. Close the add-in database and open a regular database. Select Tools ➣ Add-ins ➣ Add-in Manager to install the new add-in database from the dialog box shown here.

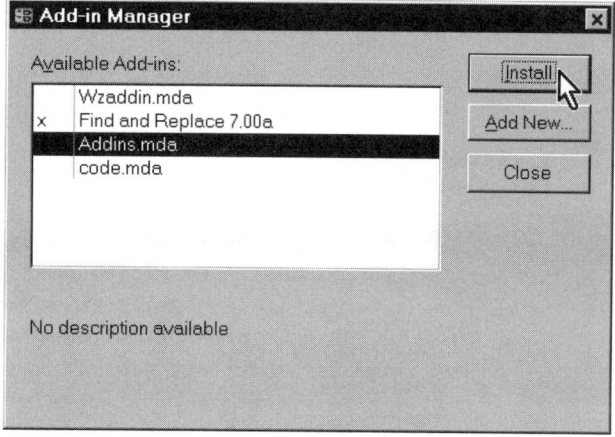

6. To check the functionality of the new Wizard, click on the TextBox tool in the Toolbox to insert a new text box on a form. The Text Box Design Wizard opens, offering you a choice of the text box styles. Click on one of the options, and then click on the Apply button. The text box will be formatted with the attributes you have requested.

The following is the Text Box Wizard code behind the form's module for Exercise 12.4:

```
Option Compare Database
Option Explicit

Dim ctlTextBox As Control
Dim ctlLabel As Control

Private Sub cmdApplyDesign_Click()
```

```
    On Error GoTo cmdApplyDesign_ClickError

        DoCmd.Close acForm, Me.Name, acSaveNo

cmdApplyDesign_ClickExit:
    Exit Sub

cmdApplyDesign_ClickError:
    MsgBox "Error No:  " & Err.Number & "; error message:
    ➥ " & _ Err.Description
    Resume cmdApplyDesign_ClickExit

End Sub

Private Sub Form_Open(Cancel As Integer)

On Error GoTo Form_OpenError

    Set ctlTextBox = Me![txtClouds]
    Set ctlLabel = Me![lblClouds]
    intTBBackStyle = ctlTextBox.BackStyle
    lngTBBackColor = ctlTextBox.BackColor
    intTBSpecialEffect = ctlTextBox.SpecialEffect
    intTBBorderStyle = ctlTextBox.BorderStyle
    lngTBBorderColor = ctlTextBox.BorderColor
    intTBBorderWidth = ctlTextBox.BorderWidth
    lngTBForeColor = ctlTextBox.ForeColor
    strTBFontName = ctlTextBox.FontName
    lngTBFontSize = ctlTextBox.FontSize
    intTBFontWeight = ctlTextBox.FontWeight
    blnTBFontItalic = ctlTextBox.FontItalic
    blnTBFontUnderline = ctlTextBox.FontUnderline
    intTBTextAlign = ctlTextBox.TextAlign
    intTBHeight = 228
    intLBBackStyle = ctlLabel.BackStyle
    lngLBBackColor = ctlLabel.BackColor
    intLBSpecialEffect = ctlLabel.SpecialEffect
    intLBBorderStyle = ctlLabel.BorderStyle
    lngLBBorderColor = ctlLabel.BorderColor
    intLBBorderWidth = ctlLabel.BorderWidth
    lngLBForeColor = ctlLabel.ForeColor
    strLBFontName = ctlLabel.FontName
```

```
            lngLBFontSize = ctlLabel.FontSize
            intLBFontWeight = ctlLabel.FontWeight
            blnLBFontItalic = ctlLabel.FontItalic
            blnLBFontUnderline = ctlLabel.FontUnderline
            intLBTextAlign = ctlLabel.TextAlign
            intLBHeight = 240

Form_OpenExit:
    Exit Sub

Form_OpenError:
    MsgBox "Error No:  " & Err.Number & "; error message:
    ➥ " & _ Err.Description
    Resume Form_OpenExit

End Sub

Private Sub grpPicture_AfterUpdate()

On Error GoTo grpPicture_AfterUpdateError

    Dim intDesign As Integer

    intDesign = Me![grpPicture]

    Select Case intDesign

        Case 1
            Set ctlTextBox = Me![txtClouds]
            Set ctlLabel = Me![lblClouds]
            intTBBackStyle = ctlTextBox.BackStyle
            lngTBBackColor = ctlTextBox.BackColor
            intTBSpecialEffect = ctlTextBox.SpecialEffect
            intTBBorderStyle = ctlTextBox.BorderStyle
            lngTBBorderColor = ctlTextBox.BorderColor
            intTBBorderWidth = ctlTextBox.BorderWidth
            lngTBForeColor = ctlTextBox.ForeColor
            strTBFontName = ctlTextBox.FontName
            lngTBFontSize = ctlTextBox.FontSize
            intTBFontWeight = ctlTextBox.FontWeight
            blnTBFontItalic = ctlTextBox.FontItalic
            blnTBFontUnderline = ctlTextBox.FontUnderline
```

```
                        intTBTextAlign = ctlTextBox.TextAlign
                        intTBHeight = 228
                        intLBBackStyle = ctlLabel.BackStyle
                        lngLBBackColor = ctlLabel.BackColor
                        intLBSpecialEffect = ctlLabel.SpecialEffect
                        intLBBorderStyle = ctlLabel.BorderStyle
                        lngLBBorderColor = ctlLabel.BorderColor
                        intLBBorderWidth = ctlLabel.BorderWidth
                        lngLBForeColor = ctlLabel.ForeColor
                        strLBFontName = ctlLabel.FontName
                        lngLBFontSize = ctlLabel.FontSize
                        intLBFontWeight = ctlLabel.FontWeight
                        blnLBFontItalic = ctlLabel.FontItalic
                        blnLBFontUnderline = ctlLabel.FontUnderline
                        intLBTextAlign = ctlLabel.TextAlign
                        intLBHeight = 240

                    Case 2
                        Set ctlTextBox = Me![txtDusk]
                        Set ctlLabel = Me![lblDusk]
                        intTBBackStyle = ctlTextBox.BackStyle
                        lngTBBackColor = ctlTextBox.BackColor
                        intTBSpecialEffect = ctlTextBox.SpecialEffect
                        intTBBorderStyle = ctlTextBox.BorderStyle
                        lngTBBorderColor = ctlTextBox.BorderColor
                        intTBBorderWidth = ctlTextBox.BorderWidth
                        lngTBForeColor = ctlTextBox.ForeColor
                        strTBFontName = ctlTextBox.FontName
                        lngTBFontSize = ctlTextBox.FontSize
                        intTBFontWeight = ctlTextBox.FontWeight
                        blnTBFontItalic = ctlTextBox.FontItalic
                        blnTBFontUnderline = ctlTextBox.FontUnderline
                        intTBTextAlign = ctlTextBox.TextAlign
                        intTBHeight = 228
                        intLBBackStyle = ctlLabel.BackStyle
                        lngLBBackColor = ctlLabel.BackColor
                        intLBSpecialEffect = ctlLabel.SpecialEffect
                        intLBBorderStyle = ctlLabel.BorderStyle
                        lngLBBorderColor = ctlLabel.BorderColor
                        intLBBorderWidth = ctlLabel.BorderWidth
                        lngLBForeColor = ctlLabel.ForeColor
                        strLBFontName = ctlLabel.FontName
                        lngLBFontSize = ctlLabel.FontSize
```

```
            intLBFontWeight = ctlLabel.FontWeight
            blnLBFontItalic = ctlLabel.FontItalic
            blnLBFontUnderline = ctlLabel.FontUnderline
            intLBTextAlign = ctlLabel.TextAlign
            intLBHeight = 324

        Case 3
            Set ctlTextBox = Me![txtInternational]
            Set ctlLabel = Me![lblInternational]
            intTBBackStyle = ctlTextBox.BackStyle
            lngTBBackColor = ctlTextBox.BackColor
            intTBSpecialEffect = ctlTextBox.SpecialEffect
            intTBBorderStyle = ctlTextBox.BorderStyle
            lngTBBorderColor = ctlTextBox.BorderColor
            intTBBorderWidth = ctlTextBox.BorderWidth
            lngTBForeColor = ctlTextBox.ForeColor
            strTBFontName = ctlTextBox.FontName
            lngTBFontSize = ctlTextBox.FontSize
            intTBFontWeight = ctlTextBox.FontWeight
            blnTBFontItalic = ctlTextBox.FontItalic
            blnTBFontUnderline = ctlTextBox.FontUnderline
            intTBTextAlign = ctlTextBox.TextAlign
            intTBHeight = 264
            intLBBackStyle = ctlLabel.BackStyle
            lngLBBackColor = ctlLabel.BackColor
            intLBSpecialEffect = ctlLabel.SpecialEffect
            intLBBorderStyle = ctlLabel.BorderStyle
            lngLBBorderColor = ctlLabel.BorderColor
            intLBBorderWidth = ctlLabel.BorderWidth
            lngLBForeColor = ctlLabel.ForeColor
            strLBFontName = ctlLabel.FontName
            lngLBFontSize = ctlLabel.FontSize
            intLBFontWeight = ctlLabel.FontWeight
            blnLBFontItalic = ctlLabel.FontItalic
            blnLBFontUnderline = ctlLabel.FontUnderline
            intLBTextAlign = ctlLabel.TextAlign
            intLBHeight = 324

        Case 4
            Set ctlTextBox = Me![txtStone]
            Set ctlLabel = Me![lblStone]
            intTBBackStyle = ctlTextBox.BackStyle
```

```
                lngTBBackColor = ctlTextBox.BackColor
                intTBSpecialEffect = ctlTextBox.SpecialEffect
                intTBBorderStyle = ctlTextBox.BorderStyle
                lngTBBorderColor = ctlTextBox.BorderColor
                intTBBorderWidth = ctlTextBox.BorderWidth
                lngTBForeColor = ctlTextBox.ForeColor
                strTBFontName = ctlTextBox.FontName
                lngTBFontSize = ctlTextBox.FontSize
                intTBFontWeight = ctlTextBox.FontWeight
                blnTBFontItalic = ctlTextBox.FontItalic
                blnTBFontUnderline = ctlTextBox.FontUnderline
                intTBTextAlign = ctlTextBox.TextAlign
                intTBHeight = 240
                intLBBackStyle = ctlLabel.BackStyle
                lngLBBackColor = ctlLabel.BackColor
                intLBSpecialEffect = ctlLabel.SpecialEffect
                intLBBorderStyle = ctlLabel.BorderStyle
                lngLBBorderColor = ctlLabel.BorderColor
                intLBBorderWidth = ctlLabel.BorderWidth
                lngLBForeColor = ctlLabel.ForeColor
                strLBFontName = ctlLabel.FontName
                lngLBFontSize = ctlLabel.FontSize
                intLBFontWeight = ctlLabel.FontWeight
                blnLBFontItalic = ctlLabel.FontItalic
                blnLBFontUnderline = ctlLabel.FontUnderline
                intLBTextAlign = ctlLabel.TextAlign
                intLBHeight = 240

        End Select

grpPicture_AfterUpdateExit:
    Exit Sub

grpPicture_AfterUpdateError:
    MsgBox "Error No:  " & Err.Number & "; error message:
    ➥ " & _ Err.Description
    Resume grpPicture_AfterUpdateExit

End Sub
```

The relevant portions of the Declarations section and the function for the example in Exercise 12.4 follow:

```
Option Compare Database
Option Explicit

Global intTBBackStyle As Integer
Global lngTBBackColor As Long
Global intTBSpecialEffect As Integer
Global intTBBorderStyle As Integer
Global lngTBBorderColor As Long
Global intTBBorderWidth As Integer
Global lngTBForeColor As Long
Global strTBFontName As String
Global lngTBFontSize As Long
Global intTBFontWeight As Integer
Global blnTBFontItalic As Boolean
Global blnTBFontUnderline As Boolean
Global intTBTextAlign As Integer
Global intTBHeight As Integer
Global intLBHeight As Integer
Global intLBBackStyle As Integer
Global lngLBBackColor As Long
Global intLBSpecialEffect As Integer
Global intLBBorderStyle As Integer
Global lngLBBorderColor As Long
Global intLBBorderWidth As Integer
Global lngLBForeColor As Long
Global strLBFontName As String
Global lngLBFontSize As Long
Global intLBFontWeight As Integer
Global blnLBFontItalic As Boolean
Global blnLBFontUnderline As Boolean
Global intLBTextAlign As Integer

Public Function TextBoxDesignWizard(strObjName As String, _
 strCtlName As String) As Variant
'Selects a color/special effect scheme for a
'text box control and its attached label
'The schemes match styles in the Form Wizard

On Error GoTo TextBoxDesignWizardError
```

```
        Dim frm As Form
        Dim ctl As Control
        Dim ctlTextBox As Control
        Dim ctlLabel As Control
        Dim strCaption As String

        DoCmd.OpenForm FormName:="frmTextBoxDesignWizard", _
    windowmode:=acDialog

        Set frm = Screen.ActiveForm
        Set ctlLabel = frm(strCtlName)
        Set ctlTextBox = ctlLabel.Parent

        'Set the text box design properties
        With ctlTextBox
            .BackStyle = intTBBackStyle
            .BackColor = lngTBBackColor
            .SpecialEffect = intTBSpecialEffect
            .BorderStyle = intTBBorderStyle
            .BorderColor = lngTBBorderColor
            .BorderWidth = intTBBorderWidth
            .ForeColor = lngTBForeColor
            .FontName = strTBFontName
            .FontSize = lngTBFontSize
            .FontWeight = intTBFontWeight
            .FontItalic = blnTBFontItalic
            .FontUnderline = blnTBFontUnderline
            .TextAlign = intTBTextAlign
            .Height = intTBHeight
            .Width = 1440
        End With

        'Set the label design properties
        With ctlLabel
            .BackStyle = intLBBackStyle
            .BackColor = lngLBBackColor
            .SpecialEffect = intLBSpecialEffect
            .BorderStyle = intLBBorderStyle
            .BorderColor = lngLBBorderColor
            .BorderWidth = intLBBorderWidth
            .ForeColor = lngLBForeColor
            .FontName = strLBFontName
            .FontSize = lngLBFontSize
```

```
          .FontWeight = intLBFontWeight
          .FontItalic = blnLBFontItalic
          .FontUnderline = blnLBFontUnderline
          .TextAlign = intLBTextAlign
          .Height = intLBHeight
          .Width = 800
       End With

   TextBoxDesignWizardExit:
       Exit Function

   TextBoxDesignWizardError:
       MsgBox "Error No:  " & Err.Number & "; error message:
       ➥ " & _ Err.Description
       Resume TextBoxDesignWizardExit

   End Function
```

This exercise showed you how to create a new Wizard to help you (or your users) format Text Box controls.

If you make any changes in an add-in database, you need to uninstall it from a regular database and then reinstall it, so that the changes will be picked up.

Form and Report Wizards

There are four methods of the Access Application object that are essential for creating Form and Report Wizards in Access: CreateForm, CreateReport, CreateControl, and CreateReportControl. While creating a complete Form or Report Wizard is a complex process that is beyond the scope of this chapter, you can start to become familiar with these methods. Creating a full Form or Report Wizard involves a thorough understanding of the way the built-in Access Form and Report Wizards function, because you need to hook your code into numerous functions and interface elements used in the screens of these built-in Wizards.

The CreateForm and CreateControl methods (and their report counterparts) are useful for creating forms and reports in general, not just in Wizards. You can use these methods from your application to create a form or report on the fly and then populate it with the appropriate controls. You can also use these methods from another Access database—or even a different Office application—using OLE Automation.

Using the CreateForm Function

The CreateForm function lets you create a form programmatically, based on a template of your choice. (If you don't specify a template, the default Access form template will be used.) This template feature is useful if you frequently need to create a form with specific properties, say for dialog boxes or pop-ups.

You can set which form to use as the default by selecting Forms ➤ Options and entering the form's name in the Form Template field.

When you create a new form from a template, the form has properties that match those of the template. If the template has its navigation buttons turned off and its ScrollBars property set to Neither, new forms you create based on the template will have the same settings. However, when you create a form from a template (whether manually after setting the Form Template in Tools ➤ Options, or from code using CreateForm), the properties of any controls you may have placed on the template won't be used. Nor will any controls on the template be copied to the new form. When you create a new control on the new form, it will have the Access default properties.

After using CreateForm to make a new form, you can use CreateControl to create and format the controls you need on the form. The following code sample illustrates the creation of a new form and a Label control with a number of its properties specified:

```
Private Sub cmdDefaultControl_Click()

    Dim frm As Form
    Dim ctlDefault As Control
    Dim ctlNew As Control

    Set frm = CreateForm(, "tmpGrayForm")
    Set ctlDefault = frm.DefaultControl(acLabel)
    With ctlDefault
        .FontWeight = 700
        .FontSize = 24
        .Width = 3000
```

```
            .Height = 3000
            .SpecialEffect = 1
            .BackStyle = 1
            .BackColor = 33023
            .TextAlign = 2
        End With

        Set ctlNew = CreateControl(FormName:=frm.Name, _
    ControlType:=acLabel, columnname:="Big Orange Label", _
    Left:=1000, Top:=1000)
        DoCmd.Restore

    End Sub
```

Although the Access Help topic states that you can create a form based on a form or form template in another database (specifying the database name in the Database argument), this does not work. According to Microsoft, this problem was discovered shortly before Access 95 shipped, and by then it was too late to change the Help file. The workaround is to always use databases loaded in memory (the current database, a library database, or a database set up as a reference under Tools ➢ References). Other external databases won't be found—you'll just get error #7870.

When you set the RecordSource property of a form immediately after creating it with CreateForm, the table or query name will not appear in the form's RecordSource property immediately. Don't Panic! It will show up after switching to Form view and then back to Design view.

Using the CreateReport Function

The CreateReport function works similarly to the CreateForm function; the code sample below creates a new report, based on the default Access report template, and adds two controls to it. The report that is created is shown in Figure 12.4.

```
    Private Sub cmdCreateReportControls_Click()

        Dim rpt As Report
        Dim ctlLabel As Control
```

```
Dim ctlTextBox As Control
Dim intTextBoxX As Integer
Dim intTextBoxY As Integer
Dim intLabelX As Integer
Dim intLabelY As Integer

Set rpt = CreateReport()
rpt.RecordSource = "tblProducts"
'Set positioning values for new controls.
intLabelX = 150
intLabelY = 200
intTextBoxX = 1500
intTextBoxY = 200

'Create unbound default-size text box in detail section.
Set ctlTextBox = CreateReportControl(rpt.Name, acTextBox, , _
"", "", intTextBoxX, intTextBoxY)

'Create attached label control for text box.
Set ctlLabel = CreateReportControl(rpt.Name, acLabel, , _
ctlTextBox.Name,"Company Name:", intLabelX, intLabelY)

DoCmd.Restore

End Sub
```

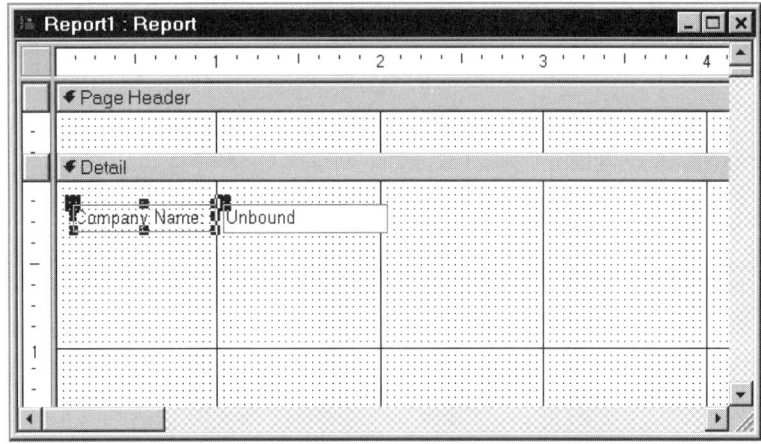

FIGURE 12.4

A form created from
a module

Builders

A Builder is generally a simpler type of add-in than a Wizard. A Builder is usually just a single dialog box or form that lets the user make choices in constructing an expression or another single data element. The Expression Builder is an example of one of the Builders that ships with Access.

Access provides three types of Builders:

- Property Builders
- Control Builders
- Expression Builders

In Exercise 12.5 you'll create a Builder that lets you select a picture for a form background. The final product is shown in Figure 12.6.

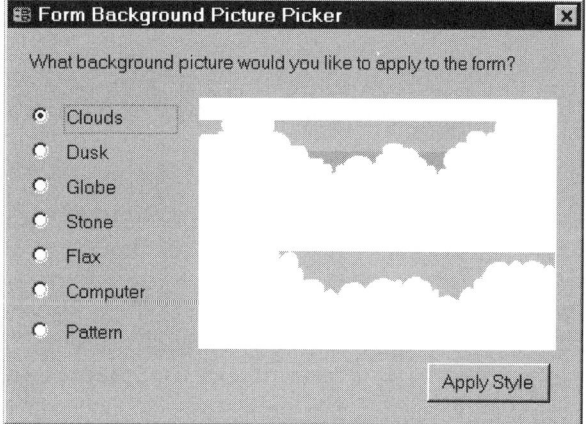

FIGURE 12.5

A Picture Property Builder

EXERCISE 12.5

Creating a Picture Property Builder

1. Add the lines in Table 12.2 to the USysRegInfo table in the Addins.mda database (the filled-in table is shown at the end of this exercise).

2. The Picture Picker form has an option group with seven buttons, and a single Image control. The Image control's Picture property is set to a different picture each time a different option button is clicked.

3. When the user clicks on an option, the Picture property (the path to the image) is stored in the strPicture global variable. The option group's event procedure is listed below:

```
Private Sub grpPicture_AfterUpdate()

On Error GoTo grpPicture_AfterUpdateError

    Dim intPicture As Integer
    Dim ctlPicture As Control

    intPicture = Me![grpPicture]
    Set ctlPicture = Me![imgBackground]

    Select Case intPicture

      Case 1
          ctlPicture.Picture = _
  "C:\Microsoft Office 95\Access\Bitmaps\Styles\Clouds.wmf"

      Case 2
          ctlPicture.Picture = _
  "C:\Microsoft Office 95\Access\Bitmaps\Styles\Sea_dusk.wmf"

      Case 3
          ctlPicture.Picture = _
  "C:\Microsoft Office 95\Access\Bitmaps\Styles\Globe.wmf"

      Case 4
          ctlPicture.Picture = _
  "C:\Microsoft Office 95\Access\Bitmaps\Styles\Stone.bmp"

      Case 5
          ctlPicture.Picture = _
  "C:\Microsoft Office 95\Access\Bitmaps\Styles\Flax.bmp"

      Case 6
          ctlPicture.Picture = "C:\Windows\Setup.bmp"

      Case 7
          ctlPicture.Picture = _
  "C:\Microsoft Office 95\Access\Bitmaps\Styles\Pattern.bmp"
```

```
    End Select

    strPicture = ctlPicture.Picture

grpPicture_AfterUpdateExit:
    Exit Sub

grpPicture_AfterUpdateError:
    MsgBox "Error No:   " & Err.Number & "; error message:   " & _
    Err.Description
    Resume grpPicture_AfterUpdateExit

End Sub
```

4. The Property Wizard's enabling function has required arguments for the form name, control name, and current value. The function initializes the strPicture variable with the current value of the Picture property, then opens the Wizard dialog box and replaces the form's current Picture property with the one selected in the dialog box. The function is listed below, together with the relevant global variables in the module's Declarations section:

```
Option Compare Database
Option Explicit

Global strColor As String
Global strPicture As String

Public Function PicturePicker(strFormName As String, _
strCtlName As String, strCurrentValue As String) As Variant
'Selects a background picture for a form

On Error GoTo PicturePickerError

    strPicture = strCurrentValue
    DoCmd.OpenForm FormName:="frmPicturePicker", _
windowmode:=acDialog
    PicturePicker = strPicture
```

EXERCISE 12.5 (CONTINUED)

```
PicturePickerExit:
   Exit Function

PicturePickerError:
   MsgBox "Error No:  " & Err.Number & "; error message:  " & _
 Err.Description
   Resume PicturePickerExit

End Function
```

T A B L E 12.2:   USysRegInfo Table Rows for a Picture Property Wizard

Subkey	Type	ValName	Value
HKEY_LOCAL_MACHINE\Wizards\Property Wizards\Picture*Picture Picker*	0		
HKEY_LOCAL_MACHINE\Wizards\Property Wizards\Picture*Picture Picker*	1	Description	Picture Picker
HKEY_LOCAL_MACHINE\Wizards\Property Wizards\Picture*Picture Picker*	4	Can Edit	1
HKEY_LOCAL_MACHINE\Wizards\Property Wizards\Picture*Picture Picker*	1	Library	|ACCDIR*addins.mda*
HKEY_LOCAL_MACHINE\Wizards\Property Wizards\Picture*Picture Picker*	1	Function	PicturePicker

This exercise has allowed you to add a Builder to your Access applications to help you set the Picture property of forms.

Menu Add-Ins

Menu add-ins either work on multiple objects or provide general Access functionality. (The Database Documentor is a built-in Access Menu add-in). Menu add-ins are always available, unlike the context-sensitive Wizards and Builders. They are listed on the Tools ➤ Add-ins menu.

In Exercise 12.6, you'll create a Menu add-in that generates an Errors table. Figure 12.6 shows how your add-in will appear on the Add-ins menu.

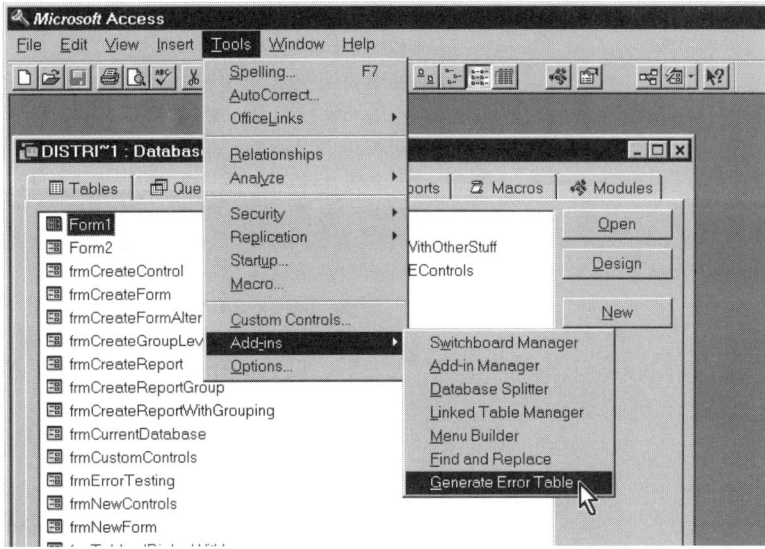

EXERCISE 12.6

Creating an Errors Table Menu Add-In

1. Add the lines in Table 12.3 to the USysRegInfo table in the Addins.mda database. (The table with the add-in rows filled in is shown at the end of this exercise.)

2. Unlike most add-ins, this one doesn't have a form. When you select this add-in from the Add-ins menu, the CreateErrorsTable sub runs, creating a new Errors table with a message telling you that the table has been created. Add this code to a module in your Addins.mda database:

```
Sub CreateErrorsTable()
        Dim dbs As Database, tdf As TableDef, fld As Field
        Dim rst As Recordset, lngCode As Long
        Const conAppObjectError = _
        "Application-defined or object-defined error"

        'Create Errors table with ErrorNumber and
    ➥ ErrorDescription fields.
```

```
Set dbs = CurrentDb
Set tdf = dbs.CreateTableDef("Errors")
Set fld = tdf.CreateField("ErrorCode", dbLong)
tdf.Fields.Append fld
Set fld = tdf.CreateField("ErrorString", dbText, 255)
tdf.Fields.Append fld
dbs.TableDefs.Append tdf
'Open recordset on Errors table.
Set rst = dbs.OpenRecordset("Errors")
'Loop through first 1000 Visual Basic error codes.
For lngCode = 1 To 1000
    On Error Resume Next
    'Raise each error.
    Err.Raise lngCode
    DoCmd.Hourglass True
    'Skip codes generating application/object-defined
    ➥ errors.
    If Err.Description <> conAppObjectError Then
        'Add each error code and string to Errors
        ➥ table.
        rst.AddNew
        rst!ErrorCode = Err.Number
        rst!ErrorString = Err.Description
        rst.Update
    End If
    'Clear Err object.
    Err.Clear
Next lngCode
'Close recordset.
rst.Close
DoCmd.Hourglass False
MsgBox "Errors table created."
End Sub
```

3. Now you're ready to install your add-in. Close Addins.mda and open another Access database. Select Tools ➢ Add-ins ➢ Add-ins Manager. Select the GenerateErrorTable add-in from the list of available add-ins.

4. Click the Install button to install the add-in, then close the dialog box. From the Tools ➢ Add-ins menu, run the GenerateErrorTable add-in.

T A B L E 12.3: USysRegInfo Table Rows for a Menu Add-in

Subkey	Type	ValName	Value
HKEY_LOCAL_MACHINE\Menu Add-ins\&*Generate Error Table*	0		
HKEY_LOCAL_MACHINE\Menu Add-ins\&*Generate Error Table*	1	Expression	=CreateErrorsTable()
HKEY_LOCAL_MACHINE\Menu Add-ins\&*Generate Error Table*	1	Library	|ACCDIR*addins.mda*

Unlike references, which have to be set separately for each database, once an add-in has been installed, it is available to all Access databases.

The USysRegInfo Table

Microsoft Exam Objective

Describe the purpose of the USysRegInfo table.

All add-ins have a system table called USysRegInfo that contains information about the add-in. Access stores this information in the Windows Registry when the add-in is installed. The Windows Registry is a database that Windows maintains where applications (including Windows itself) can store information they need.

The USysRegInfo table has four fields:

- **Subkey:** The Registry subkey to create when registering the add-in. The main key can be either HKEY_CURRENT_ACCESS_PROFILE (used in case Access is started with the /Profile command-line option to enable an Access profile) or HKEY_LOCAL_MACHINE. The first record for each add-in has only the subkey (typically HKEY_LOCAL_MACHINE); the remaining records for the add-in define values for the last key in the Registry subtree. The HKEY_LOCAL_MACHINE\Wizards\Property Wizards\Picture\Picture Picker string, for example, creates a Registry key for a Property Wizard.

If you enter the HKEY_CURRENT_ACCESS_PROFILE subkey in the USys-RegInfo table, and you don't have Access Profiles enabled, the Registry information will be written to the HKEY_LOCAL_MACHINE subkey instead.

If you create a Builder for an object that already has one, you will get a Choose Builder dialog box when you create a new object of that type. The dialog box will show the default MS Builder and your custom Builder.

- **Type:** The Type field contains an Integer value. The values it can contain are:
  - 0   First record of a new add-in
  - 1   Creates a String
  - 4   Creates a DWORD
- **Valname:** The name of the value in the Registry.
- **Value:** The actual value stored in the Registry.

See the USysRegInfo help topic for further information on Registry values for the USysRegInfo table.

Online Help

Microsoft
Exam
Objective

Provide online help in a Microsoft Access application.

You may want to create a special Help file for your application, and distribute it with the run-time version. When the users of your application request help, your custom Help file will be displayed. The ADT includes the

Help Workshop, a Microsoft application used to create Help files (*.HLP)
that you can distribute with your application.

Creating a Windows Help File for Your Application

You can use the Microsoft Help Workshop to create Help files for your
application. Or you can use a third-party application such as WexTech's
Doc-to-Help or Blue Sky's Robohelp.

If you don't include a custom Help file in your run-time application, an error
will occur when users select commands on the Help menu or press the F1
key (unless you remap the F1 key).

Integrating Access and Help

The first step in incorporating your custom Help file into a run-time application is to include it with your application when you distribute it. If you are
using the Setup Wizard you will you need to select the Help file (Appname.hlp)
as one of the files to include with your application in the Wizard's File List
screen. See the *Using the Setup Wizard* section later in this chapter for more
details.

In addition to creating a Help file accessible through the Help menu, you
can also create context-sensitive Help links between your application and your
customer Help file. Incorporating context-sensitive Help into a run-time application requires you to do more than just add the Help file to the application.
For each object (Form, Report, or Control) you must also assign a specific
Help topic by setting the object's HelpContextID and HelpFile properties.
With these properties correctly filled in, when the user selects an object and
presses the F1 key, the designated topic of the specified Help file is displayed.

To implement context-sensitive Help, you must map the HelpContextID properties of your Access objects to the context strings in the Help system. See the
Help Workshop Help file (Hcw.hlp) for more information on this mapping.

If you press F1 when a control has the focus, but no information has been
entered for the HelpContextID and HelpFile properties, the Help Topics
dialog box will be displayed.

The Access Developer's Toolkit

The Access Developer's Toolkit (ADT) is a set of developer's tools for Access 95, including:

- A Setup Wizard for preparing run-time Access applications to distribute
- A royalty-free run-time distribution license
- The Microsoft Replication Manager
- A number of extra OLE custom controls that can be used to enhance your Access applications

The Run-Time Version of Access

A run-time application prepared with the ADT allows users to add, delete, and modify records, but not to change the structure of database objects or code. Basically, users can modify the data—but not the design—of the database. As noted below, run-time applications are not immune to modification—for real assurance that users can't modify an application's design you need to secure the application. However, for many uses where security is not paramount and you just need to rule out accidental or casual modification of a database's design, a simple unsecured run-time application will meet your needs.

When you prepare an application for distribution using the Setup Wizard, you are actually preparing a package of files. These files include the run-time version of Access, a number of supporting files that are needed for Access to run, and the .MDB file(s) that you created. In addition, you may need to add some extra files required by certain components such as Help files, OLE custom controls, or library databases needed to support add-ins.

 Unlike Visual Basic, Access does not create executable files for distribution. When you use the ADT Setup Wizard to create a run-time Access application to distribute, the application is not conveniently packaged into a single executable file with an accompanying .DLL. Instead, the application consists of a large number of separate files that Setup installs to the appropriate locations on the user's computer.

The ADT includes a royalty-free run-time license, which permits the developer of an application to distribute it to users who don't have Access.

Using OLE Custom Controls

OLE custom controls (formerly called custom controls, or .OCX controls) are controls that can be used on Access forms and reports. These controls are used in addition to the built-in controls that are available from the form toolbox.

See Chapter 3 for a discussion of the built-in form and report controls.

Access itself includes one OLE control (the Calendar control) and the ADT includes a number of other OLE custom controls. Still more can be downloaded from CompuServe or the Internet (see Table 12.4). This section will discuss use of OLE controls in general from Access and the ADT (with a focus on several of the most useful).

T A B L E 12.4: OLE Custom Controls Used in Access 95

OLE Controls in Access	Separate OLE Controls in ADT	Windows Common Controls in ADT	OLE Controls from Internet
Calendar	Common Dialog	ImageList	32-bit Tab
	Data Outline 1.1	ListView	Chart FX
	DBList	Progress Bar	Caller ID
	RichText	Status Bar	Multi-select List Box
	Slider	TabStrip	Image
	Spin Button	TreeView	FMS Total Access Components
			FMS Total Access Memo

You can't assume that an OLE control developed for VB 4.0 will work in Access. VB OLE controls use extensions to the OLE Custom Control specification not supported by Access. While some VB or other OLE controls may work with Access, you can't depend on a control to work unless it was specifically developed to work with Access (see KB article Q146612).

Some of the OLE custom controls distributed with Access or the ADT are updated versions of Access 2.0 controls (the Calendar control and Data Outline control, for instance). Other controls, like the RichText control, are new to Access 95.

While the Calendar control has its own Help topic, the OLE custom controls included with the ADT are not documented as well as the standard Access controls. ADT Help does include lists of methods, properties, and events for some of the OLE controls, but there is little general explanatory material on how to use them.

You don't insert an OLE control the same way as a standard control—they aren't in the toolbox, but are inserted from a command accessed from the Insert menu. However, you can add an OLE control to the toolbox using the Customize Toolbars dialog box (see Figure 12.7), as you will in the next exercise.

See Chapter 3 for a discussion of the Access toolbox.

FIGURE 12.7

The Customize
Toolbars dialog box

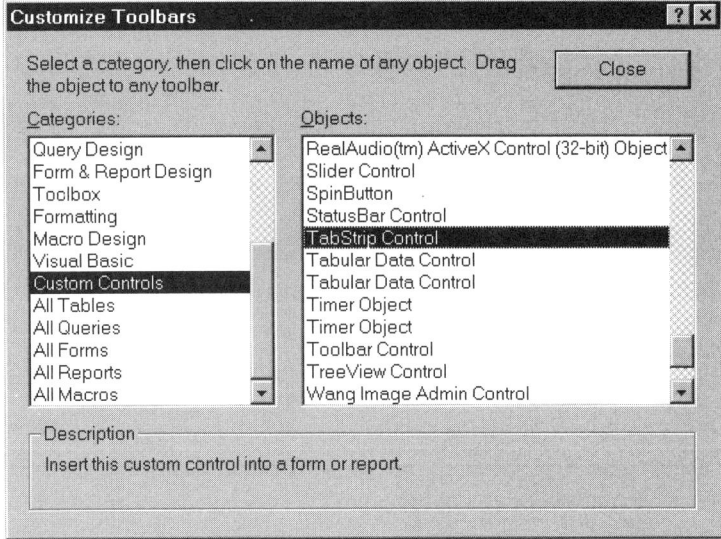

Once you have inserted an OLE control, you generally need to do some programming to make it functional, since most of the events and methods of OLE controls are not available from the control's properties sheet.

If you use a certain OLE custom control frequently, you may want to have it conveniently available in the toolbox along with the standard controls. In Exercise 12.7, you'll add the TabStrip control to the toolbox.

EXERCISE 12.7

Placing a Custom Control in the Toolbox

1. Right-click on the gray background area of the toolbox or any toolbar, and select the Customize command from the fly-out menu.

2. On the Customize Toolbars dialog box, select the Custom Controls category.

3. Select the TabStrip control in the Object list, and drag it to the toolbox.

4. Click on the Close button to close the dialog box.

5. The TabStrip control now appears in the toolbox.

Distributing an OLE Control

To distribute an OLE custom control with an application, you simply need to include the supporting .OCX file in the list of Setup files. Similarly, if you have created a library database to support one or more custom add-ins, you need to include the library database .MDA file among your Setup files.

Writing to the Registry

In previous versions of Access (and Windows), custom .INI files were used to store and retrieve information used by applications. You can still use .INI files, but the new Windows 95 Registry offers a superior way to store information.

Entries in the Registry are referred to as keys. Each key consists of a key name, a subkey, and a value name. The three parts of the key are used to organize the information that you store. Typically, the *key name* is the name of the application that is writing the value. The *subkey* is used to organize the data for the application into groups. Finally, the *value name* identifies the information that is being stored. For instance, the Sales Order application might store a variety of control information in the Registry, including data about the company. Within the company information group, the application could store the company name under the value name "CompanyName." The key would be written as

```
SalesOrder/CompanyInfo/CompanyName
```

Figure 12.8 shows how the CompanyName entry would look using RegEdit, a tool for editing the Registry included in Windows 95.

F I G U R E   12.8

RegEdit, showing the sample Company-Name entry

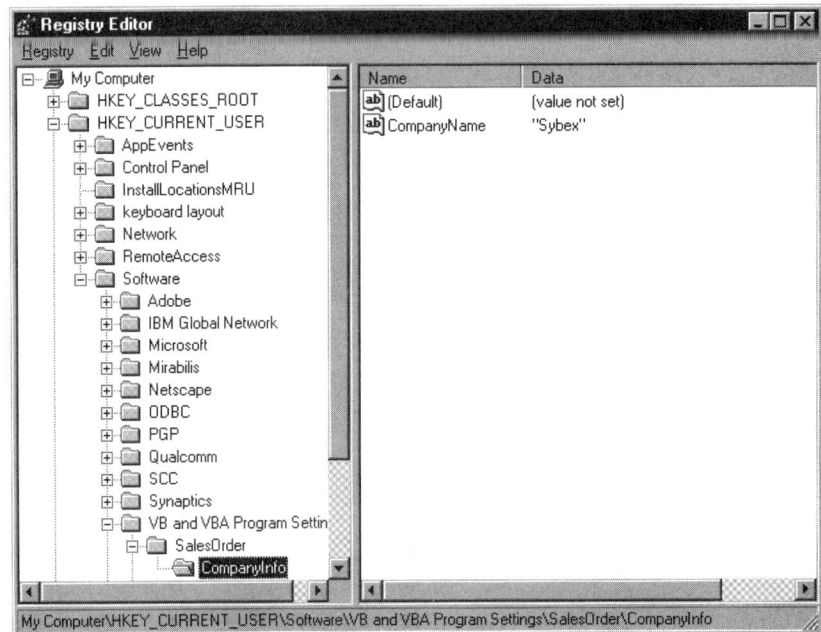

As a database developer you could think of the Registry as a table with three fields that make up its primary key.

As a developer, you can create custom keys in the Registry using VBA statements. The keys you create are stored under the VB and VBA Program Settings key. Once a key is created you can use it to store information for your application. Storing application information in the Registry has several advantages over storing it in a table in the database:

- The information is preserved even if the application has to be reinstalled.

- The same information is available to a user in different databases. For example, if several different databases need the company name then the Registry would be a good place to store it rather than in any particular Access database.

- Information can be retrieved from the Registry with a single line of code, as opposed to creating a recordset to retrieve information from a table.

To write a value to the Registry you use the SaveSetting statement. The syntax for the SaveSetting statement is:

```
SaveSetting KeyName, Subkey, ValueName, Value
```

To write the company name to the Registry, you would use:

```
SaveSetting "SalesOrder", "CompanyInfo", "CompanyName"
➡ "Sybex"
```

This line would write the name Sybex to the key "SalesOrder/CompanyInfo/CompanyName".

To read a value from the Registry you use the GetSetting function. Its syntax is:

```
var = GetSetting(KeyName, Subkey, ValueName[,Default])
```

The function accepts a key name, a subkey, and the name of a value. You can also provide an optional default value. If the key/subkey/valuename combination isn't found in the Registry, GetSetting will return the Default parameter. To read the company name into the strCompName variable you would use:

```
strCompName = GetSetting("SalesOrder", "CompanyInfo",
➡ "CompanyName" "No Name")
```

With this command, if the company name isn't found, the string "No Name" is returned.

Finally, the DeleteSetting statement will delete a key. The DeleteSetting statement is passed a key, a subkey, and the name of the value to be deleted. The syntax for this statement command is:

```
DeleteSetting keyname, subkey, valuename
```

To delete the company name entry from the Registry you would use

```
DeleteSetting "SalesOrder", "CompanyInfo", "CompanyName"
```

No error is returned if `DeleteSetting` does not find the specified key.

Exercise 12.8 will allow you to read, write, and delete settings from the Registry using a form you create (shown in Figure 12.9).

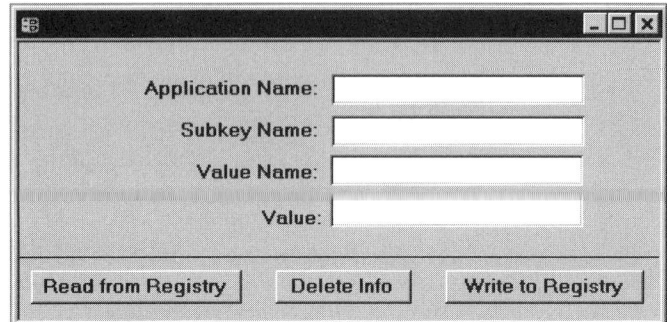

FIGURE 12.9

A form for updating the Windows Registry

EXERCISE 12.8

Working with Registry Keys

1. Open an Access database and create a form called **frmRegTest**. Add it to the controls in the following list.

Control Name	Control Type	Control Source/ Row Source
txtApplicationName	Text Box	="TestReg"
txtSubkeyName	Text Box	
txtValueName	TextBox	
txtValue	Text Box	
cmdGetCustomSettings	Command Button	See code listing below.
cmdWipe	Command Button	See code listing below.
cmdSaveCustomSettings	Command Button	See code listing below.

2. Add procedures for the three command buttons to save, retrieve, or delete custom Registry information (these procedures are listed at the end of this exercise).

3. Enter a subkey name in txtSubkeyName, a name for the value in txtValue-Name, and a value in txtValue. Click on the cmdSaveCustomerSettings button to write your entries to the Registry. To retrieve your entries, enter a key and value in the txtSubkeyName and txtValueName text boxes and click on the cmdGetCustomerSettings button to retrieve the value or cmd-Wipe to delete the setting.

4. Select Run from the Windows Start menu, and type **Regedit** to open the Windows Registry. Open the HKEY_CURRENT_USER\Software key, and you should see the keys for the TestReg application with the values you created when you entered data into the form.

These are the procedures added in Exercise 12.8 for the three command buttons to save, retrieve, or delete custom Registry information:

```
Private Sub cmdGetCustomSettings_Click()

On Error GoTo cmdGetCustomSettings_ClickError

    Dim strAppName As String
    Dim strSubkey As String
    Dim strValueName As String
    Dim strDefault As String

    strAppName = Me![txtApplicationName]
    strSubkey = Me![txtSubkeyName]
    strValueName = Me![txtValueName]
    Me![txtValue] = GetSetting( _
       AppName:=strAppName, Section:=strSubkey, KEY:= _
       strValueName, Default:=strDefault)

cmdGetCustomSettings_ClickExit:
    Exit Sub

cmdGetCustomSettings_ClickError:
    MsgBox Error$
    Resume cmdGetCustomSettings_ClickExit

End Sub
```

```
Private Sub cmdSaveCustomSettings_Click()

On Error GoTo cmdSaveCustomSettings_ClickError

   Dim strAppName As String
   Dim strSubkey As String
   Dim strValueName As String
   Dim strValue As String

   strAppName = Me![txtApplicationName]
   strSubkey = Me![txtSubkeyName]
   strValueName = Me![txtValueName]
   strValue = Me![txtValue]
   SaveSetting AppName:=strAppName, Section:=strSubkey, _
      KEY:=strValueName, Setting:=strValue

cmdSaveCustomSettings_ClickExit:
   Exit Sub

cmdSaveCustomSettings_ClickError:
   MsgBox Error$
   Resume cmdSaveCustomSettings_ClickExit

End Sub

Private Sub cmdWipe_Click()

On Error GoTo cmdWipe_ClickError

   Dim strAppName As String
   Dim strSubkey As String
   Dim strValueName As String

   strAppName = Me![txtApplicationName]
   strSubkey = Me![txtSubkeyName]
   strValueName = Me![txtValueName]
   DeleteSetting AppName:=strAppName, Section:=strSubkey, _
      KEY:=strValueName
   Me![txtValueName] = Null
   Me![txtValue] = Null

cmdWipe_ClickExit:
   Exit Sub
```

```
cmdWipe_ClickError:
   If Err = 94 Then
      MsgBox "Please supply missing data"
      Exit Sub
   ElseIf Err = 5 Then
      MsgBox "Could not find relevant data in Registry"
      Exit Sub
   End If
   Resume cmdWipe_ClickExit

End Sub
```

Using the Setup Wizard

Microsoft
✓ *Exam*
Objective

Prepare an application for distribution using the Setup Wizard.

The Setup Wizard is part of the ADT. You run the Setup Wizard to gather all the files that make up your application and package them with the run-time version of Access. The setup files (on one or more floppy disks, or stored on a network computer) can then be used to install your application on any computer. As part of preparing the setup files used to install the application on your user's computers, the Wizard will ensure that any OLE controls you use in your application will be installed correctly.

The Setup Wizard will take you through a number of steps to create your setup disks. Here are the steps you should follow in creating an application with the Setup Wizard:

1. Place all the files you will need for the application (.MDB, .ICO, .BMP, and others) in one folder. (This is not necessary, but it is convenient.)

2. Run the Setup Wizard from the Microsoft ADT program group.

3. The Setup Wizard startup screen offers two options. Select Create a new set of setup options…, and then click on the Next button.

4. On this screen of the Setup Wizard, click on the Add button to add the database and supporting files you need for the application. Typically, these will be one or two .MDB files, an .ICO file for the application's icon, and perhaps a .BMP file for a custom splash screen.

To use a .BMP file as a splash screen for your application, copy or rename a .BMP file to create a file with the same name as your application. You can find a selection of distributable .BMP files in the \Microsoft Office\Access\Bitmaps\Dbwiz folder.

5. To install your application in the application folder, assign the .MBD, .ICO, and .BMP files to the $(AppPath) Destination Folder. Any OLE customer control files (.OCX) should be assigned to $(WinSysPath) Destination Folder, to install them to the \Windows\System folder.

6. Highlight the main application file and check the Set as Application's Main File checkbox. If you have split your application into a database and application MDB, you should select the application MDB. Click on the Next button to go to the form that allows you to create shortcuts.

7. On the next screen, create two shortcuts: one shortcut to open the application, and one to repair and compact the application. Check the Run-Time checkbox for the Open shortcut, so it will be opened using the run-time version of Access, even if the user has the full version of Access. Click on the Next button to move to the Registry keys form.

Checking the Run-Time checkbox does not secure the application; a user with the full version of Access could still open the .MDB directly in Access, bypassing the shortcut. However, it ensures that the run-time version will be used when the application is started from the shortcut, as it normally would be.

8. On the next screen, add any Registry keys you want to be present when the application first starts, and initialize them with appropriate values. Click on the Next button.

When you use the SaveSetting statement to write to the Registry, the information is written to the HKEY_CURRENT_USER key. When you write to the Registry from the Setup Wizard, the information goes in the HKEY_LOCAL_MACHINE key.

9. The optional component screen lets you specify the Access components to be included in your application. The Microsoft Access Run-Time Version option should always be checked, and the Workgroup Administrator is often needed; other components are only needed in special cases. Click on the Next button.

You can distribute any type of files with an Access setup disk set. For example, you could include a Word template used to generate mail-merge documents from the Access database.

10. The Setup Wizard lets you create three different kinds of setups using the screen that appears next: Typical, Compact, and Custom. This screen of the Setup Wizard lets you order your application's components, assign them to component groups, and decide which component groups should be included in which installation type—Typical, Compact, and Custom. After you are finished with this screen, click on the Next button.

The new Setup Wizard in the Access 95 ADT can create compressed network setups (the old version only created uncompressed network setups). This saves considerable hard drive space when users need to install over the network.

It is a good idea to give your database and supporting files DOS 8+3 file names (such as MyFile.MDB), to prevent problems when installing on systems that don't support long file names. However, you can safely use a longer name for the internal database name, which appears in the title bar.

11. The second-to-last form in the Wizard lets you specify a file (say, a batch file) to run after the setup is completed. Click on the Next button.

12. On the last form, you specify the folder where you want to store your disk images or network installation files. The Access 95 ADT lets you create two or even all three types of installations in one process, which is very convenient. Click on the Save button to save a setup template for this installation, and click on the Finish button to start generating the setup files.

Microsoft ✓ ***Exam*** ***Objective***   **Choose the best way to distribute a client/server application.**

For client/server applications, the best disk image option is compressed network files. This option is best because it allows you to do installations over the network, storing the setup files on the server.

Microsoft ✓ ***Exam*** ***Objective***   **Distribute OLE custom controls with an application.**

If you are distributing a run-time application that contains custom controls, you need to include the necessary .OCX files in your distribution files. Some OLE custom controls have individual .OCX files, and others require the multi-control Comctl32.OCX file. Table 12.7 lists the files needed for some of the more commonly used OLE controls.

	OLE Control	File Required
TABLE 12.5 Files Required to Distribute OLE Custom Controls	Calendar control	Msacal70.ocx
	CommonDialog control	Comdlg32.ocx
	Data Outline control	Msdboutl.ocx
	ImageList control	Comctl32.ocx
	Rich Text control	Richtx32.ocx
	Spin Button control	Spin32.ocx
	TabStrip control	Comctl32.ocx
	TreeView control	Comctl32.ocx

It is no longer necessary to include specific DLLs in the setup files to support various .OCX controls, as it was in Access 2.0.

You can now copy the files from their disk images to one or more floppies and distribute your application. If you open the Registry Editor after installing the application on your users' computers, you will see a new key under the HKEY_LOCAL_MACHINE key, with the custom application information.

In the future, when you need to prepare a new version of the application, all you need to do is run the Setup Wizard, select the template you saved, and click on the Finish button to regenerate the setup files.

Distributing Functionality

Once the setup files have been generated (and copied to disks in case you selected the 1.44 Floppy Disk installation type), users can run Setup.exe from a floppy disk or network folder to install the custom application on their computers. The Setup program has the same interface as commercial Microsoft applications, so it should be familiar to users (see Figure 12.10).

FIGURE 12.10

The setup program created by using the Setup Wizard

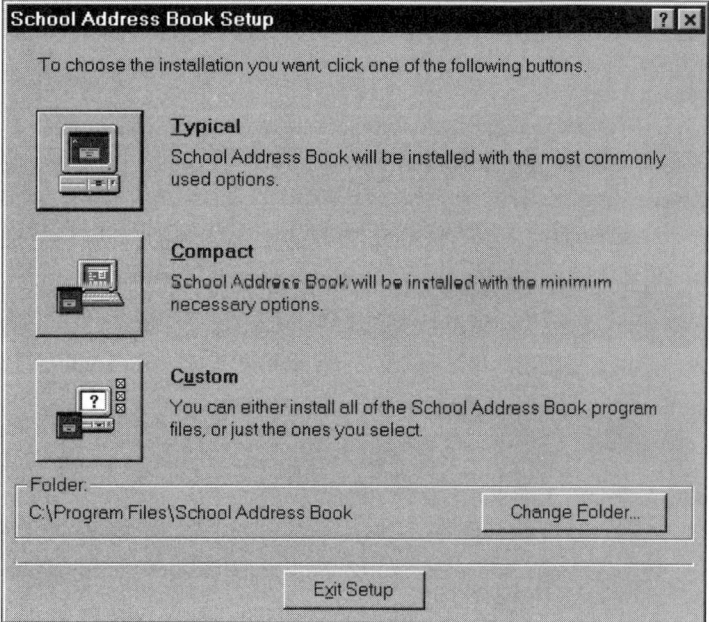

After the user installs the application, your application appears on the Start menu as a program group.

There are some differences in functionality between a run-time application and an application run in regular Access:

- Users can't modify the design of database objects.

- Users can't view or modify code.

- The database container is unavailable (the F11 key is disabled).

- No toolbar is available—just the standard menu bar.

- The new Access 95 filter-by-form capability is not supported.

- The CloseCurrentDatabase method is not supported; if you use this command in an application, replace it with DoCmd.Quit before preparing the distributed version.

Applications created by the Database Wizard use the CloseCurrentDatabase method, so you will need to modify any applications you create with one of the Database Wizards.

Optimizing Distributed Applications

Microsoft
Exam
Objective

Optimize performance in distributed applications.

With a discussion of distributing Access applications we must discuss the factors that involve distributing a run-time version of your application. With little effort we could determine that a run-time application would not include any of the features of Access that would be used to create the application in the first place. This is not surprising. Some of the other objects and features that are not included are as follows:

- A custom help file must be built if there is to be a help system with the distribution.

- Error handling must be built in. On an error, ADT displays a simple dialog box and exits the application rather gracelessly.

- A majority of the commands are no longer available via the menus. Their functionality remains, but it must be accessed with code.

All of this means that, for the most part, you must code the functionality of Access into your applications. Obviously, this means that some preparation is required.

To prepare an application for run-time distribution there are a number of points you'll need to cross off your "to do" list. Optimizing an application for distribution is much like optimizing a database, so the points we covered for that task are applicable here as well. Some of the following items are merely icing on the "vertical cake," but ignoring them would make for a rather hostile user environment. Let's look at the main points that need to be considered.

Security

For most distributed applications there is at least some small concern for security. Whether it be to limit access to site personnel or to make a credit card transaction safe from larcenous individuals, security is part of the puzzle.

Forms

Distributed applications are based around forms. A lack of forms will make a bad distributed application. The starting point for an application is usually a *Switchboard window* that directs the user to other switchboards or forms for data entry.

A switchboard is a graphical phonebook of sorts that points to forms for data entry or other switchboards. A user does not enter data directly into a switchboard.

Interface

The interface, other than the form displays, is made up of custom menu items and custom toolbars. These allow the user greater access to the functions you integrate into your application.

Startup

In order to present the user with an easy way to start the application, you set various Startup options. These include naming the application, setting the form used when the application is run, and other options such as:

- Allowing custom toolbars and menus
- Allowing the toolbars to be modified
- Defining an application icon
- Allowing default menu shortcuts

Error Handling

As mentioned before, if an error is encountered in the run-time version of Access, the application will unceremoniously dump the user out without an explanation. All error handling must be coded into the application to prevent such mishaps.

Help File

Help is not automatically provided for in any custom-built application, much less a run time application. A help file must be built and attached to the forms and objects that the developer wishes to provide online help for.

Summary

Distributing an Access application is by no means simple, but this chapter has moved you several steps closer to understanding the theory behind this often complex problem. In this chapter, you've learned about the principles and conditions that are involved in testing and debugging your application, without which your distribution would probably crash and disappoint your customer. It's always smart to spend more time on thinking of creative ways to avoid a problem than you spend on developing the application in the first place. Of course, this brings up the issue of error handling in add-in modules. Since this is important to the sanity of your targeted users, it's very important to make sure all errors that may come up have a comprehensible dialog box to describe the error to that user.

You've also learned about the USysRegInfo table, which provides detailed information about whatever add-ins you may have in your application. Because this involves messing around with the Windows Registry, it can be dangerous; but if you use it well, your applications will benefit. This chapter has also covered the basics of developing a customized solution for providing Help in your application. When users know that comprehensive online help is available, they feel more comfortable with the product.

Since we are creating an application that's final environment will probably be an office in some large (or small) building somewhere, we've examined the factors involved in developing one. Fortunately, in this situation the Setup Wizard does most of the heavy lifting for you.

Finally, we covered a trio of topics at the end of the chapter. We discussed the best way to distribute the application and which custom OLE controls to include with it. We also took a look at some of the ways you might optimize your application.

Review Questions

1. Simply distributing the application with the run-time version of Access doesn't stop users from modifying the application because:

A. You must apply security to a run-time version of an Access application for it to run.

B. Users could open the application with the full version of Access.

C. Users could use F11 to open the Database window and add objects.

D. You should compile your code first to make it unreadable.

2. A user calls to say that an application has suddenly started failing with a Function Not Found message. You recognize the function as a member of a library. The most likely cause is that the user has:

A. Compiled the application database

B. Moved the application database

C. Compiled the library database

D. Moved the library database

3. In your library you have some code that executes an OpenForm command. The form must be in:

A. The library MDB

B. The application MDB

C. Either A or B

D. Neither A nor B

4. You can deliver an Access Add-in as:

A. A Wizard, Library, or Builder

B. A Library, Builder, or Menu Add-in

C. A Menu Add-in, Builder, or Wizard

D. A Builder, Wizard, or Library

5. You have a form that will help users set the properties that a label should have whenever a label is added to a form. You should deliver it as:

A. A Wizard

B. A Builder

C. A Menu Add-In

D. None of the above

6. Access looks to the Windows Registry to find out about how to use your add-in. You should put the Registry information about your add-in:

A. In the Registry

B. In the USysRegInfo table

C. In the Setup Wizard

D. In the documentation

7. You want to write some code to create a report. To add a control to the report you would use:

A. CreateControl

B. CreateReportControl

C. CreateForm

D. CreateFormControl

8. You need to prevent users from modifying an application's design or examining the code. Some of the users have the full version of Access on their systems, and some don't. Which of the following methods is the best way to achieve this goal?

A. Prepare a run-time version of the application, without security, and distribute the application in the form of setup disks or network files.

B. Prepare a secured version of the application and distribute the .MDB files to the users.

C. Secure the application; then prepare a run-time version of the secured application and distribute the application in the form of setup disks or network files.

D. Prepare a run-time version of the application, and secure it; then distribute the application in the form of setup disks or network files.

9. To store a value in the Registry it must have:

A. A key name

B. A subkey name

C. A valuename

D. All of the above

10. To retrieve a value from the Registry, you would use:

A. The GetSetting function

B. The ReadSetting function

C. An API call

D. The GetSetting statement

11. This question applies to the run-time version of Access. To have a specific Help topic appear when the user presses the F1 key and the focus is on a control on your form, you must set:

A. HelpContextId to a valid ContextID.

B. The Help option in Tools ➤ Options.

C. The form's HelpFile property.

D. You can't have context-sensitive help in a run-time application.

12. If you can use a control with Visual Basic, then:

A. You can use it with Access if you modify the Registry settings.

B. You can use it with Access.

C. You can't use it with Access.

D. You might be able to use it with Access.

13. You want to distribute a run-time application that uses the Calendar control. What modifications do you need to make to the setup files so that the user will be able to use the control?

    A. Include the MSACal70.ocx file in the Setup file list.

    B. Include the MSACal70.ocx and OC25.dll files in the Setup file list.

    C. You cannot distribute this OLE control.

    D. Include the MSACal70.ocx and OC25.dll files in the Setup file list. Prepare a batch file using Regsvr32.exe to run after Setup is complete, to register the control on the user's system.

14. Data should be stored in the Registry if:

    A. You need it to be available to users of your application working on different databases on the same computer.

    B. You need it to be available to users running both Access 2.0 and Access 95.

    C. It is not of a data type that can be stored in an .INI file.

    D. You need it to be available to users of your application working on different databases in a multiuser environment.

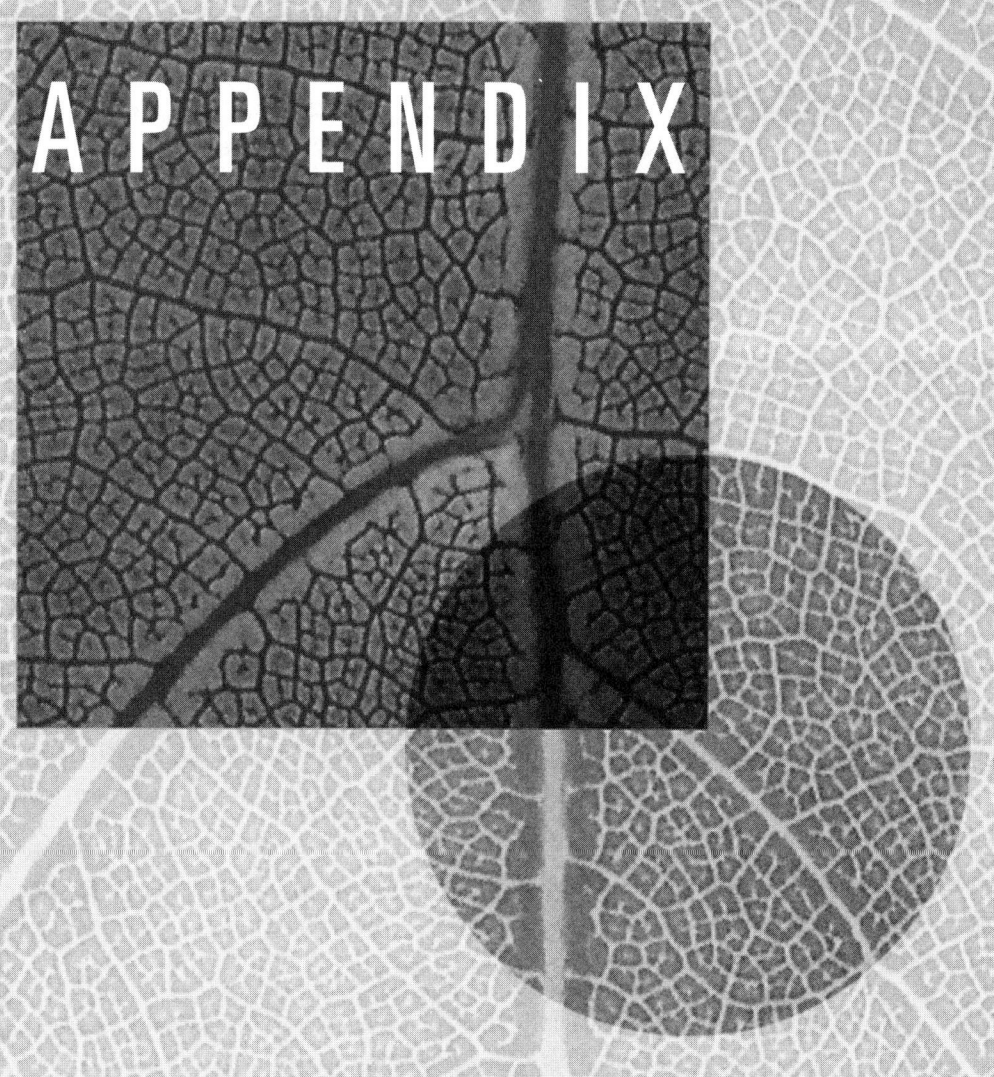

APPENDIX

Review Questions and Answers

Chapter 1

1. Below is the table design for a library; it contains information about books and borrowers. Which fields should be in a separate Book table?

   A. Title, DateLastBorrowed, Address

   B. Title, DateLastBorrowed, BookID

   C. Title, BookID, PhoneNumber

   D. Title, BookID, Address

	Field Name	Field Description
TABLE 1.1 Library Table Design Elements	BookID	Book's unique identifier in the library
	Name	Library member's name
	Title	Book title
	Address	Library member's address
	PhoneNumber	Library member's phone number
	DateLastBorrowed	Last time the book was borrowed by a library member

Answer: B. The Title, DateLastBorrowed, and Author fields all provide information about a book. The other choices mix information about borrowers (Address) and books (Title). (See the section *Which Information?*)

2. Which field(s) should be removed from the following table design to put the table in first normal form?

   A. LastName, FirstName, MiddleName

   B. BirthDate, HireDate, StartDate, TerminationDate

   C. Hours1WeekPrior, Hours2WeeksPrior, Hours3WeeksPrior

   D. DepartmentCode

	Field Name	Field Description
TABLE 1.2 First Normal Form Elements	EmployeeId	Employee number
	LastName	Employee Last Name
	FirstName	Employee first name
	MiddleName	Employee middle name
	Birthdate	Employee Birthdate
	HireDate	Date employee hired
	StartDate	First date employee worked
	TerminationDate	Date employee left employ
	Hours1WeekPrior	Hours worked last week
	Hours2WeekPrior	Hours worked 2 weeks ago
	Hours3WeekPrior	Hours worked 3 weeks ago
	DepartmentCode	Department employee assigned to

Answer: C. This answer depends on the business situation. For instance, you might feel that three name fields are repeating data. However, one of the tests for a repeating field is to determine if the user will ever ask a question that requires all of the fields to be examined. Since it would be an unusual company that would ask for all the employees where any part of their name is "Sharon", these three fields are probably not repeating fields. The same criteria could be applied to the date fields: the question "List all employees that were born, hired, started work, or terminated in December" doesn't seem likely. A question like "Which week had the most hours worked in it" does seem reasonable in many business situations, though, and so these fields should be broken out and given their own table.

3. When building a new database you should

   A. Cycle between investigation and design before creating your database

   B. Cycle between investigation and design and creation

   C. Complete the investigation before beginning the design stage

   D. Defer creating the database until the design is complete

Answer: A. The process of creating a database involves constant interplay between the investigation, design, and creation stages. Access has the flexibility that you need to allow you to switch between the three phases.

4. An entity is

   A. A record in a table in your database

   B. Something that you store information about

   C. A database

   D. A complete information item

Answer: B. An entity is anything that you will store data about in your database. During the investigation phase you determine what your entities will be and then define them in the design phase.

5. A database system with narrow scope

   A. Has a small audience

   B. Has very few tables

   C. Takes up very little room on your hard disk

   D. Has a small user interface

Answer: A. The scope of the database is tied directly to the size of the application's audience. The more kinds of users there are whose needs will be met by the database, the larger the scope will be.

6. To determine which entity a piece of information belongs to

   A. Apply the rules of normalization

   B. Create a sample database to test performance

   C. Investigate the way the business works

   D. None of the above

Answer: C. The demands for determining which entity a piece of information will belong with varies from business to business. While the rules of normalization are very useful, they apply only after you have designed your tables. You will define the entities that make up your database prior to creating your tables.

7. With Microsoft Access, you shouldn't create your database until after you have completed the design stage because

   A. It is very difficult to make changes in the database after it is created

   B. If the database is created too early, it causes the design stage to be poorly done

   C. The database design isn't fully ready to be implemented until after the design stage

   D. With Access you can create the database before the end of the design stage

Answer: D. Access makes it very easy for you to make changes in your database design. As a result, you can use Access as part of your database design process. When working with Access, you will probably find yourself creating the database before the end of the design stage.

8. A table is a relational table only if it

   A. Consists of rows and columns

   B. Is fully normalized

   C. Has a primary key

   D. Is stored in a relational database

Answer: C. The defining characteristic of a relational table is that it has a unique identifier for each record—a primary key. In math, a relation is a formula that produces one unique number for each value given to it. A relational table must be able to produce one (and only one) record for each key requested. No duplicates are allowed.

9. A candidate key is a key that

   A. Consists of only one field

   B. Could be used as a primary key

   C. May or may not use fields in the table

   D. Is small enough to be used effectively

Answer: B. There may be several fields that will uniquely identify each record. These are referred to as the candidate keys. One of them will be used as the primary key.

10. Tables are frequently left in

   A. First normal form

   B. Third normal form

   C. Both of the above

   D. Neither of the above

Answer: B. Data warehousing applications frequently leave their data in first normal form to make reporting easier. While this exposes the data to update anomalies, data warehouses usually only have data added to them rather than having existing data updated, which minimizes the problems. Most operational systems are left in third normal form as the benefits of taking the system to fourth or fifth normal form do not justify the costs of managing the additional tables.

11. First normal form

   A. Eliminates repeating fields

   B. Ensures that all fields depend on the primary key

   C. Eliminates redundant data

   D. Ensures that update anomalies do not occur

Answer: A. First normal form eliminates repeating fields. Update anomalies are eliminated by second and third normal form.

12. When a table is moved to first normal form and a new table is created

   A. The old table's primary key is expanded to include the key of the new table

   B. The new table's primary key becomes a foreign key in the old table

   C. The new table's primary key includes the old table's primary key

   D. None of the above

Answer: C. When the new table is created, its structure includes the primary key of the original table in order to link the two tables together. However, to make the key of the new table unique, additional fields must be used to define the new table's primary key.

13. A foreign key is

   A. A primary key with multiple fields

   B. A key that is not used to enforce referential integrity

   C. A key that allows duplicates

   D. A key that is a primary key in another table

Answer: D. A foreign key is a field (or fields) in one table that is the primary key of another table. A foreign key links multiple records in the table it is part of back to a single record in the table where the key is a primary key.

14. You change the value of a field in a record. As a result, the foreign keys of several other tables are also changed. This is an example of

   A. Cascading Updates

   B. Cascading referential integrity

   C. Referential integrity using foreign keys

   D. Cascading Deletes

Answer: A. A foreign key is a field (or fields) that is the primary key of another table. Cascading updates allow you to change the value of a primary key and have all of the foreign keys based on that primary key updated. While C is also an acceptable answer, the correct term for this is cascading updates.

15. You are unable to enforce referential integrity when creating a relationship in the Access Relationships window. The most probable cause is

   A. The data in the tables is inconsistent

   B. The database is corrupt

   C. Cascading Deletes has not been selected

   D. Cascading Deletes has been selected

Answer: A. You cannot apply referential integrity to two existing tables if those tables already contain data that would violate the integrity rules.

Chapter 2

1. To declare a string and two integer variables you would use:

A. Dim strName as String
Dim intOne, intTwo As Integer

B. Dim strName As String
Dim intOne As Integer, intTwo As Integer

C. Dim strName As String
Dim intOne As Integer; intTwo As Integer

D. Dim strName As String
Dim intOne As Integer, Dim intTwo As Integer

Answer: B. Multiple variables may be declared on one line separated by commas, but the Dim keyword is not repeated and each variable must be given its own datatype.

2. What will be displayed when the following code executes?

```
Dim strValue As String*3
strValue = "Peter Vogel"
Debug.Print strValue
```

A. "Pet"

B. "Peter"

C. "Peter Vogel"

D. An error will occur

Answer: A. Since the string is limited to three characters, only the first three characters of the literal will be displayed.

3. Adding Option Explicit to your Module will:

A. Require you to declare all your variables

B. Start all arrays with position 1

C. Compare strings based on their actual values

D. Compare strings based on their characters

Answer: A. Answer B describes Option Base 1, while answers C and D describe the Option Compare statement.

4. An array is declared as `Dim DispArray(5) As String`. The array can hold how many items?

   A. 4

   B. 5

   C. 6

   D. None, this is an improper declaration

Answer: C. Since arrays start at position 0 (in the absence of an Option Base statement), an array with a final position of 5 can hold 6 items.

5. To test that the value in intTest is greater than 200 you would use:

   A. If intTest > 200 Then

   B. If intTest >= 199 Then

   C. If intTest < 200 Then

   D. If intTest <= 199 Then

Answer: A. The > operator tests for "greater than." The >= operator tests for "greater than or equal to."

6. In your comparisons you do not want "S" to be equal to "s". You should add which statement to your module?

   A. Option Compare Text

   B. Option Compare Exact

   C. Option Compare Binary

   D. Option Explicit

Answer: C. Binary causes characters to be compared based on their internal storage where "S" and "s" have different codes. Option Explicit is used to control variable declarations. The other Option Compare statements will test True when comparing "S" and "s".

7. If you want to ensure that a loop is executed at least once, you should:

   A. Not put the code in a loop

   B. Use the Skip keyword

   C. Put the test in the While statement

   D. Put the test in the Loop statement

Answer: D. By putting the test in the Loop statement you have the test done after the code block is executed at least once.

8. How many times will this loop be executed?

```
For intCounter = 3 To 8 Step 2
Next intCounter
```

A. 2

B. 3

C. 4

D. 5

Answer: B. intCounter begins at 3, which is less than the loop's limit of 10, so the loop executes. The counter then is incremented to 5, still less than the limit of 10, and so executes again. The counter goes to 7, executing again. After executing with intCounter set to 7, the counter is incremented to 9, which is greater than 8, terminating the loop.

9. To create a read-only property on a form you would:

A. Add Property Get and Property Let procedures to your form

B. Add only a Property Get procedure to your form

C. Add only a Property Let procedure to your form

D. You can't create a read-only property

Answer: C. The Property Let procedure is run when a property is read (it is used in a VBA statement with an implied Let).

10. To open a second copy of the CustomerUpdate form you would use:

A. DoCmd.OpenForm CustomerUpdate

B. DoCmd.OpenForm "CustomerUpdate"

C. Set frm = New Form_CustomerUpdate

D. CustomerUpdate.New

Answer: C. The DoCmd methods won't open a second copy of a form.

Chapter 3

1. Which of the following is not a section in an Access form?

   A. Form Header

   B. Page Footer

   C. Group Header

   D. All are valid sections

Answer: C. Forms do not have grouping capabilities.

2. When does a form's Form Header appear?

   A. When the form is displayed on the screen

   B. When the form is printed

   C. Both A and B

   D. Neither A nor B

Answer: C. A form's header appears both when a form is displayed and when it is printed. A form's Page Header appears only when a form is printed.

3. To tie a form to a table or query you would use the form's _____ _____ property.

   A. Record Source

   B. Row Source

   C. Control Source

   D. None of the above

Answer: A. The Row Source property is used by list and combo boxes to specify where the rows they display (but do not update) are to be drawn from. The Control Source property is used by controls to specify which field in the Record Source they are to display and update.

4. You have set the form's Filter property but the form still displays all of the records. You must:

   A. Set the FilterOn property on the properties list.

   B. Set the FilterOn property using VBA.

   C. Select Filter ➤ View.

   D. Do nothing. The filter must be incorrect.

Answer: B. The form's FilterOn property must be set to True before a filter that you have set will take effect. This can only be done from VBA.

5. You have set a form's Record Lock property to No Locks. As a result:

A. No record locks will be used on the recordset.

B. Optimistic locking will be used on the recordset.

C. Pessimistic locking will be used on the recordset.

D. The recordset will be a snapshot.

Answer: B. You can't have a recordset without some kind of locking. No Locks simply limits the lock on a record to the time that it is actually being written. This is called optimistic locking, as it assumes that no changes will occur to a record between the time you view it and the time that you change it.

6. When a user is unable to change a record because it is being viewed by another user, this is called:

A. Optimistic locking

B. Pessimistic locking

C. Table level locking

D. No Locks

Answer: B. Pessimistic locking is implemented when a record is locked as soon as it is viewed by another user.

7. The smallest level of locking for the Jet database engines is:

A. Field level

B. Record level

C. Page level

D. Table level

Answer: C. The Jet engine does not lock records. Instead, the Jet engine locks a 2KB page around the record that is being locked.

8. When a form's default view is set to Form and its Views Allowed is set to Datasheet, how will the form initially display?

A. As a Datasheet

B. As a Form

C. Neither, an error is raised

D. Either, depending on how the user opens the form

Answer: A. Once the Views Allowed is set, it doesn't matter what the default view is.

9. You want a user not to do anything else in your application until they have completed all the entries in a form and closed it. You should:

A. Set the form's Dialog property to No.

B. Set the form's Popup property to Yes.

C. Set the form's Modal property to Yes.

D. This can't be done in Access (without a Windows API call).

Answer: C. A pop-up window is independent of the Access window but still allows you to interact with the rest of the application. There is no Dialog property.

10. To remove a command button from a form at run-time using VBA code, you would:

A. Set the Transparent property to True

B. Set the Locked property to True

C. Set the Visible property to False

D. Use VBA to delete the control

Answer: C. While setting the Transparent property of a control to True would make the control disappear, it would still be active and could be clicked on. Only setting the Visible property to False causes the button to effectively disappear from the form.

11. You have set the Cancel property of a command button to True. You now set another button's Cancel property to True. The result is:

A. Both buttons will be activated when the user presses the Esc key.

B. Neither button will be activated when the user presses the Esc key.

C. The first button set will be activated when the user presses the Esc key.

D. The second button set will be activated when the user presses the Esc key.

Answer: D. Only one button can have its Cancel property set to Yes, and the last button set is the one that retains the setting.

12. To have a list box display only the second field of a query but update the field it is bound to with the first field in the query, you must set the following properties:

   A. Bound Column = 2, Column Count = 2, Column Widths = 1;1

   B. Bound Column = 1, Column Count = 2, Column Widths = 0;1

   C. Bound Column = 2, Column Count = 1, Column Widths = 0;1

   D. Bound Column = 1, Column Count = 2, Column Widths = 1;0

Answer: B. The control source must be bound to the field that is to be used (the first field). The Column Count must be set to the maximum number of fields involved. The Column Widths must be set in the first column to 0 in order to suppress its display.

13. To create a list box that would allow the user to select multiple entries using the Ctrl and Shift keys, you would:

   A. Set the Select property to Extended

   B. Set the Multi-Select property to Extended

   C. Set the Select property to True

   D. Set the Multi-Select property to True

Answer: B. The Select property is used from VBA code to determine which items in a list box have been selected.

14. A report will display data in the order of

   A. The primary key of the table.

   B. The sort order of the underlying Record Source.

   C. The order in the Sorting and Grouping dialog box.

   D. It depends on how the report is opened.

Answer: C. The order of the report is determined only by the setting in the Sorting and Grouping dialog box. If the dialog box is not used, the order of the lines in the report is not guaranteed.

15. To prevent the page header from displaying on the first page of the report, you would:

   A. Set the Page Header/Footer property to Not with Report Header

   B. Set the Page Header/Footer property to Skip First Page

   C. Set the First Page Property to False

   D. Use VBA code

Answer: A. Since the Report Header always prints on the first page of the report, setting the Page Header/Footer property to Not with Report Header ensures that the page headers do not appear on the first page of the report.

16. You have grouped your data by department and want to have each department print on a separate page, with the first page of the report displaying the first department. To do this, you would:

   A. Create a department header and set its Force New Page property to After Section.

   B. Create a department header and set its Force New Page property to Before Section.

   C. Create a department footer and set its Force New Page property to After Section.

   D. Create a department footer and set its Force New Page property to Not With Report Header.

Answer: C. Setting the Force New Page property on the header will cause the first department to print on the second page of the report.

17. To prevent a group from printing only some of its entries at the bottom of a page, you would set:

   A. The Widows/Orphans property to Yes

   B. The Widows/Orphans property to Keep Together

   C. The Keep Together property to Yes

   D. The Keep Together property to Widow/Orphan Control

Answer: C. This selection keeps the entire group together on one page.

Chapter 4

Questions 5, 7, 8, 10, 11, and 12 use the in formation in the following tables.

Customer Table Definition

Field	Type	Size	Notes
CustName	Char	20	Primary Key
SalesRep	Char	20	
CreditCardNumber	Integer		
CustSales	Currency		

SalesRep Table Definition

Field	Type	Size	Notes
RepName	Char	20	Primary Key
TotalSales	Currency		

1. SQL consists of:

   A. DML

   B. DDL

   C. Both A and B

   D. Neither A nor B

Answer: C. The SQL language includes statements both for defining data structures (DDL—Data Definition Language) and manipulating the data in those structures (DML—Data Manipulation Language).

2. Some typical DML commands are:

   A. Select, Update

   B. Create, Drop

   C. Drop, Update

   D. Select, Alter

Answer: A. Select and Update are both Data Manipulation commands. Select is used to retrieve data and Update is used to change it. Drop (to remove tables and indexes), Alter (to change existing table structures), and Create (to define new tables) are all DDL commands.

3. Which of the following is a valid command to create a table?

   A. Create Table NewTable

   B. CreateTable NewTable (my field VarChar(5))

   C. Create Table NewTable (Myfield String)

   D. Create Table NewTable MyField Integer

Answer: C. Create and Table must be two separate words in SQL. A field name may include blanks only if it is enclosed in brackets (such as [my field]). The list of fields for a table must be enclosed in parentheses.

4. To create an index that will not permit records with duplicate values or Nulls in the indexed fields, you would use:

   A. Create Index NewIndex On NewTable (NewField) With Unique, Ignore Null

   B. Create Index NewIndex On NewTable With Primary

   C. Create Index NewIndex On NewTable (NewField) With Primary

   D. Create Index NewIndex On NewTable (NewField) With Unique, Disallow Null

Answer: C. Primary indexes do not permit either Nulls or duplicate records, so specifying "With Primary" is sufficient to meet the demands of the question. The Unique keyword is a predicate and must precede the field list. Ignore Null does not prevent records with Nulls in the key fields to be added to the database.

5. The SalesRep and Customer tables must reference each other. The Customer table must not have a value in the SalesRep field that is not in the SalesRep table. The appropriate command to create this constraint when creating the Customer table is:

A. Create Table Customer
(CustName Char(20),
SalesRep Char(20) Constraint RefSales References SalesRep)

B. Create Table SalesRep
(RepName Char(20) Constraint RefSales References Customer)

C. Create Table SalesRep
(RepName Char(20) Constraint RefSales References
Customer.SalesRep)

D. Create Table Customer
(CustName Char(20), SalesRep (20) Constraint RefSales
References SalesRep.CustName)

Answer: A. The table whose records are being controlled must reference the table that the controlling records are created in. In this case, the Customer records are controlled by the entries in the SalesRep table so the Customer field must reference the SalesRep field. When a field references the primary key of another table, it's not necessary to specify the table but the reference must be to the field in the other table. Since D refers to the CustName field (and not the RepName field), it is also incorrect.

6. You know that creating indexes on fields can speed up queries that join two tables. After creating the Foreign Key in the previous question, in order to speed up joins between the Customer and the SalesRep tables you should:

A. Create an index on the SalesRep field in the Customer table

B. Create an index on the RepName field in the SalesRep table

C. Both A and B

D. Neither A nor B

Answer: D. Since defining a field as Foreign Key or a Primary key automatically creates an index on that field, it is not necessary to add any more indexes.

7. Which of the following statements would speed up a query that listed all customers in order by the SalesRep field and, where a salesperson has more than one customer, list the customers in alphabetical order?

A. Create Index Rep on Customer (CustName,SalesRep)

B. Create Index Rep on Customer (SalesRep, CustName)

C. Create Index Rep on Customer, SalesRep (SalesRep, CustName)

D. None of the above

Answer: B Since customers are to be listed in order by SalesRep first, that field must be the first field in the index. An index must be on one table only.

8. Most customers won't have an entry in the SalesRep field. To speed up a query that finds customers for a specific salesperson, you would use:

A. Create Index FindRep on Customer(RepName) Not Null

B. Create Unique Index FindRep on Customer(RepName)

C. Create Index FindRep on SalesRep(RepName) With Disallow Null

D. Create Index FindRep On Customer (SalesRep) With Ignore Null

Answer: D. The Disallow Null option prevents records with Nulls from being added to a table. The option that the question requires is Ignore Null, which causes records with Nulls to be left out of the index. The index cannot be unique since a salesperson may have many customers and so may appear in the index many times.

9. You need to change the CustomerCreditCard field from numeric to string. To do this you would:

A. Use the Alter command

B. Use the Create Table…Alter command

C. Back up and restore the database

D. Create a new table and copy the data to it

Answer: D. The Alter command in Access SQL will not allow you to change a field's data type. The table will need to be re-created with the new data type and the data copied to it.

10. The following query, called from a program, fails with a message indicating a parameter was missing.

Select *
From SalesRep
Where RepName = Forms!SalesRep!RepName

The most likely cause is:

A. The SalesRep form is not open.

B. The query parameter is missing.

C. The RepName field is empty

D. The table has no records in it.

Answer: A. The query has a Where clause the compares the RepName field on the SalesRep form to a field on the table. If the form is not open, Access treats the reference to the form as a parameter and, since no value was provided for the parameter, fails with a Parameter Missing error message.

11. Which of the following SQL statements correctly extracts records from the Customer and SalesRep tables?

A. Select *
From Customer Join SalesRep
on RepName = CustName

B. Select *
From Join Customer, SalesRep
On RepName = CustName

C. Select *
From Inner Join On Customer, SalesRep
Where RepName = CustName

D. Select *
From Customer Inner Join SalesRep
On RepName = CustName

Answer: D. The format of the From clause is `tablename Inner Join tablename` followed by an On clause that provides the criteria for selecting rows from the Cartesian product.

12. Prior to applying a Foreign Key constraint, you want to find all of the Customers who have a SalesRep that doesn't appear in the SalesRep table. The syntax for this query is:

A. Select CustName, SalesRep
From Customer
Where SalesRep Is Null

B. Select CustName, SalesRep
From Customer Inner Join SalesRep
Where RepName Is Null

C. Select CustName, SalesRep
From Customer Left Join SalesRep
On SalesRep = RepName
Where RepName Is Null

D. Select CustName, SalesRep
From Customer Right Join SalesRep
On SalesRep = RepName
Where RepName Is Null

Answer: C. In order to have Customer records included in the result, even if there is no match in the SalesRep table, you must use an outer join. The Left Join forces all the records in the table on the left side of the Join (the Customer table, in this case) into the result.

13. You have written a query that joined a table of 15 records to another table. You expected to get 15 records back, however, there are only 12 records in the result. The query result includes several duplicated records, which you expected. The most likely cause is:

A. You included Distinct in the query

B. You included DistinctRow in the query

C. You included Unique in the query

D. You must include All in the query

Answer: B. Of the alternatives offered, only Distinct or DistinctRow could be used to eliminate duplicate records (Unique is used when defining constraints). Had Distinct been included in the query, there would have been no duplicated records. However, DistinctRow eliminates records based on duplicate values that are not displayed—so some duplicate records may appear in the query results, because it is undisplayed fields that make the rows distinct.

14. Which query will find the five salespeople with the most sales?

   A. Select Top 5 RepName
      From SalesRep

   B. Select Top(5. RepName
      From SalesRep

   C. Select Top 5 RepName
      From SalesRep
      Order By RepName

   D. Select Top 5 RepName
      From SalesRep
      Order by TotalSales

Answer: D. The Top predicate allows you to restrict the records in the query to a specified number. To get the top five salespeople by sales, the query must be sorted by sales.

15. To total the sales for customers you would use:

   A. Select CustName, Sum(CustSales)
      From Customer
      Group By CustSales

   B. Select CustName, Total(CustSales)
      From Customer
      Group By CustSales

   C. Select CustName, Sum(CustSales)
      From Customer
      Group By CustName

   D. Select CustName, Total(CustSales)
      From Customer
      Group By CustName

Answer: C. In a summary query, each field in the field list must either be in a summary function (like Sum) or referenced in the Group By clause (but not both).

16. Some of the salespeople are also customers of the company. To list all of the customers and salespeople, with any records that are in both tables listed twice, you would use:

   A. Select CustName
      From Customer
      Union

Select RepName
From SalesRep

B. Select CustName
From Customer
Union All
Select RepName
From SalesRep

C. Union
Select CustName
From Customer;
Select RepName
From SalesRep

D. Union All
Select CustName
From Customer;
Select RepName
From SalesRep

Answer: B. The Union statement by itself will eliminate any duplicate records extracted from the two tables. Union All is required to keep duplicate records in the result.

17. To delete all the Customer records where there has never been a value assigned to the SalesRep field, you would use:

A. Delete *
From Customer
Where SalesRep = Null

B. Delete *
From Customer
Where SalesRep Is Null

C. Delete *
From Customer
Where SalesRep = " "

D. Delete *
From Customer
Where SalesRep Is " "

Answer: B. To test if a field contains the Null value, you must use the Is Null test.

Chapter 5

1. Access users have been opening a linked Excel worksheet and making changes in it, which has led to problems with Excel users who need to maintain control over the data. You want to ensure that Access users can't edit the worksheet. Which of the following is the best method?

    A. Change the control to an Image control by right-clicking it and selecting Change to Image Control from the context menu.

    B. Set the control's Enabled property to False.

    C. Set the control's Locked property to True.

    D. Change the control's OLE Type property to Image.

    Answer: A. B and C both work to some extent, but the user might be able to switch to Design view and change these properties so that the worksheet could be edited. D is wrong—there is no such selection and, in any case, that property is read-only. See Exercise 5.7 for details.

2. You have a linked OLE worksheet on a form, and you want to freeze it at a certain point in time, so it won't change when the original Excel worksheet is updated. Which of the following methods is the best way to do this?

    A. Change the control's OLE Type property to Embedded.

    B. Delete the control, then insert the object again, this time leaving the Linked check box in the Insert Object dialog box unselected.

    C. You can't change a linked control into an embedded control.

    D. Click the control, select Edit ➢ OLE/DDE Links on the Access menu, then click the Manual Update option button with the link highlighted.

    Answer: D. B would work too, but it is less convenient. A won't work, because this property is read-only. C is wrong—you can only change the control to embedded by using the method described in D. See the *Automatic vs. Manual Updating of Linked Objects* section for details.

3. You have a table of name and address data in Access, which you need to merge to a Word mail-merge letter from time to time. The computer you are working on has only 12MB of memory. Which of the following methods is the best way to implement this functionality?

    A. Write WordBasic code using the CreateObject function to get the data from Access, using the DAO object model.

B. Use the Word Mail Merge Helper to link to the Access table.

C. Write an Access function to export the table to Word Mail Merge format using the TransferText method, and use the resulting text data table as the Word mail-merge document's data source. Run the function from Access when you need to do the mail merge.

D. Use the Merge It command on the OfficeLinks drop-down list on the Access menu to merge the data to the Word mail-merge letter.

Answer: C. It is an effective method to use in this situation and is the right answer, as it uses minimal memory because it doesn't require Word and Access to run simultaneously. A is wrong—Word is not an OLE controller application, and there is no CreateObject function in WordBasic. B and D will both work on a computer with lots of memory, but they use too much memory to be practical for a computer with, say, 12MB of memory. See the *Controlling Word* section for details.

4. You have imported an Excel worksheet into Access, and you have prepared several grouped reports from the data. You would like to be able to print these reports from a command button in Excel. What is the best way to do this?

A. Write Excel VBA code to create an instance of Access using the CreateObject function, and use the OpenReport method of the DoCmd object in the Access object model to print the reports.

B. Write Excel VBA code to create an instance of Access using the CreateObject function, and use the OpenReport method of the DoCmd object in the DAO object model to print the reports.

C. Select the Print from Access command from the OfficeLinks drop-down list on the Excel menu.

D. You can't print an Access report from Excel.

Answer: A. B is wrong; the DoCmd object is in the Access object model, not the DAO object model. C is wrong; there is no such button on the Excel toolbar. D is wrong; the method in A works to print an Access report from Excel. See the *Controlling Access from Excel* section for details.

5. Users complain that every time they open a form with a linked Excel chart, there is a long delay while the chart is updated. The chart's data really doesn't need to be updated more than once a month or so. How can you modify the control to prevent these long delays while allowing users to update the chart when needed?

   A. Change the linked OLE object control into an Image control by right-clicking it and then selecting Change To Image Control from the context menu.

   B. Change the linked OLE object control into an embedded control by changing its OLE Type property to Embedded.

   C. Change the linked OLE object control's Update type to Manual by clicking the control, selecting Edit ➤ OLE/DDE Links on the Access menu, and then clicking the Manual Update option button with the link highlighted.

   D. Change the Update Type property in the control's properties sheet from Automatic to Manual.

Answer: C. It prevents automatic updating, while allowing manual updating. A is wrong, since it won't allow updates in the future. B is wrong, because the OLE Type property is read-only. D is wrong; there is no Update Type property in the control's properties sheet. See the *Automatic vs. Manual Updating of Linked Objects* section for details.

6. Let's say that you write code to create a Word document and insert text into it, and then run the code. But after the code stops, the new Word document is not open. How can you keep the Word document open after the code has run?

   A. Put objWord.Preserve at the end of the code.

   B. Put a Stop command at the end of the code.

   C. There is no way to keep a document created by the CreateObject function open after the code finishes running.

   D. Open Word before running the code.

Answer: D. Word is a multiple-instance server, so if you create a new Word document with CreateObject when Word is open, the new document is created as a child document, and Word (and your document) remains open after the code stops.

7. You should use the _____ function when you want to set a reference to an existing document.

   A. GetObject

   B. UseObject

   C. CreateObject

   D. GetFile

Answer: A. GetObject can open a specific file; CreateObject just opens the application.

8. To free memory used by an Excel OLE Automation session, use the _____ command:

   A. objExcel.Quit

   B. objExcel.Close

   C. objExcel.Exit

   D. Set objExcel = Nothing

Answer: D. A closes Excel, but only setting the Excel object to Nothing frees the memory.

9. Which of the following are correct ways to declare and set an Excel object (select two)?

   A. Dim xcl As Excel.Application
      Set xcl = New Excel.Application

   B. Dim xcl As New Excel.Application

   C. Dim xcl As Object
      Set xcl = CreateOject("Excel.Application")

   D. Dim xcl As Object
      Set xcl = New Excel.Application

Answer: Both A and C will work, although A will work only if you have checked the Excel Type Library entry in the Tools ➤ References dialog box.

10. To create a server entered by the user at run-time, use
_____.

A. GetObject

B. The New keyword

C. CreateObject

D. You can't create a server in this manner.

Answer: C. CreateObject can be used to create a server from a user entry, as in the following code.

```
Set obj = CreateObject(InputBox("Enter a class name"))
```

Chapter 6

1. The DAO object model is hierarchical because:

A. Some objects inherit properties from other objects.

B. Some objects are lower in priority than others.

C. Some objects can only be accessed from other objects.

D. It represents a hierarchical database structure.

Answer: C. All DAO objects except the DBEngine object can only be accessed through the methods or properties of other DAO objects.

2. In order to determine if you can make updates to the database you should:

A. Check the Updateable property

B. Trap for update errors

C. Check the ReadOnly property

D. Use the DBStatus method

Answer: A. While you could try an update and catch the error, checking the Updateable property of the Database object is simpler and cleaner.

3. To work with the tblCustomer table in a database you would use:

    A. Set tbl = dbs.Tables("tblCustomer")

    B. Set tbl = dbs. tblCustomer

    C. Set tbl = Tables("tblCustomer")

    D. Set tbl = dbs.TableDefs("tblCustomer")

Answer: D. There is no Tables collection in DAO.

4. Which of the following objects is created automatically by DAO?

    A. WorkAreas(1)

    B. Workspaces(0)

    C. Workspaces(1)

    D. DBEngine(0)

Answer: B. DAO creates the DBEngine and the first Workspaces object. The Workspaces collection is zero based, so the first object in it is number 0. The other collections don't exist.

5. To add a table to a database with DAO you would use:

    A. The CreateTable method of the DBEngine object

    B. The CreateTableDef method of the Database object

    C. The CreateTableDef method of the DBEngine object

    D. The CreateTable method of the Database object

Answer: B. There is no CreateTable method (you are creating not a table but the table structure, hence the name CreateTableDef) and it belongs to the Database object.

6. To create a table that wouldn't appear in the database window you would use:

    A. tbl.CreateTable(,,False)

    B. tbl.Visible = False

    C. tbl.Hide = True

    D. tbl.Attributes = dbHiddenObject

Answer: D. The Attributes property controls whether a table is visible or a system table, among other characteristics.

7. When using the CreateField method you must supply:

   A. No parameters

   B. The name parameter

   C. The name and type parameters

   D. The name, type, and size parameters

Answer: A. The CreateField method can be used without any parameters, but you must set the appropriate properties of the Field object before appending it

8. To create a date field you would use:

   A. tbl.CreateField("Afield",dbDate)

   B. fld.Date = True

   C. tbl.CreateField("Afield,dbDate,8)

   D. fld.Type = Date

Answer: A. The date data type does not accept a field size and the field's type property must be set to one of the predefined constants like dbDate.

9. When creating a field you must provide the size parameter for _____ fields.

   A. Integer

   B. OLE

   C. Text

   D. B and C

Answer: C. Only the Text field requires a field size.

10. You attempt to read the Caption property of a field property and get an error message because:

   A. The Caption property is write-only.

   B. Field objects don't have a Caption property.

   C. You were reading the property into a string variable instead of a Text variable.

   D. The Caption property hasn't been created.

Answer: D. The caption property is an Access-defined property and is not always present. There are no Text variables (they are a SQL data type).

11. To determine the last time a table's data was updated, you would check:

A. The LastUpdated property.

B. The results of the LastUpdate method.

C. The DateUpdate property.

D. You cannot check this from DAO.

Answer: D. The LastUpdated property is the last date that the table's definition (or structure) was changed, not when the data in the table was altered.

12. Which of the following code would successfully add a property to a field?

A. Set prp = tbl.CreateProperty("NewProp",dbText,"Avalue")
fld.Properties.Append prp

B. Set prp = fld.CreateProperty("NewProp",dbText,"Avalue")
fld.Properties.Append "NewProp"

C. Set prp = tbl.CreateProperty("NewProp",dbText,"Avalue")
fld.Properties("Avalue").Append

D. Set prp = fld.CreateProperty("NewProp")
fld.Properties.Append prp

Answer: A. You don't have to create a Field property from a Field object. D is wrong because you must set the Property object's type and value before appending it.

13. The steps for adding an index to a table are:

1. Add the index to the indexes collection of the table.

2. Create the index.

3. Add a field to the index.

4. Create a field.

The correct order in which to perform them is:

A. 1, 2, 3, 4

B. 2, 4, 3, 1

C. 4, 3, 1, 2

D. 4, 3, 2, 1

Answer: B. You cannot add a field to an index after it has been appended, and you must create the index before adding a field to it.

14. Setting an index's Primary property to True has what effect?

   A. The Required property will be set to True.

   B. The Unique property will be set to True.

   C. A and B.

   D. Neither A or B.

Answer: C. A primary key is always Unique (no duplicate records) and Required (no Nulls allowed).

15. Which of the following code snippets will create a relationship between the tblCustomer table and the tblCustomerAddress table where each customer can have several addresses?

   A. dbs.CreateRelation ("ARel", "tblCustomerAddress", "tblCustomer")

   B. dbs.CreateRelation ("ARel", "tblCustomer", "tblCustomerAddress")

   C. dbs.TableDefs("tblCustomer").CreateRelation ("ARel", "tblCustomerAddress")

   D. dbs.CreateRelationship ("ARel", "tblCustomer", "tblCustomerAddress")

Answer: B. CreateRelationship is a method of the database object. The second parameter is the name of the primary table (the one with a single record).

16. The primary benefit in creating a QueryDef is:

   A. Improved performance

   B. Smaller query size

   C. Larger recordsets

   D. Ease of use

Answer: A. Creating a QueryDef allows you to save a query in a compiled state, which saves on compile time when you execute the query.

17. The following code snippet fails because:

Set qdf = dbs.CreateQueryDef("","Update tblSalesRep Set Salary = Salary * 1.1")

Set rst = qdf.OpenRecordset()

  A. The query is missing its Where clause.

  B. The query has no name.

  C. CreateQueryDef is a method of the Table object.

  D. The OpenRecordset method shouldn't be used.

Answer: D. For action queries, you must use the Execute method.

18. The GetCustomer QueryDef has a parameter called Customer-Number. The correct code to set that parameter is:

  A. dbs.QueryDefs("CustomerNumber") = "1234"

  B. dbs.QueryDefs("GetCustomer").Parameters("CustomerNumber") = "1234"

  C. dbs.Parameters("CustomerNumber").QueryDefs("GetCustomer") = "1234"

  D. dbs.Parameters("CustomerNumber") = "1234"

Answer: B. The Parameters collection is a property of the QueryDef object, which is a member of the QueryDefs collection, which, in turn, is a property of the Database object.

19. After executing a Delete query you determine the number of records deleted by checking the _____ property.

  A. RecordCount

  B. RecordsAffected

  C. RecordsDeleted

  D. UpdateCount

Answer: A. RecordCount is the number of records accessed in a recordset.

20. To retrieve the date that the Customer form was created you would use:

  A. dbs.Documents("Customer").Containers("Forms")

  B. dbs.Documents("Forms").Containers("Customer")

  C. dbs.Containers("Forms").Documents("Customer")

  D. dbs.Containers("Customer").Documents("Forms")

Answer: C. Form information is stored in Document objects that are in the Documents collection of Container objects.

Chapter 7

1. You need to find the record in a recordset that was last changed. Which of the following is the right way to do this?

   A. Use the LastModified property.

   B. Use the LastUpdated property.

   C. Use the MoveLast method on an indexed recordset.

   D. Use the EOF property.

   Answer: A. The LastModified property will take you to the record that was modified most recently. MoveLast will take you to the last record in index order, EOF will take you beyond the last record, and LastUpdated only gives you the date the table structure was last modified.

2. Which of the following code samples will ensure that you get an accurate count of records in a dynaset?

   A. rst.RecordCount

   B. rst.EOF
   rst.RecordCount

   C. rst.MoveLast
   rst.RecordCount

   D. rst.Count

   Answer: C is correct. With dynasets, you need to access all the records in a recordset to get an accurate count with RecordCount, and MoveLast is the most convenient way to do this.

3. Assuming that the recordset and relevant field are both updatable, which two of these code samples would update the record?

   A.
```
Dim dbs As DATABASE
Dim rst As Recordset

Set dbs = CurrentDb()
Set rst = dbs.OpenRecordset("tblShippingMethods")
With rst
    .AddNew
    !ShippingMethod = "Flying Packets"
    .UPDATE
    .Close
End With
```

B.
```
Dim dbs As DATABASE
Dim rst As Recordset

Set dbs = CurrentDb()
Set rst = dbs.OpenRecordset("tblShippingMethods")
rst.MoveLast
rst.Delete
```

C.
```
Dim dbs As DATABASE
Dim rst As Recordset

Set dbs = CurrentDb()
Set rst = dbs.OpenRecordset("tblShippingMethods")
With rst
    .MoveLast
    .Edit
    !ShippingMethod = "Fast Deliveries"
    .Close
End With
```

D.
```
Dim dbs As DATABASE
Dim rst As Recordset
Dim strFind As String

strFind = "[ShippingMethod] = 'Fast Deliveries'"

Set dbs = CurrentDb()
Set rst = dbs.OpenRecordset("tblShippingMethods",
dbOpenDynaset)
With rst
    .FindNext strFind
    !ShippingMethod = "Faster Deliveries"
    .UPDATE
    .Close
End With
```

Answer: A and B are correct. A has the Edit method before the edit, and the Update method after it to save the record. B has the Delete method, which doesn't require the Update method to make the deletion.

4. Which property should you check to determine whether a record was found before trying to edit a record?

    A. Found

    B. NotFound

    C. Match

    D. NoMatch

Answer: D.

5. Use the _____ method to add a new record to a recordset.

    A. Add

    B. Append

    C. AddNew

    D. NewRecord

Answer: C.

6. You need to be able to return to the record you were on if a Find* method fails. Which of the following would work?

    A.
```
Dim dbs As DATABASE
Dim rst As Recordset
Dim varBookmark As Variant

Set dbs = CurrentDb()
Set rst = dbs.OpenRecordset("tblShippingMethods",
dbOpenTable)
With rst
    varBookmark = .Bookmark
    .INDEX = "PrimaryKey"
    .Seek "=", 2
    If .NoMatch Then .Bookmark = varBookmark
    Debug.Print !ShippingMethod
    .Close
End With
```

    B.
```
Dim dbs As DATABASE
Dim rst As Recordset
Dim strBookmark As String

Set dbs = CurrentDb()
Set rst = dbs.OpenRecordset("tblShippingMethods",
dbOpenTable)
```

```
    With rst
        strBookmark = .Bookmark
        .INDEX = "PrimaryKey"
        .Seek "=", 2
        If .NoMatch Then .Bookmark = strBookmark
        Debug.Print !ShippingMethod
        .Close
    End With
```

C.
```
Dim dbs As DATABASE
Dim rst As Recordset

Set dbs = CurrentDb()
Set rst = dbs.OpenRecordset("tblShippingMethods",
dbOpenTable)
With rst
    .INDEX = "PrimaryKey"
    .Seek "=", 2
    If .NoMatch Then .Bookmark
    Debug.Print !ShippingMethod
    .Close
End With
```

D.
```
Dim dbs As DATABASE
Dim rst As Recordset
Dim varBookmark As Variant

Set dbs = CurrentDb()
Set rst = dbs.OpenRecordset("tblShippingMethods",
dbOpenTable)
varBookmark = .Bookmark
With rst
    .INDEX = "PrimaryKey"
    .Seek "=", 2
    If .NoMatch Then .Bookmark = varBookmark
    Debug.Print !ShippingMethod
    .Close
End With
```

Answer: A is correct. It uses a variable of Variant type to represent the bookmark, and sets it for each record before doing the search, so as to enable returning to that record if the search fails.

7. Which two of the following code samples will iterate through all the records in a table-type recordset?

A.
```
Dim dbs As Database
    Dim rst As Recordset

    Set dbs = CurrentDb
    Set rst = dbs.OpenRecordset("tblContacts")

    Do While Not rst.EOF
        Debuq.Print rst![LastName]
    Loop
```

B.
```
Dim dbs As Database
    Dim rst As Recordset

    Set dbs = CurrentDb
    Set rst = dbs.OpenRecordset("tblContacts")

    Do While Not rst.EOF
        Debug.Print rst![LastName]
        rst.MoveNext
    Loop
```

C.
```
Dim dbs As Database
    Dim rst As Recordset

    Set dbs = CurrentDb
    Set rst = dbs.OpenRecordset("tblContacts")

    For Each fld In rst
        Debug.Print rst![Last Name]
    Next fld
```

D.
```
Dim dbs As Database
    Dim rst As Recordset

    Set dbs = CurrentDb
    Set rst = dbs.OpenRecordset("tblContacts")

    Do Until rst.EOF
        Debug.Print rst![LastName]
        rst.MoveNext
    Loop
```

Answer: B and D are correct. A won't go to the next record, and C won't work, because the For Each...Next construct only works for collections, and a recordset is not a collection.

8. You write the code below to open a recordset clone, based on a form's recordset, and move to a new record in the recordset clone. After running the code, which record are you on in the form's recordset?

```
Private Sub cboSearch_AfterUpdate()

    Dim strSearch As String

    strSearch = "[LastName] = " & Chr$(34) & Me!
    ➡ [cboSearch] & Chr$(34)
    Me.RecordsetClone.FindFirst strSearch

End Sub
```

A. The same record as the recordset clone

B. The first record

C. The same record as the form

D. At the beginning of the file (BOF is True)

Answer: C is correct. The recordset pointers of the form's recordset and the recordset clone are independent, and the search only moved the pointer in the recordset clone. You need to set the form's bookmark equal to the recordset clone's bookmark to get the two recordsets synched.

9. When you add new records to a table-type recordset with its Index property set to a valid index, the new records are placed:

A. At the end of the recordset

B. In indexed order

C. At the beginning of the recordset

D. In a random location

Answer: B is correct.

10. If a recordset's LockEdits property is set to True, _____ locking is in effect for the recordset.

A. Optimistic

B. Pessimistic

C. Read-only

D. Write-only

Answer: B is correct.

Chapter 8

1. You need to use a variable (intChoice) declared as Public in the frmOrders form's CBF module. Which syntax is correct?

   A. You can't reference a variable located in another form's module.

   B. Forms!frmOrders.intChoice

   C. frmOrders.intChoice

   D. frmOrders!intChoice

   Answer: B. You can reference a variable in another form or report module, so long as it is declared as Public.

2. You create the following function and run it three times, with the argument 5. What is the number in the message box on the third time the function is run?

   ```
   Public Function RunningCount(ByVal intInput As Integer) As
   ➡ Integer

       Static intCount As Integer

       intCount = intCount + intInput
       RunningCount = intCount

       MsgBox "Running Count: " & intCount

   End Function
   ```

   A. 5

   B. 0

   C. 15

   D. 10

   Answer: C. The previous value is preserved and 5 is added to it each time you run the function.

3. You close the module containing the function in question 2 and run the function again. What is the count in the message box?

   A. 0

   B. 15

   C. 10

   D. 20

   Answer: D. Although the module is closed, the application is still running, so the static variable's value was preserved.

4. You close the entire application, then reopen it and run the function in question 2 again. What is the count in the message box?

   A. 5

   B. 10

   C. 15

   D. 20

Answer: A. Closing the application cleared the static variable's value, so you are starting over again.

5. You are having problems with code failing at a certain point when you run it. Which two of these strategies would be helpful in debugging the code?

   A. Set a breakpoint in the code, highlight the line of code before the problem area, and select Run ➤ Set Next Statement.

   B. Set a breakpoint in the code, highlight the line of code before the problem area, and select Run ➤ Set To Cursor.

   C. Set watches on the variables used in the problem area of code, set a breakpoint in the code before the problem area, and step through it, observing the values of variables as they change in the Debug Window.

   D. Set a breakpoint in the code, highlight the line of code after the problem area, and select Run ➤ Set Next Statement.

Answer: A and C. Set Next Statement should be used before the area you want to step through; Set To Cursor should be used to stop execution before a problem area (it won't help you debug the problem area). Setting watches and stepping through the problem area will give you maximum information for debugging the problem.

6. You have a procedure that calls a number of other procedures, all of which have been debugged. Your procedure has problems and needs debugging. Which of the following tools should you use in this case (assuming you have set a breakpoint in your code before the problem area)?

   A. The Step Into button on the VB toolbar

   B. The F8 function key

   C. The F5 function key

   D. The Step Over button on the VB toolbar

Answer: D. The Step Over button will step through your procedure line by line, but will skip over the already debugged called procedures.

7. You write a function to make certain changes to data on forms, using the Forms collection in your code. After running the function with no error messages, you open a form and find that its data has not been changed. What is the most likely reason?

   A. There is an error in the code.

   B. The form whose data wasn't changed was closed when the function was run.

   C. The For Each…Next construct doesn't work with collections.

   D. All forms have to be closed for the code to work.

Answer: B. The Forms collection includes only the currently open forms.

8. You write a function in a CBF module, using the Me keyword to reference a control on a subform's main form, then move the function to a standard module. When you run the function, you get an "Invalid use of Me keyword" compile error. How can you fix this problem?

   A. Change the Me keyword into a specific form reference, such as Forms![frmAuthors].

   B. Call the function from an event procedure on the form.

   C. Change "Me" to "Forms".

   D. Change the reference to Forms![frmAuthors]!Me.

Answer: A. You can't use the Me or Parent keywords from standard modules; you have to use specific form references, or iterate through the Forms collection.

9. You need to manipulate the Access window in a way that can't be done with Access VBA. What tool would be helpful here?

   A. The Windows API

   B. The Office API

   C. Assembly language

   D. C++

Answer: A. You can make API calls in Access VBA to use functions stored in the DLLs that comprise the Windows API.

10. An "Invalid Use of Null" error message when running a function most likely results from:

  A. Trying to assign a Null to a variable whose data type can't accept Nulls

  B. Trying to assign an empty string to a variable whose data type can't accept Nulls

  C. Trying to save a record with no value in a field whose Required property is set to Yes

  D. Trying to save a record with no value in a field whose Allow Zero Length property is set to No

Answer: A. C would result in a "Field *fieldname* can't contain a null value" message, and B and D won't cause an error.

Chapter 9

1. What is the difference between a single- and a multi-tiered application?

  A. The total number of tables equals or exceeds five.

  B. Queries are sent to the back-end using ODBC SQL.

  C. All joins are of the left outer variety.

  D. In a multi-tier application the interface code can be located on the workstation.

Answer: D. A Single-tier application retains all data, logic, and interface code in one file.

2. What is the most effective use of a multi-tiered application?

  A. To increase productivity in a small workgroup

  B. To increase activity in a small workgroup

  C. To improve access speed in a large workgroup

  D. To separate the front-end from the back-end

Answer: C. A and B do not necessarily apply as they are small workgroups and put a much lighter load on the server and the application. D is a byproduct of the answer, not an answer unto itself.

3. Which of the following are possible applications of the Total Access model?

   A. A small office with few workstations and no major traffic requirements

   B. A data warehousing facility

   C. A high volume sales environment with 150 salespersons

   D. A law firm where the system is used to store and retrieve client information

Answer: A, B, and D. These are all examples of low- to mid-volume network activity. C would present a problem to the Total Access Model as it requires more back-end activity and greater security.

4. Which front-end/back-end combination works best with ODBC? (Select two.)

   A. Access/Access

   B. Access/FoxPro

   C. Access/SQL Server

   D. Access/Text File

Answer: Any of these would work well with ODBC since there are drivers available for all of the back-ends represented here. However, A and C are the most common and efficient combinations of the lot.

5. What are the three types of outer join?

   A. Left, right, and obtuse

   B. Far, near, and center

   C. Left, right, and full

   D. There are only two: left and right

Answer: C. The left, right, and full outer joins are the three valid join types.

6. What does separating the interface from the system logic accomplish?

   A. Gives you a thinner application

   B. Increases modularity

   C. Streamlines the data

   D. Streamlines the codebase

Answer: B. By separating the logic code from the interface code the system becomes more scalable, and, therefore, easier to manage as the uses of the application grow. A is somewhat correct, but this applies only to the interface application, in this case, Access. Splitting a database does not decrease the amount of code; to the contrary, it increases it somewhat.

7. What are the benefits of using SQL Server as a back-end? (Select two.)

  A. Simpler indexing

  B. Less code

  C. Scalability

  D. Better network performance

Answer: C and D. Since SQL is more or less an industry standard, it lends itself to a larger number of solutions. This relates to network performance due to front-end vendors' common choice to optimize their solutions for SQL.

8. Under what circumstances would you use linking rather than importing?

  A. As a way of making the incoming data native, which improves data warehousing.

  B. Linking is required if the solution calls for ODBC.

  C. The solution calls for immediate access to the latest data.

  D. As a much more efficient way of handling archived data.

Answer: C. Linking allows databases to share data that is updated and accessed often. Linking does not make the data native, nor does it require the use of ODBC, unless the solution calls for a back-end other than Access.

9. What is the best reason for trapping your application's errors?

  A. It benefits the end-user and the developer because it allows them to understand more clearly what the problem is.

  B. It lowers support costs.

  C. It prevents the error from occurring in the first place.

  D. It promotes end-user troubleshooting techniques.

Answer: A. Trapping allows the user to more clearly describe the problem to support. Also, the developer spent time creating the error trapping code, which affords the developer a better understanding of the potential problems with the application. Trapping does not lower support costs significantly (it merely makes help desk work less stressful), nor does it prevent errors from happening.

10. Which of these are ways a system administrator can care for a database? (Select two.)

    A. Compact the database to improve speed and eliminate unused space.

    B. Use Norton Utilities to identify and replace corrupted objects.

    C. Repair the database for improved overall performance.

    D. Add RAM to the server.

    Answer: A and C. Neither B nor D are correct. Norton Utilities does not include Access repair utilities. Adding RAM does not introduce benefits that directly affect the database.

11. Which of the following are ways to optimize a server for best operation?

    A. Defragment your hard drive regularly.

    B. Don't use wallpaper or desktop themes.

    C. Eliminate the Office shortcut bar.

    D. All of the above.

    Answer: D. Performing routine upkeep on your server will ensure smooth operations.

12. Which of the following are ways to speed up the back-end? (Select two.)

    A. Split your database.

    B. Eliminate unnecessary graphics.

    C. Utilize ODBC connectivity for all queries.

    D. Make use of SQL pass-through.

    Answer: A and B. ODBC and SQL both add overhead to a multi-user environment. More specifically, using ODBC exclusively eliminates the benefits of using a native back-end. Also, using pass-through adds overhead if the queries also require updates to the original data, which requires more operations be executed, which in turn can add overhead.

Chapter 10

1. Why should you set permissions in a secured database for Groups rather than for Users?

   A. To make it easier to administer.

   B. There is no such thing.

   C. So that the database will compile.

   D. You can't assign permissions directly to Users anyway.

   Answer: A. Administering individual permissions for users is time-consuming, tedious, and unnecessary.

2. If your database is replicated, you can:

   A. Use the database password feature to implement share-level security.

   B. Use the database password feature to implement user-level security.

   C. Implement security using share-level security.

   D. Implement security using user-level security.

   Answer: C. All users must be members of the Users group. If you create a new user in the UI, they are automatically added to the Users group, but not when you create them in code.

3. Which query property and setting allows you to create row-level or column-level security on your tables?

   A. The Caption set to User's.

   B. The Description set to Owner's.

   C. Run Permissions set to Owner's.

   D. Access does not support row-level or column-level security.

   Answer: D. The database password feature (or share-level security) is not available with a replicated database.

4. How do you distribute a secured library database without requiring your users to log on?

   A. Secure the library database normally, assigning permissions to custom groups. Remove the password from the Admin user and distribute the workgroup file used to secure the database.

   B. Secure the library database normally. Remove the Admin account from the Admins group and revoke all permissions from the Users group to view the code in the library database. Do not distribute the workgroup file with the database.

   C. Simply remove the Admin account from the Admins group and clear the password for the Admin account.

   D. Secure the library database normally. Delete the Admins group so it will not have administer permissions on the library database. Do not distribute the workgroup file with the database.

Answer: A. Omitting any of the necessary steps involved in securing your database can cause security not to work.

5. Which database property can you set to prevent users from being able to hold down the Shift key and bypass your Startup options or AutoExec macro when opening a database?

   A. AutoShiftOff

   B. AutoShiftOn

   C. AllowBypassKey

   D. BypassStartup

Answer: C. You can create the AllowBypassKey property in code to disable users bypassing your Startup form or AutoExec macro.

6. Which two properties of a Document or Container object can you check in code to see if a user has permissions set for a given object? Which logical operator do you use?

   A. The Permissions property and the AllPermissions property along with the logical AND operator.

   B. The Permissions property and the AllPermissions property along with the logical OR operator.

   C. The Permissions property and the AllPermissions property along with the logical AND NOT operator.

D. The DocPermissions and ConPermissions properties along with the logical OR operator.

Answer: B. If the Admin account is removed from the Admins group and is only a member of the Users group, then the Admin user in an unsecured environment will only have permissions that you assign to the Users group in a secured database.

7. Which logical operator(s) do you use to set specific permissions on an object without affecting the user's existing permissions?

   A. XOR

   B. AND

   C. OR

   D. IIF

Answer: B

8. Which logical operator(s) do you use to remove permissions on an object without affecting the user's existing permissions?

   A. XOR

   B. AND NOT

   C. OR NOT

   D. IF NOT

Answer: C

9. Which is the best method to use when relinking tables and what permissions do you need to set for users in the source table database in order for them to use this method?

   A. The .Connect property. No permissions are needed on the underlying tables.

   B. The TransferDatabase action. No permissions are needed on the underlying tables.

   C. The .RefreshLink method. No permissions are needed on the underlying tables.

   D. The .AttachTable method. No permissions are needed on the underlying tables.

Answer: B

10. When you create a new user in code using the CreateUser method, what additional step do you need to take?

    A. None. The CreateUser method alone is sufficient.

    B. Add the new user to the Admins group.

    C. Add the new user to the Users group.

    D. Create a new custom group for the new user.

Answer: A. Remember that you need to grant Open/Run permissions on the table database itself and to grant full permissions on the links in the destination database.

Chapter 11

1. Which of the following methods will enable a regular Access database for replication?

    A. Drag a copy of the database and drop it onto the Windows Briefcase icon.

    B. Drag a copy of the database and drop it onto a shared network folder.

    C. Write code to set the database's Replicable property to "Synchronize."

    D. Use the built-in Access menu commands.

Answer: A and D. You can use both the Windows Briefcase and the Access menus to convert a database to a replica.

2. When you create a replica in code, how do you make it the Design Master?

    A. Set its Replicable property to Design Master.

    B. You don't need to do anything. A Design Master is created automatically if none exists.

    C. Set its DesignMasterID equal to its ReplicaID.

    D. Set its DesignMasterID property to True.

Answer: C. Setting a replica's DesignMasterID equal to its ReplicaID designates it as the Design Master.

3. How can you schedule synchronizations for users at different locations over a WAN?

A. Drag everyone's replica into the Windows Briefcase located on a central server.

B. Use the scheduling services available in the Replication Manager.

C. Write code to copy the replica to the different locations.

D. Use the built-in Access menus.

Answer: B. The Replication Manager provides the only scheduling capabilities for synchronizations in Access.

4. How is each record in a replicated table distinguished from the same record in other replicas?

A. Each record is identified by its ReplicaID, or GUID.

B. Each record is identified by its Replication ID, or GUID.

C. Each record is identified by its AutoNumber field set to Random instead of increment.

D. Each record is identified by its AutoNumber field set to a GUID.

Answer: B. The Replication ID, or GUID, is added to a table to uniquely identify each record.

5. How is each replica in a Replica Set distinguished from the other replicas?

A. By its unique Replication ID

B. By its Replicable property

C. By its name

D. By its unique ReplicaID

Answer: D. Each replica has a unique ReplicaID.

6. If there is a conflict during synchronization, how does Access determine the winning record?

A. The record with the most changes wins.

B. The most recently changed record wins.

C. The record with the fewest changes wins.

D. Neither record wins. Both are written to the conflict table so you can choose later.

Answer: A. The record with the most changes will be written to the table.

7. What happens to the losing record in a synchronization conflict?

   A. It is deleted.

   B. It is saved in a conflict table in the winning replica.

   C. It is saved in a conflict table in the losing replica.

   D. The system administrator is notified by e-mail.

Answer: C. The losing record in a synchronization conflict is saved into a conflict table named *<tablename>*_Conflict.

8. Jackie is editing a record in one replica and changes the Last Name field. Pat is editing the same record in another replica and changes the First Name field. The record was edited only once in each replica since the last synchronization. What happens when the two replicas are next synchronized?

   A. Both replicas reflect the changes to the Last Name and First Name fields.

   B. Both replicas end up with a conflict table showing the field that was different from the one saved in the current replica.

   C. The replica with the lowest ReplicaID wins, and the losing record is written to the Conflict table in the winning replica.

   D. The replica with the lowest ReplicaID wins, and the losing record is written to the Conflict table in the losing replica.

Answer: D. In the case of a tie, the replica with the lowest ReplicaID wins and the losing record is written to a Conflict table in the losing replica.

9. Which of the following applications would be a good candidate for replication?

   A. An order entry system where salespeople are out on the road taking orders on their laptop computers

   B. A ticket selling operation with multiple branches in the same city

   C. A banking application with a high volume of transactions

   D. An online trading system for an investment bank

Answer: A. Replication is well suited to the "traveling salesman" scenario. Applications requiring a high degree of data consistency or have a high transaction volume are better suited to a client/server architecture.

10. Identify some of the changes the Jet database engine makes to a replicated database:

    A. New tables, fields, and database properties are added. Queries now run across multiple replicas.

    B. New tables, fields, and database properties are added. These are stored in the Replication Manager for future reference.

    C. New tables, fields, and database properties are added. The behavior of AutoNumber fields is changed from Increment to Random.

    D. New tables, fields, and database properties are added. The data type of all AutoNumber fields is changed from Long Integer to GUID.

Answer: C. New tables, fields, and database properties are added. The behavior of AutoNumber fields is changed from Increment to Random.

11. How do you keep an object from being replicated?

    A. Write code to set its Synchronization property to False before replicating the database.

    B. Write code to set its KeepLocal property to "T" before replicating the database.

    C. Write code to set its Replicable property to False before replicating the database.

    D. Write code to set its Replication ID property to Null before replicating the database.

Answer: B. Objects can be kept local by creating and setting the KeepLocal property before the database is replicated.

12. Jackie is editing a record in one replica and changes the Last Name field to Cartman. Pat is editing the same record in another replica and also changes the Last Name field to Cartman. The record was edited only once in each replica since the last synchronization. What happens when the two replicas are next synchronized?

    A. Both replicas have the same value in the LastName field. No conflict is recorded.

    B. Both replicas end up with a conflict table showing the field was changed. The old value is kept in each replica.

    C. The replica with the lowest ReplicaID wins, and the losing record is written to the Conflict table in the winning replica.

    D. The replica with the lowest ReplicaID wins, and the losing record is written to the Conflict table in the losing replica.

Answer: A. Access is smart enough to detect when potential conflict records are identical and no conflict occurs.

Chapter 12

1. Simply distributing the application with the run-time version of Access doesn't stop users from modifying the application because:

   A. You must apply security to a run-time version of an Access application for it to run.

   B. Users could open the application with the full version of Access.

   C. Users could use F11 to open the Database window and add objects.

   D. You should compile your code first to make it unreadable.

   Answer: B. You don't need security to use the run-time version of Access, and the run-time version prevents the Database window from being displayed. Compiling your code has no effect on its readability.

2. A user calls to say that an application has suddenly started failing with a Function Not Found message. You recognize the function as a member of a library. The most likely cause is that the user has:

   A. Compiled the application database

   B. Moved the application database

   C. Compiled the library database

   D. Moved the library database

   Answer: D. The References list item for a library holds the complete path name for the library. As a result, if the library is moved to a new directory, the application database cannot find it.

3. In your library you have some code that executes an OpenForm command. The form must be in:

   A. The library MDB

   B. The application MDB

   C. Either A or B

   D. Neither A nor B

   Answer: C. While the library code will look first in the library database, if it doesn't find the form there, it will look for it in the application MDB.

4. You can deliver an Access Add-in as:

   A. A Wizard, Library, or Builder

   B. A Library, Builder, or Menu Add-in

   C. A Menu Add-in, Builder, or Wizard

   D. A Builder, Wizard, or Library

Answer: C. As soon as a database gets a USysRegInfo table and appears on the Add-ins, list it is a Wizard, Builder, or Menu Add-in and not just a library anymore.

5. You have a form that will help users set the properties that a label should have whenever a label is added to a form. You should deliver it as:

   A. A Wizard

   B. A Builder

   C. A Menu Add-In

   D. None of the above

Answer: B. A single form that updates a number of properties would be best classified as a Builder. Only if the routine had a number of forms would it be classified as a Wizard. Menu Add-ins are not invoked when a control is added to a form.

6. Access looks to the Windows Registry to find out about how to use your add-in. You should put the Registry information about your add-in:

   A. In the Registry

   B. In the USysRegInfo table

   C. In the Setup Wizard

   D. In the documentation

Answer: B. While putting the information in the documentation isn't a bad idea, the information must be in the USysRegInfo table where Access will transfer it to the Registry when it installs the add-in.

7. You want to write some code to create a report. To add a control to the report you would use:

A. CreateControl

B. CreateReportControl

C. CreateForm

D. CreateFormControl

Answer: B. CreateForm creates a form; CreateControl adds a control to a form; CreateReportControl adds a control to a report.

8. You need to prevent users from modifying an application's design or examining the code. Some of the users have the full version of Access on their systems, and some don't. Which of the following methods is the best way to achieve this goal?

A. Prepare a run-time version of the application, without security, and distribute the application in the form of setup disks or network files.

B. Prepare a secured version of the application and distribute the .MDB files to the users.

C. Secure the application; then prepare a run-time version of the secured application and distribute the application in the form of setup disks or network files.

D. Prepare a run-time version of the application, and secure it; then distribute the application in the form of setup disks or network files.

Answer: C. Users both with Access and without it will be able to use the application, and neither type of user will be able to modify the design or examine the code. A is wrong, because users with the full version of Access will be able to modify the design or examine the code. B won't work because users without Access won't be able to use the application. D is wrong, because setting up security creates new files, and you would have run the Setup Wizard again to re-create the run-time application with security. Also, setting up security generally takes a lot of testing and verification, and it is best to get this over with before preparing the run-time application.

9. To store a value in the Registry it must have:

   A. A key name

   B. A subkey name

   C. A valuename

   D. All of the above

Answer: D.

10. To retrieve a value from the Registry, you would use:

   A. The GetSetting function

   B. The ReadSetting function

   C. An API call

   D. The GetSetting statement

Answer: A. Since GetSetting returns a value, it is a function. While an API call was required in Access 2.0, it is no longer necessary in Access 95.

11. This question applies to the run-time version of Access. To have a specific Help topic appear when the user presses the F1 key and the focus is on a control on your form, you must set:

   A. HelpContextId to a valid ContextID.

   B. The Help option in Tools ➤ Options.

   C. The form's HelpFile property.

   D. You can't have context-sensitive help in a run-time application.

Answer: A. You can have context-sensitive help in Access by setting your controls' HelpContextId property to valid Context IDs in the Help file for the application.

12. If you can use a control with Visual Basic, then:

   A. You can use it with Access if you modify the Registry settings.

   B. You can use it with Access.

   C. You can't use it with Access.

   D. You might be able to use it with Access.

Answer: D. Some controls that work with Visual Basic have extensions not supported by Access. Others are fully functional, and yet others are partially functional. As a result, you must consult the control's documentation to be sure that the control has been tested with Access.

13. You want to distribute a run-time application that uses the Calendar control. What modifications do you need to make to the setup files so that the user will be able to use the control?

   A. Include the MSACal70.ocx file in the Setup file list.

   B. Include the MSACal70.ocx and OC25.dll files in the Setup file list.

   C. You cannot distribute this OLE control.

   D. Include the MSACal70.ocx and OC25.dll files in the Setup file list. Prepare a batch file using Regsvr32.exe to run after Setup is complete, to register the control on the user's system.

Answer: A. This answer is correct, Setup takes care of registering the control. B is incorrect as supporting DLL files are not needed with Access 95. C is wrong because the control is distributable. D is wrong because Setup takes care of registering the control.

14. Data should be stored in the Registry if:

   A. You need it to be available to users of your application working on different databases on the same computer.

   B. You need it to be available to users running both Access 2.0 and Access 95.

   C. It is not of a data type that can be stored in an .INI file.

   D. You need it to be available to users of your application working on different databases in a multiuser environment.

Answer: A. Users in different databases (on the same computer) can all access the same Windows Registry. In a multiuser environment (D), users won't necessarily use the same Registry. B is wrong because Access 2.0 can't access the Registry, even if it is running on Windows 95.

Index

Note to the Reader: Throughout this index **boldfaced** page numbers indicate primary discussions of a topic. *Italicized* page numbers indicate illustrations.

G

H

O

Q

X

MCSE CORE REQUIREMENT STUDY GUIDES FROM NETWORK PRESS

Sybex's Network Press presents updated and expanded second editions
of the definitive study guides for MCSE candidates.

ISBN: 0-7821-2220-5
704pp; 7¹/₂" x 9"; Hardcover
$49.99

ISBN: 0-7821-2223-X
784pp; 7¹/₂" x 9"; Hardcover
$49.99

ISBN: 0-7821-2222-1
832pp; 7¹/₂" x 9"; Hardcover
$49.99

ISBN: 0-7821-2221-3
704pp; 7¹/₂" x 9"; Hardcover
$49.99

ISBN: 0-7821-2256-6
800pp; 7¹/₂" x 9"; Hardcover
$49.99

A $50.00 SAVINGS!

MCSE Core Requirements
Box Set
ISBN: 0-7821-2245-0
4 hardcover books;
3,024pp total; $149.96

Microsoft® Certified
Professional
Approved Study Guide

STUDY GUIDES FOR THE MICROSOFT CERTIFIED SYSTEMS ENGINEER EXAMS

Master Your
WINDOWS® 98
Destiny

WITH THESE BESTSELLING SYBEX TITLES

MCSD: Access® 95 Study Guide

Exam 70-069: Objectives

NOTE Exam objectives are subject to change at any time without prior notice and at Microsoft's sole discretion. Please visit Microsoft's Training & Certification Web site (www.microsoft.com/Train_Cert) for the most current listing of exam objectives.